TING HSIEN
A North China Rural Community

LIAO TI PAGODA—COMPLETED A.D. 1055

"It is said that all the trees on Chia Shan were cut down
to provide fuel to burn the bricks for the pagoda."

TING HSIEN
A North China Rural Community

Sidney D. Gamble

Foreword by Y. C. James Yen

Field work directed by
Franklin Ching-han Lee

Stanford University Press
Stanford, California

To

C.G.C.

L.N.G.

D.L.G.

A. van N.G.

Stanford University Press
Stanford, California
Copyright 1954 by the International Secretariat,
Institute of Pacific Relations
L.C. 68-13743
Printed in the United States of America

First published in 1954
by the Institute of Pacific Relations
Reissued in 1968 by Stanford University Press

Foreword

As a people the Chinese attach little importance to facts or exactness. If a Chinese is asked what is the population of China, he would say about four hundred million; another would say about four hundred fifty million; still another, about four hundred seventy-five million. The common Chinese expression ch'a-pu-tou, meaning "nearly this" or "about that", is widely used by the educated and the uneducated alike. Being exact is not an outstanding virtue of the Chinese people.

However, in the modern world where science has played such a vital part in bettering human lives, the Chinese can no longer ignore it and continue with the attitude of ch'a-pu-tou. They have to learn to appreciate facts as well as to gather facts. This is what makes the pioneering survey work of Mr. Sidney Gamble, over a quarter of a century ago, so significant in the stimulation of a fact-finding consciousness among the educated and the students of social sciences.

Mr. Gamble did his pioneering work in social surveys first in Peking in 1918. This resulted in his publishing an admirable study of the life in Peking, entitled *Peking, A Social Survey*, which created wide interest among students of social sciences and rural reconstruction workers.

Through his years of hard experience in China, Mr. Gamble learned that it was not a simple matter to gather facts, especially accurate facts, in a country like China. In the first place, during the 1920s there were few, if any, organizations doing a similar kind of survey which could be used to help supplement or check one's facts. In the second place, the people, as a rule, were suspicious of any kind of investigation because the investigators might be government agents gathering information for more taxes or even conscription. In the third place, even if the people were good-natured and willing to cooperate, being illiterate and uninformed, they were not able to answer intelligently or accurately many of the questions concerning economics or education.

Mr. Gamble came to be associated with the Chinese Mass Education Movement in 1926 when the Movement first went to Ting Hsien to initiate its first rural reconstruction pilot plant in a county of 400,000 people located in Hopei province, some six hours by train from Peking. At that time the Movement undertook only a literacy and literature program. The survey work consisted of preliminary experimental studies. Experience with life in the villages plus the first results of the survey work soon demonstrated the need for the Movement to expand its program to include the economic and social betterment of the rural people.

The Movement realized that without accurate knowledge of the economic and social conditions of the people it would be impossible for it to plan rural reconstruction intelligently. It was also demonstrated that because of the educational program and the cordial teacher-student relationship first established between the Movement and the local people by village People's Schools and strengthened later through cooperatives, health clinics, and agricultural improvement programs, the villagers were not only willing but also able to answer questions intelligently. Even more important, they understood that these facts were necessary as a scientific basis for the Movement to formulate its rural reconstruction program for the betterment of their county. Many of the literate members of the community served as assistants in the social investigation.

With Mr. Gamble's expert knowledge and assistance and the cooperation the Movement had from the village people, an effective partnership was formed to carry out a hsien wide survey. It played such an important part in the Movement's rural reconstruction program that a separate Department of Social Survey was organized, one of the earliest of its kind in China. This first pilot survey carried out in Ting Hsien served as a pattern for other rural reconstruction centers, and Ting Hsien came to be known as the "Scientific Ting Hsien".

The Department of Survey published the results of its studies in three volumes in Chinese: *Ting Hsien, A Social Survey*; *Ting Hsien Yang Ke*; and *Ting Hsien Village Industry*. These books exerted influence all over China, especially among the students of social sciences and the rural reconstruction workers. Later, even provincial governments, such as Szechuan in West China and Kiangsi in Central China, established, upon the advice of the Movement, special Bureaus of Survey as an integral part of their reconstruction programs.

This idea and practice of social surveys has been an indispensable aid to social planning. It has also proved to be a real education to the workers concerned with social and economic problems. It taught them to learn from the people, however humble and illiterate. It taught them to base their program upon the felt needs and the vital problems of the people. All this might sound commonplace today, but it was not so commonplace a quarter of a century ago when the survey was undertaken. I believe this social survey has contributed more than any other single factor to a scientific approach to the social and economic problems of the Chinese peasants. The same approach has been found valuable and helpful to the Philippine Rural Reconstruction Movement, with which the International Committee of the Mass Education Movement is today cooperating in a program to help raise the living standard of the rural people of the Philippines.

During recent years it is heartening to see the increasing interest manifested in the betterment of the rural people everywhere. Rural reconstruction workers as well as students of the social sciences should find Mr. Gamble's book educative and stimulating. Mr. Gamble has not only made a real contribution to the rural reconstruction program in China, but his work will also serve as a guide and an inspiration to conscientious students and workers who are interested in raising the economic and social standard of the underdeveloped peoples of the world.

New York, October, 1953   Y. C. JAMES YEN

Contents

List of Tables

Chapter II. Population and Other Vital Statistics

Chapter VI. Government

Chapter VIII. Taxes

Chapter IX. Education

Chapter X. Farm Land: Ownership and Operation

Chapter XI. Wells and Irrigation

Chapter XII. Farm Operation: Costs and Returns

Chapter XIII. Money, Exchange, and Credit

Chapter XIV. Buying and Selling

Chapter XV. Industry

Chapter XVIII. Religion

Chapter XX. Calamities

Chapter XXI. Geography

List of Figures

Preface

O N THE BROAD coastal plain of North China there are thousands of villages, towns, and walled cities, the centers of life for the rural agricultural population. This study deals with the organization and activities of a group of 454 of these centers, a sample hsien in that area. A hsien is the Chinese political unit that corresponds most nearly to the American county. Our material, collected from 1926 to 1933, gives a picture of how, during those years, the residents of one political unit lived, worked, organized their political life, studied, played, and worshiped. Japanese invasion, civil war, and a revolutionary Communist government have brought many changes to the area. Our study, made almost at the end of the pre-World War II era, gives a base line from which to measure the many changes brought by the new day.

When Chang Tso-lin moved his troops into the Peking area in 1925 he effectively prevented our making any move to initiate a proposed study of the social, political, and economic life in the villages outside of Peking. The postponement turned out to be a very fortunate one, for a year later we were able to join forces with the Chinese National Association of the Mass Education Movement when it started its Ting Hsien experiment.

The origin of the Ting Hsien experiment goes back to World War I, when a Thousand Character System (Ch'ien Tzu K'e) was developed whereby Chinese laborers in France were taught, in two months' time, studying two hours a day, enough characters so that they could read simple newspapers giving news of the war and could write letters home to China. After the war, experiments were conducted in China to adapt the system to Chinese conditions. Literacy campaigns were carried on in several cities. The basic vocabulary was developed by determining the frequency of word use in one and one half million characters used in current written material. To test the system in a rural area and adapt it for use in the villages a group of Chinese scholars moved to Ting

Hsien in the fall of 1926 to begin what turned out to be ten years of study, experiment, testing, and growth.

At the invitation of the village elders of Chai Ch'eng, a village in the eastern part of Ting Hsien, Association headquarters were first established there. Work was carried on in a group of 62 villages which we have called the "Experimental District". Later on, at the request of the hsien leaders, the Association moved its headquarters to the county seat, and expanded its program to cover the entire hsien. In the city the Association work and staff were housed in the buildings of the old examination hall.

Social research was added to the basic educational program when the Movement first went to Ting Hsien. Agricultural, economic, political, social, and health programs were gradually added as the needs were shown and opportunities for experiment became available.

Ten years of life and work in Ting Hsien gave the members of the Movement thorough grounding and experience in rural work before they had to evacuate ahead of the Japanese in 1937. By that time the educational program had attracted country-wide interest, the Thousand Character System was in use throughout the country, and the national Ministry of Education had a department of Mass Education. During the war days in China, 1937–1945, it is estimated that more than 45,000,-000 Chinese were taught to read by the Mass Education Movement's system.

The local influence of the Movement in Ting Hsien is well illustrated by an action of one of its village Alumni Associations. Hearing that illegal gambling was going on in one of the houses in the village, members of the Association raided the house. The village head and the vice-head were found among the players. After lecturing the men on their crime and their duty to set an example for the village, the Alumni Association group decided that, rather than take the culprits to the hsien city and there lay a charge against them in the magistrate's court, which would mean a considerable loss of time and money for all concerned, they would use their standing as a community organization and levy an extra-legal fine of $3.00 on the culprits and use the money for the Association's program. The next morning the money for the fine was sent to the Association, together with a contribution of $2.00. This type of community spirit developed by the Movement brought about especially strong resistance when the Japanese invaded Ting Hsien in 1937.

We fully realize that much of our material has been secured from people who do not usually think in mathematical and statistical terms, to many of whom "several tens" is a reasonable approximation, and who are generally suspicious of anyone asking detailed and intimate questions. At the same time the very happy relationships between the staff of the Mass Education Movement and the Ting Hsien people made it possible for us to overcome much of this suspicion and to secure the best possible approximation to complete and accurate figures. Comparison of the figures secured from a variety of sources has shown an agreement which indicates that they give a reasonably true picture of the local conditions.

There was fighting, requisitioning of supplies, and looting in the Ting Hsien area in 1928 when the Nationalist forces came in from the south to capture Peking and unify the country. Troop movements through Ting Hsien in 1931 made it necessary hurriedly to pile our records in a small room and brick up the door. Fortunately the actual fighting was to the north and the disturbance was quickly over. Our records were not touched. Aside from those two short periods, the time of our study was relatively quiet and stable. The worldwide depression of the early 1930s affected prices and the economic life of Ting Hsien, but most of our field work had been finished by that time. As our study was made during a time when life in Ting Hsien, in spite of the two periods of military activity, was relatively normal and as the study was made under unusually favorable auspices, we feel that our findings can be taken as reasonably typical of life in Ting Hsien and as a good sample of rural life in North China.

Some questions must remain unanswered because the material was not available to us, others because the author of this report was not able to spend as much time in the field as had originally been planned and because the necessary delay in tabulating and analyzing the material, plus the political developments in North China, made it impossible to go back to the original records, to rearrange tables, and to get answers to questions that could not be cleared by correspondence.

All dollar figures are Chinese silver dollars. Cents are Chinese dollar decimals unless otherwise noted. From 1926 through 1933 the value of the Chinese dollar varied from U.S. $0.49 to U.S. $0.197, the exchange rate from 2.04 to 5.10.[1]

The Chinese characters for place names, names of gods and emperors, and Chinese terms have not been given as they are not sufficiently pertinent to our report to warrant the additional printing costs.

When we began our study in 1926 the Chinese name for China's capital was Pei Ching, North Capital. Its English name was Peking. In 1928 the Nationalist Government moved the capital to Nanking and changed Pei Ching to Pei P'ing, North Peace. When the Communist forces captured Pei P'ing in 1949 they made it their capital and changed the name back to Pei Ching. Whenever we have referred to the city we have called it Peking.

The Chinese language report of our survey has been published in three volumes. The first, the general survey (*Ting Hsien She Hui Kai K'uang Tiao Ch'a*, by Franklin Ching-han Lee) and the second, a collection of the dialogues of the local yang ke, or planting songs (*Ting Hsien Yang Ke*, by Franklin Ching-han Lee and Shih-wen Chang) appeared in 1933. The third, the report of our study of village industry (*Ting Hsien Nung Ts'un Kung Yeh Tiao Ch'a*, by Shih-wen Chang) was issued in 1936. A considerable amount of new statistical material, which was not available when the Chinese reports were written, is given here for the first time.

In our report we have included material that we hope will be helpful and suggestive to those who are experts in the various fields we have tried to cover. In presenting our statistical studies we have attempted to satisfy two groups. For the general reader we have pointed out and discussed, in the text, the outstanding figures of the different studies. For the specialist we have given the figures in complete tabular form. All photographs in the volume were taken by the author.

Grateful acknowledgment is made to the *American Journal of Sociology* and to the *Far Eastern Quarterly* for permission to use material on foot-binding, savings societies, and farm families that has appeared earlier in their pages, and to Dr. J. L. Buck for permission to quote from his studies of North China agricultural families. I am indebted to Mrs. L. Carrington Goodrich for making available to me material on the Chinese gods; to Dr. Goodrich for his counsel and ad-

---

1. National Tariff Commission, *The Shanghai Market Prices Report*, Shanghai, Oct.–Dec. 1933.

vice; to Mr. H. C. Chang for help with many detailed problems; to Marjorie Forsyth, Gertrude Shafer, and Miriam S. Farley for their help with the preparation of the manuscript; to the Institute of Pacific Relations for its generous help with the publication of this report. Though the book is issued under the auspices of the Institute, responsibility for all statements of fact or opinion rests solely with the author.

Credit for much of the success of our studies must be given to Franklin Lee, who, as head of the Social Survey Department of the Mass Education Movement, was in charge of the staff and the field work. To him and to the many others who helped in the work of collecting, tabulating, translating, and interpreting our material I would express my indebtedness and my appreciation of the way they met and solved many difficulties, of their care in handling the many details, and of their success in securing information.

To Dr. Y. C. James Yen, founder and leader of the Chinese National Association of the Mass Education Movement, I would express my admiration for his vision and leadership and my grateful appreciation of his willingness to add social research to the Ting Hsien program. I am indebted to him for the thrill of seeing research findings promptly made the basis of a developing program, and for the opportunity of living and working, for a time, with a group of people who by their ability, service, and self-sacrifice have proved how much can be done for better education, better livelihood, better government, and better health in the villages of China.

SIDNEY D. GAMBLE

New York, June, 1953

Glossary
(including currency, weights, and measures)

AN, nunnery or Buddhist temple.

BLACK LAND, land not entered on tax rolls.

CASH, bronze coin, par 1/1000th of a TAEL.

CATTY, 1⅓ pounds.

CENT, 1/100th of a dollar.

CHIANG YU, salty soy bean sauce.

CHIEN, space between two roof trusses, generally from 10 to 12 feet square. In smaller houses a room is one chien.

CH'IEN TZU K'E, 1,000 characters, Mass Education basic vocabulary.

CH'ING MING, third of third month, spring tomb festival, Arbor Day.

CH'Ü, district, q.v.

CHOU, administrative unit over several hsien, discontinued in 1913.

CHU JEN, second classical degree.

COPPERS, copper coins; single copper = 10 cash, double copper = 20 cash.

DISTRICT, political division of hsien.

DOLLAR, silver coin containing seven mace, two candareens, 0.72 Chinese ounces silver, 890 fine.

EXPERIMENTAL DISTRICT, sixty-two villages in east part of hsien, where first studies were made.

FENG-SHUI, wind-water, good or evil influences of a locality.

FU, administrative unit next smaller than a province and larger than a chou, discontinued in 1913.

HANG, business organization, gild.

HE, 1/10th of a SHENG.

HSIEN, political administrative unit equivalent to a county.

HSIEN CHIH, county history.

HSIU TS'AI, first classical degree.

KAOLIANG, a non-saccharine sorghum grown for its grain; for its leaves, used as a stock food; and for its stalk, used in construction work.

KE, 1/10th of a SHENG.

KUAN, Taoist temple.

KUOMINTANG, Nationalist Party.

LI, one-third of a mile.

LI, administrative district of hsien, discontinued in 1845.

LIANG, a Chinese ounce, 1/16th of a catty.

LIKIN, transit duties.

LIN, administrative unit of five families.

LÜ, administrative unit of 25 families, five LIN.

MIAO, temple.

MU, one-sixth of an acre.

PAO-CHIA, mutual protective organization, similar to LIN and LÜ. Chia = 10 families; pao = 100 families.

PAO WEI-TUAN, local militia.

PEI CHING, North Capital, Chinese name of Peking.

PEI P'ING, North Peace, name given Pei Ching by Nationalists in 1928.

P'ENG, mat shed.

PICUL, 100 catties, 133⅓ pounds.

SHENG, one-tenth of a TOU.

SZU, Buddhist temple.

TA YU NIEN, especially good year, included in list of calamities.

TAEL, one Chinese ounce of silver bullion.

TAEL CENT, 1/100th of a tael.

TAN, a bag, usually of grain, 10 TOU.

TOU, a peck measure for grain, 20 catties of millet, 19 catties of wheat, 17 catties of kaoliang.

YANG KE, planting songs—name given local plays.

YAMEN, magistrate's office.

YÜAN, dollar.

YÜEH, local government district of hsien, 1845–1912.

NOTE: Ting Hsien indicates the county, Tinghsien the city which was the county seat. The North China pronunciation of both is approximately Ding She-en.

TING HSIEN
A North China
Rural Community

CHAPTER I

Summary

TING HSIEN, the model hsien of Hopei province, lies on the western side of the flat North China coastal plain, 37 miles south of Paoting, the provincial capital, and 128 miles south of Peking, the national capital. Its climate is generally cold and dry in winter, hot and wet in summer. Monthly mean temperatures for the years 1927–29 ranged from 22.8° F. to 80.8°F. The annual average was 54.5° F. The average precipitation was 19.1 inches. Seventy per cent fell in July and August, another 14 per cent in June and September. The June–September rainfall, for the years 1914–29, varied from 24.6 mm. to 828.1 mm.

About 500 B.C. the area was named Chung Shan Kuo, Middle Hill Kingdom, and it was generally known by that name for most of the next 1,800 years. The tomb of Liu Sheng, the King of Chung Shan who died in 113 B.C., is still one of the sights of Tinghsien, the hsien city.[1] The pagoda was finished in 1055. In 1368 the Emperor Hung Wu changed the name to Ting, "in order to pacify the country", after the overthrow of the Liao dynasty.

The hsien history tells of 145 calamities in 1,821 years (106–1926). There were 35 floods and 28 droughts. Locusts were mentioned 21 times and hail 17 times. Losses caused by armies and battles were listed only once, in 1900, the year of the Boxer rebellion. Seven extra good years, with bumper crops and very low prices, were included in the list.

The T'ang and Sha rivers that flow from west to east across the hsien have often been the scenes of bloody battles as the armies of the succeeding dynasties have fought up and down the coastal plain. In 1401 Yen Wang and his army swept through Ting Hsien on the way to Nanking. He besieged, assaulted, and captured the walled hsien city and so depopulated the area that it is said that at that time "the roof swallows nested in the trees". The area was repopulated later by bringing in

1. Ting Hsien indicates the county, Tinghsien the hsien city.

large numbers of famine sufferers from Shansi. Many of the present Ting Hsien families trace their lineage back to ancestors who came from Shansi at that time.

Foreign troops occupied Ting Hsien after the allied forces captured Peking in 1900. When the armies of Wu P'ei-fu and Yen Hsi-shan fought against Chang Tso-lin's Fengtien army in 1926–28, there was fighting in the streets of the hsien city on two occasions. The victorious troops levied special taxes for "saving the hsien" and there was a good deal of looting by the troops throughout the countryside. A sample of the 62 villages in the Experimental District indicated the 1927–28 war loss, assessments, and looting to be at least $1,000,000.[2] In 1926 the provincial land tax was double and in 1927 triple the usual amount.

The area of the hsien was 480 square miles. It was divided into 454 areas, each of which was controlled by one of the political divisions of the hsien, i.e., the city and the 453 towns and villages. Seventy-six per cent of the hsien land was arable. The amount of arable land in the 454 areas varied from 245 to 32,500 mu (a mu is 0.166 acres). Seventy-three per cent of the areas had less than one square mile of farm land. The average amount per family was 20.4 mu.

The population of the hsien was some 408,300, the population density 850 per square mile. Our census counted 70,034 families. A census of individuals was possible only for sample groups of families. Our most representative sample, 5,255 families, averaged 5.83 persons per family. Fifty-five per cent of these families had not more than five members. Seventy-eight per cent had not more than seven members.

All our family studies showed that the size of the family was closely related to the amount of family income. In one group the average was 3.8 persons for the families with not more than 10 mu of land and 13.5 for those with more than 100 mu. In another group it was 3.8 for families with annual incomes between $100 and $200 and 9.3 for those receiving betwen $400 and $500 per year.

The head of the family and his direct descendants were 82 per cent of the family group. In 4 per cent of the families a woman was the recognized head of the family.

The sex division was 51.5 per cent male, 48.5 female, but for those over 50 years of age the masculinity rate (males per 100 females) was only 91.3.

2. All dollar figures are Chinese silver dollars.

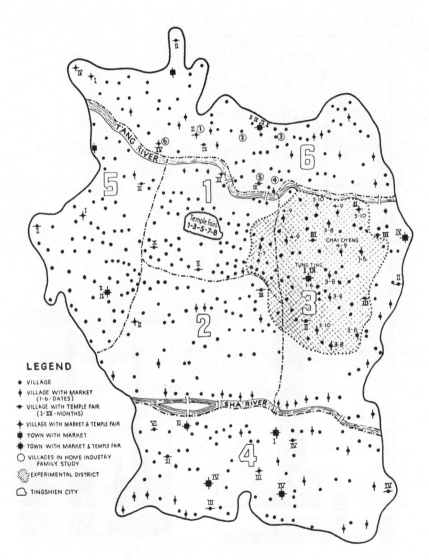

FIGURE 1. MAP OF TING HSIEN

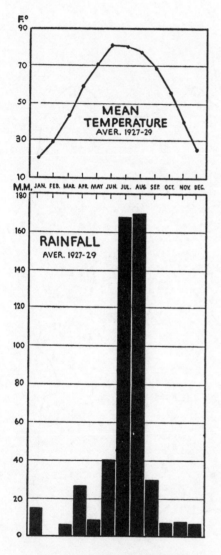

FIGURE 2. RAINFALL AND
TEMPERATURE,
1927–1929

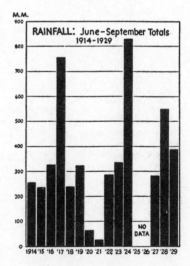

FIGURE 3. RAINFALL,
JUNE TO SEPTEMBER,
1914–1929

In the 5,255 families 93 percent of the females and 79 per cent of the males over 14 years of age were married. There were only five unmarried females over 21 years of age, but 1,177 males, 13.7 per cent of those over 21, were still single. Two nine-year-old males were married, but 12 was the youngest age of the married girls.

The age at marriage, particularly of the boys, was greatly influenced by the economic status of the family. In a group of 766 couples 41.4 per cent of the grooms were under 15 (by Western calculation) when they were married. In the poorer families, those with less than 50 mu, the proportion under 15 was 33 per cent. For the wealthier families, those with 100 mu or more, it was 80.5 per cent. In 69.6 per cent of the couples the wife was older than her husband, in some cases as much as 11 years older.

Concubines were reported by less than 0.5 per cent of the families. Widows could and did remarry. Divorce was possible but rare.

The amount of foot-binding among women of different ages showed how, even in the country villages, a social custom that was able to defy the edicts of the early Manchu emperors disappeared in 25 years.

Home ownership was almost universal. Less than one per cent of our sample families paid rent. The average residence area was about 100 x 50 feet. The average house had some six chien (rooms) but that included the barn and store-rooms as well as the family living quarters. Two-thirds of the families had either three or four persons per bedroom.

The families named Wang, Chang, and Liu together were 30 per cent of the 10,445 families in the 62 villages of the Experimental District. In 11 of the 453 villages all the families had the same name.

In a group of 515 families 88 per cent of the males and 80 per cent of the females over 12 years of age were doing farm wark. Eighteen per cent of both sexes reported primary, non-farming occupations. Twelve per cent of the males and 51.5 per cent of the females were doing some home industry.

Twelve months of accounts of 34 families showed that the average annual food consumption per adult male equivalent of families in different income levels was almost the same, some 550 catties of sweet potatoes, 420 catties of vegetables, 375 catties of grains and flours, and 19 catties of all other foods. The average value of the food used was $28.00 per capita, or $35.45 per adult male equivalent per year.

The proportion of the family budget used for food decreased from

65 per cent for the $100–$200 group to 54 per cent for the $400–$500 group, that for fuel from 8.3 to 5.3 per cent. The proportions used for rent and clothing showed almost no change. Miscellaneous expenses increased from 15.3 to 30.9 per cent. The average per capita income was $43.70 per year, but some families lived on as little as $2.50 per person per month.

In a group of 400 farm families the estimated per capita income was $55.10 per year. In 1,220 home industry families it was $34.20 per year. Our figures for agricultural production and gain from industry seem to indicate for the hsien an average per capita income of between $50.00 and $60.00 per year.

Political organization began at the five-family level. Regulations promulgated by the provincial government required that the village families be organized into lin, groups of five families with a headman who should be responsible for the members of the group. Five lin were combined to make a lü, 25 families. This was similar to the old pao-chia system of 25 and 100 families. The regulations being issued by the provincial government seemed to indicate an attempt on the part of the central and provincial government agencies to establish closer po-litical controls over the hsien government and the villages.

Village affairs were handled by a village head and a vice-head, who ordinarily were appointed by the village leaders. An attempt was being made to have the village heads elected by popular vote. The 453 villages ordinarily financed with their own funds their night watchmen, home guard, crop watching, and schools. Assessments levied on the farm land controlled by the village were usually the principal source of village income. In eight villages local jealousies and separatist interests had brought about the establishment of two village administrations in the village area.

The hsien was divided into six administrative districts, whose officials were ordinarily the intermediaries between the hsien government and the villages.

The hsien magistrate was the chief executive and judicial officer. Subject to his approval the administrative work was carried on by three sections and four bureaus, the judicial work by the local court. There had been attempts to make the local court responsible only to the higher provincial court, but the magistrate still had to review and approve the decisions.

The magistrate was appointed on the recommendation of the provincial governor and held office at his pleasure. An active, energetic magistrate could contribute a great deal toward the development of the hsien, but most incumbents showed but little initiative and attempted few changes. Their general motto seemed to be "maintain order, produce the usual revenue, make changes only on orders from above". The office was the lowest official position. According to custom no local man could be appointed. Three years was ordinarily the maximum term of office. Actually 24 men held 25 appointments as magistrate during the 27 years from May 1901 to September 1928. Seventeen of the appointments lasted less than one year, only five more than two years. Sun Fa-hsü (1914–16) was unique in actively stimulating the opening of schools and the development of model political programs. Sample figures from the Experimental District indicate that possibly as many as 200 schools were opened and 2,000 temples discontinued during his term of office.

A hsien salary scale that paid the head of a bureau $40 a month, experts $27, section managers $24, and clerks $18 could not help but encourage incumbents to take advantage of their position to increase their income.

The 1929 expenditure budget totaled $107,866, exclusive of the cost of the magistrate's office and of the court. Those items were part of the provincial budget. Thirty-six per cent of the hsien budget was allocated to education, but some of the schools reported that they did not receive the amount budgeted for them. Twenty-five per cent was designated for the police force.

The Kuomintang, or Nationalist Party, had a separate hsien-wide organization, financed by a grant of $16,800 from hsien funds. The Anti-Litigation Society was directed by the magistrate to hear and, if possible, settle all lawsuits before they came before the court. The Merchants' Association Bureau of Public Judgment on Commercial Matters was to act as conciliator and arbitrator in commercial disputes.

Government records and the estimates of tax officials indicated that the national, provincial, and hsien governments received about $500,-000 per year in taxes from Ting Hsien. How much the people paid the tax collectors could not be determined as the collection of the various sales taxes and some of the license taxes was regularly farmed to the highest bidders and their collection costs and profits could not be es-

timated. Nor was it possible to secure figures on the amounts collected
by the villages to meet the cost of their activities.

The annual land tax (which averaged approximately 10 cents per
mu), the tax on land transfers (12.6 per cent), and the tax on recorded
mortgages (5.3 per cent) formed 35 per cent of the governmental receipts, the salt tax 24 per cent, sales taxes 23 per cent, wine and tobacco
taxes 9 per cent, and stamp, likin, and special assessments 9 per cent.

The national government received 28 per cent of the total tax collections, the province 45 per cent, and the hsien 27 per cent. Some of
the provincial money came back to the hsien to pay for the magistrate's
office and the hsien court. Six thousand dollars came as a special grant to
the model hsien.

Chai Ch'eng was the model village of the model hsien. The story of
its organization and activity gives a picture of a village that was a leader
in many civic programs. It shows some of the new ideas that the Revolution of 1911 brought to the countryside, how some of these succeeded
and were gradually adopted, how some were tried and generally dis-
carded, and how some Western forms of political organization were
tried but were not widely adopted because they had not been adapted
to Chinese conditions.

The leadership of the Mi family, through the years, helped to make
the village a pioneer in education, well drilling, road repair, tree planting, and sanitation. They were the ones who persuaded the Mass Education Movement to take Ting Hsien for its rural experiment station and
to make Chai Ch'eng its first headquarters.

Chai Ch'eng's educational position is indicated by the fact that it
was the home of 33 of the 272 men and of 11 of the 32 women in the
Experimental District who had education beyond the junior middle
school. Its model village program brought an annual grant from the
hsien government of $600.

Sample studies showed that only some 20 per cent of the population
over six years of age were literate, approximately 37 per cent of the
males but only 3 per cent of the females. That progress was being made
on the literacy problem was shown by two studies. In a group of 500
families the literacy figure for the 45–49 year age group was 20.3 per
cent, but for the 11–14 year group it was 57.3 per cent. In the 366 families in Chai Ch'eng the 11–24 year age group was 53 per cent literate, 65
per cent of the males and 36 per cent of the females.

The government was attempting to make school attendance compulsory but the total number of students was equal to only 22 per cent of the children between 5 and 14 years of age. Four hundred and forty-seven schools and 18,666 students, 15,377 males and 3,289 females, were reported to the hsien Bureau of Education in 1928. In 1931 there were also more than 20,000 students in the People's Schools (Mass Education classes).

In the regular schools the teaching staff totaled 575, one for every 32 students. In the Experimental District the average teacher's salary was $90 per year for the lower primary and $150 a year for the higher primary schools.

The average cost per student was $8.20 per year. It was $5.10 in the boys' lower primary schools, $25.20 in the boys' higher primary, and $90.00 in the girls' normal school. The cost for the six weeks' course of the People's School was about 40 cents per pupil.

The school expenditure of $153,000 was financed by $117,000 from local village funds and $36,000 from the hsien government. The average income of the lower primary schools was $227 per year but 14 received less than $125 per year. The higher primary schools spent an average of $3,000 per year, the middle, normal, and vocational schools up to $8,800. Money for the village schools came from land rent, interest, village land assessment, village land transfer taxes, sales taxes, tuition, and hsien subsidy.

Middle school graduates were reported by two-thirds and college and technical school graduates by one-third of the villages, but more than one-third of the middle school graduates and almost three-quarters of the college graduates were away from home. There were four returned students from Japan and one from France. One boy was studying in France and one in the United States.

Over 92 per cent of the families owned some land, over 96 per cent farmed some land. The average farm owning family had four plots of ground with an area of 21.9 mu (3.6 acres). The average farm operating family farmed 21.2 mu. The per capita average for the hsien was 3.6 mu (0.6 acres). The largest family holding was 660 acres, but only 132 families, 0.2 per cent, owned as much as 50 acres and only 9.0 per cent as much as 50 mu (8.3 acres).

Rented land was farmed by 30 per cent of the farming families, but only 4.8 per cent were full tenants. Just under 6 per cent of the land owning families rented land to others. Only 0.7 per cent were non-farming landlords. Twelve per cent of the crop area was rented. Cash rents varied from 50 cents to $7.50 per mu. The average return to the landlord was not more than 6 per cent of the land value. The cash and cash-crop rent charges averaged between 35 and 40 per cent of the value of the crop. Some 55 per cent of the farm land was irrigated. The water came from 40,000 wells. Another 20,000 wells inside the villages furnished water for domestic use. The average figures for the wells were: depth 21 feet (none were more than 45 feet deep), lift 13 feet, cost of digging $65, labor about 50 days' work. The estimated labor cost of irrigating was about 20 cents per mu. The drought of 1920 was a great stimulus to well digging and during the next 10 years the number of irrigation wells was more than doubled.

Twenty-eight per cent of the land was double cropped. Grain was planted on 80 per cent of the crop area, beans and peas on 20 per cent, vegetables on 10 per cent, and cotton on 9 per cent. The estimated total crop value was $16,000,000, an average of $11.25 per mu, $40 per capita. Five crops, millet, wheat, sweet potatoes, cotton, and black beans, were worth more than $1,000,000 each, peanuts and kaoliang over $500,-000 each. These seven crops together were more than 80 per cent of the total yield.

A sample of 400 farm families reported that they consumed 76 per cent of their farm produce. Cotton, peanuts, sesamum, and wheat were the principal money crops. Ninety-three per cent of the cotton, 92 per cent of the peanuts, 86 per cent of the sesamum, and 42 per cent of the wheat crop were sold. These four crops together were 86 per cent of the total amount sold. The proportion sold increased with an increase in the size of the farm, from 12.5 per cent for the 1–10 mu group to 31.3 per cent for the over 100 mu group.

The values of the farm houses, implements, and animals were closely related to the size of the family farm. The averages per mu were: houses about $9.00, implements $1.25, animals $1.95.

The estimated cost of farm operation, for a group of 244 farm owners, was $8.45 per mu. This included the value of the labor of the farm family and animals, the rent value of the land, and the value of any seed or other items produced on the farm, as well as any money expenditure. The cost was about 70 per cent of the yield. The accounts of 285 grain and cotton growers showed a weighted cost equal to 87 per cent of the yield. In both groups the value of the family labor was aproximately one-third of the total cost.

In a group of 515 families full time laborers were employed by 2 per cent of the families with less than 50 mu of land, by 30 per cent of the families with from 50 to 99 mu and by 72 per cent of the families with 100 mu or more.

Wages for experienced farm workers ranged from $25 to $60 per year, $3.50 to $7.00 per month, up to 40 cents a day in the busy season. Food, which was furnished by the employer, cost about $3.00 per month. The wage rates had gone up about 200 per cent in 18 years.

The silver yüan (dollar) was the basic monetary unit and the generally accepted standard of value at the time of our study. Earlier the copper cash was the unit for most retail sales while silver bullion (taels) was used for official accounts and for wholesale transactions. A regularly quoted exchange rate indicated the varying relative value of the two monetary units. Parity of exchange was generally taken as 1,000 cash per tael, 720 cash per dollar, but for the 75 years from 1857 through 1931 the annual average exchange rates were all above par.

In 1857 the average rate was 1,093 cash per dollar. It was 4,090 in 1931. From 1857 to 1892 the trend of the annual rates was practically level, although there were fluctuations of 20 per cent both up and down. From 1892 to 1905 there was an almost continuous decline to the minimum rate of 758. The trend was then sharply reversed and, except for three years, the rate rose continuously during the next 24 years. After 1918 the rate of increase was greatly accelerated. From 1857 to 1931 the overall increase was 274 per cent. The 1892–1905 decrease was 33 per cent, the 1905–1929 increase 469 per cent.

A study of the credit needs for the three years 1929–31 of the 526 families living in five neighboring villages found that 32 per cent of the families borrowed in 1929 and 58 per cent in 1931. Declining commodity prices and the extra taxes and assessments connected with the fighting in 1931 were largely responsible for the increase. The total amount borrowed increased 133 per cent, from $21,000 to $49,000. The average per borrowing family went up 30 per cent, from $123 to $160.

The term of practically all of the loans was one year or less. Almost all of them came due after the fall harvest or before Chinese New Year. Seventy-five per cent were for 10 or 12 months. Usually less than 10 per cent were for six months or less.

The interest rate varied from nothing to 3 per cent per month. It was 2.0 per cent per month for just over one-third of the loans and 22 per cent of the total amount borrowed. It was more than 2.0 per cent per month for almost one-quarter of the loans and 11 per cent of the amount borrowed. The average rate was 1.80 per cent per month.

Forty per cent of the loans were made to refund old debts, 26 per cent to provide farm capital, and 7 per cent for business capital. The loans for family living expenses averaged only $30, those for weddings and funerals $70. Some families reported that the proceeds of their loans were used for gambling and the purchase of narcotics.

The records of a sample mutual savings society of 31 members, which met three times a year for 10 years, showed in detail one of the ways by which the village residents secured considerable amounts of money without resorting to the moneylenders. In our sample society the order in which the members took the fund collected at each meeting was decided by bidding rather than by lot. Before a member could receive the fund he had to have its repayment assured by two guarantors. Even when they were handling their own money the members apparently accepted as reasonable an interest rate of some 1.5 per cent per month.

The organizer of the society received 120,000 cash at the first meeting. He repaid that amount over the next 10 years in 30 instalments of 4,000 cash each. At the second meeting the low bidder received 67,800 cash. Over the 10 years he paid 120,000 cash. The last member received 120,-000 cash but had paid in only 57,800 cash.

The rapid depreciation of the copper coinage during the life of the society brought some surprising differences in the silver equivalents of the amounts the members paid and received. The first man received the equivalent of $99.30 but repaid the equivalent of only $64.21. The next 10 members all paid more than they received. The next 12 members paid less and the last eight members paid more than they received. The last member to take the fund received 207.6 per cent of his copper payments, but in terms of silver the amount was only 95.3 per cent of what he had paid.

The popularity of the savings societies was shown by the fact that in three villages the number of known members added up to 60.6 per cent of the male population of the villages. There were, of course, many multiple memberships.

Buying and selling was carried on by 2,228 stores in the city and villages, by thousands of itinerant peddlers, in 83 periodic markets, and at 50 temple fairs. One-third of the villages had no stores, another 22 per cent had only one.

The city, with 654 stores, with a market held 12 days a month instead of the usual six, and, with eight temple fairs, was the natural trading center of the hsien. Twelve of the city stores were over 100 years old. One family reported that it had been making eye medicine for more than seven generations. The 654 stores employed 2,761 workers. Fifteen per cent were apprentices. Just over one per cent were women. Eighty-two per cent of the stores were in rented quarters. In Tung T'ing, one of the market towns, 86 per cent of the stores owned their premises.

Wages plus bonuses were less than $65 per year for most of the store employees. Food was furnished by the employers, and cost $4.00 a month in the villages and $4.50 in the city.

Industry was that of a non-mechanical agricultural area. Power was almost entirely animal or human. Most of the tools were hand tools. The principal machines were the animal and hand powered stone mills for grinding grain, the animal powered Persian wheel for irrigation, the foot powered cotton gin and cotton batting machines, the hand driven spinning wheel and the hand and foot powered looms used to process the locally grown cotton.

Approximately one-third of the population over 14 years of age, 18 per cent of the males and 50 per cent of the females, were engaged in some industrial work. Some 90 per cent of the industrial workers were working at home. Most of the home work was a part time occupation. Over 95 per cent of the working females were engaged in spinning, weaving, or both. Forty-three per cent of the hsien industrial output was produced by industrial shops with paid workers, 57 per cent by home industry.

Every village had some home industry. Some reported as many as eight different occupations, but only four types of work—spinning, weaving, bean curd and small noodle making—were reported by more than 20 per cent of the villages, and only seven were reported by more than 5 per cent of the villages.

The estimated value of the industrial output in 1931 was $8,570,000. Home industry produced goods worth $4,860,000. Cotton products were 56 per cent of the total output, metal work only 1.9 per cent. The estimated profit of the shops, after paying wages and other expenses, was

$500,000. The estimated gain of the 36,000 home industry families was $880,000, an average of $24.50 per family per year. For our selected group of 1,220 home industry families the average was $37.00 per family. It was $11.25 per family for our 400 farm families and $12.50 per family for all the families in the hsien.

The home industries in which the average gain was less than $10.00 per person per year included 90 per cent of the home industry workers. For the thread spinners the average was only $2.90 per year.

Cotton spinning was reported by 437 of the 453 villages, weaving by 378 villages. In 1882 58 per cent of the families in a sample village were weaving. Fifty years later the figure was 86 per cent.

In 1892 the price of chuang cloth, a type of undyed cotton cloth woven for export to northwest China, was 700 cash per piece. During the next 10 years there was no change in price, but then seven increases in 18 years doubled the price. After 1922 the price was set in terms of silver. In 1931 the copper equivalent of the silver price was 4,908 cash. The silver equivalent of the 1892 copper price was 62 cents per piece. In 1931 the silver price was $1.20 per piece. In 40 years the price, in terms of copper, increased 600 per cent, in terms of silver 94 per cent.

The annual meeting of the cloth gild regularly fixed a maximum price for chuang cloth. From 1892 to 1922 it was from 5 to 9 per cent above the reported market price. From 1923 to 1931 it was from 18 to 29 per cent higher.

The number of pieces of chuang cloth shipped from Ting Hsien was 600,000 in 1892, 4,000,000 in 1915, and after 1919 about 1,000,000 per year. Shipments decreased 76 per cent in six years, but in spite of that fact the copper price went up twice during that time for a total of 27 per cent. The price evidently was very closely controlled by the gild. Over 82 per cent of the chuang cloth shipments went to Chahar and Suiyuan.

Pig bristle sorting, with an estimated output of $760,000, was, in terms of value, the second largest home industry. It was concentrated in two villages in the southern part of the hsien some 10 miles from the railroad and was carried on by only 80 families and 445 workers.

The yang ke, or planting songs, of Ting Hsien were one of the noteworthy findings of our survey, as they were quite different from the yang ke of other parts of China. In some places they were simple folk songs. In Peking and Shantung the term was applied to the entertain-

CITY WALL—SOUTH GATE

TOMB OF LIU SHENG, KING OF CHUNG SHAN, 154–113 B.C.

CARVED STONE IN SPRING GARDEN

DOMESTIC WELL WINDLASS

PERSIAN WHEEL—LIFTING WATER FOR IRRIGATION

WINNOWING GRAIN

BROOM PLANT,
PRESSED AND
READY FOR USE

MEASURING GRAIN

DRIED NOODLES

MAKING GOURD LADLES

CITY STREET—MARKET DAY

FOOD SHOP

FEATHER DUSTERS
FOR SALE

BARBER SHOP

KETTLE COVER

PREPARING COTTON CLOTH WARP

MAKING SUN DRIED BRICKS

BLACKSMITH SHOP

AIRING HIS BIRDS

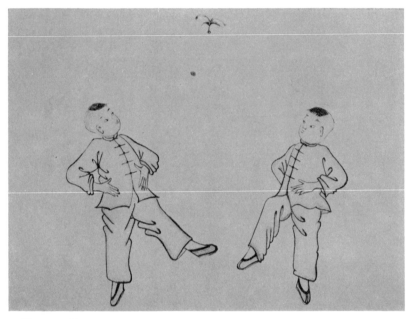

KICKING SHUTTLECOCK

BEATING STICKS

Funeral—"Libation in the Road"

Dragon Headed Catafalque

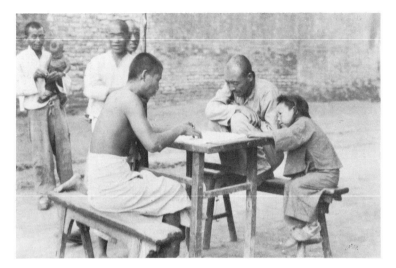

ROADSIDE CHESS GAME

SWORD DANCERS

K'UEI HSING, GOD OF LITERATURE

PAPER AND KAOLIANG CANGUE

Worn on 1st of 10th moon to remind worshipers
of the reality of Ch'eng Huang and protect them from evil.

SHRINE ERECTED TO
SPIRIT OF OLD TREE

ment provided by groups of stilt walkers. In Shanghai they were street dances. The Ting Hsien yang ke were plays given in costume, by groups of locally resident amateur or semi-professional actors, sometimes in connection with temple fairs, sometimes for special celebrations or times of recreation. Local tradition says that originally they were songs written for the rice planters by the poet Su Tung-p'o (1036–1101) when he was magistrate in Ting Hsien.

The five groups of yang ke players in the Experimental District would indicate a total of some 36 groups in the hsien. Usually a group numbered about 15 men, actors, musicians, and stage hands.

The plays, 48 of which we were able to transcribe, covered a wide variety of subjects from filial piety to slapstick humor. The older people complained that the plays had become increasingly rough, vulgar, and boisterous. The District Bureau of Education finally tried to suppress them on the ground that they were a social and moral menace, but it could not enforce its prohibition.

Troupes of traveling professional actors were engaged for some of the temple fairs and by some villages and city organizations for special celebrations. The cost of a three or four day engagement was about $130. Worship of the gods was usually closely connected with the plays. A shrine was erected opposite the stage and many of the people attending the plays combined worship and recreation.

Different community groups, whose acts must have required considerable rehearsing, provided entertainment at New Year's time, usually during the feast of lanterns. One group carried a twisting, turning, gaily painted, candle illuminated dragon through the streets. Another group carried individual lanterns and after many individual maneuvers put the lanterns together to form the figure of a fisherman or a farmer. The Lion Show Society had a red and a green lion which played with embroidered balls and danced for the crowd. Some 70 or 80 players showed their agility and prowess with different kinds of weapons in a show that went on for about eight hours.

There were many kinds of individual and group games, different versions of drop the handkerchief, hide and seek, button, button who has the button, hopscotch, and kicking the shuttlecock. Board games, resembling checkers and chess, were popular during the warm summer days. A few lines on the ground, a few pieces of brick or stone, were all the equipment needed for most of them.

Our 34 family accounts showed an average annual recreation expenditure of $1.02 for wine, $1.22 for tobacco, and $1.70 for other amusements.

The New Year is the festival that every one celebrated in Ting Hsien with vacations, family gatherings, feasting, and new clothes. Many families invited the spirits of their ancestors to return home and join the celebration. Many included worship of the gods and spirits in their celebration. The other big festivals were the fifth of the fifth month and the 15th of the eighth month. Most of the months had days of special but minor celebrations. Some families burned incense and offered special prayers to the gods on the first and 15th of every month.

As everywhere, birth, marriage, and death were important family events observed with special forms and customs. Some were used to insure happiness and good fortune, others to propitiate evil influences, others to assure the spirit of the deceased a safe, easy journey to the other world and comfort and well-being there. The expenses of weddings and funerals were almost always on a scale that brought economic difficulty to the families involved. Funeral expenses ranged from $40 for a poor family to $600 or more for a wealthy family. Wedding expenses for lower class families were some $50 for the groom's family and $80 for the bride's family.

Eight hundred and seventy-seven Taoist, Buddhist, Confucian, Official, and Individual temples, three Mohammedan mosques, and eight Catholic and Protestant Christian churches were the outward expression of religion in Ting Hsien. The village temples were divided 41 per cent Taoist, 26 per cent Official, 25 per cent Buddhist, 6 per cent Individual, and 2 per cent Miscellaneous. Some of the gods were pure spirits, others were heroes and famous men of earlier times who had been deified by the Emperor and given rank and title in the spirit world. The spirit chosen to be the god of the city wall held the same rank in the spirit world that the local official held in the temporal world.

Kuan Yin, in her various manifestations, was the principal deity in 91 per cent of the Buddhist temples. The most popular Taoist deities were the Wu Tao, the San Kuan, the Niang Niangs, Chen Wu, and Yü Huang. Kuan Yü and the Dragons were the chief Official gods. The King of the Horses and the King of the Insects were the principal deities in three-quarters of the Individual temples. Most of the village temples were small one chien buildings. The average size was only 1.6 chien.

Between 1882 and 1928 the 62 villages in the Experimental District gave up 331 temples, 76 per cent of the original number. Three-quarters of the discontinued temples were abolished in 1914 and 1915 when Sun Fa-hsü was magistrate. Before 1882 all but one of the Experimental District villages had one or more temples. The single exception was a village in which 72 per cent of the families were Mohammedans. In 1928 there were no temples in one half the villages. The reports indicate that a large proportion of the discontinued temples were converted to village use as schools, village offices, or public storehouses.

Fifty temple fairs were held in the city and 35 different villages. These three or four day celebrations combined worship, recreation, and business and were greatly enjoyed. The gods were worshiped, troupes of actors provided entertainment, local wares and products were displayed for sale, and visiting merchants set up booths to sell articles brought in from the cities. Attendances of five and ten thousand persons per day were not unusual.

Various Buddhist and Taoist societies encouraged their members to engage in contemplation, abstinence, and good deeds. Women were accepted as members by at least two-thirds of the Taoist societies.

Mohammedanism has been part of the religious life in Ting Hsien for more than 300 years. The two village mosques had a membership of 1,415, representing 255 families living in five villages in the Experimental District.

The Catholic work was in charge of a French priest. There were some 5,800 members, who belonged to some 1,100 families. Protestant Christianity was represented by the Congregational Church and the Salvation Army. They reported a membership of 1,025.

A Ting Hsien proverb says:

> Don't blame heaven if you haven't
> Dug your cabbage before the winter solstice.
> Don't be sorry for yourself if you haven't
> Protected your onions before the coming of the first frost.

PART 1. FAMILY STUDIES

CHAPTER II

Population and Other Vital Statistics

THE POPULATION of Ting Hsien was generally estimated to be, in round numbers, forty 10,000s or 400,000 persons. The total could only be estimated, for no complete census had been taken in the hsien. The families had been counted, but individuals had been counted only in sample groups of families. Our count of the families living in the hsien multiplied by 5.83, the average number of persons per family in a 7.5 per cent sample, gave a total population of 408,300, only 2.1 per cent more than the generally estimated 400,000.[1]

The average population density for the hsien was 95 persons per square li, 850 persons per square mile of total area. It was 1,100 persons per square mile of crop area. In determining these figures the area and population of the hsien city and its three suburbs have been included, as 72 per cent of their area was cultivated land. In America the population density per square mile of total area in 1930 was 649.8 in Rhode Island, 537.4 in Massachusetts, and 136.4 in Illinois.[2] Buck found the population density in a Hopei district 100 miles south of Ting Hsien to be 1,171 persons per square mile of farm area.[3]

According to our count there were 70,034 families in Ting Hsien in 1931. They were living in the hsien city, 10 "towns" and 443 "villages". We have not attempted to differentiate between the "towns" and "villages" for while the "towns" generally had more families than the "villages" there were some "villages" that were larger than the neighboring "town". Seventy-two of the "villages" held periodic markets, not all of them as large as those of the "towns" but very similar.

1. In 1947 the Ministry of the Interior reported the Ting Hsien population to be 445,474.

2. U.S. Census, 1930.

3. J. Lossing Buck, *Chinese Farm Economy* (University of Chicago Press, 1930).

There were 2,169 families in the city, and 67,865 in the 453 "villages" and "towns".

The number of families in the individual villages ranged from six to 1,200. Twenty per cent of the villages had less than 50 families, 46 per cent had less than 100 families, and 75 per cent had less than 200 families. Only seven, 1.5 per cent, had as many as 500 families. The average was 150 families per village, or 154 families if the hsien city is included.

The following figures show how the villages and families were divided in the six administrative districts of the hsien.

District	Villages	Families	Average No. of Families per Village	Average No. of Mu per Family
1	71	6,555	92	23.8
2	63	8,062	128	22.8
3	83	15,939	192	21.5
4	73	16,010	220	19.7
5	73	7,864	108	19.1
6	90	13,435	149	19.8
City	—	2,169	—	6.2
	453	70,034	150	20.4

It will be noted that in the different districts the number of villages varied from 63 to 90, the number of families from 6,555 to 16,010, and the average number of families per village from 92 to 220. We have not been able to find any reason for the wide variation in the averages. There were four market towns in the 4th District, the one with the largest average, but while there were two market towns in both the 3rd and the 5th District the average in the 5th District was 50 per cent more than in the 3rd. There was no market town in the 1st District as the city was its market center. If the city and 1st District are added together the average was 121 families per "village".

In contrast to the wide variation in the average number of families per village, there was only a small difference in the average amount of crop area per family in the six districts. It ranged from 19.1 mu in the 5th District to 23.8 mu in the 1st District. The average for the entire hsien, including the city and its three suburbs, was 20.2 mu per family.

A complete study of any part of the Chinese population is a difficult task. The people, especially those living in the country, are fearful lest the figures be used as a basis for taxation or for the recruiting of soldiers and laborers for the army, or laborers for public works projects such as dyke and road building. Reports given to Government enumerators are often very incomplete and sometimes attempts have been made to "persuade" the census takers, counting not individuals but families, to send in figures much below the actual number.

Our investigators naturally met some of this same suspicion when they were counting the families and still greater difficulties when securing detailed reports from individual families. Boys were sometimes omitted lest information about them make it possible to cast their horoscope and exert an evil influence over them; young men because of possible military service. Young girls would be left out because some families feel they do not amount to much; unmarried women because it was felt that the fact that they were unmarried reflected on the family. These difficulties were overcome, at least partially, by the fact that the study was made by representatives of the Mass Education Movement, and the matter had been discussed beforehand with the village heads in order to clear up any misunderstandings and obtain their active help and cooperation. In many villages they accompanied the investigators from house to house, and their knowledge of the individual families often made it possible for them to remind the family heads of some members that they had "overlooked". In one town we counted 200 more families than the official figure.

A "family" in this study included the present members of the family and the absent relatives who shared in the family budget. A person living alone was counted as a one-person "family." Employees were not included as they were listed with their own families.

Our population figures were secured by an extensive study of the number of families living in the hsien and by intensive studies of five different groups of families that together included 8,464 families and 49,609 individuals. Two of the studies were definite population studies. In the others securing the figures on the size of the families was incidental to the collection of other material.

The groups of families, their location, the number of families and persons included, the date of the study, the size of the average family, and the masculinity rate (males per 100 females) were:

Study	Families	Persons	Year	Location	See Chapter	Average Size of Family	Masculinity Rate
1	400	2,536	1927	Experimental District	III	6.3	108
2	34	205	1928	Experimental District	V	6.0	107
3	515	3,571	1929	Experimental District	II	6.9	106
4	5,255	30,642	1930	1st Dist., 80 per cent of families	II	5.8	106
5	2,260	12,655	1932	6th Dist., 6 villages	IV	5.6	112

The averages for the first three groups cannot be considered typical community figures as the groups were not random samples. They all included more than an average number of middle class and well-to-do families. The 34 and the 515 family studies included no one-person "families".

In our first studies our field workers found it easier to get the wealthier families to cooperate. We had no figures to indicate what was the average distribution of the families in different property and income groups. We wanted to have enough of the middle class and wealthier families so that the group figures would show what, if any, difference there was in the average size of the families in the different income groups.

That the size of the family was definitely related to the size of the family income was one of the first facts shown by our studies. Whether the family income was estimated in dollars or the income groups were divided according to the size of the family farm, it was clearly evident that, on the average, the size of the family increased as the family income increased. This did not necessarily mean an increase in the number of children in the family but in the number in the group living together. There were relatives who were willing to make use of any increased income. In some cases the family membership and the family income were both large because the family had not been "divided"; brothers and their families were still living together.

In our first study, of 400 farm families, the size of the average family increased from 3.8 persons for families with not more than 10 mu of land to 13.5 persons for those with more than 100 mu. In our third study the families with less than 10 mu of land averaged 4.7 persons; those with 100 mu or more averaged 12.9 persons. In our fifth study the average was 4.1 persons for the families with no land and 13.2 for those with 100 mu or more.

With a 100 per cent increase in the size of the family farm there was a tendency for the size of the average family to increase some 30 per cent in the 515 families, 35 per cent in the 400 farm families, and some 40 per cent in the 1,220 home industry families.

In the second study the size of the average family increased from 3.8 persons for the group with incomes of less than $200 per year to 9.3 persons for those whose annual income was between $400 and $500. With a 100 per cent increase in the family income the size of the family tended to increase over 50 per cent, but the small number of families in the different income groups makes for a large probable error in this figure.

From these figures it is quite evident that unless the economic status of the families in a sample group closely follows that of the entire community the averages of the sample group will not be typical.

The 5,255 family group is our most typical family sample and therefore the one whose average family, 5.83 persons, is nearest in size to the average family in Ting Hsien. In that study we attempted to include all the families living in the 1st District, but as six of the 71 villages refused to cooperate and a few individual family reports had to be omitted because of incomplete or evidently incorrect reporting, the 5,255 families finally included were 80 per cent of the families in the district and a 7.5 per cent sample of all the families in the hsien.

The average size of the 2,260 families in six villages was 5.6 persons, slightly less than the 5.8 average for the 5,255 families. As the villages were chosen for study because of the amount of their home industry they possibly included a larger than normal proportion of lower income families and would therefore have a lower than normal average family. The average for the 1,220 home industry families that we studied in detail was 5.2 persons per family.

The individual families in the 5,255 family group varied in size from one to 65 persons. There were 194 families with only one member and 402 with two members. These two groups were 11.3 per cent of the entire number. It was generally stated that the Chinese "large family" system prevailed in Ting Hsien, but 55 per cent of the families had from one to five members, 78 per cent had not more than seven members, and 91.3 per cent had from one to 10 members. Only 37 families, 0.7 per cent, had more than 20 members, and only 13 families had more than 25 members. The largest group of families was that with four mem-

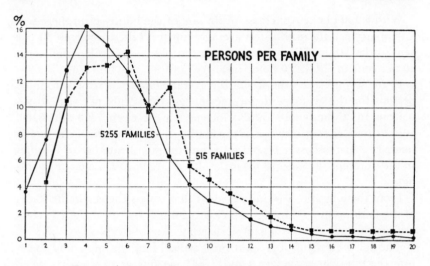

FIGURE 4. SIZE OF FAMILIES, 515 AND 5,255 FAMILIES

bers. It had 852 families, almost one-sixth of the families studied. Figure 4 shows the per cent distribution of the different sized families in the 5,255 and the 515 family groups.

One-third of the individuals in the 5,255 families belonged to families with from one to five members and four-fifths to those with from one to 10 members. Only 7.2 per cent belonged to families with more than 15 members and 3.2 per cent to families with more than 20 members.

In the 515 families of the Experimental District the size of the families varied from two to 22 members. The average, 6.9 persons per family, was 1.1 more than for the 5,255 families in the 1st District, but, as stated above, the 515 families were not an average group. No single member "families" were included and the families selected were chosen partly on the basis of the amount of land they owned. Nineteen per cent of this group owned 50 or more mu of land, compared with 7.8 per cent of the families in the hsien. The families with over 100 mu were 3.5 per cent of the 515 families, but only 1.2 per cent of all the families in the hsien. (See Chapter X.)

In the home industry group the size of the families varied from one to 30 members. Fifty-one per cent had less than five members and 93.4

per cent had less than 10 members. The corresponding figures for the 5,255 families were 40.5 and 88.4 per cent.

Five hundred and seven individuals, 1.4 per cent of the members of the 5,255 families, were away from home when our study was made. Only seven of these were females. This number did not, of course, include any married daughters as they would be counted as members of their husband's family. Peking and Tientsin, with cheap railway transportation available, offered industrial and educational opportunities that attracted at least some of the residents of Ting Hsien.

Composition of the Family

From the family records it has been possible to study the relationship between the various members of the family. The relationship given here is that of the individual to the male head of the family, or to the deceased husband of the female head. There were 54 different kinds of relationship listed in the 5,255 families and 39 in the 515 families. They covered a range of seven generations, from grandfather to great-great-grandson. The Chinese list is lengthened by their concise differentiation of relationships: elder brother, younger brother, father's elder brother, father's younger brother. The same differentiation is applied to aunts, sisters-in-law, nieces, and nephews. The relationships in four groups of families are shown in Table 4.

While the "large family" system, with several generations and coordinate branches of the family living together and pooling their economic resources, has been the typical family system in China, our relationship figures seem to show that there was a tendency and possibly a growing tendency for the brothers to divide the family after their father's death. The Ting Hsien families were generally small. Only 8.7 per cent of the 5,255 families had more than 10 members. Not more than two generations were represented in 51.4 per cent of the 515 families.

The head of a Chinese family is usually the oldest male in the family group. However, it is possible for a father, who wants to retire, to pass the headship to one of his sons. Ordinarily it will go to his eldest son, but, in some instances, personal qualities and the choice of the family will give the leadership to a younger son. In the 5,255 families there were 84 and in the 515 families 23 men whose younger brothers were heads of families. In special family situations the headship may even pass to a brother rather than to a son on the death or retirement of the head of the family.

If a son is still young when he succeeds to the headship of the family someone of the older generation, often his mother or perhaps an uncle, who may have come to help the family, will act for him, but in his name, until he is older.

Some authorities say that a woman is never recognized as the head of a family, but in 211 cases, 4.0 per cent of the 5,255 families, a woman was listed as the head of the family. In the 515 families the proportion was smaller, only 1.2 per cent, but in six families in that group a woman was the recognized head.

If the different relatives are divided into four groups, parents, head of the family and his descendants, brothers and their dependents, and other relatives, we find that the family head, his immediate family, and direct descendants were some 82 per cent; brothers, both older and younger, their wives and descendants, some 12 per cent; the older generations, fathers, mothers, grandfathers, uncles, uncles' wives, some 5 per cent of the group. Other relatives were only some 0.2 per cent. The figures in Table 4, for three different groups of Ting Hsien families, are generally so similar that it seems probable that they are typical for Ting Hsien and the neighboring rural areas. As they are very similar to the division found by Buck[4] in his study of farm families in North China, it seems probable that they also are typical for the rural areas of North China.

The ages of the family heads in the 515 family group ranged from under 15 to over 80. Fifty-four per cent were between 30 and 49, while 32 per cent were between 50 and 69 years of age. Four per cent were over 70 years old. Three family heads were under 15 and 13 were under 20. The six female heads were all between 30 and 54 years of age.

Twenty per cent of the male family heads in the 5,255 families and 14.4 per cent in the 515 families were not married. Even though there were some family heads who were below 15 years of age and in the 515 families 17.5 per cent of the male heads were 60 years of age or older, it would seem that one in five and one in seven were high proportions to be without mates.

There were 22 concubines in the 5,255 families and eight in the 515 families.

4. Buck, *op. cit.*

The proportion of sons was almost exactly twice that of daughters. This difference would be expected as the married daughters would not be listed as members of the family. Daughters-in-law did not quite make up the difference between sons and daughters.

There were 21 adopted sons in the 5,255 families and four in the 515 families, so the proportion of families adopting was well under one per cent. One family in the 515 family group had a son-in-law living with them. He probably was taking the place of a son in carrying on the family line.

One married daughter was listed in the 5,255 families and two future daughters-in-law. The custom of rearing a son's fiancee evidently was not general in Ting Hsien, but many of the boys were so young when they were married that their wives might well be listed as their fiancees. In the 5,255 families 100 boys, who were still under 14 years of age, were reported as married. This was 6 per cent of the boys from nine to 13 years of age. Nineteen per cent of the 13 year old boys were married. In a group of 1,843 married men living in three market towns, 14.8 per cent were married before they were 14 years old. In the 515 families, 25 per cent of 766 married men were under 14 when they were married.

A Chinese family with five generations living together under the same roof is said to be particularly blessed. We have been told that in the older days such an occurrence was given special notice by the Emperor. In the 515 families there was one family with five generations and 42 families, 8.2 per cent, with four generations. The two and three generation families were 49.0 and 40.2 per cent of the group. Thirteen families, 2.5 per cent, had only one generation. There were several families in the 5,255 group that may have had five generations, but this item was not taken from the records.

Sex Distribution

Fifty-one and one-half per cent of the members of the 5,255 families and 51.4 per cent of the 515 families were males. If those who were away from home, but were still counted as members of the family, are omitted, the figure for the 5,255 families was 51.2 per cent male. There had not been enough movement to the cities to make any large change in the sex division of these rural families.

In the larger Chinese cities the population was from 57 to 63.5 per cent male. Many men leave their families behind them when they go to work in the city. Long hours, the difficulties of local transportation, the cost of living in the city, and the fact that many men regularly lived where they worked, often made it better for a man to go to the city alone. Furthermore his parents would expect their daugher-in-law to stay at home and look after them.

The masculinity rates (number of males per 100 females) for four of our groups of families ranged from 105.5 to 108. These figures were only slightly higher than the 105 of the rural non-farm population in the United States. The index of our home industry families was 112, only slightly more than the 111 of the U.S. rural farm population.[5] The U.S. figures for 1930 are used as they correspond with the time of our study.

Age Distribution

The ages given in this study are figured according to the Western rather than the Chinese method of calculating age. According to the Chinese system a child is one year old when born and two years old on the next Chinese New Year. When the study of the 5,255 families was made each person's Chinese age and birthday were recorded. They were also asked the name of the "animal" in the Chinese year cycle to which they belonged. From this the Western age was easily figured. The Western ages for the other groups have been determined by reducing the Chinese age by one year.

The age distribution by five year age groups of the members of the two groups of Chinese families and of the rural farm and rural non-farm population in the United States are shown in Figure 5. The graphs for the two Chinese groups are similar except that the 515 families have a slightly larger proportion under 25 years of age, 53.5 per cent, as compared with 50 per cent for the 5,255 families. The difference is especially large in the under five group. The 515 families reported 15.2 per cent of their members under five; the 5,255 families, 12.4 per cent. We have not been able to discover any reason for the large proportion of young children in the 515 families except the fact that there were no single-person families in that group and a much smaller proportion of the families had from two to five members, 41 per cent as compared with 51.3 per cent of the 5,255 families.

5. U.S. Census.

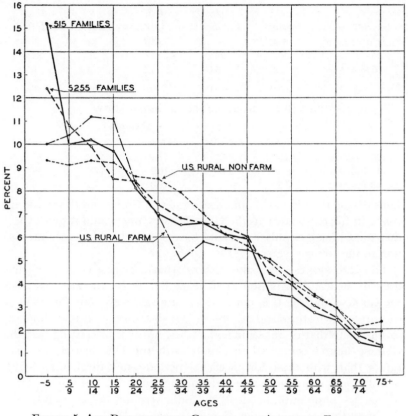

FIGURE 5. AGE DISTRIBUTION, CHINESE AND AMERICAN FAMILIES

In both the 5,255 and the 515 family group 50 per cent of the family members were between 15 and 49 years of age. In Buck's[6] families the proportion was 51 per cent. Under 15 years of age, the figures were: 5,255 families, 33.1 per cent; 515 families, 35.4 per cent; Buck's families, 35.5 per cent. Those 50 years of age and over were 16.8 per cent, 14.6 per cent, and 14.3 per cent.

The similarity of the age distribution in the 5,255 Chinese families and in the population of the United States in 1930[7] is shown by the following figures:

6. Buck, *op. cit.*
7. U.S. Census.

Age	5,255 Families	515 Families	U.S. 1930	U.S. 1880	U.S. 1940
Under 35	64.2	66.8	63.1	74	59.4
35–64	30.3	28.2	31.4	23	33.7
65 and over	5.5	5.0	5.5	3	6.9
	100.0	100.0	100.0	100	100.0

A slightly different age grouping tells a similar story.

Age	5,255 Families	515 Families	U.S. Rural Farm	U.S. Rural Non-Farm	U.S.
25 and over	50.0	46.7	44.6	51.2	52.3
50 and over	16.8	14.6	16.3	17.9	17.2
60 and over	8.5	7.7	8.0	9.6	8.5

Considering the high birth and death rates in China and the steady increase in life expectancy in the United States, one would rather expect that the Chinese population would have a considerably larger proportion in the younger years.

The U.S. figures given above show what a large change there has been in the age distribution in 60 years. Except for the fact that both the Chinese and the U.S. population were relatively stable in 1930, it was probably fortuitous that the U.S. age distribution at that time was so similar to that of our Chinese families, but it is interesting that the Chinese figures compared so closely with the U.S. figures for 1930 rather than with those for an earlier period when the United States population was so much more rural and agricultural. The rapid growth of the U.S. population before 1900 would account, in part at least, for the higher proportion under 35 years of age in 1880.

Buck, in his study of Chinese families, reported that he found a possible tendency for the Chinese to give their ages in even rather than odd numbers. For his 2,640 families with 14,952 members, the division was 59.7 per cent in the even years and 40.3 in the odd years, using the Chinese age basis.[8] The preponderance, of course, was in the odd years when the ages were figured by the Western method. The figures were quite consistent in the different ten year age groups. The range in the percentage in the even years was from 53.5 in the 61–70 year group to 63.6 in the group over 80. The males were 60.2 per cent even, the females 58.8.

In the 34 families included in our family budget study (see Chapter

8. Buck, *op. cit.*

V) just the opposite was true. In that group of 205 persons 55.1 per cent of the ages were given as odd and 44.9 per cent as even. There was a wide divergence in the figures for the 10 year age groups, from 28.5 per cent odd in the 71–80 year group to 75 per cent odd in the 61–70 year group. These wide differences probably were due to the relatively small numbers in the groups.

In our group of 5,255 families, we found the same tendency as in the 34 families. The division, however, was much more nearly even, but the odd years outnumbered the even by a ratio of 52 to 48. The ratios for the 10 year age groups were close to the average, varying not more than 1.5 per cent above or below the average, except in the over 90 group, where the small number of three individuals made a 67–33 division necessary.

For the females the 10 year age group division range was from 50.7 to 53.4 per cent odd, except in the over 90 year group. For the males the range was from 50 to 54.4 per cent odd.

To allow for the fact that the 10 year age groups all started with an odd year and that the natural decrease tends, therefore, to make the odd numbers larger than the even, we have refigured the odd-even division by 10 year age groups, omitting the one year group. When that was done the total group divided 50.4 per cent odd and 49.6 per cent even. Five of the 10 year age groups were still above 50 per cent odd, but four, the two youngest and the two oldest, had a majority in the even years. This would seem to show that by using the technique of getting the animal of the year in which a person was born we were able to eliminate any tendency there may have been to give ages in either even or odd years.

Age and Sex Distribution

The graphs in Figures 6 and 7 show that while the age distribution of the sexes in the 5,255 Chinese families was fairly similar, there was a definitely larger proportion of females in the higher age groups. The average masculinity rate was 106, but for the five year age groups from five to 44 years the rate was regularly 110 or more. The maximum was 113 in the 15–19 year group. After 45 the rate declined until in the 55–59 year group it was below 100, and the females outnumbered the males. From then on, the preponderance of females increased until in the 80–84 and 85–89 year groups the masculinity rate was only 47. It

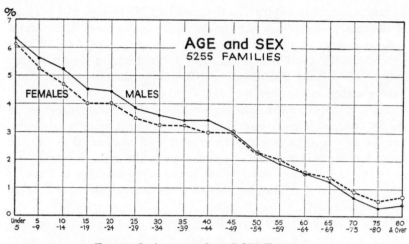

FIGURE 6. AGE AND SEX, 5,255 FAMILIES

was zero for the 90 and over group, in which there were three females but no males. For all of those 50 or over the rate was 92.7.

The greater fluctuation in the masculinity rates for the different age groups in the 515 families probably was due to the smaller number of persons involved. For those 50 and over the rate was 87.1.

In the U.S. rural non-farm families, although the average masculinity rate was 105, slightly less than that of the Chinese families, the females outnumbered the males only in the 15–19, 20–24, 80–84, and 85 and over groups. The maximum rate, 115.1, was in the 45–49 and the 50–54 year age groups, rather than in the 15–19 year group, which had the highest rate for the Chinese families.

In the U.S. rural farm families, where the average masculinity rate was 111, the females outnumbered the males only in the 30–34 and 85 and over groups. The masculinity rate increased group by group from 99.4 in the 30–34 year age group to a maximum of 146.5 in the 70–74 year group. It was 87.5 in the 85 and over group, more than twice the rate for the 5,255 families. From the graphs in Figure 7 it would appear that life on the U.S. farms was especially hazardous for females over 40 while in the older groups in China the hazards of masculinity were much greater than in the United States.

The age distribution of Chinese and U.S. males is shown to be fairly similar by the percentage distribution in the five year age groups. The

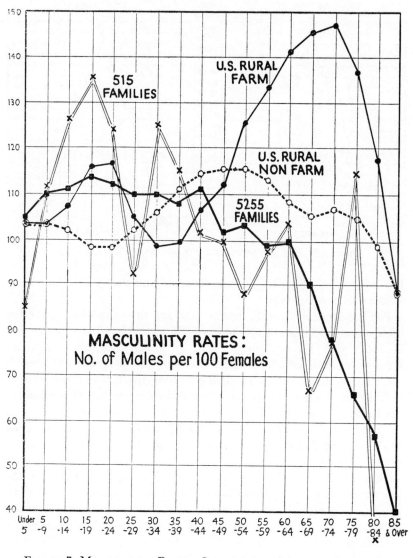

FIGURE 7. MASCULINITY RATES, CHINESE AND AMERICAN FAMILIES

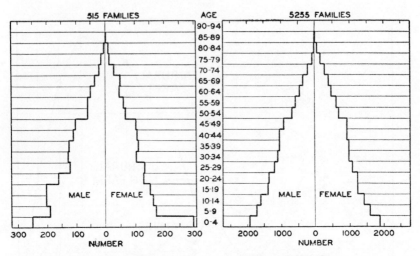

FIGURE 8. AGE AND SEX PYRAMID, 515 AND 5,255 FAMILIES

U.S. figures, however, are smaller below 15 and then larger for almost all the higher age groups.

For the females the U.S. figures were less than the Chinese for the groups under 10 years of age, higher from 15 to 44 and less for the ages 55 and above. Twenty-four per cent of the Chinese women were 45 years of age or older, 22.5 per cent of the U.S. women. The difference is not large, but it is rather surprising to have the figures show a larger proportion of Chinese women in the older age groups. Conditions of life in Ting Hsien would lead one to expect the opposite.

The pyramids in Figure 8 show the age and sex distribution of the 515 and the 5,255 families by five year age groups. As would be expected in an area with high birth and death rates, the pyramids both have a broad base. They both show relatively high death rates in the lower age groups, only slight decreases in the groups from 25 to 49 years of age, and then a sharp reduction in the number in the groups above 49 years of age. The 50 to 54 year age group of the 515 families was born in the years from 1875 to 1879. Those of the 5,255 families were born from 1876 to 1880. Those years included the big famine of 1877 and 1878. The hsien history says that at that time there was nothing growing on the land for thousands of li, that many refugees died along the road and the hungry people even resorted to cannibalism. Such a time would necessarily reduce the birth rate and the number of survivors in the older groups. The difference between the numbers in the 50–54 and the 45–49 year age groups would seem to point to a rapid recovery in the birth rate soon after the famine.

The 1920 famine was shorter than that in 1877 and less severe, and evidently more adequate relief was provided. No sharp drop is shown in the age groups covering that period.

Marital Status

All but 14.4 per cent of the members of the 5,255 families over 14 years of age had been married. Of the males over 14, 21.2 per cent were unmarried but only 6.6 per cent of the females. In the United States 34.1 per cent of the males 15 years of age or over were single and 26.4 per cent of the females.[9] To give the complete picture of the marital condition of the Chinese families it is necessary to go below the usual 15-year limit, as 169 males and 33 females under 15 were married. Two of the 169 males were nine years old, three were 10, and 16 were 11 years old. Twelve was the youngest age at which any girls were married. For the entire group, including all ages, the proportion married was males 53.5 per cent, females 62.7 per cent, total 58 per cent.

In the 515 families 54.6 per cent of the entire group were or had been married. Of the males of all ages, 51.5 per cent were married and 58.5 per cent of the females. The different age distribution of the members of the two groups of families probably accounts for at least part of the difference in the proportions married.

There were 80 widowers in the 515 families, 8.5 per cent of the males who had been married. One hundred and sixty-four men, 17.4 per cent of those who had been married, had lost by death at least one wife. Thirteen had lost two, and two had lost three wives. One hundred and one men had remarried. Eleven had married three times and one was living with his fourth wife.

There were 143 widows listed, 14.1 per cent of the women who had been married. Widows can and do remarry in Ting Hsien. Twenty women were reported as having been married twice. Two of these had lost their second husbands. The total number of women who had been widowed was 161, which was 15.8 per cent of the women who had been married.

9. U.S. Census.

The United States census reports widowers as 7.1 per cent of the males and widows as 15.1 per cent of the females who had been married. Seven per cent of the Ting Hsien widows and 17.5 per cent of the widowers were under 30 years of age. Four of the widowers but none of the widows were under 20.

There evidently was a definite relationship between the proportion of males who were widowers and the amount of land owned by their families. While the widowers were 4.3 per cent of the males in the 515 families, they were 5.1 per cent in the families with less than 50 mu, 3.2 per cent in the families with 50 to 99 mu, and 0.8 per cent of the males in the families with 100 or more mu. The one widower in the latter group had lost his wife before he was 15. While a possibly lower female mortality in the wealthier families might account for some of the differences in the percentages, most of the difference appears to be the result of a higher remarriage rate in the families with the larger farms.

For the widows the figures do not show the same sort of variation. They were 9.4 per cent of the females in the families with less than 50 mu, 5.6 per cent in the 50 to 99 mu group, and 7.0 per cent in the 100 mu and over group. For the entire group the figure was 8.2 per cent.

Sixty-one per cent of the men who had lost their first wives had remarried, but only 14 per cent of the women who had lost their first husbands.

Twenty-two plural marriages were reported by the 5,255 families and eight by the 515 families. Affecting less than one per cent of the families, concubinage was not a large factor in this rural area. The desire for sons was given as the reason for taking a concubine. As might be expected, the amount of land owned by the family definitely influenced the amount of concubinage. In the 515 families, the rate was one in 18 for the families with over 100 mu, but only one in 183 for the families with less than 50 mu.

Two divorces were reported in the 515 families. The field investigators reported that, in one family, the difficulty arose over the fact that the bride's family felt that they had been cheated by the marriage middle-man. Even though the groom's family had 35 mu of land and an income of $120 a year from selling bread and other supplementary occupations, her parents felt that his economic status was not what they should have for their daughter. Trouble developed between the families and the couple separated about a year after their marriage.

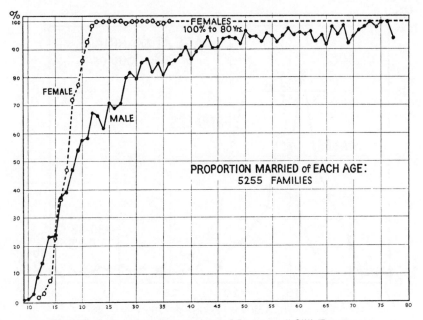

FIGURE 9. AGE AND PROPORTION MARRIED, 5,255 FAMILIES

In the second family the bride did not heed the teachings of her new home. She was flirtatious and quarreled almost constantly with her husband and her mother-in-law. A divorce was finally arranged and she returned to her family. The man remarried in less than a year. The reporter made special note of the fact that the man's second wife had borne him a son.

Age and Marriage

Early and well-nigh universal marriage was very definitely an integral part of the Chinese rural social system. This was particularly true for the women. No unmarried females over 35 years of age were listed in the 5,255 families. There were only three over 22 and only five over 21 years of age. This was only 0.66 per cent of the women over 21. The graph in Figure 9 shows how rapidly the proportion married increased from 1.4 per cent of the 12 year old girls to 100 per cent of those 23 years old. The big jump from 48 per cent for the 17 year old girls to 72 per cent for those 18 years old shows clearly that, as least in that group

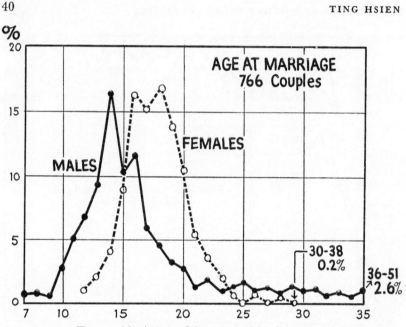

FIGURE 10. AGE AT MARRIAGE, 766 COUPLES

of families, the largest number of girls were married when they were 18.

A large proportion of the boys were married before they were 15, but the males as a group did not marry early as universally as the females. Of those who were over 21 years of age 13.7 per cent were still single. One hundred per cent of the 23 year old females were married, but only 66.3 per cent of the males. Not until they were 39 years of age were 90 per cent of the males married. Above 50 years of age the proportion was generally about 95 per cent married. Only in three years in the seventies were 100 per cent of the males married.

In the United States, 14.3 per cent of the males and 10 per cent of the females between 35 and 44 years of age were single. For those between 55 and 64 the figures were males 10.1 per cent, females 8.9 per cent.[10]

The figures for the 515 families do not give the ages of the married and unmarried, but a special study was made of the "age at marriage" of 766 couples in those families. The group included no second marriages. For the men the age at marriage ranged from seven to 51, for the women from 12 to 38. The average age was men 17.2 and women

10. U.S. Census.

17.7. Figure 10 shows that the largest number of boys, almost one in six, were married when they were 14 years old. Almost one-half, 47.5 per cent, were married in the four years from 13 through 16, and almost two-fifths, 38.1 per cent, in the three years from 14 through 16. Sixteen per cent were under 13 years of age and just over 10 per cent were over 25.

The largest number of girls, 16.8 per cent, were married when they were 18, the next largest group, 16.1 per cent, when they were 16 years old. The three years from 16 through 18 included 48.2 per cent of the girls. Eight girls were married when they were 12 and 16 when they were 13 years old. Fourteen and one-half per cent were married before they were 16, but only 7.2 per cent when they were over 21 and less than 2 per cent when they were more than 23 years of age.

A very similar story is told by a study made of 1,843 men and 2,059 women living in three market towns. The average age at marriage was the same for the girls, 17.7, but it was 1.5 years higher for the boys, 18.6. Again, the largest number of boys were married at 14 and the largest number of girls at 18. Thirty-four per cent of the boys were married when they were from 13 to 16 years of age and 29.5 per cent in the three years from 14 through 16. The 9.8 per cent who were under 13 were a smaller proportion than in the 515 families. There was a larger proportion in the higher ages, 27.1 per cent in the 17 through 21 group and 17.1 per cent in the over 25 group.

Fifty-eight per cent of the girls were from 16 to 18 years old when they were married. One in eight was married before she was 16, 6.5 per cent after they were 22, but only 2.7 per cent after they had reached 24 years of age.

The influence of the family's economic situation on the age at marriage is very clearly shown when the 766 couples in the 515 families are divided into three groups according to the amount of land owned by their families, under 50 mu, 50–99 mu, and 100 mu and over. Figure 11 shows that in all three groups 14 was the most popular age for the boys and 18 for the girls. However, the average age for the girls marrying into the families with 50 or more mu of land was a full year less than for those marrying into families with less than 50 mu, 16.8 as compared with 17.8. For the boys the difference was much more marked. Their average age at marriage was 18.4 for the families with less than 50 mu. It dropped to 15.6 in the 50 to 99 mu group and to the surprisingly low

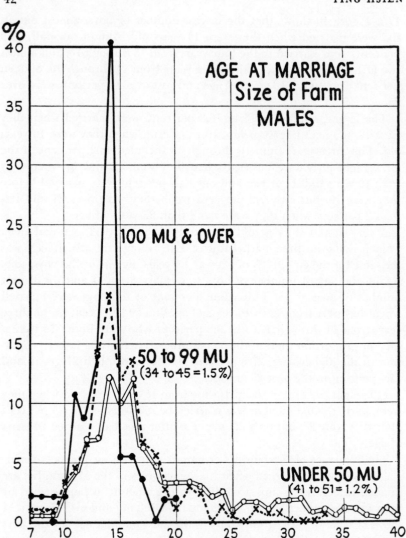

%

AGE AT MARRIAGE
Size of Farm
MALES

100 MU & OVER

50 to 99 MU
(34 to 45 = 1.5%)

UNDER 50 MU
(41 to 51 = 1.2%)

FIGURE 11A. AGE AT MARRIAGE AND SIZE OF FAMILY FARM,
766 COUPLES: MALES

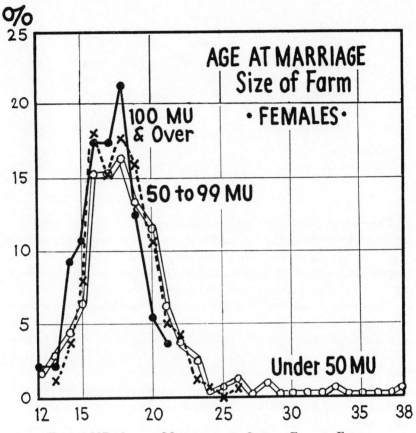

FIGURE 11B. AGE AT MARRIAGE AND SIZE OF FAMILY FARM,
766 COUPLES: FEMALES

average of 13.2 in the families with 100 mu or over. The youngest age at marriage was seven for the males and 12 for the females. The oldest age was 51 for the males and 38 for the females.

The following figures, giving in summary form the proportions of the males and females in the 766 couples who were married before they had attained given ages, show how the age at marriage varied for the sexes and how it was affected by the economic status of the family. The effect was very striking for the boys, less so, but still very noticeable, for the girls.

Males

Size of Farm	Under 13	Under 15	Under 18	Over 22	Total No. of Couples
Under 50 mu	14.7	33.3	61.0	20.3	490
50–99 mu	15.6	48.9	80.7	5.2	219
100 mu and over	26.3	80.5	94.6	1.8	57
Total	15.8	41.4	69.3	14.6	766

		Females			16–20
Under 50 mu	1.4	8.6	44.9	4.8	60.7
50–99 mu	–	4.5	45.1	1.9	76.7
100 mu and over	1.8	12.4	57.8	0.0	73.7
Total	1.0	7.8	46.0	3.7	72.6

The outstanding figures are those showing that while only one-third of the males in the couples in the families with less than 50 mu of land were married before they were 15 years old, the proportion was 80.5 per cent in the families with 100 mu or more. In the latter group 40 per cent of the males were married when they were 14 years of age.

The lower income families often cannot help delaying their son's marriage when faced with the cost of the wedding celebration and the problem of feeding another "mouth." In some of the lower income families in Peking the expenditures for a wedding often amounted to four or five months' income.[11]

It will be noted that nearly three-quarters of the girls were between 16 and 20 years old when they were married. Detailed figures are given in Table 8.

The influence of the family's economic status is also shown in the distribution of the 766 couple study. The average was 1.2 couples in the families with less than 50 mu of land, 2.7 in the 50 to 99 mu group, and 3.2 in the group with 100 mu and over.

Groups were working in Ting Hsien to reform the marriage customs. Hence, at the time of our study, the age at marriage probably was higher than it had been some years earlier and it has probably gone up since then. The Customs Improvement Club of Chai Ch'eng attempted to set the minimum age as 20 for boys and 16 for girls.

11. Sidney D. Gamble, *How Chinese Families Live in Peiping* (Funk and Wagnalls, New York, 1933).

Ages of Husband and Wife

The age figures of the 766 couples in the 515 families showed that in 69.6 per cent of the couples the wife was older than her husband. In 24.6 per cent the husband was the older. In only 44 couples were the husband and wife the same age. Where the wife was the older, the difference in age ranged from one to 11 years with the largest number two and three years older. In four out of five of those couples the difference was not more than five years. The average difference was 3.8 years.

Where the husband was older the difference in age ranged from one to 28 years. In 31 per cent of these couples the difference was 10 or more years. The average difference was eight years.

For the entire group the wives were, on the average, eight months older than their husbands. The greater number of older wives offset the greater age difference when the husband was the older.

A study of 1,540 couples in three market towns does not tell quite the same story. In that group the division was 48 per cent of the wives older than their husbands and 46.3 per cent of the husbands older than their wives. The average differences in age were almost the same, 7.9 years where the husband was older and 3.9 years where the wife was older. Because of the more even division, the average difference in age for the entire group was the husband 1.8 years older.

A difference in the economic condition of the 515 farm families and the 1,540 market-town families may account for some of the differences in the figures for the two groups. In the families with 100 or more mu the wife, on the average, was 3.6 years older than her husband. In the 50 to 99 mu group, the difference was only a little over one year. In the under 50 mu group the husbands were, on the average, seven months older than their wives. The more well-to-do groups evidently arranged marriage for their sons when they were very young, but they did not ordinarily pick out a very young girl as a daughter-in-law. She would not be physically able to carry the burden of serving her parents-in-law or of child bearing.

In the 515 families there were 97 couples in which one of the partners had been married more than once. Even in this group there were 20 wives who were older than their husbands. The average difference in age was three years. In the 68 couples where the husband was older the average difference in age was 12 years.

Birth and Death Rates

A study made by the health department of the Mass Education Association found the crude birth rate to be 40.1 per 1,000, the crude death rate 27.2 per 1,000. The infant mortality was 199 per 1,000 live births, the maternal death rate 13.0 per 1,000 live births.

These figures verify the general report that the population was gradually increasing. The only figures we were able to secure that would give any indication of population growth over a period of years were from the elders of one village. They said that the number of families had increased steadily from 155 in 1882 to 180 in 1932, a growth of 16 per cent in 50 years. (See Chapter XV.) The increase, of course, could be the result of division of families rather than an increase in the number of persons, but the steady growth in the number of families seems to indicate at least some growth in population.

A health study of the students in 25 village primary schools showed that 58.5 per cent of the children had trachoma and 26.2 per cent ringworm.

Foot-binding

Foot-binding was almost universal among the women over 40 years of age in the 515 families (99.2 per cent). None of the girls under 13 years of age had bound feet. The figures for the intervening five year age groups show how a cultural pattern, which in the past had successfully defied an imperial ban, had disappeared within 30 years.

The origin of the Chinese custom of foot-binding is uncertain, but apparently it began about one thousand years ago. It is first definitely mentioned in connection with the court of the southern T'ang dynasty at Nanking, 937–75 A.D. This court practiced a life of luxury and enjoyed the sight of dancing girls, their feet clad with "bow-shoes", the upturned toes of which resembled the bow of a Roman galley. The small feet of the sought-after dancers may have started the style, but it hardly explains the spread and long continuance of foot-binding, which has meant so much limitation, discomfort, and pain to so many individuals over so many years.

In the twelfth century the highly influential scholar-philosopher, Chu Hsi (1130–1200) was, according to Dr. Lin Yutang, "enthusiastic in introducing foot-binding in southern Fukien as a means of spreading Chinese culture and teaching the separation of men and women."

Although apparently accepted as part of Chinese culture in central China, the custom does not seem to have penetrated northern China to any great extent under the Liao, the Chin, or the early Yuan dynasty. By the first part of the fourteenth century, however, it must have become fairly general for Friar Odoric of Pordenone, who was in northern China for three years during the period 1322–28, says in his travelogue: "And with the women the great beauty is to have little feet; and for this reason mothers are accustomed, as soon as girls are born, to swathe their feet tightly so that they can never grow in the least."[12] Other early European or Western Asiatic travelers do not comment on the custom. Some Chinese authors of the twelfth, thirteenth, and fourteenth centuries, in mentioning the practice, apparently accept it as part of their mores.

The early Ming emperors, a Chinese dynasty, did not bandage the feet of their palace women, although foot-binding was practiced by a considerable proportion of their subjects.

When the Manchus, who did not practice foot-binding, came into power they endeavored to prohibit the custom among their Chinese subjects. Their first proscription was issued in Mukden in 1638. In 1645, the second year of his reign as Emperor of China, Shun Chih issued another edict against foot-binding and attempted to enforce it throughout the country. K'ang Hsi withdrew the ban as he found that while he could force the Chinese men to wear queues he could not compel the Chinese women to give up binding their feet. The custom, however, was not tolerated by the Manchu emperors in their palaces or in the banners (sections of the army).

Among the Chinese, objection to the practice apparently did not begin to crop up until the late eighteenth and early nineteenth centuries. Yüan Mei (1716–99), Li Ju-chen (ca. 1763–ca. 1830), and Yu Cheng-hsieh (1775–1840) all wrote against it. In 1896–98 K'ang Yu-wei (1858–1927) made it one of the reforms for which he struggled.

The Protestant missionaries have steadily worked against the practice and have been one of the many influences that have combined to arouse public opinion against foot-binding and bring about the discontinuance of the custom.

Among the females in the 515 families who were born before 1890, and so were forty years of age or over in 1929, foot-binding was prac-

12. Sir Henry Yule, *Cathay and the Way Thither*, rev. Cordier, printed for the Hakluyt Society (London, 1916).

tically universal, 99.2 per cent. One wonders how it was that four women in that group did not have bound feet. (See Table 9.)

There were six women with unbound feet in each of the next two younger five year age groups, born between 1890 and 1899. The increase in numbers was not large but the proportion with unbound feet rose to over five per cent in each group. Even in the rural communities, a few families were beginning to accept new ideas and leave their daughters' feet unbound, despite the fact that later on it might be difficult to find husbands for the girls.

Many new ideas came in after Boxer year, 1900, and the spirit of change evidently reached the Ting Hsien countryside with considerable rapidity. Eighteen and one-half per cent of the girls born during the five years from 1900 through 1904, for whom foot-binding would ordinarily start from 1903 through 1907, did not have their feet bound. In the next five-year age group, 1905–9, the proportion more than doubled, reaching 40.3 per cent.

The biggest change of all came in the group born from 1910 to 1914. These were the years of the Revolution and the founding of the Republic. New ideas were being adopted in many fields and many old customs were breaking down. The proportion of girls with unbound feet was 80.5 per cent—double that of the next older five-year age group.

In the 1915–19 group, 94.4 per cent of the girls had unbound feet. The 5.6 per cent with bound feet were all born before 1917. All the girls under thirteen years of age were reported to have natural, unbound feet.

If these figures are typical we can say that foot-binding came to an end in Ting Hsien in 1919. Knowing the general conservatism of the countryside it is remarkable to see how this old and well-nigh universal custom, which had lasted almost one thousand years and had successfully defied imperial authority, disappeared completely in these Ting Hsien families in a period of about thirty years, about one generation.[13]

The queue, which had been practically universal with the men before 1911, disappeared very rapidly after the downfall of the Manchus. In 1929 only three were left among the 1,835 males in the 515 families.

13. See Samuel Couling, "Anti-footbinding" and "Footbinding", *Encyclopedia Sinica* (Oxford University Press, London, 1917); Lin Yutang, *My Country and My People* (Reynal and Hitchcock, New York, 1935); Lin Yutang, *T'ien Hsia Monthly*, vol. I, pp. 127–50; Paul Pelliot, *T'oung Pao*, 1920–21, p. 179; K. Chimin Wong and Lien-teh Wu, *History of Chinese Medicine*, 2nd ed. (Tientsin Press, Ltd.)

Their wearers did not belong to the very old group, but were men between 46 and 55 years of age.

A surprisingly small number of persons with physical disabilities were reported in the 515 families. The total was 25. Only three of these were females. There were three blind men and three men and one woman were blind in one eye. Two men were dumb and six were deaf. Lameness was serious enough to be reported for four men and two women. Two men had paralyzed arms and two paralyzed fingers.

With less than one per cent of the group reported as having physical disabilities one cannot but wonder whether the report was incomplete or whether the extra difficulties of life had eliminated others who might have been stricken.

Home Ownership

Home ownership was almost universal for these Ting Hsien families. The figures are 98.8 per cent for the 5,255 families and 96.3 per cent for the 515 families. In a group of families living in Peking only 21.2 per cent owned their homes.[14]

About two-thirds of the non-owners were given the use of their homes, so house rent was paid by only 0.4 per cent of the 5,255 families and by 1.4 per cent of the 515 families. The small proportion of home renters makes it evident that a large proportion of those classed as tenant farmers owned their homes, even though they rented all of the land they farmed. In the 1st District 11.4 per cent of the families were tenant farmers, in the hsien only 4.7 per cent.

The high percentage of home ownership indicates very definitely that Ting Hsien had a steady, settled population and that almost all of the families had been in the area long enough to accumulate the funds needed to buy their homes. Quite a number of the families said that their ancestors came to Ting Hsien about 500 years ago.

In the 71 villages in the 1st District the average family residence area was 2.1 mu, about 100 x 150 feet. In that area the family would have its living quarters, housing for any animals, and storage for all farm equipment and for its food, fodder, and fertilizer.

The total residence area in the 71 villages varied from eight to 800 mu. Sixteen villages had less than 50 mu each. Fourteen had 300 or more mu. The average per family varied from 0.4 mu to 8.2 mu, but

14. Gamble, *op. cit.*

only five villages had an average of more than 4.0 mu per family. In 57.8 per cent of the villages the average residence area was less than two mu per family.

A study of the residence area of 357 families living in two villages gave detailed figures of relatively crowded conditions that would be typical of the more crowded 25 per cent of the villages in the 1st District. The average residence area was 0.78 mu, about 70 x 80 feet. More than 30 per cent of the families had less than half a mu, 60 x 60 feet. Only four families had as much as 2.5 mu. The largest home place was 10 mu. (See Table 11.)

The estimates of the average value of the land inside the villages, as given by the elders of the 453 villages, ranged from under $100 per mu to $1,000 and over. In 28.8 per cent of the villages the average value was under $200 per mu. In 18 per cent it was given as $400 or more per mu. There were only three villages with an estimated value of $1,000 or more per mu. The median value was between $250 and $299 per mu.

The size of the houses, counting all the rooms used for the family living quarters and for farm purposes, ranged from one to 60 chien for the 5,255 families and from one to 34 chien for the 515 families. A chien, the space between two roof trusses, generally varied from 10 x 10 to 12 x 12 feet. The number of chien usually corresponds closely with the number of rooms, but is not always the same, for it is possible to have a half chien room or a two or three chien room. In our study rooms and chien are assumed to be equal.

The average number of rooms per family was 6.2 for the 5,255 families and 6.8 for the 515 families. For the renting families, the averages were 2.9 and 2.7 rooms, while for those who borrowed or were given the use of their homes, the averages were 1.8 and 2.0. The average number of persons per chien was 1.1 and 1.0. (See Table 13.)

Figure 12 shows that the largest number of families had three rooms, then in order five, six, and four rooms. These four groups included 58.8 per cent of the 5,255 families and 52.5 per cent of the 515 families.

According to one of our investigators a three room house consisted of the family bedroom at one end of the house, a room at the other end which was storeroom, barn, and granary combined, and a middle room with a built-in stove, which served as kitchen and living room. At night chickens, a pig, and even a donkey were kept in the middle room lest they be stolen. The door of the house usually opened into the middle

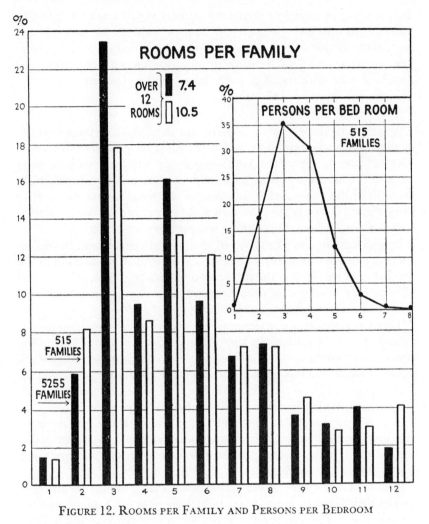

FIGURE 12. ROOMS PER FAMILY AND PERSONS PER BEDROOM

room. In the bedroom there was ordinarily a built-in brick bed or k'ang with a flue under it so it could be heated in winter.

The 515 families reported that they had from one to 12 bedrooms, with the average three per family. Seventy-three per cent of the families had from one to three bedrooms per family.

When the families were asked what was the largest number of persons sleeping in their bedrooms, the answers varied from one to eight. Sixty-six per cent had either three or four persons. Almost half, 46.4 per cent, reported more than three persons. The average was 2.3 persons per bedroom, which would seem to indicate that, on the average, the homes of these rural families were not especially crowded.

Economic Activity

A sample of the economic activity and the family occupational life in the villages was secured by asking the 1,282 males and 1,176 females over 12 years of age in the 515 family group what was their primary work and what, if any, was their secondary occupation. Eighty-eight per cent of the males and 80 per cent of the females were doing farm work. Only 18.6 per cent of the men and 18.5 per cent of the women reported a primary occupation that was non-farming.

Besides farming the men reported 55 different primary and 56 secondary occupations. There was, of course, a great deal of duplication in the two lists. For the women the lists were much shorter, nine primary and 12 secondary non-farming occupations. Similar occupations have been combined in the figures in Table 14.

Thirty per cent of the males and 38 per cent of the females reported secondary work. Farming was the primary work for most of these. Secondary work could be done during the winter months or other slack times on the farm. Only 12 of the men with non-farming primary occupations reported any secondary work. For 11 of those the secondary work was farming, evidently helping out during the busy seasons.

Only 3.7 per cent of the males and 1.3 per cent of the females reported that they were idle or had no occupation. The women apparently did not ordinarily think of home making as an occupation, for only 3 per cent gave that as their vocation.

Seventy-nine per cent of the males were working on the farms operated by their families. Nine per cent did some farm work for wages. Five per cent did both types of farm work. No women reported doing farm work for wages. Thirty-eight of the families, 7.4 per cent, owned no land; 22 families, 4.3 per cent, farmed no land. These proportions were practically the same as those for the entire hsien (see Chapter X).

Six and one-half per cent of the males were engaged in selling, either in stores or as itinerant peddlers. One woman was selling cakes. Almost 10 per cent of the males worked as laborers, skilled or unskilled, as carpenters, masons, barbers, watchmen, sheep herders, or cotton ginners, but only 2.9 per cent reported such work as their primary occupation. Government work, including the police force and the army, employed 2.1 per cent of the males. Nine reported government work as a secondary occupation but they were village officers, heads of street organizations, or engaged in other community work, all of which was usually unpaid.

The apprentice system was used by some stores in the villages but was not a large economic factor in the countryside. There were only four apprentices in the 515 families. On this basis the total for all the village families was some 530 apprentices.

The small number of students, 48 males and three females, indicates the small amount of school work done by the adolescents in the rural areas. Twenty-four men were engaged in teaching or school administration.

Twelve per cent of the males and 51.5 per cent of the females were doing work classed as Home Industry (see Chapter XV), making articles for sale and receiving their pay from profits rather than from wages. For all but seven of the 156 males their home industry was a secondary occupation. Those seven reported weaving as their primary work.

Spinning, weaving, or both, were reported by 9.7 per cent of the males and 50.4 per cent of the females. Only five males did any spinning. Of the females doing spinning and weaving, 81.6 per cent did only spinning, 1.3 per cent did only weaving, and 17.1 per cent did both.

Chinese Surnames

One hundred and ten surnames were represented in the 10,445 families in the 62 villages of the Experimental District. There were 1,419 families named Wang and 856 named Chang. The Liu families were third with 828. Then followed the Li, Ma, Chao, and Chen families. The Yang, Wu, and Shih families were also included in the first 10-family groups, all of which had over 200 families each.

At the other end of the list, there were 15 names that were represented by only one family each. Thirty-nine names had less than 10 families each, while 51 names had less than 25 families.

The number of family names or clans represented in the different villages varied from one to 26. The average was 8.5. In Wang Chia Chuang, a village of 80 families, everybody was named Wang. In another village with 64 families there were 44 Wang families and 20 Liu families. In almost half of the villages the largest clan included over 50 per cent of the families in the village, while in some 20 per cent of the villages, the proportion was over 70 per cent. In almost one quarter of the villages the two largest clans together included over 90 per cent of the families in the village. In 58 per cent of the villages they included more than 70 per cent of the families. In 11 of the 453 villages of the entire hsien all the families had the same name.

The largest clan in each village varied in size from under five to over 250 families. In 21 per cent of the villages the largest clan had 100 or more families, while in one-third of the villages the largest one had between 50 and 99 families. In 44 per cent of the villages of the 4th District the largest clan had 100 or more families, but in the 1st District the ratio was only four per cent.

One hundred and sixty-two clans, 30 per cent of those in the Experimental District, reported that they owned some property in common. For two-thirds of the land-owning clans the value of the property was less than $1,000. The others ranged in value up to $4,000.

One hundred and fifty-six clans reported expenses for the business of the clan. These were relatively small amounts as the total was less than $20 a year for 55 per cent and under $40 a year for 93 per cent of the clans reporting group expenses. The largest amount reported was $200 a year. The reports do not give the details of these expenses nor do they show whether the income from the clan property was sufficient to meet them. Care of the family tombs and the cost of an "eating meeting" were some of the expenses met from the income from clan property (see Chapter XVII).

TABLE 1. FAMILIES PER VILLAGE

Families	Villages	Per Cent	Families	Villages	Per Cent
Under 50	90	19.8	300–349	16	3.5
50–99	118	26.1	350–399	10	2.2
100–149	71	15.7	400–499	10	2.2
150–199	60	13.3	500–599	3	0.6
200–249	35	7.7	600 and over	4	0.9
250–299	36	8.0	Total	453	100.0

Minimum 6   Maximum 1,200

TABLE 2. SIZE OF FAMILIES

	5,255 Families Per Cent of		515 Families Per Cent of	
Persons	Families	Persons	Families	Persons
1–3	24.1	10.0	14.8	5.8
4–6	43.7	36.8	40.4	29.3
7–9	20.6	27.0	25.9	29.5
10–12	7.1	13.2	10.7	16.7
13–15	2.5	5.8	4.4	9.1
16–18	0.8	2.4	2.2	5.2
19–21	0.6	2.1	1.4	3.9
Over 21	0.6	2.7	0.2	0.5
	100.0	100.0	100.0	100.0

TABLE 3. SIZE OF FARM AND PERSONS PER FAMILY

Mu	515 Families	Mu	400 Families	Mu	1,220 Families
1–9	4.7	1–10	3.8	None	4.1
10–29	6.4	11–20	4.8	Under 25	4.7
30–49	7.8	21–30	6.2	25–49	6.7
50–99	10.6	31–40	6.7	50–74	10.6
100 and over	12.9	41–50	8.4	75–99	14.1
Average	6.9	51–100	9.4	100 and over	13.2
		Over 100	13.5	Average	5.2
		Average	6.3		

TABLE 4. FAMILY RELATIONSHIPS: PERCENTAGE DISTRIBUTION

Parents:	5,255 Families	515 Families	34 Families	North China[1]
Grandfather	*	*	–	–
Grandmother	0.2	0.1	0.5	0.2
Father	0.7	1.2	1.9	0.9
Mother	4.3	3.8	5.3	4.1
Stepmother	*	*	–	–
Mother-in-law	*	–	–	–
Father's brother	0.1	0.1	–	0.1
Father's brother's wife	0.2	0.1	–	0.1
	5.5	5.3	7.7	5.4

Family Head and Descendants:

	5,255 Families	515 Families	34 Families	North China
Male head	16.5	14.3	16.6	16.9
Female head	0.7	0.2	–	–
Wife	13.1	12.2	14.1	14.3
Concubine	0.1	0.2	–	–
Son	20.7	22.1	25.4	21.1
Son, adopted	0.1	0.1	–	–
Son-in-law	–	*	–	–
Daughter	10.6	11.8	13.7	11.8
Son's wife	7.8	8.0	7.3	8.4
Son's concubine	*	–	–	–
Son's fiancee	*	–	–	–
Grandson	5.9	6.8	2.4	6.4
Granddaughter	4.9	5.9	3.9	4.3
Grandson's wife	0.7	0.8	–	0.2
Great-grandson	0.3	0.3	–	0.1
Great-granddaughter	0.2	0.3	–	–
Great-grandson's wife	*	–	–	–
Great-great-grandson	*	–	–	–
Great-great-granddaughter	*	–	–	–
	81.6	83.0	83.4	83.5

Brothers and Descendants:

	5,255 Families	515 Families	34 Families	North China
Sister	0.3	0.7	0.5	0.7
Brother	3.8	3.6	5.4	3.3
Wife	2.5	2.2	2.0	2.6
Son	3.0	2.4	–	2.4
Daughter	1.5	1.6	1.0	1.8
Son's wife	0.8	0.9	–	–

(continued on next page)

(TABLE 4 CONTINUED)

(Brothers and Descendants:)	5,255 Families	515 Families	34 Families	North China[1]
Grandson	0.5	0.2	–	0.2
Granddaughter	0.3	*	–	0.1
Grandson's wife	*	*	–	–
Great-grandson	*	–	–	–
Great-granddaughter	*	–	–	–
	12.7	11.6	8.9	11.1
Other Relatives:	0.2	0.1		

* Less than 0.1 per cent.
[1] J. Lossing Buck, *Chinese Farm Economy.*

TABLE 5. MASCULINITY RATES

Age	5,255 Families	515 Families	U.S. Rural[1] Farm	U.S. Rural[1] Non-Farm
Under 5	104	85	103	103
5–9	110	111	104	103
10–14	111	126	107	102
15–19	113	135	115	98
20–24	112	124	116	98
25–29	110	92	105	102
30–34	110	125	99	106
35–39	108	115	100	111
40–44	111	102	106	114
45–49	102	100	113	115
50–54	103	88	125	115
55–59	99	98	134	113
60–64	100	104	141	109
65–69	90	67	145	106
70–74	78	78	147	107
75–79	66	114	137	105
80–84	47	36	117	99
85 and over	40	0	88	88
Average	106	106	111	105

[1] U.S. Census.

TABLE 6. AGE AND SEX
(per cent in five-year age groups)

	5,255 Families			515 Families			North China[1]	U.S.[2]
Age	Total	Male	Female	Total	Male	Female	Total	Total
Under 5	12.4	12.3	12.5	15.2	13.6	17.0	12.5	9.3
5–9	10.8	11.0	10.7	10.0	10.3	9.7	11.5	10.3
10–14	9.9	10.1	9.6	10.2	11.1	9.3	10.5	9.8
15–19	8.5	8.8	8.2	9.8	11.0	8.6	10.3	9.4
20–24	8.4	8.6	8.2	8.1	8.7	7.4	7.4	8.9
25–29	7.4	7.5	7.2	7.0	6.5	7.5	8.5	8.0
30–34	6.8	6.9	6.7	6.5	7.0	5.9	6.9	7.4
35–39	6.6	6.6	6.6	6.6	6.8	6.3	7.3	7.5
40–44	6.4	6.6	6.3	6.1	6.0	6.2	5.9	6.5
45–49	6.0	5.9	6.2	5.9	5.7	6.0	4.9	5.7
50–54	4.4	4.4	4.5	3.5	3.2	3.9	4.7	4.9
55–59	3.9	3.8	4.0	3.4	3.3	3.5	4.2	3.8
60–64	3.0	2.9	3.1	2.7	2.7	2.8	2.4	3.1
65–69	2.5	2.3	2.7	2.4	1.9	2.9	1.6	2.3
70–74	1.7	1.4	1.9	1.4	1.1	1.6	0.9	1.6
75–79	0.8	0.6	1.0	0.8	0.9	0.8	0.3	0.9
80–84	0.4	0.2	0.5	0.4	0.2	0.6	0.1	0.4
85 and over	0.1	0.1	0.1	–	–	–	0.1	0.2
	100.0	100.0	100.0	100.0	100.0	100.0	100.0	100.0
Total persons		15,780	14,862		1,835	1,736		

[1]J. Lossing Buck, *Chinese Farm Economy.*   [2] U.S. Census, 1930.

TABLE 7. AGE AT MARRIAGE

| | 515 Families | | 3 Market Towns | |
	766 Couples		1,843	2,059
Age	Males	Females	Males	Females
Under 10	1.3	–	0.7	–
10	2.8	–	1.1	–
11	5.0	–	3.1	–
12	6.7	1.0	5.0	0.8
13	9.4	2.1	4.9	1.8
14	16.2	4.6	11.9	4.9
15	10.2	6.9	6.7	5.0
16	11.8	16.1	10.8	23.3
17	5.9	15.3	7.0	10.0
18	4.7	16.8	6.4	24.5

(continued on next page)

(TABLE 7 CONTINUED)

	515 Families 766 Couples		3 Market Towns 1,843	2,059
Age	Males	Females	Males	Females
19	3.1	13.8	6.0	7.2
20	2.6	10.6	4.7	11.6
21	3.0	5.6	3.7	4.4
22	2.7	3.5	2.9	2.6
23–25	3.9	2.4	7.9	2.3
26–28	2.9	1.1	6.7	0.8
29–31	3.4	–	4.3	0.5
32–34	1.0	0.1	2.4	0.2
35 and over	3.4	0.1	3.8	0.1
	100.0	100.0	100.0	100.0

TABLE 8. AGE AT MARRIAGE AND SIZE OF FAMILY FARM
(766 couples in 515 families)

Age	Under 50 Mu		50–99 Mu		100 Mu and over	
	Male	Female	Male	Female	Male	Female
Under 10	0.8	–	1.4	–	5.3	–
10	2.9	–	3.2	–	1.8	–
11	4.5	–	4.6	–	10.4	–
12	6.5	1.4	6.4	–	8.8	1.8
13	6.7	2.7	14.1	0.9	14.0	1.8
14	12.0	4.5	19.2	3.6	40.2	8.8
15	10.0	6.1	11.8	7.8	5.3	10.4
16	11.7	15.1	13.6	17.8	5.3	17.5
17	5.9	15.1	6.4	15.0	3.5	17.5
18	4.9	16.1	5.5	17.4	–	21.1
19	3.5	13.1	2.7	16.0	1.8	12.3
20	3.5	11.3	0.9	10.5	1.8	5.3
21	3.5	6.1	2.7	5.0	–	3.5
22	3.3	3.7	2.3	4.1	–	–
23–25	5.2	3.0	1.4	1.4	1.8	–
26–28	3.9	1.4	1.4	0.5	–	–
29–31	5.0	–	0.5	–	–	–
32–34	1.4	0.2	0.5	–	–	–
35 and over	4.8	0.2	1.4	–	–	–
	100.0	100.0	100.0	100.0	100.0	100.0
Couples	490		219		57	

TABLE 9. AGE OF FEMALES WITH BOUND AND UNBOUND FEET
(515 families)

Age	Unbound Feet	Bound Feet	Total	Per Cent Bound
Under 5	294	–	294	–
5–9	169	–	169	–
10–14	152	9	161	5.6
15–19	120	29	149	19.5
20–24	52	77	129	59.7
25–29	24	106	130	81.5
30–34	6	97	103	94.1
35–39	6	103	109	94.5
40 and over	4	488	492	99.2
	827	909	1,736	

TABLE 10. RESIDENCE AREA PER FAMILY
(village averages, 1st District)

Mu	Villages	Per Cent	Mu	Villages	Per Cent
Under 0.5	2	2.8	3.0–3.4	7	9.9
0.5–0.9	16	22.6	3.5–3.9	3	4.2
1.0–1.4	15	21.1	4.0–4.4	2	2.8
1.5–1.9	8	11.3	4.5–4.9	2	2.8
2.0–2.4	10	14.1	5 and over	2	2.8
2.5–2.9	4	5.6	Total	71	100.0

TABLE 11. RESIDENCE AREA, TWO VILLAGES

Mu	Families	Per Cent
Under 0.5	113	31.7
0.5–0.9	138	38.6
1.0–1.4	72	20.2
1.5–1.9	19	5.3
2.0–2.4	11	3.1
2.5 and over	4	1.1
	357	100.0

TABLE 12. AVERAGE VALUE OF LAND IN VILLAGES

	Villages	Per Cent		Villages	Per Cent
Under $100	16	3.5	350–399	22	4.9
100–149	50	11.0	400–499	42	9.3
150–199	65	14.3	500–599	30	6.6
200–249	85	18.8	600 and over	9	2.0
250–299	54	11.9	Total	453	100.0
300–349	80	17.7			

TABLE 13. ROOMS PER FAMILY
(percentages)

Rooms	5,255 Families	515 Families
1–3	30.7	27.2
4–6	35.3	33.8
7–9	17.5	18.8
10–12	8.8	9.7
13–15	3.4	4.8
16–18	2.1	3.1
19–21	1.1	1.6
22–24	0.3	0.6
25 and over	0.8	0.4
	100.0	100.0
Average rooms	6.2	6.8
Persons per room	1.1	1.0

TABLE 14. OCCUPATIONS OF FAMILY MEMBERS OVER 12 YEARS OF AGE
(515 families)

Males

Occupation	Primary	Secondary
Farming	993	14
Hired farm labor	64	55
Merchant	25	11
Peddler	7	40
Store employee	6	6
Apprentice	4	–
Skilled labor	17	65
Unskilled labor	13	30
Home industry, misc.	–	32
——, weaving	7	112
——, spinning	–	5
Doctor	2	5
Education	19	5
Government	11	9
Military	15	–
Student	48	–
Unemployed	40	–
No occupation	2	–
Away from home	8	–
No data	1	–
	1,282	389

Females

Occupation	Primary	Occupation	Secondary
Farm work	943	Spinning and weaving	428
Spinning and weaving	165	Dyeing	4
Home work	44	Bean curd making	3
Students	3	Bread steaming	2
Miscellaneous work	2	Cotton picking	2
Selling	1	Miscellaneous work	2
Sewing	1	Noodle making	2
Begging	1	Cotton ginning	1
None	15	Sewing	1
No data	1		445
	1,176		

CHAPTER III

Four Hundred Farm Families

Four hundred farm families living in the 62 villages of the Experimental District were studied in 1927 in order to secure figures that would give a picture of their economic life and activities. Two hundred and two families, 50.5 per cent, lived in Chai Ch'eng, the village where the Mass Education Movement had its headquarters. The other villages had from one to seven families in the study. The 202 Chai Ch'eng families were 55 per cent of the families living in that village.

The 400 families were a 4 per cent sample of the farming families in the Experimental District. The total number of families in the District was 10,445, but generally some 3.5 per cent of the families were not farm operators. They were landlords, business men, artisans, and hired laborers.

Contact with the families studied was generally made through the teachers of the Mass Education schools. Answers to a questionnaire covering farm size, ownership, operation, production, value of farm lands, houses, implements, number of farm animals, details of farm income and expense, age and sex of the members of the family, and amount of family income and expense were secured from the head of the family. The figures given here are the tabulations of the answers to that questionnaire. Being based on reports and estimates, they cannot have complete accuracy, but their consistency, when the families are grouped according to the size of their farm and the type of farm ownership, seems to show that they give reasonably accurate pictures of the farm families in the Experimental District and very probably for all of Ting Hsien.

While we attempted to make the group of 400 families as nearly typical as possible, our area of choice was necessarily affected by the families' willingness to cooperate in, to them, a new and unusual study and their readiness to answer many intimate questions. The group therefore probably had a higher than average intellectual level. We know that it included more than the average number of the larger and wealthier farms. Because of this difference the families have been divided into groups according to the size of their farms, in order to give a picture of farm activity on different economic levels rather than just for our particular group of families. The farms with not more than 50 mu of land have been divided into five groups, each with a range of 10 mu, and the larger farms into two groups, one with more than 50 but not over 100 mu, the other with over 100 mu. To avoid the constant use of decimals and for ease of designation the group with not more than 10 mu is called the 1–10 mu group, the group with more than 10 mu but not over 20 mu the 11–20 mu group. The families also have been divided into three ownership groups, owners, part-owners, and tenants.

Land Ownership and Area

Land ownership is always a basic question in any study of farm families. Sixty-one per cent of the 400 families were listed as owners, owning all the land they operated; 33.8 per cent were part-owners, renting part of the land they farmed; 5.2 per cent were tenants who rented all of their land. (See Table 15). The 202 Chai Ch'eng families included in the study were divided 58 per cent owners, 38.5 per cent part-owners, and 3.5 per cent tenants. Our 1931 figures for the entire hsien divided the farming families 70 per cent owners, 25.2 per cent part-owners, and 4.8 per cent tenants. In the six districts of the hsien the proportion of owners ranged from 50.6 to 78 per cent, so it is difficult to find a typical sample.

The total area farmed by the 400 families was 12,377 mu, approximately 3.2 square miles. This was 5.5 per cent of the total farm area of the 62 villages. As a higher proportion of land than families was included in our study, the average size of the 400 farms, 30.9 mu, just over five acres per family, was some 39 per cent larger than the average of all the farms in the Experimental District, 22.2 mu, 3.7 acres per family. It was 46 per cent larger than the hsien average of 21.2 mu, 3.5 acres per farming family. In Chai Ch'eng the average was 26 mu per family.

The averages for our different ownership groups were owners 36.5 mu, part-owners 25.3 mu, and tenants 14.3 mu.

Two and four-tenths per cent of the land was operated by the tenant group and 27.6 per cent by the part-owners. Seventy per cent was farmed by the owner group. The part-owners rented 34 per cent of their farm area. Only 11.8 per cent of the total crop area was operated by renters. With 88.2 per cent of owner operation there would be very few of the problems resulting from landlordism and tenancy.

The number of crop mu reported was 15,044. The amount of double cropping therefore was 2,667 mu and the index of double cropping 121. Buck[1] in his land study gave the double cropping index for Hopei province as ranging from 125 to 155. For our three ownership groups there was but little difference in the index. The range was 117 to 124. The lowest was for the tenants, the highest for the part-owners.

We do not have an estimate of the amount of uncultivated and waste land held by the 400 families, nor do we have any figures giving the area of their houses. The latter, of course, were all in the villages and separate from the farm lands. In the 62 villages the cultivated land was 83.3 per cent of the total area; houses 4.7 per cent; roads, graves, and other uncultivated land 12.0 per cent.

A comparison of the averages of the different farm groups shows that many of the differences are directly related to the differences in the size of the farms; the amounts per mu are apt to be quite similar. That being the case, the figures for our 21–30 mu group, with an average farm of 25.6 mu, are probably much more typical for the 62 villages of the Experimental District and for all of Ting Hsien than the averages for the entire 400 families, whose average farm had 30.9 mu. Because of this difference in the averages we have given in the text many more figures for the different sized farm groups than would be the case if we were presenting the 400 farms as a typical and average group.

How the farms were distributed according to size and ownership is shown in Table 16. It will be noted that there were no part-owner or tenant families in the over 100 mu group and no tenant families in the 41–50 mu group. Only three tenant families had more than 20 mu. They operated different sized farms, so the three upper tenant groups had only one family each. Their figures, of course, cannot be taken as typical for those groups. For both the owners and part-owners, the largest group was the 11–20 mu group, 25 and 41.1 per cent respectively. Fifty-two per cent of the tenants were in the 1–10 mu group. Forty-five per cent of all the farms had from one to 20 mu. Their total area was only 18 per cent of the land. The 25 per cent of the families who had over 40 mu had 55 per cent of the land.

1. J. Lossing Buck, *Land Utilization in China* (University of Chicago Press, 1937).

Size of Family

The 400 families included a total of 2,536 persons, an average of 6.3 persons per family. The total, however, included 64 year-round workers who lived with the families. If they are omitted, the size of the average family was 6.2. How the average size of the family increased as the size of the farm increased, from 3.8 persons for the families with 10 mu or less to 6.7 persons for those in the 31–40 mu group and 13.5 persons for those with over 100 mu, is shown in Table 17. If the 64 full-time workers are omitted, the average family was 8.2 for the 41–50 mu group, 8.8 for the 51–100 mu group, and 11.8 for the over 100 mu group. These were the only groups with enough full-time workers to affect the size of the average family. Ordinarily, we have not omitted the full-time workers as they were given their board by their employers and so were part of the family "mouths".

In other studies of Chinese families, we have regularly found that as the amount of the family income increased the average size of the family increased. In this study increased size of farm holding usually indicates increased family income. From the figures, it appears that there was a tendency for the average size of the family to increase some 35 per cent with a 100 per cent increase in the size of the farm.

The amount of land farmed by the family also appears to have a definite influence on both the number and the proportion of children in the family. The average number of children from one to 10 years of age, Chinese count, increased from 0.6 per family for the 1–10 mu group to 3.2 for the over 100 mu group. The proportion of children was 15 per cent in the families with 30 mu or less, but it was 24 per cent for the families with more than 100 mu.

The population density was 785 persons per square mile of crop area. It was about 650 per square mile if an average area for the home sites in the villages is added to the cultivated area and an allowance made for graves, roads, and wasteland.

For the 400 families the average amount of land per person was 4.8 mu, 0.8 of an acre. For the 1–10 mu group, the average was less than one-third of an acre per person. Table 17 shows how the amount increased as the size of the farm increased until the average for the over 100 mu group was five times the average for the 1–10 mu group.

The 2,536 members listed by the 400 families were divided 1,348

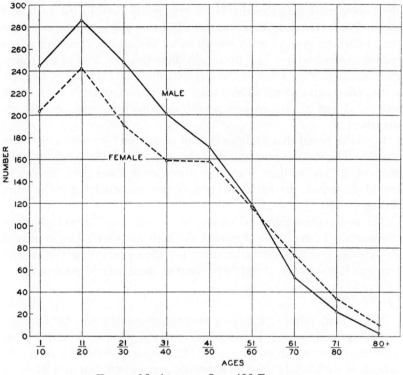

FIGURE 13. AGE AND SEX, 400 FAMILIES

males and 1,188 females, or 53.2 per cent male. If the 64 year round
farm workers are subtracted from the number of males, the families
were 52 per cent male, a masculinity rate of 108. This is slightly higher
than the figures for our 515 and 5,255 family groups, and practically the
same as for the rural population of the United States, but less than the
111 rate of the United States rural farm population.[2]

The age and sex distribution of all the families is shown by 10-year
age groups in Figure 13 and Table 18. The ages are given according to
the Chinese count, whereby a child is one year old when born and two
years old at the next Chinese New Year. It is particularly noticeable
that in this group of families the number of both males and females was
larger in the 11–20 year age group than in the 1–10 year group and that

2. U.S. Census.

there were more males in the 21–30 year group than in the 1–10 year group. We cannot determine whether this unusually large proportion in the 11–20 year group was the result of an incomplete report or represented an unusual age distribution in these families. Part of the difference, undoubtedly, is due to the fact that the 1–10 year group, Chinese count, covers an average of only nine and one-half instead of ten years. Our 5,255 and 575 family groups did not show the same unusual age distribution.

It will be noted that 54.3 per cent of those over 50 years of age were females. The females outnumbered the males in all the groups over 60 years of age and as there were only three more males than females in the 51–60 group, the females probably outnumbered the males after the age of 55.

The field reports listed 457 males and 44 females as "able to recognize characters". Thirty-four per cent of the males, but only 3.7 per cent of the females, had had some education. For the entire group, the proportion was 19.8 per cent. It was 24 per cent of those over 10 years of age.

Farm Capital

The capital value of the farm property owned by the 400 families, including land, houses, implements, animals, trees, seed, and fodder, totaled $1,020,900, an average of $2,552 per farm. For the owners, the average was $3,320. It was $1,538 for the part-owners, but only $152 for the tenants. (See Table 19.) The difference in these figures is largely due, of course, to the fact that the tenants included nothing for land owned and the part-owners included the value of only two-thirds of the land they used. Land value represented 82 per cent of the total reported capital. If the land is omitted, the average capital amounts were owners $569, part-owners $306, and tenants $152.

The larger size of the farms of the owners and part-owners was partly responsible for the difference in these figures, as our study showed that the amount of capital, other than land, was generally related to the size of the farms, though the owners' figures were usually larger than the part-owners', and the part-owners' larger than the tenants'. The averages per mu for the three ownership groups were owners $16.00, part-owners $12.20, and tenants $10.65. In all three groups, the highest amount per mu was in the 1–10 mu group, largely because of a high per mu value of the houses. If both house and land are omitted, the capital per mu was $6.35 for the owners, $4.55 for the part-owners, and $2.95 for the tenants.

Along with the averages for the three ownership groups, the detailed figures of the 1–10, the 21–30, and the over 100 mu owner groups are given in Table 19 to illustrate the variations in the land value and other capital items of the different sized farms.

The total value of land, buildings, and equipment of the individual owners ranged from less than $500 to over $10,000. It did not go above $6,500 for any of the part-owners and was less than $500 for all of the tenant families. Sixteen owner families reported capital of more than $10,000. This was one more than the number of families with over 100 mu of land. Almost one-half, 48 per cent, of the owners reported capital of over $2,500, but only 15 per cent of the part-owners had more than that amount. In both the owner and part-owner groups, the largest number of families had from $501 to $1,000 of capital. Fifty-eight per cent of the entire group of 400 families had not more than $2,000 of capital. The fact that none of the tenant families reported more than $500 of capital is indicative of their financial status and of many of their problems and relationships. (See Table 20.)

The total land value of $889,010, shown in Table 21, includes the value of the rented land as well as that of the land owned. While the average value for the 12,377 mu was $71.80 per mu, the land owned by the operators averaged $76.60 and the rented land $35.30 per mu. The value of the rented land would seem to have been underestimated for the gross return per mu in the 1–10 and 11–20 mu groups was larger for the tenants than for either the owners or the part-owners.

The reports do not give any totals for irrigated and unirrigated land, but, judging from the value figures, probably at least two-thirds of the area had water available. The Chai Ch'eng families had an average of more than one well per family.

The average value of the farm houses was $280, but the amounts for the different ownership groups and the different sized farms varied from $75.80 for the tenants with 1–10 mu to $1,200 for the owners with over 100 mu.

How the average house value increased with the size of the farm is shown in Table 22. The figures given there are for all the families regardless of ownership classification.

While the value of the house increased with the size of the farm, it did not correlate closely with the amount of land farmed. The average was $9.05 per mu, but for the different sized farm groups the amount varied from $7.25 per mu for the 11–20 mu group to just twice that amount, $14.50, for the 1–10 mu group. The latter figure was unusually high because $100, the average house value for that group, was probably close to the minimum needed to provide a room for the family and a place for farm tools and produce. For the groups with the larger farms, the value of the house usually increased more rapidly than the size of the farm. It was $9.75 per mu in the over 100 mu group. The house value did not, however, represent an increasing proportion of the farm capital. It averaged 10.4 per cent for the owners, 12.4 for the part-owners, and 72.1 for the tenants.

The field reports did not include figures on the size of the houses, but for the 34 families included in our family budget study (see Chapter V), the average house had 6.7 chien and was valued at $360. The residence area of the families in the Experimental District averaged 1.13 mu per family, a plot about 80 by 100 feet. The reports did not state how many of the 400 families owned their homes, but other studies showed that home ownership in Ting Hsien was almost universal.

The farm implements were valued at $39.15 per farm. For the three ownership groups the averages ranged from $31.35 for the part-owners to $45.60 for the owners. As the size of the farm increased the average value of the implements increased from $9.00 for the 1–10 mu group to $35.77 for the 21–30 mu group and to $119.20 for the families with more than 100 mu. This was a wide range, but the figures per mu showed that the amount of equipment owned was closely related to the size of the farm. For the different sized farm groups the amounts varied from $0.95 to $1.55 per mu. The average was $1.25 per mu. The amount per mu was smallest for the tenants and largest for the owners. (See Table 22.)

The cost of different types of farm implements varied from 10 cents for a sheng measure to $100 for a Persian water wheel. Brooms, made from locally grown broom plants, cost from 10 to 30 cents. Wooden forks, made by steaming a tree crotch with three limbs and then tying it to a ladder to shape it, cost from 70 to 80 cents, a flail from $4.00 to $5.00. Peanut sifters were listed as costing $8.00 to $9.00, but not many of the farmers owned them as they could be rented for 40 cents per day. (See Table 23.)

The farm animals reported included 36.3 horses, 76 cows, 109.5 mules, and 135.6 donkeys. These were all used as draft animals. The fractional figures for donkeys, mules, and horses are correct, for 56 families reported that they owned one-half or one-third of an animal. Three hundred and thirty-four farms, 83.5 per cent, had at least a fraction of a draft animal. Ninety-five per cent of the families in the 21–30 mu group and all of the families with more than 30 mu owned at least part of a draft animal. Thirty per cent of the families with 20 mu or less and 63 per cent of the families with 1–10 mu had none. We wonder how 21 families in the 1–10 mu group managed to support a family and even a part of a donkey on a farm of less than 1.6 acres. More than one animal was reported by 9.4 per cent of the owners and 4.5 per cent of the part-owners. We do not have the details of how the families who owned shares in a draft animal divided its work, the cost of its upkeep, and its care, but we can imagine some of the difficulties and arguments that could arise.

Eighty-one per cent of the families had pigs and 84 per cent had chickens. Generally from 90 to 100 per cent of the families with more than 20 mu had pigs. The proportion was 71 per cent for the families with 11–20 mu and 45 per cent for the families with 1–10 mu. Of the tenant families with 1–10 mu only 18 per cent kept a pig. The families with pigs had an average of 1.6 animals per family. The owners with more than 50 mu and the part-owners with from 31 to 50 mu averaged more than two pigs per family, but the part-owners in the 51–100 mu group had 1.5 pigs per family.

Ninety-two per cent of the families with more than 20 mu kept some chickens. In the 1–10 mu group 58 per cent had some fowl. The average number was 4.6 for the families keeping chickens. In the different sized farm groups the average ranged from 1.9 for the 1–10 mu owners to 6.9 for the over 100 mu owners. One tenant family with 36 mu had 13 birds.

Only 13 families, 3 per cent, had ducks and smaller numbers of families kept geese, sheep, and rabbits. (See Table 24.)

The average value of the farm animals was $50.40 per farm. For the owners the average increased from $8.15 for the 1–10 mu group to $42.20 for the 21–30 mu group and $238.45 for the over 100 mu group. For the part-owners the average varied from $6.60 to $91.60. The value per mu for the owner groups ranged from $1.20 to $1.95, with the average $1.71 per mu. For the part-owners and tenants the averages were somewhat smaller. (See Table 22.)

Trees on the farms and around the houses were estimated to be worth $30,125. Five-sixths of this amount was reported by the owners. Only $100 was reported by all the tenants. For the owners the average was $102.35 per farm. It was $20.60 for the 1–10 mu owner group and $144.85 for the 51–100 mu group. There was a big increase in the over 100 mu group, where the average was $404.15. All of the owner groups had an average of over $100 except the two with 20 or less mu. For the part-owners the averages were less than $75 for all groups and only $8.40 for the 1–10 mu group. For the tenants the averages were all less than $6.25, except for the 31–40 mu group. The one family in that group reported that it had $20 worth of trees. All the tenants' trees, of course, were around their houses in the villages.

Seed that was on hand and reported as farm capital averaged $8.75 per farm but was very largely an owner and part-owner item: $10.15 for the owners, $7.30 for the part-owners, but only $1.80 for the tenants. The amount for fodder was just half that for seed with none reported by the tenants. Fertilizer was such a small item that the 400 families reported a total of only $15.40 on hand.

Farm Income

Eighteen different crops were grown on the 400 farms. The total estimated value of the annual crop yield was $139,235, an average of $348.00 per farm. The average per mu was $11.25.

The average crop yield per mu shows a very consistent agreement for the different ownership groups and for the different sized farm groups. For the three ownership groups the difference in the averages was only 25 cents. The amounts were tenants $11.10, owners $11.20, and part-owners $11.35. There was a slightly wider range in the different sized farm groups. There, except for the tenant groups with only one family, the variation was from $10.60 to $12.35. For the owners the range was from $10.70 in the over 100 mu group to $12.35 in the 21–30 mu group. The average did not show any tendency to increase as the size of the farm increased. For the owners the 1–10 mu and the 41–50 mu averages were the same and they were only five cents more than the over 100 mu average.

Millet (ku-tzu) was the most generally grown crop. It was raised on all but two of the farms and was grown on 30.3 per cent of the crop mu and 36.8 per cent of the crop area. Glutinous and panicled millet were grown on a total of 3.9 per cent of the crop mu. The millets, therefore, were raised on just over one-third of the crop mu and 41.5 per cent of the crop area. The figures for both crop mu and crop area are given because of the 21 per cent double cropping.

Wheat and cotton were the next largest crops. Wheat was grown on 90 per cent of the farms and 9.9 per cent of the crop mu, cotton on 74 per cent of the farms and 9.1 per cent of the crop mu. Together they took 23.1 per cent of the crop area. The three crops, millet, wheat, and cotton, together accounted for 53.2 per cent of the crop mu and 64.6 per cent of the crop area.

Kaoliang, black beans, and sweet potatoes are the only other crops that had over five per cent of the crop mu. Sweet potatoes were grown on 95 per cent of the farms, black beans on 57 per cent. Rice was not grown by any of these families for only in another part of the hsien do springs provide the necessary water.

Sixty-two per cent of the crop mu and 75.2 per cent of the crop area were used for different kinds of grain.

Different varieties of beans, black, green, yellow, and white, were grown on 11.8 per cent of the crop mu. Root plants, sweet potatoes, peanuts, and turnips had 10.5 per cent. Miscellaneous vegetables were grown on 2.3 per cent and sesame on 4.3 per cent.

The millets produced the largest value, almost $35,000. Sweet potatoes were next with some $16,500. The cotton crop totaled some $15,000. Wheat was the only other crop valued at more than $10,000, but by-products, such as kaoliang leaves and stalks, bean vines, animal products, etc. were reported as amounting to $20,820.

Sweet potatoes, vegetables, peanuts, and cotton gave the largest return per mu, $16.20 for sweet potatoes, $10.95 for cotton. Green and white beans gave the lowest return, only $2.95 per mu. This, undoubtedly, was due to the fact that the beans generally were grown with another crop, kaoliang, panicled or glutinous millet. Those grains show a return of from $4.15 to $4.70 per mu, while the return from millet was $7.05 per mu and from wheat $9.10 per mu.

The farmers reported that they used 76 per cent and sold 24 per cent of the crops they produced. The chief money crops, judging by the proportion sold, were peanuts with 93 per cent, sesame with 92 per cent, cotton with 86 per cent, and wheat with 42 per cent. Green and yellow beans and buckwheat were the only other crops of which more than 8 per cent was sold. The bean figures were 15 and 18 per cent. The products sold represented a value of $33,330, an average of $83.30 per farm.

Cotton brought in the most money, $12,850; peanuts were next with $6,685, and sesame third with $4,590. Wheat with $4,435 and millet with $1,915 were the only other crops of which over $1,000 worth was sold. These five crops brought in some 91.5 per cent of the amount received. Complete figures are given for each crop in Table 25.

The proportion of the farm products sold increased as the size of the farm increased. For the owners it went from 12.5 per cent for the 1–10 mu families to 31.3 per cent for the over 100 mu group. For the part-owners the figures were very similar except that the 1–10 mu group sold only 7.8 per cent. The 1–10 mu tenant group reported selling 21.1 per cent of their crops, but the 11–20 mu group only 12.4 per cent. (See Table 26.)

Besides the crops used and sold, the families reported the sale of animals and animal by-products amounting to an average of $10.50 per farm. The amount was $2.50 for the 1–10 mu owners and $19.20 for the over 100 mu group. The owner and part-owner averages were practically the same, $10.90 and $11.00. The tenants reported only $3.00 per family or less than one-third the average for the other groups.

Miscellaneous farm income added an average of $5.50 per family. There was also a reported increase in the farm capital of $16.95 per family during the year. This came from the saving of farm products, such as seeds and fertilizer, the unsold increase in the number of farm animals, etc. When these are added to the crop income shown in Table 25, the reported gross income of the farms totaled $149,282, an average of $373.20 per farm. For the owners it was $427.55 with the amount increasing from $83.50 per family in the 1–10 mu group to $1,392.80 for the over 100 mu group. The part-owners' average was $305.90 and the tenants' $174.65. Again the differences in the averages were almost entirely due to the differences in the size of the average farms. The gross return per mu varied from $12.00 for the owners to $12.25 for the tenants. In the different sized farm groups, the averages ranged from $11.25 per mu for the 41–50 mu group to $13.10 for the 31–40 mu group. There appeared to be some tendency for the amount per mu to decrease when the size of the farm increased beyond 40 mu, but it was not regular nor was the amount large.

The very small differences in the per mu averages for the three ownership groups and the relatively close agreement of the averages for the different sized farm groups seem to indicate that, on the average, the reports on the 400 farms have been reasonably complete and accurate.

Farm Expenses

The cost of farm operation, including the estimated value of the family and animal labor used on the farm, as well as the amounts spent for hired labor, rent, fertilizer, fodder, seed, taxes, implements, and house repair, totaled $63,359.20, an average of $158.40 per farm, $5.15 per mu. This was 42.4 per cent of the reported farm income. (See Table 27.)

The owner group reported the largest average expense, $166.10 per farm, and the tenants the lowest, $108.85. However, it was just the reverse for the expense per mu. That was $4.70 for the owners, $6.05 for the part-owners, and $7.65 for the tenants. The differences were largely the result of the rent paid by the tenants and part-owners. If we equalize the amounts by adding the rent value of the land owned by the owners and part-owners and the average hsien taxes on the rented land, the average cost of operation would be $8.45 per mu for the owners, $8.55 for the part-owners, and $7.75 for the tenants. If, on the other hand, we deduct rent and taxes from the different groups, the owner and part-owner costs were $4.60 and $4.70 per mu and the tenants' $3.90 per mu.

For the different sized farm groups the per mu operating cost varied from $4.00 to $5.45 for the owners, from $4.95 to $6.50 for the part-owners, and from $6.25 to $9.90 for the tenants. The lowest amount was usually in the 1–10 mu groups, the largest in the 11–20 or the 21–30 mu groups.

The value of the family and animal labor has been estimated and included as a farm expense. If these non-cash items are omitted, the money spent for the farm operation averaged only $59.00 per farm per year, or $1.90 per mu. Again, because of the rent item, the tenants had the largest average cash cost, $63.90. The part-owners' average was the smallest, $51.00. The owners spent $12.00 per farm more than the part-

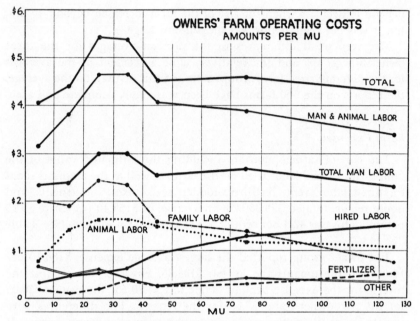

FIGURE 14. FARM OPERATING COSTS, 400 FAMILIES

owners, principally because of the 10 mu difference in the average size
of the farms. The average cash outlay per mu for the three ownership
groups was $1.75 for the owners, $2.00 for the part-owners, and $4.50 for
the tenants. The 1–10 mu owners operated with an average cash expenditure of only $8.15 per farm per year.

If rent and taxes are omitted, as well as the non-cash items of farm
expense, the money spent for farm maintenance and operation was only
72 cents per mu for the tenants, 70 cents for the part-owners, and $1.65
for the owners.

The value per mu of the labor and other items applied to their land
by the owners of the different sized farms is shown in Figure 14. As
might be expected, the amount of family labor per mu ordinarily decreased and the amount of hired labor increased as the size of the farm
increased. The larger expenditures reported by the 21–30 and 31–40
mu groups would seem to indicate somewhat more extensive cultivation
by those families. The extra labor investment was reflected in larger
yields. The average amounts for those two groups were both over $12.00

per mu. For all but one of the other groups the amount was less than $11.00 per mu. The average was $11.20 per mu.

The amounts spent per mu for the different expense items by the three ownership groups are given in Table 27. For the average family only rent and labor (family, animal, and hired) amounted to more than $10 per year. For the three ownership groups only three items, again the amounts for rent and family and animal labor, were more than $1.00 per mu per year.

With no rent charge to meet, the owners could pay more for hired labor than the part-owners or the tenants. They paid $36.80 while the tenants paid an average of only $1.45 and the part-owners $5.75. The amounts per mu were tenants 10 cents, part-owners 23 cents, and owners $1.04.

Sixty-four full-time laborers were employed by 44 families. All but two of these families were in the owner group. There were none in the tenant group. Only three owner families in the over 100 mu group did not employ a full-time worker. The other families in that group averaged just over two workers per family. Fifty-four per cent of the 51–100 mu owners, 33 per cent of the 41–50, and 4 per cent of the 31–40 mu owners reported year-round laborers. The two part-owner families with full-time workers were in the 41–50 mu and the 51–100 mu groups. No family with less than 30 mu employed year-round labor.

Day labor was used sometime during the year by 152 families, 38 per cent. Forty-eight per cent of the owners, 21 per cent of the part-owners, and 24 per cent of the tenants used some day labor. For the owners the figures increased from 14 per cent for the 1–10 mu group to 68 per cent for the 31–40 mu group and 93 per cent for the over 100 mu group. The spring and fall harvests were naturally the times when most of the day labor was used.

The average number of days' work per owner family using day labor was 61. The figure varied from 19 for the 1–10 mu group to 43 for the 21–30 group and 101 for the over 100 mu group. For the part-owners the average, for those using day labor, was 28 days. The largest average was 52 days in the 11–20 mu group. The other averages varied from 10 to 29 days. Ten days was the average for both the 31–40 and the 41–50 mu group. The five tenant families used an average of 19 days of hired labor apiece.

Children were employed to help with the farm work by 22 families,

16 owners and six part-owners. The children evidently were employed on a daily basis and usually for a relatively short period.

One hundred and seventy-two families, 43 per cent of the entire group, reported that they had some hired labor during the year. For the ownership groups the proportions were owners 56 per cent, part-owners 23, and tenants 24 per cent, practically the same proportions as used day labor. For the owner groups the proportion varied from 14 per cent for the 1–10 mu group to 72 per cent for the 31–40 mu group, 88 per cent for the 51–100 mu group, and 100 per cent for the over 100 mu group. For the part-owners the proportion increased from 15 per cent for the 11–20 mu group to 64 per cent for the 51–100 mu group.

The average number of days of labor used by the reporting families was 217 for the owners, 55 for the part-owners, and 19 for the tenants. For the 1–10 mu owner group the average was 19 days. It was 645 days for the over 100 mu group. The part-owner averages generally ranged from 28 to 70 days except in the 41–50 mu group. There, one family reported having 310 days of hired labor, 300 days from one full-time worker and 10 days from men hired by the day. At least some men classed as "full-time workers" did not work during the winter season.

The average expenditure for labor in the 1–10 mu group was $2.20 per farm for the owners, 60 cents for the part-owners, and 55 cents for the tenants. For the 21–30 mu group, the average was $11.75. In the 51–100 mu group, the average amounts were tenants $6.00, part-owners $17.55, and owners $82.60. For the over 100 mu owners the average was $191.85. The larger farms required increasing amounts of labor beyond that available in the farm families. The field reports did not give the rates on which these amounts were calculated, but wages for a year-round laborer in 1931 were given as $45.00 plus room and board. First-class day laborers averaged 35 cents a day plus board, but the amount varied widely with the season. The rate, naturally, was highest at harvest time. The expenditure for labor and the reported number of days worked gives an average wage for all the laborers, year-round, day, and child of 30 cents a day.

The estimated value of the family labor used on the farm averaged $57.60 for the 400 families. The amount was $29.90 for the tenant group, $65.15 for the part-owners, and $56.30 for the owners. This was one instance where the part-owner figures were regularly larger than those for the owners. For the different sized farms the averages ranged from

$9.15 for the 1–10 mu tenant group to $129.45 for the 51–100 mu part-owner group. For the over 100 mu owners it was $89.80.

If the value of the family labor and the cost of the hired labor are added together, the average amount of man labor used was $2.65 per mu. It was $2.20 for the tenants, $3.10 for the part-owners, and $2.65 for the owners. For both the 1–10 mu and over 100 mu owner groups the amount was $2.30 per mu. The highest owner amount was $3.00, the average for the 21–30 mu and the 31–40 mu group.

The reported value of the animal labor averaged $41.50 per farm. For the tenants the amount was $15.05. For the part-owners it was $36.15, more than double the tenant average, while for the owners the average was $46.75, just over three times the tenant figure. The per mu averages were much closer. They were tenants $1.05, part-owners $1.45, and owners $1.30.

Land rent averaged $53.60 per farm for the tenants and $31.55 for the part-owners. The average per mu was $3.65. For the different sized tenant farms the average rent per mu varied from $3.20 for the 1–10 mu group to $4.90 for the 31–40 mu group. It must be remembered that there was only one family in the latter group. The other single family tenant groups reported rents of $3.50 and $4.50 per mu. The village land owned by Chai Ch'eng was rented at $3.00 per mu. The records seem to show that the rented land was all let on a cash rather than a share basis.

Fertilizer cost the owners $11.15, the part-owners $5.60, and the tenants $2.50 per year. The owners spent almost twice as much per mu as the tenants, but even for the owners the average was only 31 cents per mu. The largest farm generally paid the most per mu, but the amount did not increase regularly as the size of the farm increased. The value of the fertilizer produced on the farm or collected by the boys was not included in these figures.

The cost of seed was the largest for the owners, $3.40, and the least for the tenants, $2.75. However, the tenants' cost per mu, 20 cents, was just twice that of the owners. The tenants apparently spent on seed the amount they saved on fertilizer, when compared with the owners.

Fodder was a very small item as most of the food for the animals came direct from the farm. The average expenditure for both owners and part-owners was $1.70. The tenant average was $2.65, owing to the expenditure of $16 and $20 by two families. From the per mu figures, it is evident that, because of the small size of most of their farms, the tenants had to buy more fodder for their animals.

The average rate for the hsien taxes was 10 cents per mu, but extras and surtaxes had raised it to 10.5 cents. The average reported by the owners, however, was 10.1 cents. It was 10.25 cents for the part-owners. It would seem that some of the owners had been able to reduce the number of mu assessed to them below their actual holdings.

The reported farm expenses do not include any amounts for village assessments. Other studies have shown levies of 10 and 15 cents per mu in villages in Hopei province, for home guard, education, crop watching, village watchmen, etc.[3]

Implement repair cost the owners $1.50 per farm, the part-owners 67 cents, and the tenants only 23 cents. House repair was another small item. The owners spent an average of $4.80, the part-owners 85 cents, and the tenants only 70 cents. For the 1–10 mu owners, the amount was $2.15 per farm. It was only $1.30 for the 41–50 mu group, but $15.15 for the over 100 mu group.

The total farm expense varied from $26.70 for the 1–10 mu owners to $528.50 for the over 100 mu owners. The average was $158.40 per farm. The cost per mu was $4.70 for the owners, $6.05 for the part-owners, and $7.65 for the tenants. The per cent of the gross yield was owners 39, part-owners 50, tenants 62.

The net return per mu, if the value of the family and animal labor is counted as one of the operating costs, was owners $7.35, part-owners $6.05, and tenants $4.50. If family and animal labor value is not deducted, the amount per mu was owners $10.25, part-owners $10.05, tenants $7.75. The farm products used by the operator's family are, of course, counted as farm income. On the basis of our 21–30 mu families, whose average farm is approximately the average for the entire hsien, Ting Hsien families had an average net income from their farms of $187.00 per year, or $293.00 if the family and animal labor is not counted as an expense.

Family Income

A report of income received from other than farm sources, labor for others, rent of land, interest on loans, home industry, and business, made

3. Sidney D. Gamble, "Hsin Chuang", *Harvard Journal of Asiatic Studies*, vol. 8, no. 1 (1944).

it possible to estimate the total family income. The average income from all sources was $347.30 per family. For the owners it was $395.55; for the part-owners $289.60; for the tenants $147.40. (See Table 28.) The owners derived less than 10 per cent of their average income from other than farm sources. The tenants received 23 per cent of theirs from non-farm sources.

Labor for others was largest in the tenant groups, an average of $10.75 per family. This was more than four times the owner average. The total amount reported by the 101 owners with more than 30 mu per family was only $25. No labor income was reported by the two tenant families with more than 30 mu, but the one family in the 21–30 mu group earned $45. The 11–20 mu tenant group averaged $19.15 per family. It is interesting to note that in the 1–10 mu group the owners had the largest average, $5.75. For the 1–10 mu part-owners and tenants the averages were $1.50 and $4.25 per family.

Rent from land was reported only by the owners. The total was $1,280, or the rent of about 350 mu. Even some of the 1–10 mu owners reported that they rented part of their holdings to others. They apparently rented some 80 mu.

Two owners reported receiving rent for a house. For one the amount was $1.00, for the other it was $8.00 per year.

Some families in all the owner groups reported receiving interest on loans. Even for the 1–10 mu group the average was $1.75. For the 51–100 mu group it was $8.55. The amount was $19.45 per family for the over 100 mu group. The total interest reported was $1,036.40. No tenant families reported the receipt of any interest. Interest rates were commonly 2.0 and 2.5 per cent per month.

Business and home industry brought an average of just over $1.00 per month per family to the tenants, $1.50 a month to the owners, and just under $2.00 a month to the part-owners. For most of the different sized farm groups the average generally was between $10 and $20 a year, except for the 51–100 mu group, where the owner average was $39.35 and the part-owner $78.90. The total received from business and home industry was $7,835, just under $20 per family per year. The average gain from home industry was $11.25 per family. For the entire hsien the average was $12.50.

If the families are ranked according to the amount of their annual income the amounts range from under $50 to over $1,000. How they

were divided is shown in Table 29. The income included the value of
the family and animal labor used on the farm, the net return from the
farm, labor for others, returns from home industry or business, rent,
and interest. One wonders how the 10 families with incomes of $50 or
less a year managed to get along. Their average income was $40.50, or
just over $3.50 per family per month. And that amount included the
value of the farm products used by the family. Those families certainly would have but little money to spend for any extras. Seven of the
10 were farm owners.

Over one-half, 52.4 per cent, of the tenant families had incomes of
not more than $12.50 a month. About one-fifth of the owner and
part-owner families were in that income range. Ninety per cent of the
tenants, almost two-thirds of the part-owners, but less than one-half
of the owner families received not more than $25 a month. None of the
tenant families had incomes of more than $500 a year, but 11 per cent
of the part-owners and 27 per cent of the owners received more than
that amount. Only 17 families, 16 owners and one part-owner, reported
incomes of more than $1,000 a year.

Income per Person

The amount of money available for family use, the cash income
from farm produce sold, labor for others, interest, home industry, and
business, minus the cash expense items of hired labor, rent, and taxes,
averaged $75 per family per year, or about $1.00 per person per month.
For the owner groups, the money income per person per year ranged
from $8.15 for the 11–20 mu group and $10.85 for the 1–10 mu group
to $17.55 for the 51–100 mu group and $19.10 for the over 100 mu group,
or from 68 cents to $1.60 per person per month.

The farm produce used by the owner families amounted to $1.30 per
person per month for the 1–10 group, and $6.60 for the families with
over 100 mu.

Added together, the cash and produce figures give a per capita income
of only $2.20 per month for the 1–10 mu owner families. The amount
was less than $5.00 per person per month until the families had more
than 50 mu of land. Even in the wealthiest families, because of the increase in the family membership, the income was only $8.20 per person
per month. For the average family the amount was about $4.25 per per-
son per month.

These figures of family cash income, produce used, and total income per person are probably the most significant of our study of the farm families for they show very clearly the 1927 basis of the monetary and economic life of Ting Hsien.

TABLE 15. OWNERSHIP, NUMBER, AND AREA OF FARMS

	Farms	Per Cent	Mu	Per Cent	Average Mu	Crop Mu[3]
Owners	244	61.0	8,667	70.0	35.5	42.8
Part owners	135	33.8	3,410[1]	27.6	25.3[2]	31.5
Tenants	21	5.2	300	2.4	14.3	16.7
	400	100.0	12,377	100.0	30.9	37.6

[1] Owned 2,248 mu; rented 1,162 mu.   [2] Owned 16.7 mu; rented 8.6 mu.
[3] Total crop mu 15,044. Index of double cropping 121.

TABLE 16. SIZE OF FARMS

	Number[1]			Crop Area[1]			Per Cent of Total	
Mu	O	PO	T	O	PO	T	Number	Area
10 and under	37	8	11	249	62	74	14	3
11–20	61	56	7	920	862	105	31	15
21–30	45	37	1	1,178	925	25	21	17
31–40	25	11	1	875	372	36	9	10
41–50	18	12	–	800	532	–	7	11
51–100	43	11	1	2,801	657	60	14	29
Over 100	15	–	–	1,844	–	–	4	15
	244	135	21	8,667	3,410	300	100	100

[1] O = owner; PO = part owner; T = tenant.

TABLE 17. SIZE OF FARM AND SIZE OF FAMILY

Size of Farm (mu)	Average Mu	Size of Family	Children 1–10 Years	Mu per Person
1–10	6.9	3.8	0.6	1.8
11–20	15.2	4.8	0.8	3.2
21–30	25.6	6.2	0.9	4.1
31–40	34.7	6.7	1.3	5.2
41–50	44.4	8.4	1.4	5.3
51–100	64.0	9.4	1.9	6.8
Over 100	123.0	13.5	3.2	9.1
Average	30.9	6.3	1.1	4.8
Owners	35.5	6.8	1.3	5.2
Part-owners	25.3	6.0	0.9	4.2
Tenants	14.3	4.1	0.6	3.5

TABLE 18. AGE AND SEX

Age[1]	Males	Females	Total	Per Cent	Average Family[2]
10 and under	245	204	449	17.7	1.1
11–20	286	243	529	20.8	1.3
21–30	248	191	439	17.3	1.1
31–40	201	159	360	14.2	0.9
41–50	171	158	329	13.0	0.8
51–60	119	116	235	9.3	0.6
61–70	53	73	126	5.0	0.3
71–80	22	34	56	2.2	0.2
Over 80	3	10	13	0.5	–
	1,348	1,188	2,536	100.0	6.3

[1] Chinese age.
[2] 64 year-round workers included.

TABLE 19. VALUE OF CAPITAL ASSETS

	Owner				Part-owner	Tenant
	1–10 Mu	21–30 Mu	Over 100 Mu	Average	Average	Average
Land	$464	$2,002	$9,821	$2,751	$1,232	–
House	111	216	1,200	345	191	$109
Implements	9	40	119	46	31	15
Animals	8	42	238	61	37	21
Trees	21	101	404	102	37	5
Seeds	1	8	38	10	7	2
Fodder	–	4	22	5	3	–
	$614	$2,413	$11,842	$3,320	$1,538	$152

| Average value per mu of land owned | | | | $77.50 | $73.95 | |

TABLE 20. CAPITAL PER FARM
(percentages)

	Owners	Part-owners	Tenants	Total
$ 500 and under	6.2	13.3	100	13.5
501–1,000	14.3	31.1		19.2
1,001–1,500	12.3	17.1		13.2
1,501–2,000	11.9	13.3		11.8
2,001–2,500	7.4	10.4		8.0
2,501–3,000	7.0	7.5		6.8
3,001–4,000	11.9	4.5		8.8
4,001–5,000	10.6	1.4		7.0
5,001–7,500	10.6	1.4		7.0
7,501–10,000	1.2			0.7
Over 10,000	6.6			4.0
	100.0	100.0	100	100.0

TABLE 21. LAND VALUE

	Area (mu)	Per Cent	Total Value	Per Cent	Per Mu
Under $40 per mu	1,295	10.5	$ 35,190	4.0	$27.20
$40–$79	4,972	40.2	300,650	33.8	60.50
$80 and over	6,110	49.3	553,170	62.2	90.50
	12,377	100.0	$889,010	100.0	$71.80

TABLE 22. VALUE OF FARM HOUSES AND IMPLEMENTS

Size of Farm (mu)	Houses		Implements		Animals	
	Per Farm	Per Mu	Per Farm	Per Mu	Per Farm	Per Mu
1–10	$ 100	$14.50	$ 9.00	$1.30	$ 6.10	$0.88
11–20	110	7.25	19.00	1.25	27.22	1.80
21–30	205	8.00	35.75	1.40	39.50	1.55
31–40	255	7.35	52.95	1.55	48.01	1.40
41–50	345	7.80	65.85	1.50	69.15	1.55
51–100	620	9.70	74.85	1.15	111.42	1.75
Over 100	1,200	9.75	119.20	.95	238.45	1.95
Average	280	9.05	39.15	1.25	50.40	1.65
Owners		9.75		1.28		1.71
Part-owners		7.55		1.24		1.45
Tenants		7.65		1.02		1.49

TABLE 23. FARM EQUIPMENT PRICES, 1931

Bag, grain	$ 1.00– 1.50	Mill, grain, flat stones	$13.00– 14.00
Basket	.20– .80	——, grain, stone roller	15.00– 20.00
Bellows	2.00– 5.00	Peanut sifter	8.00– 9.00
Broom	.10– .30	——, rent per day	.40
Cart	80.00–90.00	Persian wheel	80.00–100.00
Cotton batting machine	40.00–50.00	Plow	3.50– 5.00
Cotton gin	30.00	Pole, carrying	.70– 2.70
Drill, stone	.70	Rake, bamboo	.60– .70
Flail	4.00– 5.00	Rope winder	.60– .70
Flour sifter, large	1.30– 1.40	Shovel, fertilizer	.50– 1.00
——, small	.70– .80	——, wooden	.30– .60
Fork, digging	.30– 1.00	Sickle	.10 and.40– .50
——, wooden	.50– .80	Spinning wheel	.50– .60
Harrow	3.00	Straw cutter knife	2.00
Hoe	1.50	Wheelbarrow, small	6.00– 7.00
Loom, metal frame	30.00	——, large	14.00– 15.00
——, wooden frame	7.00– 8.00	Whip	.50– 1.00
Measure, grain, sheng	.10	Windlass, irrigation, with	
——, grain, tou	.60– .70	ropes and baskets	4.00– 5.00
		Winnowing machine	15.00

TABLE 24. FARM ANIMALS

	Farms	Per Cent	Animals
Cows	86	21.5	76
Horses	37	9.3	36⅓
Mules	92	23.0	109½
Donkeys	148	37.0	135⅔
Draft animals	334[1]	83.5	–
Pigs	323	80.8	536
Chickens	335	83.8	1,474
Ducks	13	3.3	25
Geese	3	0.8	5
Sheep	8	2.0	26
Rabbits	6	1.5	49

[1] Families with fractional draft animals—56.
Families with more than one draft animal—29.

TABLE 25. FARM PRODUCTS

	Per Cent Crop Mu[1]	Per Cent Crop Area	Amount Produced	Average Value per Mu	Per Cent Sold
Millet	30.3	36.8	$32,240	$ 7.05	6
——, glutinous	2.2	2.7	1,485	4.45	3
——, panicled	1.7	2.0	1,055	4.15	–
Wheat	9.9	12.1	10,630	9.10	42
Kaoliang	7.9	9.6	5,600	4.70	3
Corn	3.5	4.2	4,530	8.65	8
Buckwheat	4.5	5.5	3,225	4.75	13
Barley	2.0	2.4	1,475	5.00	1
Black beans	6.5	7.9	6,080	6.25	3
Green beans	2.8	3.6	1,325	2.95	15
Yellow beans	2.0	2.4	1,270	4.35	18
White beans	0.5	0.6	200	2.95	–
Sweet potatoes	6.8	8.2	16,475	16.20	2
Turnips	–	–	510	–	–
Vegetables	2.3	2.9	5,215	14.80	6
Peanuts	3.7	4.1	7,200	13.05	93
Cotton	9.1	11.0	14,905	10.95	86
Sesame	4.3	5.2	4,995	7.70	92
By-products	–	–	20,820	–	3
Total and average	100.0	121.2	$139,235	$11.25	24

Amount sold—$33,330; average per farm—$83.30.
Grains sold—12.2 per cent.
Animals and animal products sold (average)—$10.50.

[1] Total crop mu—121 per cent of crop area.

TABLE 26. SIZE OF FARM AND PROPORTION OF CROPS SOLD

Size of Farm (mu)	Per Cent Sold				Production per Mu
	Owners	Part-owners	Tenants	Total	
1–10	12.5	7.8	21.1	13.5	$12.55
11–20	14.2	20.2	12.4	16.9	12.45
21–30	21.6	20.3	17.8	21.0	13.10
31–40	21.6	24.2	56.0	23.2	12.50
41–50	23.5	29.3	–	25.8	11.25
51–100	27.1	26.0	27.0	26.9	11.60
Over 100	31.3	–	–	31.3	11.30
Average	24.4	22.9	22.2	23.9	12.05

Average value of production per mu: owners $12.00, part-owners $12.10, tenants $12.25.

TABLE 27. FARM EXPENSES

	Per Mu			Average	21–30 Mu
	Owner	Part-owner	Tenant	per Family	Group
Hired labor	$1.04	$0.23	$0.10	$ 24.50	$ 11.75
Fertilizer	.31	.22	.18	8.80	6.75
Fodder	.05	.07	.18	1.75	2.90
Seed	.10	.12	.20	3.25	2.20
Implement repair	.04	.03	.02	1.15	.80
House repair	.14	.03	.05	3.25	3.45
Hsien taxes, owner	.10	–	–	3.55	2.65
——, part-owner	–	.07	–	1.70	1.65
Rent, part-owner	–	1.25	–	31.55	32.15
——, tenant	–	–	3.75	53.60	112.50
Est. value family labor	1.60	2.60	2.11	57.60	65.10
——, animal labor	1.32	1.43	1.05	41.50	41.15
Total or average	$4.70	$6.05	$7.65	$158.40	$153.45
Labor per mu, man				$2.65	
——, animal				1.35	
Land rent, average per mu				3.65	

TABLE 28. SOURCES AND AMOUNTS OF FAMILY EARNINGS

	Owner	Part-owner	Tenant	21–30 Mu	Total
Farm net	$257.15	$154.00	$ 65.70	$187.00	$212.30
Labor on own farm (family, animal)	102.65	99.90	47.60	106.00	99.40
Labor for others	2.55	8.00	10.75	3.85	4.85
Rent of land	5.30	–	–	–	3.20
Interest on loans	3.95	.55	–	1.25	2.60
Home industry	10.95	12.45	7.80	11.95	11.25
Business	7.15	10.90	5.25	3.95	8.30
Other	5.85	3.80	10.30	6.05	5.40
	$395.55	$289.60	$147.40	$320.05	$347.30
Per person per month	$ 4.85	$ 4.05	$ 3.03	$ 4.30	$ 4.53

TABLE 29. FAMILIES AND AMOUNT OF INCOME
(percentages)

	Owner	Part-owner	Tenant	Total	Average Amount
$ 50 and under	2.9	0.7	9.6	2.5	$ 40.50
51–100	6.9	3.7	19.0	6.5	81.25
101–150	12.3	16.3	23.8	14.3	127.10
151–200	11.1	15.6	19.0	13.0	175.15
201–300	14.3	28.2	19.0	19.3	246.30
301–500	25.4	24.4	9.6	24.2	394.65
501–1,000	20.5	10.4	–	16.0	647.90
Over 1,000	6.6	0.7	–	4.2	1,283.45
	100.0	100.0	100.0	100.0	$ 347.30

CHAPTER IV

Home Industry Families

IN ORDER to round out our study of village home industry (see Chapter XV) and secure more complete and detailed figures than was possible in our hsien wide survey, a family by family study was made, in 1932, of six neighboring villages in the 6th District north of the T'ang River. Their location is shown on the hsien map on page 5. The villages varied in size from 120 to 1,100 families. The total in the six villages was 2,260. Seventeen hundred and forty families, 77 per cent, reported some home industry. In the individual villages the proportion varied from 70 to 96 per cent.

The number of persons in the 2,260 families was 12,655, an average of 5.6 persons per family. In the individual villages the average number of persons per family varied from 4.5 to 6.9. In the 5,255 families in the 1st District the average family had 5.8 persons.

The six villages had a total of 30,521 mu of farm land, an average of 13.5 mu (2.25 acres) per family and 2.4 mu (0.4 acres) per person.[1] This was only two-thirds of the hsien average. In the individual villages the average amount of land per person ranged from 1.1 to 5.3 mu. The largest village had the smallest amount of land per family, 9.5 mu. The smallest village had the largest average per family, 27.5 mu.

Besides having the smallest amount of land per family, the largest village also had the smallest proportion of families engaged in home industry, 70 per cent. The home industry families, however, compensated, at least in part, for their smaller farm income by more industrial work. The average time they worked during the year was over 50 per cent more than the average of the next most active village and more than twice the average of the village with the least industrial activity.

It had been our original intention to study all of the home industry

1. It was reported (1950) that the Central People's Government land program allowed a family to hold 2.5 mu per person.

families in the six villages, but when we found that in one village all of the 770 home industry families were weaving reed mats it seemed reasonable to take a random sample of 250 families as representative of that village and its industry. That sample, plus all of the home industry families in the five other villages, made the total number of families studied 1,220. Our composite figures for the six villages are based on the 1,220 families. We have not attempted to interpolate, from the 250 family sample, figures for all of the 770 home industry families in the mat weaving village.

In size the home industry families ranged from one to 30 members with the average 5.2 persons. This was 0.4 less than the average for all families in the six villages but the difference was not unexpected. In an agricultural community the poorer and therefore the smaller sized families would more generally be the ones to supplement their income from agriculture with income from industry. Fifty-one per cent of the home industry families had less than five members. Only 6.6 per cent had 10 or more members.

The sex division was 53 per cent male, 47 per cent female. This was a higher proportion of males than the 51.4 per cent of the 5,255 families and the 51.2 per cent of the 515 families. Part of the difference again was undoubtedly due to the larger proportion of small families in the home industry group. Fifty-one per cent of the 1,220 families had less than five members as compared with 37.4 per cent in the 5,255 families and 27.8 per cent in the 515 families. Figures for the home industry families definitely indicate that there is generally a higher proportion of males in the smaller families. In one group of families, which averaged 4.1 persons per family, 56.3 per cent were males. In another group, averaging 8.1 persons per family, 50 per cent were males.

The average number of workers per family was 2.7: 1.1 males and 1.6 females. Just under 40 per cent of all the males in the home industry families were working and just over 65 per cent of the females. The ease with which spinning can be carried on as a part time occupation was apparently the principal reason for the high proportion of females working.

The number of families and individuals engaged in the different industries in the six villages shows that processing the locally grown cotton was the chief industry of the Ting Hsien area. Except for the families in the mat weaving village there were only 14 home industry families that did not have one or more members working on cotton, ginning, beating, spinning, or weaving. This was only 1.5 per cent of the home industry families in the five villages. Only 12 females and 72 males in those villages were non-cotton workers, 0.6 per cent of the female workers and 5.4 per cent of the male workers. If the families in the mat weaving village are included, 80 per cent of the workers in the 1,220 families were working on cotton.

More than one industry was reported by 27 per cent of the families. There were 321 with two industries and eight with three. Ginning, spinning, and weaving was one series. Spinning, weaving leg bands, and making brooms was another.

Two kinds of work were reported by 10.5 per cent of the female workers but only 1.1 per cent of the males. None reported more than two. Spinning and weaving covered all the duplications for the 10 males and all but four of 210 duplications for the females.

The villages show an interesting concentration of industry. One village had only mat weaving. Some thread was spun in that village but it was all used in binding the mats so was not listed as a separate activity. All the bags were woven in one village. All but two of the 124 families weaving belts and leg bands lived in one village. Two-thirds of the industries reported were found in only one of the six villages. Bean curd making, cotton ginning and spinning, and cloth weaving were the only industries reported by five villages.

The items covered in our study of the 1,220 families made it possible to relate the family's land holdings to the size of the family, sex distribution, number of workers, and the proportion of the males and females working. The figures are given in Table 33.

Small land holdings were the rule. Eleven per cent of the families had no land and 82.2 per cent had less than 25 mu. Less than 1.0 per cent had 100 or more mu. As the amount of land held by the family increased the size of the average family generally increased. It was 4.1 persons for the landless families and 14.1 persons for those with 75–99 mu. As mentioned above the proportion of males decreased as the amount of land and the size of the family increased.

The average number of male workers per family did not change appreciably except in the highest group. Generally it was about 1.0 per family. In the 100 mu group, however, the average was only 0.1 male worker per family. For the females the average number of workers per family increased as the size of land holdings and the size of the family increased. It was 1.2 for the landless group but three times that for the 75–99 mu group.

The proportion engaged in home industry decreased for both the males and the females as the land holdings increased. The highest top figures were 45.0 per cent for the males and 69.2 per cent for the females. Both were in the under 25 mu group. If we assume that from 25 to 30 per cent of the females were girls too young to work (in our 5,255 families 25.3 per cent of the females were under 12 and 29.2 per cent were under 14 years of age), it seems evident that almost all of the older females in the families with less than 25 mu were doing some home industry. Even in the families with 100 or more mu of land 45.3 per cent of all the females were reported as working in home industry. Spinning is easy to do and the extra personal income undoubtedly appealed.

Detailed figures for three villages showed that from 40 to 57 per cent of the home industry workers began working before they were 15 years of age and that from 92 to 96 per cent began before they were 20 years of age. In one village there were two men who said they began working before they were 10 years old. There were two men and three women who began after they were 50 while one man and one woman said they started after they were 60 years old. Eleven persons said they had worked 65 or more years. Two women claimed to have worked 70 years.

The value of the annual industrial output was estimated to be $279,-715, an average of $230 per family and $85 per worker. The average profit was estimated to be 16.4 per cent, $37.60 per family and $13.95 per worker per year. For the entire hsien the average income from home industry was estimated as $12.50 per family.[2]

The profit figures for the males and females show a wide range in the different villages. For the males the amount varied from $10.50 to $34.45. For the females the lowest amount was an average of $3.65 per year, one cent a day. In four villages the amount was less than $8.20 per year. The highest amount was $24.05 but that was in the mat weaving village, where it was impossible to separate the work of the men and the women and both had to be given the same average. If the division could be made, the average for the females would undoubtedly be considerably lower and that for the males correspondingly higher.

While we found it difficult to get an accurate estimate of the amount

2. See Chapter XV.

of time worked during the year we have taken the workers' estimate of the time they spent on home industry, reduced it to 10 hour days and figured the average earnings per day. The average number of full working days reported in the different villages varied from 81 to 190 for the males and from 51 to 190 days for the females. The top figures for the men and women were the same as they were for the mat weaving village, where no sex division was possible. The figures indicate that generally the males engaged in home industry worked an equivalent of between three and four months of full time days a year, the females between two and three months.

The amount of earnings per full working day showed considerable consistency even though they had to be based on estimates. For the men the amount was around 15 cents per day. For the women it was eight or nine cents per day, less than one cent an hour.

The total annual income from all sources was estimated to be $226,-460. Twenty per cent of the income came from the profit on home industries. The average income was $185 per family and $34.20 per person. These average amounts were only 53 and 63 per cent of the corresponding averages for the 400 farm families. In the six villages the average annual income per family varied from $152 to $249, the amount per person from $30 to $39.50.

The reported expenditure averaged $155 per family, $29.70 per person. There was an apparent surplus of $30 per family, but probably much of this was the result of omissions in estimating the family expenditure and the actual surplus was considerably less than that amount. Thirty per cent of the families reported a deficit.

In one village four of the 274 home industry families reported incomes of less than $50 per year. These probably were the three single person families, all males, and one of the two person families. Twenty families reported expenditure of less than $50 per year. This was two-thirds of the one and two person families in the village. Only one out of eight of the families reported incomes of $25 or more per month. For all the home industry families in the village the average income was $178 per family, $39.50 per person. The expenditure was $138 per family, $31 per person per year.

TABLE 30. FAMILIES, PERSONS, LAND, HOME INDUSTRY FAMILIES,
WORKERS
(six villages)

Families, total	2,260	Persons, total	12,655
With home industry	1,740	Average, all families	5.6
Per cent of total	77.0	In 1,220 families	6,365
Home industry families studied	1,220	Average	5.2
		Males	3,371
		Females	2,994
		Per cent male	53.0

Farm land, total mu	30,521
Average per family	13.5
Average per person	2.4
In five villages (mat weaving village omitted)	
Average per family	17.3
Average per person	3.2
Home industry families	15.4
Average per person	2.8

Workers, 1,220 families	3,288
Average per family	2.7
Males	1,329
Females	1,959
Per cent male	40.4
Average per family	
Males	1.1
Females	1.6
Males working	39.4%
Females working	65.4%

Size of Home Industry Families

Persons	Families	Per Cent	Persons	Per Cent
Under 5	622	51.0	1,990	31.3
5–9	517	42.4	3,258	51.1
10–14	58	4.8	661	10.4
15–19	14	1.1	233	3.7
20–24	5	0.4	112	1.8
25 and over	4	0.3	111	1.7
	1,220	100.0	6,365	100.0

TABLE 31. FAMILIES, HOME INDUSTRY FAMILIES, PERSONS, LAND—PER VILLAGE

Village	Total Families	Average No. of Persons	Average No. of Mu	Home Industry Families	Per Cent in Industry	Average No. of Persons	Per Cent in Industry	Average No. of Mu
1	340	4.5	12.1	274	80.6	4.5	72.3	12.7
2	180	6.9	17.2	174	96.7	6.7	50.5	14.9
3	250	6.5	18.5	229	91.6	6.5	34.7	16.5
4	120	5.2	27.6	92	76.7	4.7	53.6	21.5
5	270	4.6	18.5	201	74.4	4.7	49.9	15.5
6	1,100	5.8	9.5	250[1]	70.0	4.5	53.5	n.d.
Total or average	2,260	5.6	13.5	1,220	77.0	5.2	51.6	

[1] 250 family sample of 770 mat weaving families.

TABLE 32. INDUSTRIES AND WORKERS

	Families	Males	Females	Totals
Bean curd	10	11	3	14
Boxes	2	2	–	2
Brooms	3	3	–	3
Buckets	1	1	–	1
Candy	1	3	–	3
Cotton ginning	20	37	13	50
Firecrackers	1	2	–	2
Flour	6	8	5	13
Hatchets	1	1	–	1
Horsehair sieves	1	1	–	1
Noodles	1	1	–	1
Oil pressing	12	30	4	34
Plows	2	3	–	3
Sausage casings	1	2	1	3
Shoemaking	1	1	–	1
Soap	8	10	–	10
Spinning	684	170	1,111	1,281
Weaving, bags	68	63	11	74
——, belts and leg bands	124	47	105	152
——, cloth	359	559	712	1,271
——, mats	250[1]	388	205	593
	1,556	1,343	2,170	3,513
Per cent duplication	27.5	1.1	10.5	6.7

[1] 250 families taken as sample of 770 mat weaving families.

TABLE 33. HOME INDUSTRY FAMILIES, AMOUNT OF LAND OWNED

Land	No. of Families	Per Cent	Total Males	Total Females	Per Cent Male	Size of Average Family
None	134	11.0	309	239	56.3	4.1
Under 25 mu	869	71.2	2,182	1,875	53.9	4.7
25–49	156	12.8	513	531	49.1	6.7
50–74	39	3.2	215	197	52.1	10.6
75–99	14	1.1	99	99	50.0	14.1
100 and over	8	0.7	53	53	50.0	13.2
	1,220	100.0	3,371	2,994	53.0	5.2

Land	Workers, Male	Workers, Female	Workers Per Family Males	Females	Total	Per Cent Working Males	Females	Total
None	134	160	1.0	1.2	2.2	43.5	66.9	53.6
Under 25 mu	982	1,299	1.1	1.5	2.6	45.0	69.2	56.2
25–49	149	330	1.0	2.1	3.1	29.0	62.0	45.7
50–74	50	96	1.3	2.5	3.8	23.2	48.7	35.4
75–99	13	50	0.9	3.6	4.5	13.1	50.5	31.4
100 and over	1	24	0.1	3.0	3.1	1.9	45.3	23.6
	1,329	1,959	1.1	1.6	2.7	39.4	65.4	51.6

TABLE 34. ANNUAL OUTPUT, PROFIT, DAYS WORKED, PROFIT PER DAY

Output, estimated value	$279,715	Profit, estimated	$45,900
Per family	$230.00	Per family	$37.60
Per worker	$85.00	Per worker	$13.95
		Average profit	16.4%

	Profit per Worker per Year		Days Worked per Year		Profit per Day	
Village	Male	Female	Male	Female	Male	Female
1	$11.95	$ 8.15	120	96	$0.10	$0.09
2	28.50	17.40	123	109	0.23	0.16
3	34.45	3.65	90	51	0.38	0.07
4	14.10	4.55	101	67	0.14	0.07
5	10.50	6.45	81	72	0.13	0.09
6[1]	24.05	24.05	190	190	0.13	0.13

[1] No sex division possible.

TABLE 35. FAMILY INCOME AND EXPENSES

Income reported, total	$226,460	Families reporting:	
Per family	$185.00	Surplus	784
Per person	$34.20	Deficit	374
Proportion from home		Balanced budget	62
industry	20.2%		———
Expenses, total	$188,925		1,220
Per family	$155.00	Amount of surplus	$45,035
Per person	$29.70	Amount of deficit	$7,560

Income and Expense Distribution
Village No. 1

Amount	Income Families	Expense Families
Under $50	4	20
50–99	53	60
100–149	65	80
150–199	61	50
200–249	22	41
250–299	35	19
300 and over	34	4
	—	—
	274	274

Average Income and Expense

Village	Income per Family	Income per Person	Expense per Family	Expense per Person
1	$178	$39.50	$138	$31.00
2	249	35.70	202	30.20
3	196	30.00	174	26.80
4	162	33.70	144	30.60
5	182	38.70	171	36.20
6	152	34.30	113	25.20
	—	—	—	—
	$185	$34.20	$155	$29.70

CHAPTER V

Family Budgets

THE DAILY accounts and records of 34 farm families give a sample of rural family budgets and figures that are at least suggestive of the way the farm families in different income levels divided their expenditure, the kinds and amounts of food included in their diet, the types and value of their housing, the relation between the amount of income and the size of the family group.

Almost no farm families keep such records, so it was necessary for our field workers to persuade a group of families to keep them for us. Since most of the families were illiterate, it also was necessary to persuade them to report their daily income and expenditure to a writer who called regularly to make the entries in the record.

As our study of 400 farms[1] showed that 76 per cent of the farm produce was used by the farm family and that the money they handled was only a small part of their real income and expenditure, it was necessary to have the families report the amounts and value of the farm produce used from day to day, as well as any money income and expenditure. This required actual weighing of the food used, at least until a reasonable basis of estimating the amount used was established and understood. Periodic weighings were also used to check the accuracy of the reports.

Because of the seasonal nature of some of the income and expenditure, it was necessary to continue the accounting for a full year. Since the lunar year was still in general use, the families felt that they had completed the year's record when they had finished 12 lunar, rather than 12 solar months. The difference between the two years is some 11 days, 3.1 per cent. Generally we have taken the records as written and based our tables on the lunar year. For the annual food consumption figures,

1. See Chapter III.

however, the reported amounts have been increased by enough to put them on the solar rather than the lunar year basis.

It is fully realized that there are many chances for error in this type of accounting, especially when it covers the period of a year and when, because of literacy problems, the entries have to be made by someone outside of the family. Previous experience with a similar study of the budgets of city families[2] made it possible to foresee and provide for some of the problems. We were able to enlist the cooperation and assistance of the village heads. The records were made, not by an outsider, but by one of the villagers. In spite of all we could do, a considerable number of families dropped out during the year. For some others the record was so evidently incomplete that they had to be eliminated. Fifty-five families started the study but only 34 completed the year's record.

A small group of 34 families that, because of the requirements of the study, had to be chosen on a highly selective basis cannot be called average for all of Ting Hsien, but the general consistency of the figures, when the families are divided into groups according to the amount of their income, is such that it is felt that the income group figures give a very informative picture of the way the rural families of different income levels divided and used their income and furnish a basis for comparison with similar figures from other areas. It is also felt that the record figures are much more accurate than those that could be secured from estimates, by the head of the family, of the previous year's expenditures.

The first of our families began its account on the first of the first month of 1928, a few more families were added the next month, but most of the group began in the third month and continued through the second month of 1929. There was a leap second month in 1929, but it was not included in our study.

The families lived in Chai Ch'eng, Hsiao Liu, and Tung T'ing. These villages were all in the Experimental District. The problem of finding available writers as well as families willing to cooperate in our study made it advisable to work in three neighboring villages rather than in one center. Three men took care of the necessary account keeping.

All of the 34 families were land owners. Seven held land under

2. Sidney D. Gamble, *How Chinese Families Live in Peiping* (Funk and Wagnalls, New York, 1933).

mortgage and five rented part of the land they farmed. Land held under mortgage was practically owned by the mortgagee. Instead of paying interest on the mortgage, the owner turned the land over to the mortgagee subject, of course, to the right of redemption. The area farmed by the individual families varied from eight to 60 mu. The total was 1,061.6 mu. Of this, 976.8 mu were owned, 53 mu were held under mortgage, and 31.8 mu were rented. The 3 per cent of rented land was low when compared with the 6.9 per cent average for the 3rd District and the 12.2 per cent average for the hsien. None of the 34 farms was large enough to warrant employing a full-time worker.

The average farm area per family was 31.2 mu, 5.2 acres. This was some 36 per cent more than the average for the Experimental District and 47 per cent more than the hsien average of 21.2 mu per farm operating family.[3] Our average family very evidently belonged to a higher income group than the average Ting Hsien family. This difficulty is overcome, to some extent, by dividing our budget families into four income groups beginning with $100 per year and with an income range of $100 per year per group. The number of families in these income groups is smaller than we would like, but, even so, their figures seem to give a reasonable picture of the distribution of family expenditure at different income levels.

How the families were divided among the different income groups and how the average number of mu per family varied with the amount of the family income from 14.8 mu for the $100–$200 group to 41.8 mu for the $400–$500 group is shown in Table 36.

The 34 families ranged in size from two to 12 persons. The total number of persons was 205, an average of 6.0 persons per family. This was only slightly higher than the average of 5.8 persons in the 5,255 families living in the 1st District.[4] As the farm of our average family contained six mu, 24 per cent, more land than the average farm in the 1st District, we should be inclined to expect more of a difference in the size of the average families. Since the families in the $200–$300 income group averaged 5.9 persons and their farms 27.7 mu, or very nearly the average figures for the families in the 1st District, it seems possible to infer that the average incomes of the two groups were fairly comparable. For our $200–$300 group, the average annual income was $262.65 per family, $44.50 per person.

3. See Chapter X.   4. See Chapter IV.

That the number in the family was very definitely related to the size of the family income is shown by the increase in the average persons per family from 3.8 in the $100–$200 group to 9.3 in the $400–$500 group.

Figure 15 shows how closely the size of the family was related to the size of the farm. The number of mu per person, in the highest income group, was only 15 per cent more than in the lowest income group. The 400 farm families[5] showed a tendency for the size of the family to increase some 35 per cent with an increase of 100 per cent in the size of the farm.

As the number of mu per person was less in the $400–$500 income group than in the $300–$400 group, we wonder whether the higher income families might not have had a fairly recent influx of relatives that had increased the size of the average family and reduced the number of mu per person. It may be, however, that, since these larger families had sources of income other than farming, they had not increased their land holdings. The families in this income group received 31.4 per cent of their income from non-farm sources. With an average surplus of some $116, they had sufficient means to purchase additional land, if desired.

The 205 family members were divided 106 male and 99 female, or 51.7 per cent male. The masculinity rate of 107 was only slightly higher than the rate for the 515 and the 5,255 families included in our population study in Chapter II.

The age distribution of the family members showed a much larger proportion in the 16–30 age group than was true in the two other and larger groups of Ting Hsien families, 35.7 per cent, as compared with 24.9 and 24.3 per cent. This was offset by smaller proportions in the 1–15 and 31–45 year groups.

The relationship distribution was practically the same as that found in the two larger groups of families. Eighty-three percent were members of the immediate family of the head of the household, or his direct descendants; 7 per cent belonged to an older generation and 10 per cent were brothers, their families, and sisters. The details of the distribution are shown in Table 4.

Only 22 per cent of the family members who were 15 years of age or older were single, 22 males and 11 females. All of the women over 24 years of age had married. Three men over 24 were still single. There

5. See Chapter III.

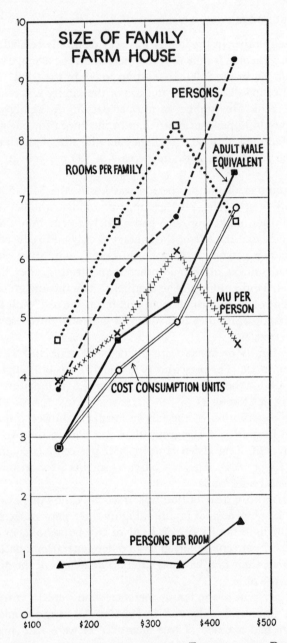

FIGURE 15. BUDGET FAMILIES: PERSONS PER FAMILY & PER ROOM, ADULT
MALE EQUIVALENTS & ROOMS PER FAMILY, LAND PER PERSON

were 48 couples in the 34 families. In 63 per cent the wife was older than her husband. In 31 per cent the husband was the elder. The average age difference was three quarters of a year, with the wife the older. There were eight widowers and 13 widows.

To allow for the differences in consumption due to differences in age and sex, the size of the families has been figured in terms of Atwater's Adult Male Equivalents and of the food scale of Cost Consumption Units developed by the United States Department of Agriculture.[6] The usual age figures in the tables of equivalents have been increased by one to allow for the difference between Chinese and Western ages. The total number of adult male equivalents was 158.5 and of cost consumption units 149.0. Figure 15 and Table 36 show that the adult male equivalents per family varied from 2.8 in the $100–$200 group to 7.4 in the $400–$500 group. Cost consumption units varied from 2.8 to 6.8.

Seventy-three of the 78 males over 14 years of age (13 foreign count) were listed as farmers. Of the five men engaged in other full-time work, two were in business, one was a teacher, one an apprentice, and one an employed laborer. Twenty farmers reported working in their spare time, weaving, peddling, making incense, paper, and teapots, beating cotton batting, herding sheep, and wagon driving. The women helped with the farm work at harvest time and did some weaving and spinning.

The families have been grouped according to the amount of their reported income unless their expenditure was larger than their income. In that case, it is assumed that the deficit was financed from some unreported source and that the amount of income was equal to the expenditure. Unspent income was considered as surplus that may have been spent for some unreported items or kept as savings, partly in money, partly in unused farm products in the family storeroom.

The average incomes of the different income groups were not far from the mid-point of the income range of each group. The minimum income reported was $107.29, or $9.00 a month. The maximum was $486.19, just over $40 per month.

Because the size of the family increased when the family income increased, the figures showing the income per person and per adult male equivalent are much more significant than those giving the income per family. The figures in Table 36 show that, for this group of families, the income per adult male equivalent was very similar in the different

6. U.S. Department of Agriculture, Bulletin 1382, January, 1926.

income groups. The same was true of the income per person figures. Generally the amounts were about $4.00 per month per person and $5.00 per month per adult male equivalent. The lowest amounts were in the $100–$200 group, the highest in the $300–$400 group rather than in the $400–$500 group. The $300–$400 group average per adult male equivalent was only 11 per cent above that of the $100–$200 group.

The sources of the family income, shown in Table 37, include three sources of farm income: crops, land rent, and other farm income. Crop income is the net income after paying the necessary operating expenses. It includes the cash income from any crops sold and the value of the crops used by the families. It averaged generally between $6.50 and $7.00 per mu. Only three families reported crop income of more than $10.00 per mu. Five families reported less than $5.00 per mu.

The averages were somewhat higher than those given by dividing the average crop income by the average number of mu per family, as eight of the families rented to others part of their land holdings. The total amount received from this source was $139.45. The records do not give the exact number of mu rented, but an average rate of $3.50 per mu would make it 40 mu. That amount has been deducted in figuring the crop income per mu.

Other farm income included the value of animals and animal products sold or used on the farm, also the value of wood from the farm trees. Four-fifths of the families received some income from this source, the amounts ranging from $6.00 to $185.00. The latter, undoubtedly, was the family that sold a horse. The next largest amounts reported were $71 and $68. All of the 27 families reporting income from animals either sold or used some pork. The majority listed eggs, nine wood. Three sold mules. The sale of the mules and the horse may have represented the sale of a capital item rather than current income, but, lacking definite information, we have counted the amount received as part of the family income.

"Miscellaneous income" included wages earned, business profit, and other occasional items. Twenty-four families reported amounts varying from 70 cents to $150. For four families, the amount was over $75. They all received $130 or more. Three of the four families were in the $400–$500 income group.

House rent was purely a bookkeeping item, entered on both the income and expense side of the family accounts, as all of the families owned their homes and paid no rent. The figures used, therefore, were the estimated rent value of the house occupied by the family. To make our figures comparable with those in other budget studies, it has been necessary to include a rent charge in the family expenses and balance it with a like amount on the income side. It averaged 5.1 per cent of the total estimated value of the houses, $12,300. The estimated value of the individual houses ranged from $120 to $920, but only four were worth more than $500. The average value was $360. The values used for the different kinds of construction were $40 per chien for a house with earthen walls and no porch, $70 per chien if the house had a porch. If the walls were brick the value was $60 per chien without and $90 with a porch.

The estimated rents of the four types of houses were 15, 20, 30, and 35 cents per chien per month, or from $1.80 to $4.20 per chien per year. The rent value of the brick walled, no porch house was higher than that of the earthen walled house with porch even though the value of the latter house was estimated to be $10 more than that of the brick walled house. The amount of housing and the relation of the rent item to the family budget is given in connection with the rent expenditure.

Ten families reported spending more money than they received. The totals for the different income groups have been averaged for the group. Two of the lowest income families had deficits of some $76. All of the families with incomes of less than $170 per year reported borrowing from $20 to $50. Two families in the $300–$400 group reported borrowing to meet deficits. Amounts borrowed were not counted as income except for the amount necessary to cover the reported deficit. Lacking inventories of the families' food supply at the beginning and end of our study, we cannot determine how much of the deficits was covered from that source and how much from other sources not noted in the family accounts.

How the family expenditure was divided by amount and per cent among the six main expense headings of food, clothing, fuel, rent, miscellaneous, and surplus is shown in Figure 16 and Table 38. It will be noted that the amounts for clothing, rent, fuel, and miscellaneous are all small, about $1.00 a month for the low income families, increasing to about $2.00 a month for the highest income group. The expenditure for food increased from some $9.00 a month for families in the $100–$200 group to $20 a month for those in the $400–$500 group. The pro-

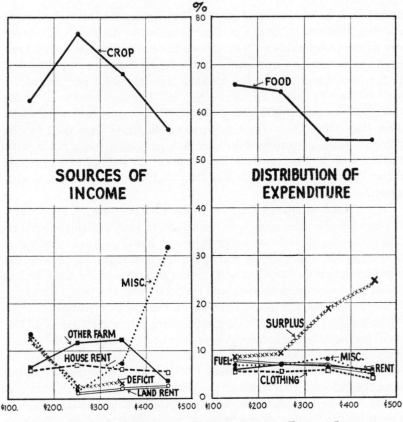

FIGURE 16. BUDGET FAMILIES: DISTRIBUTION OF FAMILY INCOME
AND EXPENSES

portionate increase in the food expenditure was fairly comparable with
that in the other expense classifications. Surplus, on the other hand, increased some eight times while the family income increased less than
three times. Some of the large increase in surplus was, undoubtedly,
due to unreported expenditure, but much of it represented family savings in one form or another.

The percentages of the family expenditure used for the different expense classifications generally followed the usual family budget pattern.
The proportion used for food decreased from 65.5 to 54.0 per cent and
that for miscellaneous and surplus together increased from 15.3 to 30.9

per cent as the family income increased. The proportions spent for rent and clothing stayed about the same, averaging 5.1 and 6.4 per cent. That used for fuel, however, instead of remaining about the same, decreased from 8.3 to 5.3 per cent, a more rapid rate of decrease than that for food. This probably was the result of the small amount of fuel used for heating by Chinese families. Expenditure for fuel for cooking and lighting would probably not increase proportionately with the family income. We found the same decrease in the per cent used for fuel by families living in Peking.[7]

The proportion of the family budget used for food by the Ting Hsien families was higher than that used by Peking families with similar incomes. The larger size of the rural families in all except the $100–$200 group would readily account for this difference. The rural families in the $400–$500 group averaged 9.3 persons, but the city families with incomes between $420 and $480 a year averaged only 5.1 persons. In the next higher city group, the average was only 3.9 persons.[8]

The proportion used for clothes was very similar in the rural and city groups, as was that used for miscellaneous and surplus together. The percentages for rent and fuel were distinctly less for the rural families.

Because of the importance of the expenditure for food, we have made a detailed study of the amounts spent for eight different groups. Millet, which is the principal grain in the Ting Hsien area, was segregated from the other grains and flours. Sweet potatoes, another large item in the family diet, were also given a separate classification. Vegetables, condiments, meat, fruit, and miscellaneous were the other groupings.

The average expenditure of the different income groups for each of the eight food groups is shown in Table 40. It will be noted that in all the income groups by far the largest amount was spent for millet; the amounts for other grains and for sweet potatoes were similar though the grain amounts were regularly larger. The amount for vegetables was about 60 per cent of that for sweet potatoes. The amounts for condiments and meat were much smaller, generally under 50 cents a month. Fruit was a very minor item with an average of some 10 cents per month.

While the amounts per family changed as the family increased, the proportionate distribution of the food expenditure remained practically the same for all the income groups. The approximate division for

7. Gamble, *op. cit.*   8. Gamble, *op. cit.*

the four income groups was 36 per cent for millet and 25 per cent for the other grains, a total of 61 per cent for grain and flour; sweet potatoes were about 21 per cent and vegetables 12.5 per cent. Condiments, meat, fruit, and miscellaneous together took only 5.6 per cent of the average family food budget.

This similarity of distribution was not found in the budgets of Peking families. There the grains and flours decreased and meat increased as the family income increased. City families with incomes from $20 to $25 per month spent some 62 per cent of their food budget for grain and flour. Condiments were 13 per cent, over four times the country figure. Fruit and miscellaneous together were 6.8 per cent, over 13 times the corresponding rural figures. Vegetables were 50 per cent larger in the farm budget. Sweet potatoes, for which the rural families used some 21 per cent of their food expenditure, were not separately listed in the city diet. Generally, the city families considered sweet potatoes distinctly a country food.[9]

The difference in the size of the families in the different income groups makes it difficult to compare their food expenditure directly, but when the amounts are expressed in terms of amounts per person or per adult male equivalent there is a great similarity between the total food figures for the different income groups and in the figures for all of the eight different food divisions. Table 39 shows how close the agreement is. Interestingly enough the amount per adult male equivalent is largest in the lowest income group, and there is a slight but regular decrease in each group as the family income increases.

The small differences in the distribution of the food expenditure and the small differences in the total expenditure per adult male equivalent in the different income groups make it seem evident that there was almost a standard diet for these Ting Hsien families and that once this was attained there was little change even with considerable change in the family income. The amounts per family changed, but generally only in response to a change in the size of the family. The standard diet evidently was available even to the families in our lowest income group. It probably would be available to other small low income farm families in Ting Hsien. The diet was amost entirely dependent on local production. The expenditure per person was so small that it would be difficult to include any considerable amount of imported food.

9. Gamble, *op. cit.*

The average food expenditure of $2.40 per month per person, $3.00 per month per adult male equivalent, and $3.30 per month per cost consumption unit gives a very definite picture of the food expenditure of these families. Buck's figure for the food expenditure of families in Hopei province was $22.94 per adult male equivalent per year.[10] This was 35 per cent below our figure but was based on figures secured some six years earlier.

In Peking the food expenditure of the families with incomes of from $15 to $25 a month was $2.55 per capita and $3.60 per cost consumption unit per month.[11]

The amounts of food per adult male equivalent used by the average family in the different income groups naturally show the same similarity as the expenditure figures. The small amounts of condiments, meat, and fruit are especially noticeable. Five pounds of meat and three and a half pounds of fruit per person per year means that those were very minor items in the general diet. (See Figure 17 and Table 40.)

The average amount of food per person per year was 1,030 catties. Per day this was 2.8 catties, or 3.8 pounds. For the average adult male equivalent the amount was 3.75 catties, 5.0 pounds per day. For the individual families the amount per person per year ranged from 780 to 1,485 catties or from 2.9 to 5.4 pounds per day.

The average daily diet of a member of these families was 17 pound ounces of grain and flour, 25 ounces of sweet potatoes, 19 ounces of vegetables, and 0.8 of an ounce of other foods. By weight the diet was 40 per cent sweet potatoes, 31 per cent vegetables, 28 per cent grains, one per cent condiments, meat, fruit, and miscellaneous.

The large amounts of millet and sweet potatoes are the outstanding items in the food list. Other areas report using sweet potatoes, but not in anywhere near the same amount. Other areas also report using more kaoliang or wheat than millet.

The 34 families reported an average sweet potato consumption of 430 catties per person per year. We have been interested to note that the farm production estimates for the hsien gave a total for sweet potatoes that was equivalent to 465 catties per person if the hsien population is taken as 408,000 persons. The 400 families estimated that all but 2 per cent of the sweet potato crop was consumed on the farm. This

10. J. Lossing Buck, *Chinese Farm Economy* (University of Chicago Press, 1930).
11. Gamble, *op. cit.*

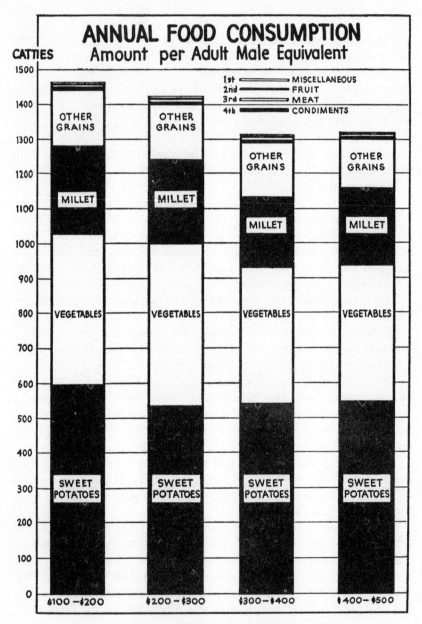

FIGURE 17. BUDGET FAMILIES: FOOD CONSUMPTION
PER ADULT MALE EQUIVALENT

would make the difference between the two sweet potato figures less than 8 per cent.

The average family expenditure for each of the different kinds of food, the number of families reporting its use, and the average amount used are shown in Table 41. The average price per catty is also given. It will be noted that some 40 per cent of the expenditure for sweet potatoes was for those that had been dried. In the dried form they are often ground and cooked as noodles in very much the same way as some of the grains. Only seven families reported using any rice during the year.

The average daily consumption of cabbage was 2.3 catties per family, of squash 1.6 catties. The leaves of the white beets were used as a green vegetable; the roots were pickled and eaten for flavoring with other food. The turnips were generally cut in strips, pickled, and used as a salt vegetable. The reported 30 catties of fennel, or anise, included the leaves and stems used as a vegetable as well as the seed used for flavoring.

The average amount of salt used was 6.0 catties (8.0 pounds) per person per year. This agrees very closely with the 6.5 catties per person reported by the salt wholesaler. (See Chapter VIII.)

Meat was used almost exclusively at festival time. About three quarters of the expenditure was for pork, the only meat item reported by all the families. Beef was used by four-fifths of the families. Dates were the only fruit used by all the families.

The clothing expenditure averaged $14.85 per family, or $2.48 per person per year. For the different income groups, the amounts per person varied from $2.10 for the $400–$500 group to $2.73 for the $300–$400 group.

The details of the average family expenditure for clothes are given in Table 42. Cloth, cotton, shoes, and stockings were the items reported by all the families. Native cloth was woven in Ting Hsien. Foreign cloth was not necessarily made abroad. The name was used to indicate both the kind of cloth and the fact that it was made outside of Ting Hsien. It was woven on machine looms. The native cloth was woven on hand looms. The cotton was the cotton batting used to line winter clothes. Eighty-six feet of native cloth, 10 feet of foreign cloth, and 4.6 catties of cotton were the average purchases. The prices were 7.0 cents a foot for native cloth, 10 cents a foot for foreign cloth, and 40 cents a catty for cotton.

Housing seemed to be relatively adequate for there were more rooms than persons in the average house. The average was 0.9 persons per room. It must be remembered, however, that the number of rooms reported included not only the living rooms of the family but storerooms for farm equipment and supplies and rooms used to house animals. How the number of rooms per family and per person varied in the different income groups is shown in Figure 15 and Table 36. The high average of 1.5 persons per room in the $400–$500 group would lead one to feel that these larger families might recently have been augmented by the addition of extra relatives and had not had time to adjust themselves to the new situation, or possibly there was not room for additional building on the home site inside the village. Certainly there was sufficient surplus in the family budget to finance additional building.

The size of the individual houses varied from three to 15 chien. The 229 chien were divided into 102 with earthen walls and 127 with brick walls. Three of the earthen walled and 23 of the brick walled rooms had porches. The rent value of the different types of houses was estimated to range from $1.80 to $4.20 per chien per year. The average rent per family was $1.55 per month, 6.4 per cent of the family expenditure. For the different income groups the average amount varied from 79 cents to $2.07 per month. (See Table 38.) All of the families owned their homes, so the rent item represents rent value rather than actual expenditure.

The type of house was not closely related to the size of the family income. Twenty-four of the families had some brick walled rooms. Thirteen of these also had earthen walled rooms. Four of the 14 families in the $300–$400 income group had only earthen walled rooms. One family in the $100–200 group had only brick walled rooms.

No rent for farm land was included in the family expenditure as that was a farm expense and was paid from the gross farm income.

Most of the $19.55 used for fuel was the value of the dried grass and stubble and wood grown on the farm or secured from neighbors. Coal, kerosene, and matches, of course, had to be imported. The distribution of the fuel costs was:

Hay and wood	$15.15
Coal	2.25
Kerosene	1.90
Matches	.25
	$19.55

The amounts reported for wood and dried grass ranged from $6 to $25. Only 20 families used any coal. Ten dollars was the most any family spent for that item. The average amount of kerosene was 13.58 catties per family per year, or just over one-half of a tin. For the individual families the amounts ranged from 5.5 to 25 catties. The average daily use was one-half Chinese ounce that cost two coppers. The price per catty was 14 cents, $3.57 per tin. The 25 cents spent for matches bought 55 boxes.

Miscellaneous expenditures naturally included a large number of different items. In this study they have been divided into 10 different groups. The amounts spent for each of these by the families in the different income groups are shown in Table 38. Most of the amounts were small. Even the highest total for all 10 groups was less than $2.50 per month. For three of the four income groups the total for miscellaneous was less than 7.0 per cent of the total expenditure.

Under the head of social expenditure were included the amounts spent for cakes sent as gifts for weddings, funerals, or the birth of a child, or bought to entertain visiting relatives; the eggs sent at the birth of a child; the special expenses for New Year; and money given to the children at New Years' or to a bride.

All the families bought some wine. The average expenditure was $1.02. Locally grown tobacco was much more generally used than the imported cigarettes. Twenty-six families used an average of 6.3 catties of tobacco. The 12 families buying cigarettes reported the purchase of 262 packages. Each package contained 10 cigarettes. The price of the tobacco was 17.5 cents a catty, of the cigarettes five cents per package. The seven families using tea leaves used an average of five ounces per family per year. The average price was just under five cents an ounce.

All of the families went to the temple fair and the theaters. The average expenditure for these amusements was 75 and 55 cents per family. Other amusements included gambling, fortune telling, watching a magician, and the cost of birds to be kept in a cage. Fortune telling and sleight of hand evidently were not very prosperous businesses for the total contribution to them was only 37 cents. The two families that bought birds spent $2 apiece.

The list of house furnishings purchased during the year included 29 items, but the only one reported by all 34 families was chopsticks. Only five items were reported by over half of the families. The average expenditure for chopsticks was 14 cents per family. Only five other items averaged as much as 10 cents per family per year, and only one, bowls, averaged as much as 20 cents.

Soap and hair cuts were the only two health items reported by all the families. The average annual expenditure was 26 cents for soap and 17 cents for hair cuts. The two families that bought toothbrushes and toothpaste spent a total of 75 cents for those items. Only four families spent any money for shaves and three for baths. The average expenditure for medicine was $1.22.

Educational items were reported by only 19 families. Their total expenditure was $18.32, an average of 96 cents. The expenditure for books was only 3.5 cents per person. Only three families said they paid school tuition. Their total expenditure was $4.12, an average of $1.37 per family.

The 70 cents spent for religion bought an average of three packages of paper money of 88 sheets each, 1.2 packages of yellow paper of 96 sheets each, and 2.7 bundles of incense. The price of the incense was five cents per bundle, of the paper 10 cents per package.

An assessment was levied on all families for the support of the army. It totaled $84.74. The amount per family varied from 60 cents to $4.80. It averaged some 8.0 cents a mu for all the land farmed by the 34 families, but it was 8.7 cents per mu for the land owned and 8.25 cents per mu on the land owned and held under mortgage. It seems clear that the owner of rented land was required to pay the assessment. Other studies generally indicated that it was the mortgagee who paid on the mortgaged land. The amounts reported by the individual families varied from 8.0 to 12.5 cents per mu on the land owned and from 4.1 to 12.5 cents per mu on the land owned and held under mortgage.

The village assessment for home guards, schools, etc. totaled $68.89. It averaged 7.1 cents per mu on the land owned and 6.7 cents per mu on the owned and mortgaged land. On the latter basis, the amounts for the individual families varied from 2.5 to 8.4 cents per mu, but for 21 of the families the amount was between 7.0 and 7.4 cents inclusive. As other studies have generally indicated that the village assessments were levied according to the number of mu a family owned or held under mortgage, it is not clear why there was such a difference in the amounts paid per mu unless the amount of the assessment was related to the quality of the land. Different rates for the three villages in which our families lived might account for some, but hardly for all, of the differences.

Miscellaneous included two payments on debts and the expenditure for the one funeral reported. The debt payments were $31.00 and $15.50. The funeral cost $13.49.

TABLE 36. AVERAGE SIZE OF FAMILY, FARM, HOUSE, INCOME

Income Group	No. of Families	Average No. of Persons	Average A.M.E.[1]	Average C.C.U.[2]	Mu per Family	Mu per Person
$100–200	8	3.8	2.8	2.8	14.8	3.9
200–300	9	5.9	4.5	4.1	27.7	4.7
300–400	14	6.7	5.3	4.9	40.6	6.1
400–500	3	9.3	7.4	6.8	41.8	4.5
Average		6.0	4.7	4.4	31.2	5.2

Income Group	Rooms per Family	Persons per Room	Income per Family	Income per Person	Income per A.M.E.[1]
$100–200	4.6	0.8	$166.75	$35.80	$58.50
200–300	6.6	0.9	262.65	40.70	59.40
300–400	8.2	0.8	345.00	46.70	64.90
400–500	6.6	1.5	454.65	46.20	61.45
Average	6.7	0.9	290.95	43.70	61.35

[1] Adult Male Equivalent.   [2] Cost Consumption Unit.

TABLE 37. SOURCES OF FAMILY INCOME

Income Group	Crop	Other Farm	Land Rent	House Rent	Misc.	Deficit	Total
			Amount				
$100–200	$103.80	$10.50	$ –	$ 9.45	$ 21.60	$21.40	$166.75
200–300	201.60	30.40	2.60	18.55	5.75	3.75	262.65
300–400	237.35	42.00	5.55	22.35	28.55	9.20	345.00
400–500	257.50	17.00	12.65	24.85	142.65	–	454.65
Average	198.25	29.30	4.10	18.55	30.95	9.80	290.95
			Per Cent				
$100–200	62.2	6.3	–	5.7	13.0	12.8	100.0
200–300	76.8	11.5	1.0	7.1	2.2	1.4	100.0
300–400	68.7	12.2	1.6	6.5	8.3	2.7	100.0
400–500	56.6	3.7	2.8	5.5	31.4	–	100.0
Average	68.1	10.1	1.4	6.4	10.6	3.4	100.0
Number reporting	34	27	8	34	24	10	

TABLE 38. AVERAGE ANNUAL EXPENDITURE

Income Group	Food	Clothing	Rent	Fuel	Misc.	Surplus	Total
			Amount				
$100–200	$109.20	$ 8.75	$ 9.45	$13.80	$11.35	$14.20	$166.75
200–300	165.70	13.45	18.55	18.70	17.75	28.50	262.65
300–400	186.40	18.25	22.35	22.40	29.60	66.00	345.00
400–500	245.65	19.65	24.85	23.95	24.50	116.05	454.65
Average	167.95	14.85	18.55	19.55	21.70	48.35	290.95
			Per Cent				
$100–200	65.5	5.2	5.7	8.3	6.8	8.5	100.0
200–300	64.1	5.2	7.1	7.2	6.8	9.6	100.0
300–400	54.0	5.3	6.5	6.5	8.6	19.1	100.0
400–500	54.0	4.3	5.5	5.3	5.4	25.5	100.0
Average	57.7	5.1	6.4	6.7	7.5	16.6	100.0

TABLE 39. AVERAGE ANNUAL EXPENDITURE FOR FOOD

Per Family

Income Group	Millet	Other Grain	Sweet Potatoes	Vege- tables	Condi- ments	Meat	Fruit	Misc.	Total
$100–200	$38.65	$28.10	$22.85	$13.30	$3.40	$2.20	$0.44	$0.26	$109.20
200–300	60.75	42.25	32.30	21.00	5.00	3.50	0.48	0.42	165.70
300–400	68.30	45.10	39.10	23.10	5.40	4.50	0.70	0.20	186.40
400–500	87.80	57.10	55.60	33.05	7.15	4.10	0.60	0.25	245.65
Average	61.05	41.40	34.90	21.10	5.00	3.65	0.57	0.28	167.95
Average per cent	36.4	24.6	20.8	12.6	3.0	2.2	0.3	0.1	100.0

Per Adult Male Equivalent

Income Group	Millet	Other Grain	Sweet Potatoes	Vege- tables	Condi- ments	Meat	Fruit	Misc.	Total
$100–200	$13.55	$9.85	$8.00	$4.65	$1.20	$0.77	$0.15	$0.09	$38.25
200–300	13.70	9.50	7.50	4.75	1.10	0.78	0.10	0.09	37.50
300–400	12.90	8.50	7.35	4.35	1.05	0.84	0.14	0.04	35.15
400–500	11.85	7.70	7.50	4.45	0.95	0.55	0.08	0.03	33.10
Average	12.90	8.75	7.35	4.45	1.05	0.77	0.12	0.06	35.45

TABLE 40. AVERAGE AMOUNT OF FOOD USED PER YEAR[1]

Income Group	Millet	Other Grain	Sweet Potatoes	Vegetables	Condiments	Meat	Fruit	Misc.	Total
			Catties per Family						
$100–200	665	465	1,685	1,250	34	13	19	3	4,134
200–300	1,030	705	2,380	2,090	52	23	8	6	6,294
300–400	1,165	765	2,880	2,130	54	27	20	3	7,044
400–500	1,525	980	4,090	2,900	72	25	12	2	9,606
Average	1,050	700	2,580	1,970	50	22	15	4	6,391
			Catties per Adult Male Equivalent						
$100–200	238	166	600	446	12.1	4.6	6.8	1.1	1,474.6
200–300	230	158	530	465	10.5	5.1	1.8	1.3	1,401.7
300–400	220	144	543	400	10.2	5.1	3.8	0.6	1,328.7
400–500	206	132	555	390	9.7	3.4	1.6	0.3	1,298.0
Average	224	149	550	420	10.6	4.7	3.2	0.9	1,362.4

[1] Adjusted for difference between lunar and solar years.

TABLE 41. FOOD USED BY AVERAGE FAMILY PER YEAR:[1]
KIND, AMOUNT, VALUE

Grains, Grain Products, Sweet Potatoes

	Catties per Family	Value per Family	Families Using	Price per Catty
Sweet potatoes	2,008	$20.08	34	$.01
Dried sweet potatoes	495	14.85	34	.03
Millet	1,017	61.05	34	.06
Wheat	147	11.20	34	.076
Beans	130	8.08	34	.063
Kaoliang	111	5.38	34	.048
Buckwheat	98	5.58	34	.057
Glutinous millet	56	2.95	34	.052
Corn	51	2.42	29	.047
Barley	38	2.31	32	.061
Panicled millet	35	1.72	26	.05
Wheat flour	9	.80	15	.09
Rice	4	.38	7	.09
Steamed twisted bread	2	.16	18	.078
Fine dried noodles	2	.20	15	.122
Cakes	1	.12	25	.10
Noodles	*	.05	10	.20
Sesame	*	.02	1	.09
	4,204	$137.35		

Vegetables

	Catties per Family	Value per Family	Families Using	Price per Catty
Cabbage	822	$7.69	34	$.009
Squash	625	3.13	34	.005
White beets	203	1.15	34	.006
Turnip strips	156	6.57	33	.042
Onions	48	.42	32	.009
Fennel	30	.37	27	.012
Spinach	9	.11	4	.012
Fresh turnips	7	.06	3	.009
Leeks	2	.04	7	.017
Egg plant	2	.02	2	.01
Bean sprouts	2	.05	15	.03
Cucumbers	1	.01	6	.01
Seaweed	1	.14	26	.17
Bean noodles	8	1.25	32	.156
Garlic	1	.03	4	.04
Bean curd	1	.04	15	.06
Thyme	*	–	1	.03
Dried vegetables	*	.02	1	.075
	1,918	$21.10		

(continued on next page)

(TABLE 41 CONTINUED)

Condiments

	Catties per Family	Value per Family	Families Using	Price per Catty
Salt	36	$3.47	34	$.091
Vinegar	5	.15	32	.034
Black oil	4	.65	34	.15
Sesame oil	2	.46	33	.25
Sauce	1	.11	23	.18
Pepper	1	.04	24	.07
Ginger	*	.05	24	.23
Starch	*	.03	7	.16
Sugar	*	.02	11	.17
Lard	*	.02	4	.26
	49	$5.00		

Meat

Pork	15	$2.74	34	$.18
Beef	5	.71	27	.145
Mutton	1	.10	8	.11
Eggs	1	.04	1	.087
Pig's liver	*	.05	1	.187
Horse meat	*	.01	2	.34
	22	$3.65		

Fruit

Watermelon	5	$.04	9	$.01
Dates	4	.22	34	.05
Muskmelon	3	.07	15	.023
Pears	1	.14	27	.124
Persimmons	1	.04	17	.057
Apricots	1	.03	10	.065
Peaches	*	.01	3	.19
Grapes	*	.01	3	.08
Red fruit	*	*	3	–
Tangerines	*	.01	1	.32
	15	$.57		

Other Foods

Elm bark	2	$.13	6	$.059
Soda	1	.05	18	.078
Barley candy	1	.06	16	.112
Sugared fruit	*	.03	14	.16
Candy	*	.01	4	.24
Peanuts	*	–	1	.12
	4	$.28		

* Less than 0.5 catty.   [1] Lunar year.

TABLE 42. AVERAGE EXPENDITURE FOR CLOTHING

	Amount	Families Reporting
Native cloth	$5.99	34
Foreign cloth	1.07	34
Cotton	1.80	34
Shoes	2.54	34
Stockings	1.45	34
Belts	.02	4
Uniforms	.11	2
Hats	.10	10
Fur	.52	2
Net	.15	1
Bedding	1.10	9
	$14.85	

TABLE 43. AVERAGE ANNUAL EXPENDITURE FOR MISCELLANEOUS ITEMS

Income Group	Social	Wine & Tobacco	Amusement	Household Equipment	Medicine & Health	Education
$100–200	$2.71	$0.95	$0.78	$0.57	$0.64	$0.02
200–300	3.15	1.19	1.35	1.03	1.41	0.26
300–400	6.15	3.51	2.56	2.48	2.99	1.03
400–500	5.50	2.88	1.20	2.25	0.80	0.44
Average	4.48	2.24	1.70	1.62	1.83	0.54

Income Group	Religion	Military Assessment	Village Assessment	Misc.	Total
$100–200	$0.37	$1.39	$0.96	$2.96	$11.35
200–300	0.57	2.19	1.70	4.90	17.75
300–400	0.96	3.25	2.72	3.95	29.60
400–500	0.73	3.10	2.65	4.95	24.50
Average	0.70	2.48	2.03	4.08	21.70

PART 2. GOVERNMENT AND EDUCATION

CHAPTER VI

Government

TING HSIEN was widely known as a Model Hsien of Hopei (Chihli) province. The magistrate Sun Fa-hsü,[1] who held office from May 12, 1914, to September 26, 1916, applied to the provincial government for permission to reorganize the area as a model hsien. The permission was granted and offices for Model Plans were opened in each of the six districts in May, 1916. In each office there were four directors who were chosen by the gentry. There were also six assistants and one secretary who took charge of the affairs of the office. The directors were to assist the magistrate in making improvements in the district and were to make suggestions and report to the yamen concerning developments in the program. The assistants, acting under the direction of the magistrate or the district directors, were to promote the public welfare and supervise the work of the village heads and vice-heads.

The plans called for a monthly conference on model hsien affairs. The gentry were invited to attend and give their suggestions. All decisions of the conference were reported to the yamen. If they were approved by the magistrate the district offices were to help enforce them. As part of the model program, schools were established, adult education was promoted, public lectures were presented, the police force was reorganized, industry, commerce, communications, finance, and the administration of justice were improved.

Under the guidance and stimulus of the magistrate Sun Fa-hsü the program evidently was very effective. Our reports show that 9 per cent of the schools in the hsien were established in 1914 and almost 35 per

1. Sun Fa-hsü, whose courtesy name was Sun Shun-chai, was born in 1869 in T'ung-ch'eng Hsien, Anhui. During the revolution of 1911 he served under Li Yuan-hung. After his service in Ting Hsien he was appointed civil governor of Shansi under Yen Hsi-shan. The fact that he came from the same distict as Tuan Ch'i-jui is given as one of the reasons for his rapid political rise.

cent in 1915. In the Experimental District 75 per cent of the 327 temples given up from 1882 to 1928 were discontinued during the three years 1914–16, when Sun was in office. The usually conservative countryside was willing to accept Sun's new proposals and program as they fitted in with the enthusiasm for change that followed the Revolution of 1911.

It is not clear how much influence the model hsien program had after Sun left Ting Hsien, but the organization was continued and provision was made for its support in the hsien expense budget. In 1929 the hsien received $6,000 from the provincial treasury for the model hsien program. This apparently was an annual grant. In 1931 Ting Hsien still had the reputation of being a model hsien.

Before the Revolution of 1911 Ting Hsien was known as Ting Chou, as it was the headquarters of a chou government. Its name was changed to Ting Hsien in 1913, when the provincial government was reorganized and the chou, administrative areas that included several hsien, were discontinued.

Under the empire a hsien magistrate ordinarily had an official staff of assistant magistrate, prison warden, patrol officers, and clerks, besides his personal staff of secretaries and confidential servants. The work of the hsien was carried on through eight executive offices: ceremonies, documents, engineering, judicial, military, personnel, taxation, and treasury.

The reorganization plan promulgated by the National Government in 1913 called for four main sections in the hsien government: home affairs, finance, education, and industry. There also were to be six sub-sections with the necessary secretaries and clerks. The magistrate Sun Chia-yu in 1913 applied for permission to make the required changes but the actual reorganization was not carried out until 1914 when Sun Fa-hsü was the magistrate. He established three instead of four sections, combining education and industry. For the convenience of the people he added an information office. The model hsien program, which gave more emphasis to public welfare work, was introduced in 1916.

In 1920 an executive committee was organized to develop plans for constructive work in the hsien.

The 1913 reorganization called for the separation of the administrative and judicial functions of the magistrate's office and the creation of a separate court of justice with assessors in charge of civil and criminal cases. The magistrate was to retain the right to review the decisions of the court. "Because of the inconvenience to the people" the separate court was abolished in the spring of 1914. Instead of having separate assessors, the judicial cases were handled by officers who were sent by the provincial government at the request of the magistrate. Ting Hsien had two such officers, one for civil and one for criminal cases.

The hsien government was reorganized again in 1928 after the forces of the Nationalist Government had taken Peking and unified the government and "the Republic had been established in the victory of the Revolution". There were then three sections and the four bureaus of public safety, finance, education, and construction. The First Section was in charge of police, fire protection, sanitation, health, relief, forest protection, and census. The Second Section was responsible for lands, agriculture, engineering, roads, bridges, waterways, labor, industry, business, schools, libraries, museums, and parks. The Third Section looked after the fiscal affairs of the hsien, appropriations for the hsien budget, taxes in money and grain, taxation on land, loans, public lands, local finance, audit, and the handling of hsien funds and hsien property. The work of each section was in charge of a section head, an assistant head, and from three to five clerks. The monthly salary of a section head was $60, of his associate from $30 to $40, of a clerk $11. The heads of the three sections and the four bureaus met weekly as the hsien government committee to discuss problems and plan for the improvement of the administrative program.

In 1928 another effort was made to establish a separate court of justice responsible to the high provincial court rather than to the magistrate. The court was organized with a judge, a judicial officer and five clerks, a prison staff of 12, a prison head, one matron, 10 guards, 10 judicial police, and 10 regular police. The budget of the court was $480 a month, or $5,760 per year. This was paid from the provincial treasury rather than from hsien funds.

In spite of the new organization the court was not entirely removed from the control of the magistrate. He generally was able to influence the high court in the appointment of the judge and he had to review and approve all court decisions before they were carried out.

The reorganization of 1928 added the Kuomintang (Nationalist Party) Board and its subsidiary organizations to the hsien political machinery. Members of the Kuomintang had been working secretly in Ting Hsien from 1924, and thus were prepared to develop an organization when the Party came to power, following the success of the Nationalist armies and the capture of Peking. The Party Board was the basic organization. It had 208 members: 82 teachers, 53 students, 20 farmers, 17 officers, 13 merchants, 5 officials, 2 soldiers, 2 policemen, and 14 others. The work of the Board was carried on by an Executive Committee with a secretarial organization, training and propaganda divisions, and an Inspection Committee. In 1929 the activities of the Board were supported by a grant of $16,800 from hsien funds.

The work of the Party Board was discontinued in 1930 because of political changes but it was begun again in 1931, after the military situation had cleared.

After its organization in 1928 the Board promptly set up five subsidiary organizations for farmers, merchants, laborers, students, and women. Each organization was to promote the interests of its special group. Executive and inspection committees usually were organized, but the subsidiary organizations evidently were set up primarily to function at the instigation of the Party Board. They were given no budgets and any incidental expenses of meetings and other activities were met from Party funds. They all sent representatives to conferences and rallies, parades, and committee meetings. Meetings of the anti-opium and the finance committees were specially mentioned.

Before 1928 labor unions were unknown in Ting Hsien. The old gilds had included both the masters and the men. After the establishment of the Party Board, labor unions were promptly organized and the General Labor Union of Ting Hsien was organized by the Tailors' Union, Shoemakers' Union, Silversmiths' Union, Carpenters' Union, and Barbers' Union.

As the Farmers' and Women's Associations covered the entire hsien the farmers had central, district, and village organizations, the women, central, district, branch, and sub-branch organizations.

The National Conference on Home Affairs, held in December, 1932, took hsien government reform as its central theme of discussion. The Conference recommended that an Institute of Political and Social Reconstruction be established in the provinces willing to experiment with the problem of rural reconstruction, that an Experiment Area be set aside as the laboratory of the Institute, and that the Area be under the direct and complete control of the Institute. This recommendation was enacted into law by the sanction of the Central Political Council, and the Hopei Institute of Political and Social Reconstruction was organized in the spring of 1933. Ting Hsien was selected as the location of the Institute and as its experimental district. The General Director of the Mass Education Movement was appointed as president of the Institute and other members of the Movement staff were given responsible positions in the Institute. Franklin Lee, head of the Movement's Social Survey Department, was appointed concurrently as director of the Survey Department of the Institute.

Magistrate

The chief officer of the hsien government was the hsien chang, or magistrate. Ordinarily he was appointed by the Central Government on the recommendation of the Provincial Governor and held office at his pleasure. Under the Manchu government it was the rule that no man could be appointed to office in his native province and that a hsien magistrate's term should not be more than three years. Those rules were also generally followed under the Republic.

While the magistrate was responsible to the provincial government and was required to carry out its orders and instructions, his position and local power as both chief judicial officer and chief administrator made it possible for him to affect greatly the life and development of the hsien. The character and quality of the administration was largely determined by him. Ordinarily the magistrates followed the customary procedures, produced the usual revenue or perhaps a small increase, and made few changes in the established routine. Coming from another province, they had no personal interest in developing the area. Their tenure of office was usually relatively short (from 1901 to 1928 the average was only 13 months) so there was little incentive to initiate a program that would take some time to carry out. The magistracy being the lowest of the appointive offices of the provincial government, the incumbents, hopeful for promotion, would not be apt to initiate any undirected changes. Occasionally a man like Sun Fa-hsü, stimulated and aided by the enthusiasm and idealism of the Revolution, made great changes.

Twenty-four men served 25 terms as magistrate in the 27 years from May 16, 1901 to September 21, 1928. One man was given two short appointments. The shortest term was one month and eight days. Four terms were less than two months, eight were less than six months, and

17 of the 25 appointments were terminated in less than one year. Two terms were more than three years. The longest was just 18 days less than five years. One wonders what personal characteristics or political conditions made it possible for the magistrate Ch'en Yen-chang to hold office from November, 1905, to October, 1910, and Fu En-te from March 5, 1920 to January 23, 1924, especially when the regular rule was that a magistrate's term of office was not more than three years.

The disturbed conditions and the political readjustments after the Boxer disturbances undoubtedly accounted for the six appointments made between May, 1901, and November, 1905. From then until January, 1924, all the magistrates served for more than one year except for two short appointments during the time of the Revolution, November, 1911, to December, 1912. The political changes brought by the revolution were evidently quickly accomplished and rapidly stabilized.

The civil wars that began in 1924, the changes in the government in Peking, the resulting changes in the government of Hopei province, and the coming of the Nationalist forces were undoubtedly reflected in the 10 appointments made between January, 1924, and September, 1928. All were less than one year and five of the 10 were ended in less than six months.

The known age range of the magistrates at the time they held office was from 37 to 54. Most of the group were between 40 and 50. Six of the 14 magistrates whose educational record was available had been trained in the old classical system. Three held the Chü-jen, two the Kung-sheng degree. Others were graduates of law school, higher normal school, or officers' training school. One had been educated in Japan.

In the reorganization of 1913 the Central Government set limits for the administrative expenditures of the hsien governments. The Chihli (Hopei) Provincial Government divided its hsien into six classes, with the amount of the hsien administrative expenditure determined by the class to which it was assigned. The money was to come from the provincial treasury and was not included in the hsien budget.

Ting Hsien at first was rated as a second class hsien and given $1,100 a month for its administrative budget. This amount was found to be insufficient and the hsien was advanced to the first class with an administrative budget of $1,300 a month. A later increase raised the amount to $1,400, but in 1919 the provincial government ordered a cut of $200 per month. At that time the monthly salary scale was magistrate

$300, his assistant $100, two section and bureau heads $40, five section heads $30, 21 clerks an average of $9.50, and 16 other employees an average of $7. Supplies and miscellaneous expenses were budgeted at $258 per month.

We were not able to secure the magistrate's budget for 1929 from the provincial records nor, of course, was there any record of the amount of income the magistrate and his staff received from their "perquisites". It was generally reported, however, that because of the low salary scale, family and political financial demands, and long established custom, the amounts were at least "generous".

With the establishment in 1933 of the Hopei Institute of Political and Social Reconstruction, the president of the Institute was authorized to nominate the Ting Hsien magistrate. This made it possible for one of the Mass Education Movement staff to be appointed magistrate and for him to fix definite salaries for all hsien employees, to abolish "legalized" commissions, to require special training for all hsien employees, and to effect reforms in the prison, the police, and the militia.

Hsien Finance

It was reported that prior to 1916 there was no regulated plan for controlling the hsien finances. Local organizations needing money would collect and use the necessary funds, but under the general centralized control of the hsien government. In 1916 a Civic Council of private citizens was organized to act as a central bureau for all hsien expenditures. The spending organizations were required to present their budgets to the Council and get the needed funds for them. In 1920 the Civic Council was changed to the Finance Board by order of the Provincial Committee. In 1925 the Board was abolished and its place was taken by a Municipal Council, which was replaced in August, 1928, by the Public Fund Bureau, which was replaced in November, 1928, by the Bureau of Finance. The budget for the operation of the bureau was $3,222 in 1929.

In December, 1928, the Ministry of the Interior organized a Government Planning Commission and made one of its responsibilities the improvement of hsien finance. The Commission, together with the Ministry of Finance, adopted the following Hsien Improvement Plan:

1. All receipts and expenditures were to be under centralized control.
2. Incidental taxes, emergency taxes, etc., all those that were not levied

by the National or Provincial Governments, must be approved by the Provincial Finance Bureau.

3. Disbursements must be made according to the budgets and needs of the different departments. If there should be a deficit because of extraordinary conditions the hsien government could ask the provincial government for aid.

4. The finances of the hsien were to be managed by the Hsien Finance Board. It was expected to keep within the adopted budget.

5. No organization except the Finance Board was to be allowed to collect funds.

6. In case of an unexpected decrease of income the Hsien Finance Board was to take action so that the work of the other hsien bureaus would not be interrupted.

7. All authorized established organizations supervising local real property were to be retained.

The following figures give the amounts in the main sections of the hsien budget for the years 1917, 1928, and 1929. These do not cover the entire cost of the hsien government, as the amounts spent for the magistrate's administrative office and for the judicial branch were part of the provincial budget and the money came from the provincial rather than from the hsien treasury.

Hsien Expenditure Budget

	1917	1928	1929
Kuomintang	–	$ 7,100	$ 16,800
Administration	$ 8,812	14,676	16,338
Police and militia	25,237	22,316	27,584
Education	30,080	37,017	39,349
Construction	1,691	1,472	1,472
Special	894	6,343	6,343
	$66,714	$88,924	$107,886

The amounts for education and construction represent the expenditure for the activities and projects of those bureaus. The operating expenses of the bureaus themselves are included in the figure of administration.

The $16,800 for Party expense was a new item in the budget, for which 1929 was the first full year. It represented the largest increase over the 1917 budget. In 12 years the total budget increased 61 per cent, the amount for administration 81 per cent, for education 31 per cent, but for the police and militia only 10 per cent.

Police

The hsien police were reorganized in 1902. At that time the hsien was divided into five districts. In 1912 the name was changed, in line with the new terminology of the Republic, and there was a change in the number and duties of the top police officers. In 1915 there was another reorganization and the hsien was divided into six districts. In each district there was one central police office and from one to four branch offices. The total number of branch offices was 13. There was a police officer and assistant in each district office and an under officer in each branch office. The number of patrolmen was given as 263. Twenty-four of these were mounted police.

The police force was reorganized again in 1928 after the Nationalist forces reached North China. The name was changed to Bureau of Public Safety. The central office force was set up with one chief officer, two section heads and an associate for each, one inspector, a clerk, a treasurer, a porter, two police officers, one for the mounted detachment, an associate for each officer, ten policemen, and ten mounted men. In each of the six district offices there was a headman, a clerk, two police officers, two mounted police, and a varying number of foot police. In the branch offices, there was regularly one police officer and 12 men. The reported expenditure for the police force was $25,237 in 1917, $20,616 in 1928, and $25,884 in 1929.

Militia

The local militia, pao wei t'uan, was put under the Bureau of Public Safety in 1928 and given a headquarters budget of $1,700, but it was organized by the people rather than by the hsien government. The home guard had long been part of the village organization. This new organization apparently was an attempt to put it on a coordinated hsien-wide basis rather than have each village organize independently. The new organization and affairs of the militia were discussed by a meeting of the village heads and their assistants, called together by the magistrate. The six districts for the militia were the same as the six police districts. Each district was divided into five sub-districts. The village elders and their assistants in each sub-district elected a representative to the district committee. These five men coopted two popular farmers and two men from the public organizations in the villages. This committee of nine nominated three men to be the head of the militia in the district. The magistrate appointed one of the three. The committee of nine also was responsible for the local budget of the militia, which it usually approved on a six month basis.

The directors were supposed to number nine in each district, but this was true of only three districts. There were five directors in the 1st District, seven in the 5th, 13 in the east half and three in the west half of the 6th.

The date given for the reorganization of the militia was the spring of 1929, except for the west half of the 6th District. It organized some five months earlier, in the latter part of 1928. When the east half of the 6th District was organized in 1929 two militia groups were kept in the district.

The district organization generally consisted of a headman, a clerk, a soldier, and a guard for each district office, with a sub-head and assistant for each of the sub-districts, a total of 14 men. The 4th District reported a slightly different organization with only three sub-heads and two assistants, an investigator, three cooks, a coolie, and two mounted police.

The number of volunteers serving under the district officers was ordinarily 45 men, but the 4th District reported 54. The total number in the militia was, therefore, some 422 men, 98 in the administration and 324 volunteers. This, of course, was the peacetime basis. Additional men were called out whenever any local crisis arose.

The reported budgets of the districts ranged from $1,000 to $1,240 per year. The total was $8,374.

The district militia committees were also called upon to decide how much each family in their district should pay for the support of the militia and toward the support of the troops stationed in Ting Hsien. This, apparently, was a new type of assessment for other taxes had helped meet the demands of the army in 1927 and 1928. The militia report says that the amount fixed by the district committees was 60 cents per family per half year, except in the 4th District, where the assessment was set at 35 cents. In the tax report the amount of the assessment was given as 35 cents per family per year.

The militia were reported to be more effective than the police of the Bureau of Public Safety in protecting the villages. Being local volunteers, they were closer to the villages. In case of trouble the police would have to be summoned from the nearest branch office. The militia were especially helpful, during the winter period of farm unemployment, in protecting the villages from robbers and other trouble makers.

Bureau of Construction

In 1920 the head of the Bureau for Encouraging the People to Work was appointed by the Provincial Department of Industry from a slate of three nominated by the hsien magistrate. Four associates were also appointed. At that time the administrative expense of the Bureau was $122 per month. This expense was financed from one cash of the 3.5 cash received by the Merchants' Gild Association from the tax on each piece of native cloth sold in Ting Hsien. If this allocation was not sufficient, the difference was to be met from the one per cent of the land tax that was allocated to expenses. In 1922 the salary of the head of the bureau was $22 a month. The associates received $10 a month.

The Bureau for Encouraging the People to Work was changed to the Bureau of Industry in 1925. In the reforms of 1928 the Bureau of Industry became the Bureau of Construction. Its three sections were Agriculture, Construction, and General. In 1929 the administrative budget of the Bureau was $5,160. It was paid from the general hsien income. At that time the salary of the head of the bureau was $40 a month. The four experts were each paid $27 a month, the three section managers $24 a month, and the clerks $18 a month.

Reports on the work of the Bureau for Encouraging the People to Work stated that, from the establishment of the Bureau, a total of 25,802 wells had been dug and 3,311,220 trees of 17 different varieties had been planted. The China International Famine Relief's well survey report gave the number of wells dug from 1916 to 1930 as 26,103.[2]

The Bureau cooperated with the People's Factory by sending teachers to the villages to instruct the people how to make braid for straw hats. The braid was bought by the factory. In 1929 a subsidy of $156 was given to the factory, but in 1930 it had to be closed.

The Bureau of Construction required the people living along the

2. China International Famine Relief Commission, Series B #49, *Well Irrigation in West Hopei*, Preliminary Report, December, 1931.

T'ang river to build extra bridges across the river besides those for
the main roads and required repairs to be made on the roads. The Bureau reported that under its encouragement another 800,000 trees were
planted and 900 additional wells had been dug.

The programs laid out by the Bureau were very extensive. In the
Agricultural Section they included the promotion and development of
silk worm culture, the growing of mulberry trees, increasing the or-
chards and forests, improving the soil and the farming implements. The
Industrial Section planned to show the people how to make oil, soap,
paper, and artificial fertilizer, how to improve the native cloth and other
home industries. They also planned to open a flour mill, organize an
electric company, and establish leather tanning. The general plans included correspondence courses, lecture programs for the farmers, agricultural and industrial exhibits, agricultural experiment stations,
farmers' forest associations and forest protection police, a monthly mag-
azine, and a general market. Lack of funds and disturbed conditions in
North China prevented the implementation of most of these plans.

Agricultural Experiment Station

An Agricultural Experiment Station was established in 1916. Twenty
mu of land were set aside for its use and $1,180 a year of the money re-
ceived from the tooth (sales) tax on cotton was allocated to its budget.
In 1919 the program was extended by opening a cotton experiment station south of the pagoda, but in 1928 the station was closed and the
land used for a public playground.

In 1917 the magistrate instructed the head of the Agricultural Experiment Station to open a tree nursery. Seven hundred mu of land
were borrowed from the girls' school and an appropriation of $166 was
made for the work. In 1918 the trees in two temples were cut down and
sold and the money was used to erect the buildings for the nursery and
additional funds were granted for the program. Considerable progress
must have been made, for in 1920 the provincial inspector approved
the program and sent a certificate of commendation.

In 1921 the girls' school was given 100 mu of land for experiments in
raising mulberry trees for the feeding of silk worms.

In 1928 an inventory of the nursery showed 5,500 Chinese cedars,
5,800 silk trees (Albizzia Julibrissin), 6,000 Chinese ash, 7,000 Lindera,
9,800 white poplar, 12,000 cedars, 75,000 thorn ash, and 250,000 mul-

berry. There were also 31 mu of German ash, 91 mu of willow bushes, and 35 mu of vegetables and other crops.

The 1929 hsien budget included $1,276 for the nursery. Forty dollars was sent to Paoting for the experimental farm there.

Bureau of Education

The Bureau of Education was the successor, after several reorganizations, of the Bureau for Urging the People to Learn which was established in 1904. At that time the magistrate and the supervisor of the middle schools joined to persuade the people to establish elementary schools. This campaign resulted in the establishment of 130 schools. The Bureau for Urging the People to Learn was organized with a director and 16 assistants, all volunteers, whose only remuneration was a small amount to cover the cost of their travel.

By 1910 the large number of assistants and the lack of individual responsibility were found to be inefficient, so the 16 volunteers were replaced by four paid assistants.

In the changes of 1913 the Bureau was abolished and its work was taken over by the educational section of the hsien government. At that time one supervisor was employed to inspect the elementary schools.

Some of the citizens, who had had experience in educational work, felt that the educational section could not adequately supervise the work of the schools. Hence they organized an Educational Committee of three members to cooperate with the village heads and their assistants in promoting the work of the schools. Before the end of 1914 the educational section of the yamen felt that it was "inconvenient" for it to continue the educational work and the Bureau for Encouraging the People to Learn was reestablished with a headman who was paid $30 a month and five assistants who each received $10 a month.

Forty-one schools were established in 1914. These included two schools with both upper and lower primary grades, and two girls' and 37 boys' lower primary schools. In 1915 the name of the lower primary schools was changed to People's Schools. In that year 159 new schools were established. Sixteen of these were for girls. Six of the boys' schools had both the upper and lower primary grades. A traveling teacher was appointed to supervise the schools. During the next four years, 60 girls' and 20 boys' schools were added and it became necessary to add an extra traveling teacher.

In 1915 the administrative budget of the Bureau amounted to $1,100 per year. In 1923 it was increased to $1,700 because of the increase in prices and an increase in the personnel of the Bureau. These funds came from the land taxes. To facilitate the educational program and the supervision of the schools the hsien was divided into 25 school districts. The program called for the establishment of an elementary school in every village with more than 500 families (only seven villages had that many families). Smaller villages were to join with a neighboring village or villages to establish a union school.

In 1923 the Provincial Department of Education ordered that the Bureau for Urging the People to Learn be reorganized as the Hsien Bureau of Education. The personnel of the Bureau consisted of a head, five inspectors, four education committee members, a treasurer, a business manager, and a clerk. The head of the Bureau was put in charge of all the educational work of the hsien, but functioned under the direction of the magistrate. The annual budget of the Bureau amounted to $3,948.

In 1929 the personnel of the Bureau still totaled 13, but there were only three instead of five inspectors. The Educational Committee had been increased to five and a secretary had been added to the list. The hsien was divided into 12 school districts, two in each District. The administrative budget for the Bureau had been increased to $6,096. The hsien budget also included $22,203 for the expenses of the middle, normal, and vocational schools, $5,100 for the city primary schools, and $10,959 subsidy for the village primary schools. Rent from village lands or general village funds provided the main support of the primary schools.

The Office for Social Education was established in 1917 as part of the model hsien program. Its function was to promote social and adult education and through those programs to improve the customs and habits of the community. There were only two on the office staff, a headman and a clerk. They were also in charge of the public library, the newspaper reading room, and the museum, and supervised the work of the Three Principles Lecture Hall. The expenses of the Office, including the library, the reading room, and the museum, totaled $648 in 1929. The budget of the lecture hall was $288. In 1930 the name of the Office was changed to the Peoples' Educational Office.

The Educational Association was established in 1907 by those who were interested in promoting education in Ting Hsien. Later on the head of the Bureau for Encouraging the People to Learn was appointed from the membership of the Association. In 1913, when the work of the Bureau for Encouraging the People to Learn was taken over by the educational section of the hsien government, the Association was abolished. The Bureau was reestablished in 1914, but the Association was not reorganized until 1917. At that time its name was changed to the Educational Weekly Association. Its chief activity was the publication of a weekly paper. A president and vice-president were elected for a term of three years. They were the editors of the paper. In 1929 the budget of the Association was $150 for the expense of publishing the weekly. The money came from general hsien funds.

The total for education in the hsien expenditure budget for 1929 was $45,444. This was 42 per cent of the budgeted items. If the non-budgeted administrative items, magistrate's office, and judiciary were added to the budgeted total the amount for education would probably be between 30 and 35 per cent of the total hsien expenditure.

Farm Association

The Farm Association was established in 1876 to promote reforestation and to protect the grain in the fields, but was discontinued because of political disturbances. It was reorganized in 1914. It was not affected by the 1928 reorganization and continued to receive a grant of $570 from the hsien Bureau of Finance.

In 1918 the hsien government required the people in the villages to organize branches of the Farm Association. Three hundred and twenty-seven were set up in the 453 villages. The branch associations tried to protect the trees and grain in their area and investigated and attempted to solve any thefts of trees or grain. This would seem to be a duplication of the function of the Green Crop Associations and an attempt on the part of the government to take over and control that work.

Merchants' Association

The Merchants' Branch Association, originally organized under the Manchu regime, was reorganized in 1914 by representatives of 95 shops. The next year the Agricultural Section issued orders that the Association should again be reorganized and the name changed. The new name was the Merchants' Association or, it might be translated, Chamber of

Commerce. Orders from the Agricultural Section and the Bureau of Industry required changes in the organization and rules of the Association in 1916 and again in 1918, if it was to register with the Section and be authorized to use a seal.

The Association's annual budget of $2,000 was part of the hsien budget. The necessary funds came from membership fees of $3, $4, and $5 a year, a fee for handling the excise stamps attached to receipts, and part of the tax on cotton cloth.

The organization of the Bureau of Public Judgment on Commercial Matters was one of the duties of the annual conference of the Association. This Bureau was to "harmonize opinions and compromise disagreements by conciliation and arbitration". The salary of the director appointed to handle the affairs of the Bureau was $20 a month. The secretary was paid $8 a month and the clerk $5.

Anti-Litigation Society

The Anti-Litigation Society was organized in 1923 and reorganized in 1925. Its purpose was to prevent litigation and to arbitrate the disputes of the people. The $635 spent for its activities was part of the budget of the Merchants' Association.

When the Anti-Litigation Society was reorganized the magistrate then in office directed that all lawsuits should be heard and, if possible, settled by the Society before they came to the yamen. Only those cases with which the Society was unsuccessful were to come before the hsien court. More than 100 cases were settled in the five years from 1923 to 1928.

Anti-Foot-Binding Society

The Anti-Foot-Binding Society was a semi-official organization founded in 1913 to persuade the women to unbind their feet and parents not to bind their daughters' feet. The magistrate was the president. The head of the Bureau of Education and the head of the Police Court were the vice-presidents. The heads of other community organizations were the members and honorary officers. For a time meetings were held the first of every month in the offices of the Bureau for Encouraging the People to Learn. Six women were appointed as district investigators and given travel fees of $20 each. Branch societies were organized in practically all the villages. Foot-binding had been so generally discontinued by 1928 that the Society was no longer active.

Other items in the Special section of the hsien budget were $600 for the model village program of Chai Ch'eng, $550 for public ceremonies, $380 for food for the poor, $27.15 for winter clothes for the poor, $216 for food for prisoners, and $2,000 for miscellaneous.

Districts

After the political reorganization in 1928 the Provincial Government promulgated rules and regulations for the establishment of from three to eight chü (districts) in each hsien, for the democratic election of the headmen of the villages, and for organizing the families in each village into lin and lü, five families to a lin and 25 families to a lü.

There were six Districts in Ting Hsien in 1928.[3] The district heads at first were appointed by the magistrate, but it was planned that later they would be elected. The appointees were to be examined and trained by the Provincial Department of Civil Affairs. The head of the district, with the help of two or three assistants, was required to carry out the orders of the magistrate, report to him the desires of the people, transmit to the villages all rules and orders affecting them, and, as the chief police officer of the district, to carry out the orders of the Bureau of Public Safety. District conferences were to be held every season to receive reports and discuss district affairs. The expenses of the district government were not to be more than $80 a month for a small district, $100 a month for a medium sized district, and $120 a month for a large district.

The regulations provided for the appointment of a supervising committee of five, three to be named by the Village Supervisory Committee of the District and two by the magistrate. The committee's primary function was to audit the accounts of the district and supervise the activities of the district head. The committee members served without salary. The amount allowed the committee for expenses was determined by

3. A map issued by the Division of Social Survey of the Hopei Provincial Institute of Political and Social Reconstruction in May, 1934, showed only five districts. The new 2nd, 3rd, and 5th Districts were the same as the old 3rd, 4th, and 6th. Nine villages on the west end of the old 2nd District had been added to the old 5th to make the new 4th District. The remainder of the old 2nd District and the old 1st had been combined to make the new 1st District.

the Village Supervisory Committee but was not to exceed $120 per year. Ordinarily the committee held only one meeting per year, on the 1st of March, but special meetings could be called by any two members of the committee.

Villages

Four hundred and fifty-three organized villages and towns carried on the local political administration of Ting Hsien. Each one controlled a village residence area and the surrounding farm land. The size of the villages ranged from six to 1,200 families, the farm areas from 245 mu to 32,500 mu.

The usual village government was a headman and a vice-head selected by and assisted by recognized influential men of the village community or representatives of the influential families. After 1928 the headmen were to be elected by the village. These men regularly served without pay. The detailed work of the village government was done by salaried clerks and secretaries.

Besides carrying on the village administration the village governments were responsible to the hsien magistrate and the district officer to pass on to the people of the village information concerning new laws and rules and regulations. The headmen were also generally responsible to the magistrate for the actions of the villagers. When there was fighting in the area the headmen were required to produce the villages' share of the requisitions and assessments levied on the hsien by the armies.

The changes that came after Boxer year, the Revolution of 1911, and the Nationalist success in 1928 all brought more and more control of the village governments by the hsien and provincial governments until, in 1929, the regulations required that a representative of the hsien government supervise the election of the village head and that the village families be organized into lin and lü groups, the leaders of which were to be responsible for their members. These sub-village organizations apparently made possible a much closer control of the rural population than previously had been the case.

The provincial regulations listed the minimum number of organizations that should be set up in each village. These included the village government, the home guard, the village school, the anti-litigation society, and the farm association.

The cost of the village administration and other activities were met from the rent of any land owned by the village and from funds raised from the land owners of the village. The assessment rate per mu was determined by the amount of money required and the amount of land in the village area. So that shops and stores that owned no land might bear their share of the cost of the village government they were, in some instances at least, rated as "owning" a given number of mu and assessed on that amount at the current rate.

The amounts of the Ting Hsien village budgets and the expenditure for administration, home guard, schools, etc., were not available for our study. Other studies in nearby areas found that in 1929 the assessments for the village services ran about 15 cents per mu.

A study of the occupations and ages of the village officers showed that over 95 per cent of the headmen and vice-heads were farmers. There was a wide range in their ages. The youngest headman was only 20 years old, the youngest vice-head 19. The oldest headman was 82, the oldest vice-head was 84. The average ages were 47 and 46. Some 5 per cent of the headmen were under 30 years of age, while 6.5 per cent were 65 or over. The youth of so many of the village heads and vice-heads would seem to indicate that in many cases they were selected because of the prestige of their families rather than for their own leadership.

There were eight more headmen than there were villages and 28 more vice-headmen. In eight villages there were two separate governments. Local jealousies and friction between different groups in these villages had reached the point where it had become necessary to divide the village geographically, divide the village income, and set up a second government. Twenty of the larger villages and towns evidently needed more than one vice-head to carry on the village program and had taken advantage of the government's regulation that permitted a village with over 200 families to have two and one with over 300 families to have three assistant heads. There were 114 villages with 200 or more families and 43 with 300 or more.

Nineteen villages had two residence areas but only one government. Later on the number of villages might be increased if the satellite areas insisted on being given separate status.

Further details of village organization and activity are given in our more complete study of Chai Ch'eng.

TABLE 44. TERMS OF MAGISTRATES

Date	Yrs.	Mos.	Days	Date	Yrs.	Mos.	Days
1. May 16, 1901		7	15	14. Mar. 3, 1919	1	0	2
2. Feb. 1, 1902	2	4	4	15. Mar. 5, 1920	3	10	18
3. June 8, 1904[1]		1	8	16. Jan. 23, 1924		1	18
4. July 13, 1904		8	23	17. Mar. 11, 1924		10	19
5. Apr. 6, 1905[1]		1	14	18. Jan. 30, 1925		3	10
6. May 20, 1905		7	19	19. May 9, 1925		1	14
7. Nov. 25, 1905	4	11	12	20. June 23, 1925		6	8
8. Oct. 7, 1910	1	1	13	21. Jan. 1, 1926		3	11
9. Nov. 20, 1911		4	5	22. Apr. 12, 1926		6	17
10. Mar. 25, 1912		8	6	23. Oct. 29, 1926		11	12
11. Dec. 1, 1912	1	6	12	24. Oct. 11, 1927		7	4
12. May 12, 1914	2	4	24	25. May 15, 1928		4	6
13. Sept. 26, 1916	2	6	7	Sept. 21, 1928			

[1] Same appointee.

TABLE 45. AGES AND OCCUPATIONS OF VILLAGE HEADS

Ages

Age	Headmen		Vice-Headmen	
	Number	Per Cent	Number	Per Cent
Under 25	7	1.5	14	2.9
25–29	18	3.9	32	6.7
30–34	46	10.0	55	11.4
35–39	51	11.1	59	12.3
40–44	53	11.5	59	12.3
45–49	79	17.1	64	13.3
50–54	81	17.6	69	14.3
55–59	47	10.2	47	9.8
60–64	49	10.6	46	9.5
65–69	16	3.5	21	4.4
70–74	7	1.5	13	2.7
75–79	5	1.1	1	0.2
80–84	2	0.4	1	0.2
	461[1]	100.0	481[1]	100.0
Oldest	82		84	
Youngest	20		19	
Average	47		46	

Occupations

	Headmen			Vice-Headmen	
	Number	Per Cent		Number	Per Cent
Farmer	439	95.2	Farmer	465	96.6
Merchant	11		Merchant	8	
Teacher	7		Teacher	3	
Doctor	2		Shops	4	
Tax collector	1		Bee-keeper	1	
None	1			481	
	461				

[1] Eight villages had two headmen, 28 had two vice-heads.

CHAPTER VII

Chai Ch'eng, A Model Village

C HAI CH'ENG was known as the model village of the model hsien and was very proud of the fact. It was so designated after the magistrate Sun Fa-hsü, appreciating the progress already made by the village, petitioned the Provincial Government in 1914 for permission to develop it as a model village that would be an example to all of Ting Hsien. This designation brought about great activity in community organization. It also meant an annual grant to the village budget of $600 from the hsien government.

According to tradition Chai Ch'eng had been a walled village for some 1,600 years, since about the time of the Eastern Tsin dynasty. It was located 30 li east of the hsien city (see map, page 5) and in 1930 it was the largest village in area in the 3rd District (11,170 mu, 20.7 square li), and the largest in number of families (366). It had more families even than the nearby market town of Tung T'ing. The village area was divided as follows:

Farm land	9,500 mu	Dry and barren	1,100 mu
Fruit trees	20 mu	Roads	50 mu
Other trees	200 mu	Inside village	300 mu

The five streets of the village were named for the five Chinese virtues, Benevolence, Righteousness, Propriety, Wisdom, and Faith. In the political reorganization of 1929 the streets were used as the basis for the political division of the village. The families were divided into five groups: i.e., those living on each of the five streets.

The population was 2,085 persons, 1,110 males and 975 females, an average of 5.7 persons per family. The masculinity rate, 114, was considerably above the 106 rate of the 515 and 5,255 families. For the five streets the size of the average family varied from 4.6 to 7.3, the masculinity rate from 138 to 97. Judging from our studies of other groups

146

of Ting Hsien families,[1] it seems probable that the wealthier families of the village were living on Propriety Street. There the size of the average family was 7.3, the masculinity rate 97. The poorer families apparently lived on Benevolence, Wisdom, and Faith Streets, where the family averages were all less than 5.0 and the masculinity rates from 117 to 138. The average family residence had an area of 0.82 mu, about 60 by 100 feet.

There were 19 different family names in the village. There were 130 Mi, 73 Ch'in, 48 Chang, 33 Han, 27 Li, 12 T'ung, and 10 Hsü families. The other names all had less than 10 families. Three names, Ch'iu, Ch'en, and Chao, had only one family each. The Mi and Ch'in clans together included 57 per cent of the population. The average Mi family had 6.4 members, the Ch'ins 4.9, the Hsüs 7.1, and the Lis 7.2.

The development of Chai Ch'eng was greatly stimulated and assisted by members of the Mi family. Mr. Mi Chien-san worked out plans for the development of a village self-government program as far back as 1902. Soon after the establishment of the Republic he organized, at his own expense, girls' primary schools and higher primary schools for both boys and girls. His son, Mr. Mi Ti-kang, went to Japan for study. He was greatly interested in the program for the development and improvement of Japanese village life and brought back many new ideas. On his return he used his enthusiasm, position, and influence to bring about the giving up of temples, the establishment of schools, and changes in the village organization. He worked especially on the development of village self-government, for it was his opinion that "only by developing self-government in the villages could the families and the nation be united. As the village government stands between the families and the hsien and provincial governments, village improvement is the foundation that will insure the control of the families, the proper government of the state, and the pacification of the country". Later he was greatly concerned to see so many of the young people, who had been educated in the modern schools, leaving the villages and going to the cities.

Because Chai Ch'eng had done so much to improve its community organization and activities under the stimulus of its forward looking leaders, it was possible for them in 1926 successfully to invite the Mass Education Association to make the village the first headquarters of its

1. See Chapters II, III, and V.

North China Experiment Station. Eleven other hsien sent invitations to the Association.

After Chai Ch'eng was made a model village in 1915 many different organizations were started as part of the village development program. Some of these functioned successfully and continuously; some were later reorganized with different names and committees but with similar activities; others continued for a time; some failed to operate after the first meeting. They were all kept, however, as part of the village organization and reported to any visitors interested in the story of Chai Ch'eng's development as a model village.

Village Government

The Self-Government Council was organized in October, 1915. It was made up of the village head, the vice-head, and eight other members representing the eight self-government districts into which the village was then divided. The Council took over the functions that had been exercised by an earlier village government, the Public Service Bureau, which had had similar powers and a fairly similar organization, with a village head and vice-head and a group of influential men as councilors. The members of the Self-Government Council were chosen by the influential men of the village rather than by popular suffrage. It met regularly once a month and at other times at the call of the village head.

The headquarters of the Council was in the village office, located at the main crossroads of the village. In July, 1915, the magistrate Sun Fa-hsü gave the village a subsidy of $300 toward the cost of erecting the village office. It was a three-room building, rebuilt from an old temple. The office hours were from 8 to 10 A.M. and 3 to 6 P.M. daily, except Sundays. The village clerk was on duty from 8 to 12 A.M. and from 1 to 6 P.M.

The work of the Council was divided into two sections, financial and non-financial. There were two officers in the financial section who dealt with taxes, current accounts, and village budgets. The four officers in the general affairs section looked after education, public safety, census, encouraging the people to work, philanthropy, construction, sanitation, conscription, records, and all other non-financial items. The village heads served on a voluntary basis. The clerks were paid regular salaries. It is not clear whether the section officers were paid, but it seems evi-

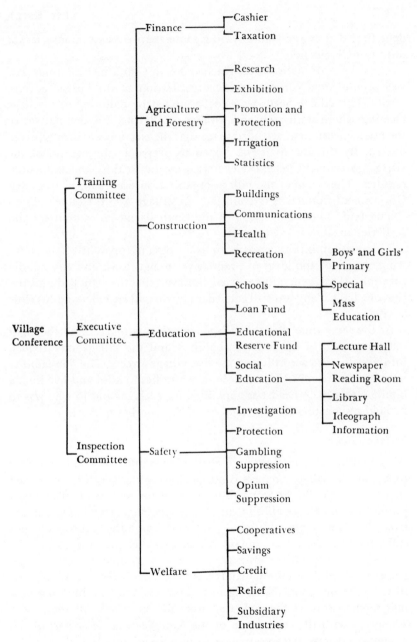

FIGURE 18. CHAI CH'ENG VILLAGE GOVERNMENT ORGANIZATION

dent that if they received anything more than expense money it was only a small stipend.

After the Nationalist forces reached North China in 1928 a new law was promulgated concerning the organization of the village governments. The village heads were to be elected by balloting at a village meeting where both men and women could vote. Representatives of the hsien government attended to see that the election was properly conducted. By this means it was hoped to overcome the control of the village government generally exercised by the wealthy and influential families. The name of the village organization was changed from Self Government Council, Tzu Chih Hui, to Village Affairs Council, Ts'un Cheng Hui. The organization of the Council and its committees and activities are shown in Figure 18.

This very ambitious organizational program apparently was an attempt to adopt the ideas of progressive foreign town and city administrations. It was generally reported, however, that the actual administration of Chai Ch'eng was still carried on by the village elder and his close advisers.

At the same time that the village council was reorganized the eight self-government districts were abolished and the village was divided into five districts according to the five village streets. The 366 families were divided into 74 lin and 15 lü, five families to a lin and five lin, 25 families, to a lü. A head was appointed for each lin and lü who was to be held responsible for the members of the families under him.

Village Finance

The village accounts were not available for our study, so a complete report on the village finances is not possible. However, it was reported that in 1904 the Public Service Bureau used the income of 405.5 mu of public land for the establishment of an elementary school. The income from that land, from additional land, and from other sources was not sufficient to meet the customary village expenses plus the cost of the school plus the other constructive activities desired by the village. Something had to be eliminated. It was the dramatic performances given to welcome the gods, the firing of firecrackers, and the building of a mat shed to protect the gods that were discontinued. All these were connected with the celebration of the New Year. At least part of the money saved was used to purchase more village land. According to the report of the village elders, the village land was increased to 589 mu. This village land was rented to residents of the village for a cash rent that was collected in the early spring. The rent money formerly was held in turn by the men working under the village head, but later was collected and managed by the Finance Committee of the village Self-Government Council. The money could not be used without the signature of the village head.

In 1931 the village income was reported to be $3,100. Of this amount some $1,800 came from land rent, $600 from the Provincial Government for the model village program, $400 from the hsien educational bureau, and $300 from the hsien government for the village schools.

An estimate of the village expenditure gave the approximate total as $3,150, some $3,000 for education and $150 for other expenses. We cannot help wondering how the village met the expenses of the home guard, the night watch, etc. that were reported by other villages, plus the special expenditure for the model village program. The records speak of village funds being used for special items such as road repair and erection of school buildings. Amounts such as the $1,500 and $3,300 used for school buildings must have been financed by special assessments, probably pro rata, on the owners of the land within the village farm area. The crop watching was financed by contributions of grain collected from the farmers.

Land Tax Collection

"In order to stir up the spirit of the village for service to the country and for the convenience of the villagers", it was proposed at a village conference, called by the village head soon after the village government reorganization in October, 1915, that the village authorities should collect and remit to the hsien yamen the land taxes assessed by the hsien on the land in the village area. A set of regulations was adopted by the village meeting and two managers were appointed from each of the eight districts to help the district leader with the collection. The taxes were collected in the third month of 1916. The village head secured from the hsien yamen a list of families and the amount of land they held. A period of ten days was set for the payment of taxes to the district leaders. They turned the money over to the finance division officers, who sent it to the hsien office. The village families found it a very convenient way of paying taxes as it saved them the time and trouble of a trip to the hsien city and dealing with the yamen. One of the village elders estimated that this cooperative system saved at least $170 that would have to be paid for meals and travel under the old individual system. That amount would mean a saving of only 50 cents per family, so the amount might very well have been considerably more.

The cooperative tax collection was one of the model village activities that took root in Chai Ch'eng and was continued year after year.

Village Granary

A village granary was organized in the latter part of 1914 to help provide against famine and other calamities and to make it possible to aid the poor of the village. The farm families were divided into three groups, according to the amount of their land. After the harvest the first-class farmers contributed 0.07 tou per mu of land, second-class farmers 0.05 tou per mu, and third-class farmers 0.03 tou per mu. The amount collected from each family was entered in the village accounts. Special contributions were specially recorded to encourage a philanthropic spirit. A manager and five assistants operated the granary.

The granary regulations provided that the villagers might borrow grain from the granary, but they should give a pledge for their loan and pay interest when they returned the grain, generally after the harvest. If they borrowed 9 tou they should return 10 tou.

When a considerable amount of grain was accumulated, the granary manager could decide, with the village head, when it was a good time to sell the grain. The money secured was to be loaned at one per cent per month.

It was proposed that in times of famine or other calamity the money held by the granary should be used to buy grain, which, together with any in the granary, should be distributed as a loan to the poor families of the village. They were expected to repay the loans, if they could, when they had a good harvest.

The collection of grain by the granary was discontinued in 1927 because of the civil war, extra taxes, and hard times. The granary funds, however, were retained. In 1931 the amount was $1,200.

Cooperative Benefit Society

The Cooperative Benefit Society was started as the result of the suggestion made by Mr. Mi Shu-p'ing that the village should advance money to purchase, from Wu Chi Hsien, cottonseed that would later be sold to the Chai Ch'eng farmers. This would save the time of the individual farmers and secure good seed for the cotton crop.

Later, about 1924, a complete cooperative organization was developed with a credit department, a cooperative store, and both a buyers' and a sellers' cooperative program. The business of the cooperative was directed by a Board of Trustees with a president and 10 members. The work was carried on by a business manager and an accountant. The capital of the cooperative, which amounted to $12,000 in 1931, was secured by the sale of shares at $50 each.

The finance and credit department was by far the most active part of the cooperative. Besides the original capital, it handled the funds of the village government and of other public organizations, the school endowment funds and the student loan fund, and savings of the villagers, and received deposits from the residents of Chai Ch'eng and of other villages. It was authorized to borrow money from banks, other organizations, and individuals. Most of the money handled by the cooperative was deposited in a money shop in the hsien city.

The society cleared its accounts at the end of every year and at the end of every three years it paid a distribution to its shareholders. The profits were divided into 12 parts. Two parts were kept as reserve, three parts were distributed to the employees as a bonus, and seven parts went to the shareholders. Before 1931 two dividends had been paid, the first one $28, the second $32 per share.

Savings Society

The Diligent and Thrifty Savings Society was organized in 1915 with a chairman and a committee of eight. One report said the village head was the chairman and the eight district leaders were the committee. The purpose was to persuade the people to save money, to create good customs, and to cultivate the habits of perseverance and honesty. All the village was invited to attend the meetings of the society and listen to lectures on savings and economy. Every family was asked to save at least 10 cents a month. The money collected was sent to the finance department of the village. The village head and the head of the finance department together determined how the money should be used to earn a profit. Interest was paid on deposits of more than $1.00. The accounts of the society were posted every year so that the villagers could see the progress made. In 1924 the amount held by the society totaled $3,000. The society was still operating in 1931.

Patriotic and Improvement Societies

A Patriotic Society was organized in 1915 to help create patriotic feelings in the village. It had a head, a secretary, and an investigator. Its duties were to persuade the members to buy government bonds, encourage the young men to enlist when the government was recruiting soldiers, and promote the purchase of home-made goods. The magistrate Sun Fa-hsü came to Chai Ch'eng to give lectures on patriotism. After he left Ting Hsien, the patriotic society was discontinued and only its name remained.

The Virtue Put Into Practice Society was organized in 1914 and was especially active in 1915. Its meetings were attended by some 150 men. Women held separate meetings with some 80 attending. After 1917 the society gradually declined and the meetings were discontinued. In 1931 only the name remained.

The Work Together Society was organized in 1915 to develop public spirit. It had a head and a committee of nine. Its purpose was to create mutual friendship, to console those who mourned, to provide mutual help in time of difficulty, and to befriend others with honesty and sincerity. No meetings were held after the first one.

The Customs Improvement Society was organized in 1915 to improve the customs and habits of the village. It was still operating in 1931. The chairman of the society was the village head. Early marriage, expensive funerals, and foot-binding were some of the customs they worked to change. In reporting on the work of the society, the officers stated that some 80 per cent of the men used to marry before they were 20 years old. In 1931 the figure was not over 40 per cent. At least 10 per cent of the girls used to marry before they were 16 years old. In 1931 no girls were marrying before they were 16. The society also reported that no girls under 16 years of age had bound feet.

Funerals used to involve visits to the temples, hiring necromancers, engaging monks, and burning paper money, paper houses, and other paper equipment for the use of the dead. Much of this expense had been given up by 1931. It was reported that none of the Chai Ch'eng families were having monks for funerals. It was also stated that the families were using bows instead of kotows in connection with funerals. The kitchen gods and the gate gods generally had been given up by the Chai Ch'eng families.

The Admire the Sages Society was organized by the school teachers in 1906 to encourage the people to imitate the good people of the past. In 1913 other educated people were included in the society membership. The Mi brothers and other prominent men gave lectures at the one or two meetings that were held every year. After 1921 meetings were held only every three years. The principal of the village school could call a meeting of the society, but it was completely inactive in 1931.

Promotion of Agriculture

From 1904 to 1908 Ting Hsien suffered from drought and the farmers had poor crops. Mr. Mi, the village head, and his assistant, Mr. Hsü, consulted with the other village elders as to how they might encourage the villagers to dig wells to provide water for irrigation. In 1906 eight wells were dug on village land as a demonstration, prizes were offered to encourage the poor farmers to dig wells, and arrangements were made whereby farmers, in need of money to finance the cost of a well, might borrow half the cost of the necessary materials. The loans were to be repaid after the harvest. Over ten years' time more than one hundred wells were dug.

Following the success of this program, the village elders encouraged the owners of small fields to dig cooperative wells where the individual fields were not large enough to warrant the digging of separate wells. There was great need for such cooperation as the study of a group of 3,763 fields belonging to 1,136 families in four other villages showed that only 7.9 per cent of the fields had 10 or more mu, and only 0.7 per cent had 25 or more mu.[2] A good well could irrigate from 25 to 30 mu.

The village elders provided that where land was held by a mortgagee he should pay his share of the cost of digging a cooperative well but he should be repaid by the mortgagor when he redeemed the property. Where land was held under lease the owners should pay the cost of the well, but should be reimbursed by increasing the rent. The village elders set up regulations for settling disagreements between mortgagors and mortgagees and between tenants and landlords over the cost of the wells and the increased rent.

Village regulations provided for the care of the public wells and the

2. See Chapter X.

cooperative wells. The latter were to be looked after in turn by the various owners. Those responsible were required to report to the village office before they covered the wells to protect them from frost. If the well was damaged because of improper coverage the person responsible was required to repair the damage and pay a fine of five dollars. The village office was to keep a record of the owners of the cooperative wells and the time when each was to be responsible for the care of the well. The regulations required that after the wells had been covered for the winter and after they had been opened in the spring the village officers visit the fields and inspect the wells to determine whether they were being kept in proper condition. The well digging program received a further impetus from the drought of 1920–21.

In 1928 Chai Ch'eng had 390 wells, 96 for the domestic use of the 366 families and 294 for irrigation. A large proportion of the crop area of the village must have been irrigated, for the average area per well was 33 mu. Chai Ch'eng had the largest number of wells of any of the 62 villages in the Experimental District, four times the average number.

Watching the ripening crops to prevent theft before harvest time was another agricultural activity of the village. The watchmen were held responsible for any loss there might be through theft. This work had been done previously by the Green Crop Society, but in 1904 the village officers and elders adopted a series of regulations and employed eight men to watch the crops before the autumn harvest. Two men were assigned to each quarter of the compass. By 1913, when the crop watching was made part of the program of the Agriculture and Forestry Society, it was possible to protect the crops with only four watchers.

The wages of the crop watchers, which one report gave as 10 cents a day plus food, were met by contributions from the land owners. These were paid in kind and were graduated according to the amount of land held by each owner. The field report states that those with from 20 to 50 mu were to pay three gills (0.03 of a tou) of grain per mu; those with from 50 to 100 mu paid five gills per mu, while those who had more than 100 mu contributed seven gills per mu. If there was any surplus it apparently was kept as a special earmarked account rather than added to the general funds of the village.

In 1905, the year after the village engaged the crop watchers, regulations were adopted to cover the protection of trees planted in the village area. Two men were engaged to watch the trees and protect them from damage and theft. Our field report said that the protection was effective and encouraged the villagers to plant trees in the village and on some 200 mu of land that were too sandy for farming, but it did not state how the work was financed or how long it was continued.

The village Agriculture and Forestry Society was organized in 1913. Mr. Mi Chu-wu and four assistants were the board. The society included in its program the promotion of well digging, deeper plowing, the use of more fertilizer, the planting of trees, and the planting of more cotton. The society also took over the crop watching program.

In 1908 a pest of worms attacked the fields just before the harvest. The farmers were inclined to do nothing because they believed the gods sent the worms as a punishment, but Mr. Mi Ch'un-ming persuaded the villagers to join together to catch and kill the worms. In 1915, when locusts were found north of the hsien city, the Chai Ch'eng farmers formed the Insect Destroying Society. The first meeting was attended by over one hundred persons. A chairman, four secretaries, and eight temporary officers were elected. An annual meeting was held during the summer to discuss how to get rid of any locusts that might appear. The villagers were advised how to clean and take care of their farms so that the locusts could be kept down.

At the time of our study it was the rule that all the village residents must help destroy pests. The village gong was rung by the managers of the society to call out the village in time of need. The regulations provided that those who were purposely absent from the meetings of the Society or from any campaign against locusts should be fined.

In discussing the efforts made to promote the village agricultural program, one of the men said "Though not much development is made, the spirit is not to be neglected".

Village Market

The village market was held on the 4th, 9th, 14th, 19th, 24th, and 29th of the lunar month. On the 14th of the 8th month, the day before the fall festival, there were 262 sellers in the food section of the market. Prices of food and other details are given in Chapter XIV.

Industrial Organization

In 1913 Mr. Mi encouraged the weavers of the village to buy a new type of iron loom to replace the old style wooden loom they had been

using. The new style machine made it possible to weave some four or
five pieces of cloth per day instead of one or two.

In 1914 the Home Industry Society was organized to continue the
iron loom promotion work and to develop a program for the judging
and encouragement of industrial production. It was reported that the
villagers bought some 60 of the new looms. The people felt the campaign had been so successful that they presented a medal to Mr. Mi for
his work on the program.

After the new looms were well established Mr. Mi encouraged the
village to engage some special weaving teachers who could teach additional people how to weave and also improve the quality of the output.
The necessary funds for the teachers were to be raised by the society.

In 1923 sock knitting machines were introduced in Chai Ch'eng. At
the time of our study five families had them.

Road Repair

In 1914 the village roads were in such poor shape and the drainage to
the east and south was so poor that the roads were apt to be washed
away in the summer rains. At the suggestion of the village heads $200
was taken from the village funds and used for the repair of the roads.
The leaders in the eight districts were directed to inspect the roads and
persuade the residents to repair them. The regulations provided that, if
the roads were in very poor condition, the whole village should plan
to repair them. Regulations were also adopted to prevent the storing
of fertilizer, fuel, and other things in the streets.

Sanitation Office

Sun Fa-hsü, when he came to Chai Ch'eng in 1915, pointed out many
unsanitary conditions in the village, fertilizer piled in the street, bad
drainage, and flooding during the summer rains. The village head and
elders met to discuss the sanitary conditions and decided to appoint two
men for each of the five streets who should compel all the families to
clean their share of the streets and to improve the sanitary conditions in
their houses. Once again the roads were repaired and the planting of
trees along the streets was encouraged.

At the suggestion of the village head a Sanitation Office was organized in October, 1915. A director and five secretaries were appointed and
regulations were adopted. The regulations provided that every day be-

fore sunset every family was to clean the street in front of its house. If fertilizer had to be put in the street it should be removed within three days. Plans were made to vaccinate the children. While the vaccination was to be arranged by the Bureau, the cost of the vaccine was to be met from philanthropic rather than village funds. It could not be determined how successful the vaccination program had been.

The field investigator commented on the fact that the village looked different because of the work of the Bureau, the streets were clean and repaired, and trees were growing along the roads. He stated that in winter the snow was cleaned off the streets in one day.

Mutual Protection

In November, 1915, the mutual protection program was organized. The village was divided into five districts, and a leader was chosen from each district to be responsible for the protection work. Two night watchmen were engaged. In case of theft all the village was summoned by the ringing of the village gong.

If any of the villagers were hurt or killed in attempting to catch a robber it was customary that they should be given a sum for medical expenses or their families be given a funeral present. No indemnity was given to the family that had been robbed. The expenses of the mutual protection program were to be paid by the entire village.

Education

Modern education was started in Chai Ch'eng in 1894 with the establishment, apparently under private auspices, of a Yü Cheng school for boys. The school was taken over by the village in 1905 when $1,500 was secured from the village treasury for the building of a schoolhouse at the east end of the village. This had five classrooms and five teacher's rooms. The new building made it possible to enlarge the school. It was enlarged again in 1913 when another $2,200 was appropriated from the village treasury for the building of three classrooms, 12 chien of rooms for the students, and five chien for the kitchen and dining rooms. This enlargement made it possible for the village to take over the higher primary class that Mr. Mi Chien-san had started at his own expense the previous year. He also was financing higher and lower primary schools for girls. When the magistrate Sun Fa-hsü saw the educational development at Chai Ch'eng he contributed first $600 and later another $350 toward the erection of additional buildings for the higher primary. The Vice-Governor of the province gave $2,000 in 1914 for buildings for both the boys' and the girls' schools.

In 1930 there were over 80 chien in the buildings of the boys' school and over 20 chien in the girls' school. The enrolment was 153 boys and 95 girls. There were four classes in the boys' lower primary and two in the higher primary. The girls had four lower primary classes, but only one in the higher primary.

In 1914 a village Educational Committee was organized to administer the village schools. All those who were higher primary graduates were automatically members of the committee. The committee met twice a year, in the new year and summer vacations, to discuss school problems. The administrative work of the committee was handled by an executive committee of nine members and four secretaries elected for a term of two years. The Educational Committee was given considerable executive power, for it discussed school budgets, school principals, and improvement of the schools.

One of the first acts of the Educational Committee was to make the village education free and universal. A special village meeting was called to discuss the problem. Twelve regulations were adopted and a special committee was appointed. All children from six to 14 years of age were to go to school and their schooling was to be free. A list of all children was to be prepared and sent to the village office one month before the opening of school and a supervisor was to notify all parents to send their children to their respective classes. The supervisor was to call on the parents if their children did not appear during the first week of school. Although there was no tuition charge, the village parents evidently found many reasons why their children should not go to school, for in 1926 the Mass Education Movement found a large amount of illiteracy among the young adults of Chai Ch'eng.

In 1927 the Educational Committee was changed to the School Board of Directors. The membership was set at 22.

In 1908 the village had no higher primary school so was faced with the problem of what it should do for poor children who wanted to continue their education after they had finished the lower primary school. Mr. Mi Feng-chi discussed the problem with the village leaders. It was finally decided to establish a village loan fund and make loans of $18 to each of seven lower primary graduates so that they might attend the higher primary school in another village. The loans were to be repaid when the boys were independent. The addition of the village higher primary classes in 1913, naturally, brought the discontinuance of the village loan plan, but Mr. Mi strongly recommended it as a very advantageous plan for families and clans.

The higher primary classes of Chai Ch'eng attracted students from nearby villages that had only lower primary schools. In some villages higher tuition was charged for children coming from outside villages, but the Chai Ch'eng records did not show any charge made for such children. The opening of higher primary classes by some neighboring villages in the late 1920s reduced somewhat the enrolment in the Chai Ch'eng schools.

The enrolment of the Chai Ch'eng boys' school ranged from 45 to 57 from 1904 to 1912, but during the next four years it increased by some thirty students per year until, in 1916, it was 175. The opening of the higher primary school in 1913 and the general stimulus to education given by the Revolution would account for the increase. In 1917 the enrolment dropped to 136 because of the heavy floods that caused some villages to give up all their school work for a year. Two years later the number was again up to 172. The maximum number was 178 in 1922 and 1923. The enrolment was down to 146 in 1929 and 153 in 1930. We do not have the year by year enrolment of the girls' school, but in 1930 it was 95. That year the total number of students, boys and girls, was 248.

The number of students graduating from the boys' higher primary school in 1931 was 17. This was considerably below the 27 graduates in 1923 and the 24 in 1927. The drop evidently was due to the opening of a higher primary school in a neighboring village and the withdrawing of its pupils from the Chai Ch'eng school. The total number of graduates in the 16 years from 1916 through 1931 was 350, an average of 23 per year.

The cost of operating the village higher and lower primary schools was given as approximately $3,000 per year. This was an average of $12.10 per student, nearly twice the hsien average of $6.40 for both higher and lower primary students.

Chai Ch'eng's school calendar was different from that of the neighboring villages. While the schools were closed for the usual New Year's vacation, they did not conform to the agricultural calendar and close for the spring and autumn harvests. They had instead a summer vacation, the only one of the 62 villages in the Experimental District to close its schools at that time.

Judging from our population studies[3] Chai Ch'eng's children of primary school age, from six to 14, numbered approximately 400. However, it is not possible to say that 62 per cent of the school age children, 73 per cent of the boys and 51 per cent of the girls, were in school, as some 10 per cent of the lower and higher primary students were over 14 years of age, and there were some higher primary students from neighboring villages. Even so, it was evident that Chai Ch'eng had a very good school record, with approximately two-thirds of the boys and nearly one-half of the girls from six to 14 years of age in school.

An educational survey of the 62 villages in the Experimental District found 276 men and 32 women who were graduates of at least junior middle school, or approximately the ninth grade in American schools. Of these, 33 men and 11 women lived in Chai Ch'eng, one-eighth of the men and one-third of the women. These proportions show very clearly Chai Ch'eng's educational progress.

After the Mass Education Movement made Chai Ch'eng its rural headquarters in 1926 it established several schools there, both to improve the educational situation in the village and to experiment with the rural education program. There were Yü Ts'ai personal training schools for the higher primary graduates and others who were capable of carrying the work, separate schools for men and women. The men's school met from 7 to 9 in the evening, the women's classes from 9 to 12 and 2 to 4. The men's subjects included literature, civics, letter writing, geography, history, village self-government, and "common sense". The women's studies were these plus home economics, home industry, Sun Yat-sen's Three Principles, abacus, penmanship, and games. There were 45 students in the men's school and 37 in the women's.

In the fall of 1927 the Movement also organized four experimental schools, two for boys and two for girls. Two were of higher primary and two of lower primary level. The boys' schools met from 7 to 9 in the evening, the girls' higher school from 10 to 12 in the morning, and the lower school from 2 to 4 in the afternoon, six days a week. The enrolment of the experimental school was 107—55 boys and 52 girls.

3. See Chapter II.

The curriculum of the lower primary classes included the Thousand Characters, penmanship, the abacus, and phonetics. The boys' higher primary courses were higher Chinese readers, letter writing, civics, history, the abacus, and agriculture. The girls' school substituted home economics for agriculture.

The Movement also established two of the Thousand Character schools in Chai Ch'eng, one for boys and one for girls. These met two hours a day, the boys in the evening, the girls in the afternoon. The eight weeks' course was designed to teach the pupils to read and write the Thousand Characters. Later it was found possible to reduce the time to six weeks.

In 1928 53 per cent of the 11–24 year age group in Chai Ch'eng were literate, 65 per cent of the males and 36 per cent of the females.

A Parent Teachers' Association was established in 1906 to bring the school and the families together. There were two meetings a year, with discussions, exhibitions, and consultations on student characteristics and problems.

Adult Education

In the field of adult education there was a Patriotic Lecture Hall and a library and newspaper reading room. The lecture hall was organized by the village head in 1914 with one director, one manager, and one investigator. It was housed in a borrowed building formerly used by a girls' school. One of the first tasks undertaken by the lecture hall was the training of the village officers in self-government, citizenship, hsien and village development programs, and model village affairs. Later a similar course was given to a group of educated villagers who might serve as village officers. These courses were given prior to the organization, in 1915, of the Village Self-Government Council.

Anyone who was intelligent, of good character and who knew the purposes of the Hall could become a lecturer if he was introduced by two members. The lectures given had to have the approval of the magistrate. The lectures were largely based on the hsien government lecture notes but also included considerable material on the Japanese village organization. The chief lecturers were the village head, the head of the higher primary school, and the school teachers.

Lectures ordinarily were given on market days. For lectures of special interest, that would attract too many listeners for the lecture hall, a stage was set up in the school grounds or other public place. Benches were provided for the audience. Records were kept of the lectures given. Necessary expenses were paid by the Lecture Hall but it did not provide food for the lecturers.

The Library and Newspaper Reading Room was established in September, 1915, as part of the Model Village program. It was located in the buildings of the higher primary school and the head of the school was put in charge of the reading room. Later the reading room was moved to the village office. The reading room was open two hours per day. The library had some 1,100 books and magazines on its shelves.

Mr. Mi Ch'un-ming and Mr. Hsü Chin contributed many of the first collection of books. Such good progress was made with the library that at the end of the year the head of the Provincial Bureau of Education contributed $100 and the magistrate Sun Fa-hsü gave a large number of books. The reading room had three daily newspapers and two monthly periodicals.

Chai Ch'eng showed a long list of organizations with many officers and committees. Some of the offices were held concurrently by the village head or the district heads and the activity was that of a sub-committee of the village government. Others were entirely divorced from the village government and were separate community organizations. Whatever the list of officers in the village organizations, it was clear to our investigators that about 20 men were responsible for the community activities of Chai Ch'eng. The quality of leadership is indicated by the fact that in 1916 Mr. Mi Ti-kang was appointed vice-chairman of the Hopei provincial government.

This story of the organization of the model village of Chai Ch'eng pictures a community that was fortunate in having more than an average number of capable leaders, that had had, through its leaders, early contact with outside ideas, and had adopted some of them in its community life. When stimulated by the energetic, active, and progressive magistrate Sun Fa-hsü, the village, in a few months, organized or reorganized many different types of community activity. When his stimulus was removed the community program lost much of its momentum, but was continued in good measure. New and progressive ideas, brought by the Mass Education Movement, gave new stimulus to village activities and development, but our survey did not attempt any study of that change.

Community Organization in Other Villages

Other villages had much less community organization than was set up under Chai Ch'eng's model village program, but at least three organizations were found in every village. They were the Village Government, the Home Guard, and an organization to protect the crops, either a Farm Association or an independent Green Crop Association. One report said that there was an Anti-Foot-binding Association in every village, but they were not active as foot-binding had been generally discontinued.

In the 62 villages of the Experimental District, only nine villages had more than the three or four general organizations. Besides those in Chai Ch'eng, the total number was only 14. About half of these were inactive because of the lack of funds for expenses. There were six different kinds: school board (3), sanitary club (2), granary (2), wartime provisions (2), anti-litigation (3), anti-opium (2).

Two villages had had granaries that collected grain during good years for use during bad times. The amount was one-half sheng or one sheng of grain per mu, but only the families with more than 20 mu of land were asked to contribute. The grain was all taken by the troops in 1927 and 1928.

The organizations to collect food for the soldiers functioned only during war times. By assessing all the families according to the amount of their land, the village head, or his deputy, and a representative group of villagers attempted to provide the rations demanded of them by the army.

The Anti-Litigation Societies were organized to provide an arbitration group to hear and attempt to settle all village disagreements before they were taken to the hsien courts. The 1929 village regulations of the Provincial Government called for the organization of an Anti-Litigation Society in every village.

Opium and opium derivatives had been enough of a problem to warrant anti-narcotic organizations in two villages, but they had both been discontinued for lack of support.

CHAPTER VIII

Taxes

TAXES in Ting Hsien were of many kinds and varieties: national, provincial, hsien, and village; direct, indirect, and transfer; permanent and temporary; regular, special, and surtaxes on regular; land, sales, manufacturing, business licenses, registration, and stamp. Some were used for general governmental purposes, some were allocated to specific accounts such as education, police protection, support of a library, poor relief, and anti-Red campaign. Some were collected by governmental agencies, others were farmed to and collected by semi-private organizations such as the business gilds or by private agencies. In some cases the records showed how much the governmental agencies received from the Ting Hsien area. In others the amount could only be estimated, as Ting Hsien was part of a larger tax district.

Our figures show approximately the amounts the government agencies received from the hsien, but how much the people actually paid can only be guessed. There were no figures available to show how much the tax collectors received from the taxes farmed to them. Nor could we discover how many people earned their livelihood collecting taxes. It must have been a large number, for there were 64 collection organizations operating from 22 centers and they had to cover the different sections of the 83 periodic markets.

Most of the taxes farmed to the highest bidder were those levied on the sale of animals and local produce, although in some instances license taxes were farmed to non-governmental collectors because of the difficulty of collection. The tax rates were nominally fixed, but even if the total amount of sales were known the amount paid to the tax collectors could only be approximated. Some sales were missed entirely by the tax agents. At festival time they were so busy with the larger sales that they made no effort to collect on the smaller ones. Sales of fruit and vegetables under 50 catties were exempt, as were sales to peddlers. Sometimes the amount of the tax was set by bargaining with the collector. Any discount would be influenced by how prosperous a year he had had and by his friendship for the buyer or seller. In some cases where the charge was to be divided between buyer and seller only one of them paid. Some of the taxes collected on Ting Hsien land were remitted to other hsien and did not appear in the Ting Hsien records.

The recorded and estimated amounts received from Ting Hsien in 1929 by national, provincial, and hsien governmental agencies totaled almost $500,000. This was divided national government 29 per cent, provincial 47 per cent, and hsien 24 per cent. The total amounted to approximately $1.25 per capita, or $7.25 per family. A rough estimate of the unreported village assessments and a guess as to the profit of the non-governmental tax collectors would make the total probably 75 per cent higher and possibly even more, perhaps $2.25 per capita, $13.00 per family per year. In 1927 the land owners were assessed the equivalent of three years' taxes. The extra, which was called an emergency tax for the anti-Red campaign and for rehabilitation, was collected for the army.

The principal national taxes were those on salt, a government monopoly; on wine, tobacco, and cigarettes; likin or transit duties; and stamp taxes. In 1927 the Peking government and in 1929 the new Nationalist government levied a special registration and inspection tax on old land deeds.

The income from the annual land taxes, transfer taxes on land, taxes on mortgages, and commodity sales taxes, was divided by the provincial and hsien governments. The proportion going to the provincial government varied from 100 per cent of the regular land tax to 34 per cent of the general sales taxes. The annual animal and cotton sales tax and the slaughter house tax were divided almost evenly. The salt gabelle paid to the province all of the "user's contribution", a surtax of $1.70 per 100 catties.

A special assessment of 35 cents per family was collected by the hsien in 1929. That was the only year this tax appeared in the records during our tax study. The amount received indicated payment by 61,237 families, some 8,800 less than the total of our family census.

Transportation taxes were levied on carts and rickshas, but no report of the amount collected was available.

The unsettled political conditions in North China during the time of our study, with troop movements in the area, brought special tax levies. The arrival of the Nationalist government in 1928 brought considerable readjustment and rearrangement in the tax program. The efforts of the various departments of the government to expand their services and take on new activities tended to increase the amount of the regular taxes and to add some new assessments.

Salt was a monopoly of the national government and the salt tax had long been one of its chief sources of income. The amount collected from Ting Hsien could be accurately estimated as the local distribution was in the hands of a single dealer. He reported the annual consumption to be some 5,500 bags of 471 catties each, a total of almost 2,600,000 catties, or some 6.4 catties (8.5 pounds) per person per year.

The basic salt tax was $2.75 per picul (100 catties), and was collected for the national government. Numerous surtaxes that had gradually been added for various purposes had been combined into one "consumer's contribution" of $1.70 per picul. This was allocated to the provincial government. The total tax, $4.45 per 100 catties, was 51 per cent of the market price of $8.70 per picul. The total Ting Hsien tax, some $115,000, was divided $71,000 to the national government and $44,000 to the provincial government.

On cigarettes the basic tax was 32.5 per cent of the wholesale price. On the Little Child brand it was $29.25 per case of 50,000 cigarettes. For 1929 the estimated consumption of all brands was 100 cases per month and the estimated annual tax $35,100.

The locally grown tobacco leaf was taxed $2.00 per 100 catties. A license fee was levied on all local tobacco dealers, varying from $2.00 a year for the peddler who carried cigarettes in his load to $48 for a store that handled only tobacco, $80 for a tobacco agent, and $400 a year for a factory branch or agent. In 1928 and 1929 the hsien tax office collected the license taxes, but it had so much difficulty in checking on all the dealers that in 1930 the larger tobacco dealers were made responsible for the collection of the license fees.

Wines and wine dealers were similarly taxed. The production tax was $1.25 per 100 catties of rice and date wine, $2.50 per 100 catties of kaoliang wine. Dealers' licenses ranged from $2.00 to $32.00 per year, manufacturers' from $64 to $128 plus a fee of from 20 cents to $4.00 for the issuing of the license. The 1929 wine and tobacco production tax collections totaled $2,450, the dealers' licenses $8,016.

Surtaxes were levied on both tobacco and wine in 1927. The tobacco surtax was 40 per cent of the basic tax and was designated for education. The wine surtax was 60 per cent of the regular tax and was collected for the army. In 1928 the wine surtax was reduced to 30 per cent and was designated for relief. Both surtaxes were discontinued in 1929 by the new Nationalist government but the loss was more than made up by a large increase in the dealers' rates. The 1929 income from that source, $8,016, was more than 3.5 times the $2,300 received in 1928. Other wine and tobacco receipts increased only $416, from $2,034 to $2,450.

Likin (transit taxes) was collected in Paoting and Shih Chia Chuang. No records were kept of the shipments addressed to Ting Hsien, but the heads of the two collection offices estimated that the taxes on the goods destined for that area amounted to some $12,500. For most items the likin was an ad valorem charge of one per cent; for some it was 5 per cent; for some it was based on weight or number, e.g., 10 cents per 100 catties of flint and bamboo, 50 cents per 100 catties of bristles, 30 cents per ton of coal, $1.50 on a noodle machine, $6.00 on a cart.

Stamps were required on practically all documents, from one cent on receipts for less than $10.00 to 10 cents on a store account book, 40 cents on a marriage license, $1.00 on a college diploma, and $2.00 on the papers for an automobile worth more than $1,000. The government apparently attempted to set stamp quotas for the hsien, but the quota figures usually were far above the actual receipts. In 1919 Ting Hsien's quota was $6,000 but the amount actually received was reported as less than $500. In 1929 the quota was $8,800, the receipts $6,340.

Ting Hsien was the head stamp office for 13 hsien. The receipts from that area were reported as just over $50,000. Twenty per cent of the total was kept by the district office for expenses. Stamp agents, of whom there were four in Ting Hsien, were paid 5 per cent on their sales. During 1926–28 almost none of the proceeds of the stamp taxes went to the national government. They were kept by either the province or the armies.

In 1913 the new Republican government decreed that all land owners must present their deeds for inspection and registration. A registration fee of 10 cents was charged on all deeds and an inspection fee of $1.00 on deeds for property worth more than $30. The next year the deeds for land worth less than $30 were taxed 50 cents each. The hsien kept 10 per cent and sent the rest to the provincial capital. The amount paid from May to December, 1914, was $52,000.

In 1927 the Peking government again issued regulations requiring that all deeds be presented for inspection and that old and new deeds be stamped according to the value of the land. The graduated fee was 10 cents for values under $50, 20 cents under $100, 50 cents under $300, $1.00 under $500, and $2.00 for all values of $500 or more. Not much was done in the matter until February, 1928. Then each village was required to register a minimum number of deeds depending on its size; at least 500 deeds by villages with from 50 to 200 families, at least 1,500 deeds by those with from 200 to 500 families, and at least 3,000 deeds by those with from 500 to 1,000 families. The collection of the inspection fee was finally passed on to the village heads and they were required to finish the work in half a month. The government was anxious to complete the program before the arrival of the Nationalist forces.

The Nationalist government also instituted a deed registration program in 1927, in order to get money for the provincial governments, but Ting Hsien was not affected until 1929, when the program was applied to Hopei province. Then the representatives of 96 hsien went to Peking to protest against a second registration program in two years, but the best they could do was to get the time of collection extended.

The regular annual land tax, which produced some 22 per cent of the tax income from the hsien, was based, according to the hsien history, on a classification of the privately owned land set up by the Emperor Wan Li (1572–1619). In order to have a uniform tax rate, but still relate the amount of the tax to the value of the land, the size of each plot of land was fixed in terms of an elastic size tax mu, larger than the standard mu. The number of standard mu in a tax mu was determined by the quality of the land. Three and one-half mu of good land, five mu of medium grade land, seven mu of poor land, and 14 mu of very poor land were equivalent to one tax mu. The land so rated was known as the o nei land (fixed number of mu). The number of large mu on the 1929 tax roll was 224,223.4. This was the same as the figure given for 1657 except for 21,361.1 mu that had been destroyed by four floods in the 19th century and therefore removed from the tax rolls.

The records show that early in the Ch'ing dynasty the taxed land was divided into three classes: (1) land owned by gentry who were exempt from the surtax imposed to replace a head tax and a national labor corvée (later this land lost its exemption and was added to class 2); (2) land of other resident owners; (3) land of absentee owners. At that time 11 per cent of the tax mu were in class 3. The first and second classes paid the same basic tax rate, 13.195 tael cents per tax mu, but for the third class the rate was 14.159 cents, 8.51 per cent higher, because of the owners' inability to perform any local labor service.

During the first part of the Sung dynasty a large military force was maintained in Ting Hsien and a considerable portion of the hsien, possibly as much as one-quarter of the arable land, was held as government land to be cultivated by the troops. The crops provided the food needed by the army. In 1659, farmers in Fang Shan Hsien and Liang Hsiang Hsien were given most of the cultivated military land in Ting Hsien to compensate them for their lands that had been taken and given to Manchu princes and officers as a reward for their services in the establishment of the new Manchu dynasty. Land used for drill grounds and barracks, or to provide food for disaster relief or income for soldiers' salaries and schools, and all uncultivated land apparently was kept by Ting Hsien.

The Ting Hsien land distributed to the Fang Shan and Liang Hsiang farmers became a tax enclave in Ting Hsien with the tax income belonging to those hsien rather than to Ting Hsien. The land had not been taxed when it was held as government property; hence it had made no contribution to the Ting Hsien budget. It was assessed when distributed to private owners, but, as it replaced land formerly assessed by Fang Shan and Liang Hsiang, but tax free in the hands of the new Manchu owners, the Ting Hsien authorities were required to collect the taxes and remit them to Fang Shan and Liang Hsiang hsien. Although all the regular land taxes belonged to the provincial government, the advantage that accrued to the remitting hsien was preserved, at least in part, for Fang Shan and Liang Hsiang hsien by transmitting the new Ting Hsien taxes through them.

A large part of the land allocated to the Fang Shan and Liang Hsiang farmers was gradually reclaimed by Ting Hsien when (1) the land was sold to Ting Hsien residents; (2) there were no heirs in a family that had been given land; (3) any of the land was confiscated; (4) land that was barren when distributed later became fertile; (5) any of the confiscated land in Fang Shan and Liang Hsiang hsien was returned to the original owner. The recovery was not complete, for the 1929 tax records indicated that Ting Hsien was still collecting taxes for Fang Shan and Liang Hsiang hsien. The amount of the enclaved land was not given.

The recovered land in groups 2 to 5 was sold to private owners and the land in all five classes was added to the Ting Hsien tax rolls. The recovered area, together with the government land, drill grounds, uncultivated land, etc., that had been kept by Ting Hsien in 1659 but later sold for private use, was known as the o wei land. It was outside the tax area as fixed by Wan Li.

The recovery of land from Fang Shan and Liang Hsiang and the sale of the government land evidently took place before 1753, for the tax records of that year and those for 1929 show the same number of o wei mu, except for 11,304 mu destroyed by floods in the 19th century and 2,680 mu transferred to Hsin Le Hsien soon after the establishment of the Republic. The 1929 total was 341,636.3 mu. The land recovered from Fang Shan and Liang Hsiang hsien was 257,546.3 mu, 72 per cent of the o wei total.

Because of the different kinds and sources of the o wei land it was assessed in eight different categories, with six different tax rates. The records do not indicate that any attempt was made to adjust the tax rates to the different values of the land within the different categories. The basic o wei rate varied from 1.0 tael cents per mu for the barracks land, the drill grounds, and the land that had been used to grow food for disaster relief, to 2.229 cents per mu for the land recovered from Fang Shan and Liang Hsiang, 3.0 cents per mu for the land for soldiers' salaries, and 13.2 cents per mu for school land. The average rate was 1.9518 cents per mu. Both the land area and the amount of tax were figured to three decimal places.

A third classification was added to the land list in 1914, when the hsien officials were asked to collect the rent on land that had been owned, tax free, by Manchu families and where (1) the family had died out; (2) Manchu landlords had paid their agents for their services by giving them land subject to a small rent charge and the agents were trying to avoid paying the rent; (3) land had been confiscated because of crime. The average rent charge was 10.43 tael cents per mu on (1), 4.45 cents per mu on (2), and 14.6 cents per mu on (3). The rent collected on (1) was paid to individuals as directed by the provincial government, on (2) to the landlords, and on (3) was apparently kept by the hsien. For its services in connection with the first two groups the hsien was paid a commission of 13 cents per tael, the equivalent of the maximum charge sometimes levied on tax payments to compensate for the taxpayer using poor quality silver when paying his tax bill. The area of the Manchu land involved was 5,584 mu.

In 1927 this Manchu land was classified and offered for sale to private owners. It was entered on the tax roll with an average tax rate of 2.937 tael cents per mu.

A head tax was part of the Ming tax program. The families were divided into three different categories and there were three classes in each category. The lowest rate was 10 tael cents per head. The classification of the family and the size of the family were reviewed and adjusted every five years. In 1713 K'ang Hsi decreed that there should be no further revision of the size of the family and that all families should pay 10 cents per head. At that time the population of Ting Hsien was given as 88,111. This was a little more than one-fifth of the 1929 population figure, but if allowance is made for some under-reporting the total was probably about one quarter of the 1929 figure. The population apparently was doubling about once per century. At that rate the average population increase was 0.75 per cent per year.

Since revision of the number of persons in the family was prohibited by Imperial decree, it was not long before the tax base had but little relation to the actual number of persons in the family. There must have been many complaints over the inequity, for only 11 years later, in the second year of Yung Cheng, the head tax was discontinued and a compensating amount was added to the land tax.

A national labor draft was instituted by the Ming emperors to provide the workers needed to build their new palaces, first in Nanking and later in Peking. Quotas were set for the provinces and passed on to the hsien. Later the labor assessment was converted into a money payment. In 1724 the amount for Ting Hsien was only 33.75 taels. This too was added to the land tax.

The head tax and the labor assessment together totaled 8,097.507 taels, 20.7 per cent of the total basic land tax. The different land tax rates were all increased by that per cent. The resident o nei owners' rate became 15.927 tael cents per tax mu, equivalent to 4.55 tael cents per standard mu of good land, 2.28 cents for the poor land, and 1.14 for the very poor land. The o wei rates varied from 1.207 to 15.932 tael cents per mu with the average 2.282 cents per mu.

In 1927 the total tax on the o nei, o wei, and Manchu land (basic rate plus the 20.7 per cent surcharge) was 47,215.02 taels.

Under the Empire there were two additional surcharges, one of 11.7 per cent to compensate for the leap months of the lunar calendar and one that averaged 3.0 per cent to compensate for the impurities in the silver bullion used in paying taxes. Together these charges amounted to 6,925.14 taels. Both were discontinued in 1914, when the solar calendar was adopted and the dollar became the silver monetary unit.

When the shift was made from taels to dollars the original tael tax rates were still retained but the exchange was figured at $2.30 per tael rather than $1.39, the par of exchange. The adjustment evidently was made partly to compensate for the revenue lost by the discontinuance of the leap month and silver quality assessments and partly to cover the increase in the general price level. The dollar rates set in 1914 were used through 1929 and presumably at least until the Japanese invasion in 1937.

At $2.30 per tael the average provincial tax rates became 36.917 cents per tax mu of o nei land (from 10.5 to 2.6 cents per standard mu), 5.249 cents per mu of o wei land, and 6.755 cents per mu of Manchu land. The total to be collected was $108,434.99. The reported delinquency for 1928 was only $244.35, an amount so small that it was easy to see why there was no ready answer to the question "What happens if the land tax is not paid?" (A delinquent owner could be jailed for the non-payment of his taxes.) The 1929 delinquency was $1,679.64.

Two other small amounts, totaling $4,572.35 in 1927 and $2,923 in 1929, were collected for the province. They were based on the number of tax receipts issued rather than on the number of mu involved. To cover the cost of the paper on which the tax receipt was written there was a charge of 40 cash per receipt in 1927 and 1928 and 20 cash in 1929. For recording a receipt the charge was 26.5 cash. The total number of receipts issued was apparently 257,860. On this basis the 64,550 land owning families had an average of four deeds per family and the area covered by the average deed was 5.5 standard mu.

Besides the basic tax collected for the province the farm land was assessed for local governmental activity, regularly by the hsien, generally by the village governments. The hsien charge originally included a regular tax, a 2 per cent surcharge of 20 cash per thousand to make up for the 20 cash regularly deducted by the money shops when they strung the cash, and an additional surcharge of 49.2 per cent designated for the police and for education. After 1914 these items were combined into a single levy. In 1927 the total was 60,206,017 cash or $16,051.91. In 1929 the rate was more than doubled. The total was $33,578.04. This was 30 per cent of the provincial levy.

Together the provincial and hsien levies for 1929 totaled $144,938. The combined rate was 48.52 cents per o nei mu (from 13.9 to 3.47 cents per standard mu) and 6.89 cents per o wei mu. The overall average was just under 10 cents per standard mu.

Most of the villages collected "crop money" from the owners and operators of the surrounding farm land, in order to pay the village expenses for crop watching, night watchmen, local police, home guard, schools, and the demands of the military forces. The rates for the Ting Hsien villages were not available but in a village about 25 miles south the charge varied from 12 to 23 cents per mu during the five year period, 1927–31. The highest rate was in 1928 when the military demands were especially heavy.[1] In 21 multi-village areas near Peking the fall "crop money" ranged from 15 to 70 cents per mu in 1929 and from 18 to 45 cents in 1930. For the individual areas the averages for the five years, 1929 to 1933 inclusive, ranged from 19.5 to 54 cents per mu. For 13 of the 21 areas the five year average was between 30 and 45 cents per mu. The average annual assessment of the 21 areas ranged from 30.6 to 36.4 cents per mu.

Transfer taxes were levied on all land sales and on mortgages. The latter were taxed as they involved a definite land transfer. The mortgagee regularly took possession of the mortgaged land and held and used it until the mortgage was repaid. The income from the land went to the mortgagee in lieu of interest on the loan.

The tax regulations required the village land supervisors, village gentry, to witness the signatures on land deeds and to see that the transfer taxes were paid within six months. Delay beyond six months brought a 100 per cent penalty. If delayed beyond one year the penalty was 200 per cent and beyond two years 300 per cent. Concealing the value of the land transferred, or the amount of the mortgage, incurred penalties of from 100 to 500 per cent depending on the amount of the discount, 100 per cent for undervaluations up to 20 per cent and 500 per cent if over

---

1. Sidney D. Gamble, "Hsin Chuang", *Harvard Journal of Asiatic Studies*, vol. 8, no. 1 (1944).

50 per cent. If there was collusion that involved the land supervisor of the village he was to be assessed twice the amount of the tax due.

The tax rates were 12.6 per cent on deeds and 5.3 per cent on mortgages. The basic rates were 6 per cent and 3 per cent and were collected for the province by the hsien. It kept 2 per cent of the total for its collection service. A surtax of 10 per cent of the basic tax was designated for education. The remaining 6 and 2 per cent represented the commission, ya yung, formerly collected by the middlemen who arranged the deals, but later taken over by the government agencies.

The basic rate and the 10 per cent surtax were paid by the seller or mortgagor. The ya yung charges were paid 60 per cent by the purchaser or mortgagee, 40 per cent by the seller or mortgagor.

The proceeds of the extra 6 per cent, ya yung, on deeds was divided 1.5 per cent for the province, 2.0 per cent for the hsien, and 2.5 per cent for the village where the land was located. The extra 2 per cent on mortgages was divided 0.5 per cent to the province, 0.8 per cent to the hsien, and 0.7 per cent to the village. The hsien and village shares were earmarked for education. The village share was reported as one of the sources of income for the village school. (See Chapter IX.)

In addition to the taxes there was a charge of 50 cents a sheet for the official deed and mortgage forms and 10 cents each for recording.

The number of deeds recorded was 4,826 in 1927, 5,660 in 1929. The three year average was 5,550. The number of mortgages was 903 in 1927, 1,110 in 1929, the three year average 1,049. The total reported value of the deeded land was $100,000 in 1927, $208,000 in 1929, the three year average $150,000. The total amount of the recorded mortgages was $24,600 in 1927, $54,500 in 1929, the three year average $37,870. The average land value per deed was $21 in 1927, $37 in 1929. The amount of the average mortgage was $22 in 1927 and $49 in 1929.

The land transfer tax on deeds and mortgages, plus the charge for the official forms and for recording, totaled $17,317 in 1927 and $33,091 in 1929. The average for the three years was $24,290. The division between deeds and mortgages was almost exactly the same for all three years, 89.3 per cent for deeds, 10.7 per cent for mortgages.

Tooth (sales) taxes, ya shui for the province and ya chüan for the hsien, were collected on most sales. Some said that the term "tooth taxes" was derived from the fact that the taxes were first levied on the sale of farm animals, transactions that regularly included the examination of the animals' teeth. Other suggested that the term was connected with the amount of talking that the middleman had to do to consummate a sale. Unlike the land transfer taxes, which were collected by the hsien tax office, the tooth taxes were regularly farmed out to the highest bidders. The tax contract usually granted the collection privilege for the entire hsien, though for some taxes two or three different collection areas were indicated. There was evidently considerable subcontracting because of the area of the hsien and the number of market centers, 83, that had to be covered. It was also reported that anyone could act as middleman and tax collector in a market if he secured a license and arranged with the next higher tax contractor for the payment of the taxes collected and with the higher up middleman for the division of the commissions involved. In the animal market the commission was generally divided evenly.

The combined tax and commission charge was usually divided by the seller and the buyer, the actual proportion paid by each depending on official tax regulations and on local customs. Where the government's rules and the local procedure differed, local usage was apt to prevail.

On most sales the middleman collected a 6 per cent fee, 3 per cent for the tax, 3 per cent for commission. Only one per cent tax was paid on cotton, but the tax agent ordinarily estimated the amount of cotton offered for sale in the market and collected the tax on that amount even if the cotton was not sold. In that case the middleman had to pay the tax. One report gave the 1929 tax as 70 coppers per picul, the middleman's gross collection on a sale as 200 coppers per picul, and his net as 130 coppers. A later report stated that there were two taxes on cotton, the tooth tax and an additional sales tax. The combined tax was given as 38 coppers per picul with the buyer paying one copper per catty and the seller nothing, or the division might be determined by the terms of the sale. A 1933 report gave the combined tax as 52 coppers and therefore the net to the middleman only 48 coppers per picul. Although the middleman might not receive any direct payment from the seller he usually managed to secure some profit on exchange when he turned over the money from the sale. It was also stated that the middleman protected himself on the matter of the taxes on unsold cotton by generally under-reporting his sales to the tax office.

On cotton cloth there was a fixed charge of two cents per piece. In the grain markets the tax was usually two coppers per tou, except for sesamum, on which the charge was four coppers per tou. The commission was the same as the tax, two or four coppers per tou. In 1931 the price of millet was 50 cents per tou, kaoliang 54 cents, wheat 88 cents, and sesamum $1.28.

There were eight different tooth taxes: (1) animals, (2) cotton and cotton seed, (3) cloth, (4) grain, (5) oil cake, fuel, vegetables, fruit, bags, thread, and belts, (6) peanuts, mats, and hemp, (7) timber, oil waste, animal hides, bones, and oil, (8) bristles. The history of the different taxes shows that most of them had long been collected for local use. About 1915 many of them were designated, at least in part, for particular purposes: cotton for an agricultural demonstration center; cotton cloth for the opening of the Chamber of Commerce, for the establishment of an industrial school, for the promotion of industry; oil cakes, vegetables, etc., for lecture halls and reading rooms; peanuts and mats for official and religious ceremonies, for the establishment of a police association, for visiting primary schools, for reading rooms; lumber and animal products for relief funds for orphans and the poor, for girls' higher primary schools. Then in 1925 Li Ching-lin, the governor of Hopei province, reformed the taxes and appropriated part of the tooth taxes for the provincial government. In fact the province took over the tooth taxes, except for a fixed amount equal to what the hsien government had been collecting. Later increases in the tooth taxes went to the province rather than to the hsien.

The amounts collected from the tooth tax contractors in 1929 ranged from $1,458 on bristles and $1,540 on cloth to $5,750 on grain and $18,130 on animals. The total was $44,313, of which $28,863 went to the hsien and $15,450 to the province. In 1927 the total for the province was $7,482. Most of the increase came in the animal tax, which went up $6,780, 59 per cent in two years. Three amounts went down during the two years, cotton by only $10 but oil cake, etc., by 12 per cent and cloth by 15 per cent. Grain and peanuts went up not more than 3.5 per cent but wood, etc., increased 33 per cent and bristles 45 per cent.

The increase in the tax receipts did not, of course, necessarily represent any increased payment for the people, except as it made the tax collectors more diligent in their work. The increase was rather an adjustment in the division of the tax income between the collector and the government and possibly the recognition of larger sales totals because of price increases. The figures also show something of the relative strength of the business and agricultural groups. In 1927 extra emergency land taxes were collected amounting to 200 per cent of the normal land tax. The increase in the tooth taxes arranged for that year but collected in 1928 was only 11.1 per cent. In 1928 the extra land tax was 61 per cent of the normal tax. The same year the government tried to secure a 40 per cent increase in the tooth taxes for 1929 but the best it could get was 10 per cent. The land owners were evidently much more vulnerable to emergency tax assessments, but as soon as the military emergency was over the extra levies were discontinued and the land tax returned to the traditional level.

When preparing for the annual tooth tax bidding the government authorities attempted to set up minimum amounts that must be bid. In 1927 six of the eight bids were above the minimum, but four of the six by not more than $10. The total for the eight contracts was $747 less than the sum of the proposed minima. The next year the minima were the bids of the previous year. Again six of the successful bids were above the minimum. Grain was only $1.00 more. The total was $4,037 above the sum of the minima. The animal tax bid was up $3,010, 26 per cent. In 1929 the authorities raised the minima so that their total was $16;145 (40 per cent) above the total of the 1928 bids, but the successful bids totaled only $3,931 (10 per cent) more than the 1928 total. All of the final bids were less than the proposed minimum and two of the eight, peanuts and bristles, were less than the amount bid the previous year. Another rise of $3,710 in the animal tax accounted for most of the increase in the total.

For both 1928 and 1929 the total increase in the tooth taxes over the amount for the previous year was within a few dollars of $4,000, an increase of some 11 per cent per year. Figures are not available to show whether this increase continued. However, the drop in prices in the early 1930s undoubtedly brought decreases in the amounts bid by the tax collectors.

Besides the eight tooth taxes the hsien and province collected an additional tax on the animal and cotton sales. In 1929 it was $42,668, only $1,645 less than the total for the eight tooth taxes. There was also a tax on the butchering of animals that totaled $9,500. These two amounts were divided approximately 54 per cent to the province and 46 per cent to the hsien. The hsien also received an additional $17,156 on peanuts and wood, an amount in which the province did not share.

The total sales tax receipts in 1929 were $113,637, divided $70,259 for the hsien and $43,378 for the province.

The 1917–29 record of the hsien tax on peanuts and wood shows how the highest bids for one of the extra sales taxes nearly trebled in 12 years and how from the low in 1918 to the maximum in 1929 the amount was almost quadrupled.

In seven years the amount was more than that for the previous year. In five years, 1918, 1920, and three successive years 1925–27, it was less. The 1918 drop of 26.3 per cent and the 1920 decrease of 18.5 per cent undoubtedly reflected the damage done by the 1917 floods and the 1919–20 drought. In both cases the succeeding year's increase more than equaled the preceding decline. Disturbed political conditions appear to be the reason for the 27.3 per cent decrease from 1924 to 1927.

The successful bid in 1917 was $6,070. In 1929 it was $17,156, an overall increase of 183 per cent. From the minimum of $4,484 in 1918 to the maximum in 1929 the increase was 284 per cent. From 1927 to 1929 the amount went up 44 per cent. During the same two years the tooth tax total increased only 22 per cent.

From our figures it would appear that the governmental agencies received only a small proportion of the taxes paid by the buyers and sellers. The hsien wheat crop was estimated to total $2,689,000. A sample of 400 farm families estimated that they sold 42 per cent of their wheat. From the sales taxes on all grains the government collected only $5,750. The sales of bristles were estimated to be some $760,000. The reported sales tax paid the government was $1,458. The sales of "export cloth" totaled some 1,000,000 pieces. Only part of the 600,000 piece output of "big cloth" was sold but it would add considerably to the sale total. For the privilege of collecting the tax of two cents per piece the cloth gild bid only $1,540.

The records do not show what, if any, year to year changes there were in the successful tax bidders. With the cloth gild dealing with the government on their tooth tax there probably would not be any other bidders. Apparently little if any change was expected in the organizations actually collecting the taxes as they were required to secure a five year certificate as well as an annual license. The tax hangs were divided into six classes according to the amount of their collections or their surplus. The five year certificates cost from $80 to $300, the annual license from $20 to $160 plus $1.20 big money for the certificate showing the renewal of the license. Later, for extra income, the $20 rate was increased to $29.55 and $35.10, the $40 rate to $58.50.

In 1925 Ting Hsien listed 64 tax collection units. There were 24 for animals, 15 for cotton and cotton seed, six for cloth, 19 for grain, two for peanuts etc., four for oil cake etc. Six agencies collected two different tooth taxes. None were listed for the wood, oil waste, animal hides and bones group, or for bristles. As there were only 80 families, living in two villages, who were engaged in sorting and selling bristles they undoubtedly made their own tax arrangements with the hsien government. It was also stated that these two groups were not listed because of lack of time for the preparation of the necessary regulations.

The 64 tax units were located in 22 different centers throughout the hsien. There were nine in the city. Nine villages had only one unit. The units were rated one second class, one third class, five fourth class, 12 fifth class and 44 sixth class. The total charge for their five year certificates was $6,290 and their total annual license fees were $2,201.70.

The city had three grain tax units, three animal units, one for mules and horses, one for donkeys and cattle, and one for pigs. Ming Yueh Tien had four animal units, one for mules and horses, and separate ones for donkeys, cattle, and pigs. Ch'ing Feng Tien among its seven units had one for the $25,000 worth of rice grown on the 2,090 mu of spring irrigated land in the 6th District.[2]

Provincial taxes on butcher shops were begun in 1915. An extra amount for the hsien was added in 1916 but the regulations provided that the hsien extra could not be more than the amount for the province. The rates were first fixed at 20 cents each for sheep and goats, 30 cents for pigs, and $1.00 for cattle. In 1916 the rate for cattle was increased to $2.00 per animal, that for donkeys was set at 60 cents, and that for horses, mules, and camels at 80 cents. Bids were to be received for three categories—pigs, cows and sheep, others—with the successful bidder for each collecting from the entire hsien. In 1925 the hsien was divided into districts and the rates increased to 40 cents for sheep and goats, and 60 cents for pigs. Cattle, etc., went up to $4.00 each to discourage their being slaughtered. In 1929 the slaughter house taxes were combined under one contract instead of three. The rate on cattle was reduced to $3.00 and the butchering of mules, donkeys, horses, and camels was forbidden.

2. See Chapter X.

The tax payment of $9,500 in 1929 was divided $5,000 for the province and $4,500 for the hsien. From 1927 to 1929 the amount increased 22 per cent, 40 per cent if the 1927 amount for horses, etc., is omitted. From 1921 to 1929 the increase was 100 per cent, 130 per cent if the 1921 amount for horses is omitted. The 1928 tax of $9,105 was divided $4,829 for pigs, $2,987 for cattle and sheep, $1,289 for mules, horses, and donkeys.

The following figures give the 1931 rates for transportation licenses:

		Day	Month	6 Mos.	Year
Carts:	1 animal	10 cops.	$0.50	$2.50	$ 4.00
	2 animal	20 "	1.00	5.00	8.00
	3 animal	30 "	1.50	7.50	12.00
	4 animal	— double 2 animal			
	5 animal	— double 3 animal			
Ricksha			$ .30	$1.50	$ 2.50

Remission or postponement of part or all of the land taxes was one method of giving general community relief when an area suffered from flood, drought, locusts, or other natural disaster. The details of such adjustments are given in Chapter XX. When there was fighting in an area the military generally collected extra taxes and levied special assessments for food, transportation, and man power. There was often looting in the actual fighting area. The extra taxes were sometimes said to be the prepayment of taxes for later years. Sometimes the extra assessment was softened by being labeled for a special need.

In 1926 and 1927 a 60 per cent surtax was added to the wine taxes. It was allocated to the army. In 1928 the extra levy was cut to 30 per cent and was designated for relief. Similar surtaxes were levied on tobacco.

When the land owners went to pay the second half of their 1926 provincial taxes they had to pay three times the usual amount. Besides the regular amount for local government activity a full year's extra taxes were collected for the army's anti-Red campaign. In 1927 an extra year's tax was collected both spring and fall, three year's taxes in one.

The extra tax collected in the spring of 1928 was 61 per cent of the year's total. It was divided 58.5 per cent for rehabilitation and 2.5 per cent for relief. In the three years the extra land taxes totaled $389,158. In addition the requisitioning and looting of the army cost Ting Hsien almost $1,000,000 in 1927 and 1928.[3]

3. See Chapter XX.

The extra taxes were discontinued after the Nationalist government took over in the summer of 1928.

TABLE 46. TAXES, 1929

National

Salt	$71,240	
Wine and tobacco	2,450	
Wine and tobacco dealers	8,016	
Cigarettes	35,100	
Likin	12,500	
Stamps	6,340	$135,646
Special deed inspection		2,528

Provincial

Land	106,755	
Receipt forms recording	2,925	
Land sales	16,803	
Mortgages	2,072	
Forms and registration	4,063	
Sales (tooth) taxes	15,450	
Animal and cotton	22,928	
Slaughter house	5,000	
Additional salt	44,000	219,996
Special land		65

Hsien

Land	33,578	
Land sales and mortgages	5,623	
Sales (tooth) taxes	28,863	
Animal and cotton	19,740	
Peanuts and wood	17,156	
Slaughter house	4,500	109,460
Special family assessment		21,438

Village

Land sales and mortgages		4,530
		$493,663

TABLE 47. TOOTH (SALES) TAXES, 1929

	Hsien	Province	Total
Animal	$ 9,500	$ 8,630	$ 18,130
Cotton, cotton seed	3,900	600	4,500
Cloth	500	1,040	1,540
Grain	4,300	1,450	5,750
Oil cake, fuel, vegetables, fruit, bags, thread, belts	3,300	165	3,465
Peanuts, mats, hemp	3,000	850	3,850
Wood, oil waste, animal hides, oil, bones	3,563	2,057	5,620
Bristles	800	658	1,458
	$28,863	$15,450	$ 44,313
Additional sales taxes			
Animal and cotton	19,740	22,928	42,668
Butcher shops	4,500	5,000	9,500
Peanuts and wood	17,156	–	17,156
	$70,259	$43,378	$113,637

TABLE 48. HSIEN RECEIPTS FROM TAXES ON PEANUTS AND WOOD

1917	$6,070	1922	$10,010	1927	$11,818
1918	4,484	1923	12,580	1928	13,553
1919	6,170	1924	16,282	1929	17,156
1920	5,560	1925	13,200		
1921	7,610	1926	12,680		

Amount from Districts, 1929

1	$3,770	4	$ 2,250
2	1,310	5	2,770
3	3,870	6	3,186
		Total	$17,156

TABLE 49. TAX COLLECTOR'S FEES, 1925

	No.	5 Year Certificate	Annual	1 Year Total
Animal	24	$2,280	$ 805	$1,261
Cotton	13	1,160	385	617
Cloth	4	640	280	408
Grain	19	1,890	651	1,029
Others	4	320	80	144
	64	$6,290	$2,201	$3,459

CHAPTER IX

Education

THE PROGRESS made in education was one of the reasons why Ting Hsien was named a model hsien. Four hundred and forty-seven schools and 18,666 students were reported to the hsien Bureau of Education in 1928. However, in spite of these favorable statistics, several sample studies showed that some 80 per cent of the population over six years of age were illiterate at the time of our study. Approximately one-third of the males over six years of age were literate but only about 3 per cent of the females. That very definite progress was being made on the literacy problem in some areas was shown by the figures for the 11–24 year age group in Chai Ch'eng. Fifty-three per cent of that group were literate, 65 per cent of the males and 36 per cent of the females.

Teaching her people to read was and still is one of China's biggest problems. It was this problem that the Mass Education Movement was attacking in Ting Hsien. It was their hope that, using the Movement's Thousand Character system, they could, within three years after they had begun their hsien wide program, by 1934, teach most if not all of the hsien's seventy thousand young illiterates to read. By that system, which actually taught some 1,200 characters in its beginning course, a person could, in two months' time (later six weeks), become literate enough to read simple books, write letters, and keep accounts. A second or post-graduate course covered another 1,200 characters.

In a study of the characters used in various kinds of written material and their comparative frequency rates in a million and a half characters the Mass Education Movement found that if a person could recognize nine characters he could read one out of seven characters in simple material. Seventy-eight characters would cover 50 per cent, 352 characters 70 per cent, and 1,169 characters 91 per cent. The Movement therefore based its first series of lessons on 1,200 characters. The combination of the characters into binomial and trinomial terms gave a total vocabulary of well over 2,000 words. In printed material published by the

Movement phonetic symbols giving the pronunciation, both sound and tone, were printed beside any new or unfamiliar characters. The meaning of the character was given by the context.

It was generally estimated that some five thousand characters were needed for general newspaper reading.

By the end of 1931 there were People's Schools (Mass Education classes) in all the 453 villages and in the 19 satellite villages. More than 20,000 students were enrolled. The estimated cost was 40 cents per pupil. This covered classroom, equipment, light, fuel, texts, materials, teaching, and supervision. By 1932 it was possible, in some villages, to organize a campaign to enroll all of the remaining illiterate young adults and "eliminate illiteracy" in those villages. By 1934 the hsien government had taken over the promotion of the literacy classes. That year there were 844 classes in 416 villages with an enrolment of 21,170, 14,080 males and 7,090 females.[1]

The 80 per cent of illiteracy for the hsien was determined from the figures for several sample groups of families, 515 in the Experimental District and 5,255 in the 1st District, and from special literacy studies of the 11–50 age group in 500 families in the Experimental District, of the 11–24 age group in the 366 families in Chai Ch'eng, of 150 of the 362 families in Tung T'ing, and of 1,633 families in the city and 536 families in the three suburbs. Those who had had at least two years of lower primary school, or two months in a People's School, i.e., had completed the first Thousand Character course, were classed as literate. In the 500 family study individuals were given a test in which they were required to recognize and write a representative sample of ten of the characters used in the Thousand Character readers. If they failed to make a perfect score they were classed as part literate but were not included in the literate group.

The 5,255 families had the lowest literacy figures: males 5 years of age and over, 30.3 per cent, females 1.7 per cent, total 16.5 per cent. For the 400 farm families the figures were males 37 per cent, females 4.0 per cent, total 21.6 per cent. Chai Ch'eng, where the first Mass Education schools were opened in 1926, had the highest literacy figure for the

1. Dr. Y. C. James Yen, head of the Mass Education Movement, has stated that during the war years 1937–1945 over 45,000,000 people learned to read by the Thousand Character System taught in classes promoted by the Mass Education Department of the Government Ministry of Education.

11–24 year group: males 65 per cent, females 36 per cent, total 53 per cent. The Tung T'ing figures were only slightly smaller: males 60 per cent, females 37 per cent, total 49 per cent. The highest figures for any one age group were in the 10–14 year group in the city. For that group the literacy figures were males 81.8 per cent, females 19.0 per cent, total 54.5 per cent, but it will be noted that the figure for the females was only about half those for Chai Ch'eng and Tung T'ing.

Literacy and family income were closely related. The effect of the amount of the family income, measured by the size of the family farm, on the educational opportunities of the family is shown very strikingly in the 515 families. Only 56.6 per cent of the families with less than 50 mu of farm land had any literate members. In the 50–99 mu group the figure was 98.8 per cent. All the families in the 100 mu and over group had at least one literate member. The effect of the size of the family farm on the proportion of the family members who were literate is shown by the following figures for the 11–50 year age group in the 500 families in the Experimental District. The figures also show how the increase, through the years, in the number of village schools and greater interest in education had increased the literacy of the younger people.

Land	Per Cent Literate	Age	Per Cent Literate
Under 25 mu	16.9	11–14	57.3
25–49	31.7	15–19	51.2
50–74	45.6	20–24	39.1
75–99	51.0	25–29	28.8
100 mu and over	58.1	30–34	22.1
Average	27.7	35–39	18.2
		40–44	22.2
		45–49	20.3

The same effect of age is shown by the literacy figures for the males and females in the 400 farm families.

Age	Per Cent Literate Males	Females	Age	Per Cent Literate Males	Females
5–10	21	6.5	51–60	35	–
11–20	55	11.5	61–70	34	–
21–30	43	3.1	71–80	18	–
31–40	30	1.3	Over 80	–	–
41–50	25	0.6	Total	37	4.0

The following figures show how, for the 515 families, the average number of students per family and the years in school increased and the average age at which the students entered school decreased as the size of the family farm increased.

Mu	Aver. Persons with Education	Per Cent of Family	Aver. Years in School	Aver. Age Entered School
Under 50	1.1	18	3.9	8.8
50–99	3.5	33	6.1	7.8
100 and over	4.5	35	7.3	7.2

Where the head of the family could read the literacy figure was 49 per cent. Where he could not read it was only 25.6 per cent.

The very definite effect of the father's occupation on literacy is shown by the following figures.

Occupation	Per Cent Literacy
Education, government, military	71
Merchant	48
Farmer	33
Manual laborer	18

China's old educational system was based on the Chinese classics and aimed to prepare the students for the government examinations. The local district examinations were held in Ting Hsien in the examination halls that, during the latter part of our study, were the headquarters of the Mass Education Movement. The old style education was given privately, by a tutor in a wealthy family, by a scholar who earned his living teaching a group of pupils who came to his home, or in schools maintained by some villages.

The first modern school of which we found a record was a private school opened in 1894. Villages began to establish schools about 1902 but it was not until after the Republic was established in 1912 that rapid progress was made. The influence of the magistrate Sun Fa-hsü, appointed in 1914, was especially strong in the establishment of schools. Many temples were given up at that time and their buildings were taken over for the new schools.

China's general educational system was a six-six-four division, elementary school six years, middle school six years, college four years. The elementary school period was divided at first, lower primary three years, higher primary three years. By governmental decree dated September 6, 1928, the division was changed to lower primary four years, higher primary two years, and the lower primary was made compulsory for all children.[2] The middle school was divided junior middle three years, senior middle three years.

In 1927 there were 449 schools in the hsien. In 1928 there were 447. Our tables for 1928 showed a total of 468 schools, but in getting the number of lower and higher primary schools we counted twice the 21 schools that had both lower and higher primary departments. There were five schools above the primary grade, boys' and girls' junior middle schools, boys' and girls' normal schools, and a vocational school.

Villages with schools had a school board responsible for the operation of the schools. Many of them also had an Educational Committee that consisted of the village head, the head of the village school board, and an undetermined number of other village leaders. This committee was responsible for the development of the educational program, the preparation of the school budget, the provision of funds to meet the budget, and overall management of the school property. They were required to keep account of all school funds and to make regular reports to the hsien Bureau of Education.

In 1923 the Provincial Department of Education ordered that the Hsien Bureau for Urging the People to Learn be reorganized as the Hsien Bureau of Education. The head of the Bureau, working under the magistrate, was put in charge of all the educational work in the hsien. Working with him were four educational committee members. They generally were some of the leading gentry and served without salary. The employed staff of the Bureau included five inspectors, a treasurer, a business manager, and a clerk. By 1930 the staff had been increased to six inspectors and a secretary had been added.

The magistrate also appointed an Educational Administrative Committee of nine members, all of whom served without pay. They, in consultation with the head of the Educational Bureau, worked out plans for the development of the overall educational program of the hsien, especially for the higher schools that were largely financed from hsien funds. The Administrative Committee prepared the educational budget, secured funds to meet it, and managed the property of the

2. Theodore E. Hsiao, *The History of Modern Education in China* (Peking University Press, Peiping, 1932).

schools under their direct control. The plans developed by the Administrative Committee were carried out by the Bureau staff.

The operating budget of the Bureau of Education was $3,953 in 1928. In 1929 the Bureau was supposed to receive $6,096 but reported that it did not get the full amount.

Other school items in the hsien expenditure budget totaled $35,930 in 1928 and $38,262 in 1929. The following details show how the amounts were distributed in 1928.

Boys' normal school	$ 9,468
Girls' normal school	8,559
Vocational school	1,484
Chung Shan middle school	360
Special higher primary schools	5,100
Subsidies to higher and lower primary schools	10,915
Ming Yueh Tien school	44
	$35,930

The only increase in 1929 was $2,332 more for the boys' normal school. The normal schools reported that they received considerably less than the amounts budgeted for them.

The $35,930 in the hsien budget for education was less than 25 per cent of the $153,134 reported expenditure for all the schools in the hsien. The balance came from village and other funds.

At the same time that the Bureau of Education was established in 1923 the hsien was divided into 12 educational districts, two in each governmental district. These districts operated under the direction of the members of the Administrative Committee. The city was a special area where the schools were sponsored by the Bureau. The School District headquarters received and passed on to the Bureau the reports of the schools and were the channels through which all bureau orders were sent to the schools.

In spite of the progress that had been made there were 124 villages, 27.4 per cent, that had no schools. Most of these must have been small villages that felt they could not afford a school. Twenty per cent of the 453 villages had less than 50 families and 46 per cent had less than 100 families. Not all the villages without schools were without educational opportunities for, in some cases, small neighboring villages joined together to establish a union school. Some villages with no schools were permitted to send their pupils to the school of a neighboring village, often paying an increased tuition rate for them.

The 1st District had the highest proportion of villages without schools, 44 per cent. At first this seemed surprising but it evidently was the result of the large proportion of small villages, 37 per cent with less than 50 families and 66 per cent with less than 100 families. In the 4th District only 10 per cent of the villages had no primary school, but in that district only 21 per cent of the villages had less than 100 families and only 8 per cent had less than 50 families.

In spite of its large proportion of villages with no schools, the 1st District had the smallest number of families per boys' primary school, 159. The 4th District had the highest number, 239 families. For the hsien the average was 201 families.

Ninety-one villages had two schools each, one for boys and one for girls, but only seven villages had two schools for boys. The latter were probably the larger market towns.

Less than a quarter of the villages, 23 per cent, had lower primary schools for girls. Only two villages had higher primary departments for girls. According to our figures there were 109 schools for girls, one for every 650 families. In the 5th District there was one girls' lower primary for every 1,573 families. The 6th District had the best record, one for every 464 families.

There were coeducational schools in 14 villages and the city but even in those schools the boys and girls usually were taught in separate classes.

In the city there were 20 schools: 15 primary schools, three of which had higher primary departments, and five higher schools. For girls there were only two primary schools (one with a higher primary department), a middle school, and a normal school. There also were two coeducational lower primary schools.

Almost all of the lower primary schools had only one teacher. At the most 18 out of 417 lower primary schools had two instructors. The combined lower and higher primary and the higher primary schools usually had four teachers. The total number of teachers for all grades was 575. Only 88 were women. In more than a quarter of the girls' lower primary schools the teachers were men. In some if not all of the higher grade schools for girls there were some men teachers.

The teachers in general were a relatively young group for 57 per cent of the men and all but four of the women were under 30 years of age. Thirteen per cent of the men were over 49 years old.

The schools reported a total of 18,666 students, 15,377 boys and 3,289 (17.7 per cent) girls. The total number was equal to some 22 per cent of the children between 5 and 14 years of age. For the males the proportion in school was about 35 per cent. For the females it was about 8 per cent. The proportion with some school experience was, of course, higher as a considerable number of the 5–14 year age group had attended school and graduated or left, inasmuch as until 1928 the lower primary was only a three year course. After 1928 it was a four year course. The students attending the higher primary, middle, normal, and vocational schools were only 3.5 per cent of the 10–19 year age group.

Table 50 gives, for the 5,255 families, the numbers of those who were in school and of those who had graduated or left school before we made our study; also the proportions of different age groups who were or had been in school.

The figures for the 515 families (Table 51) in the Experimental District show the number of students in the different types of schools, the number who had left school, and the number of years they had spent in study. The record seems to be much better than for the 5,255 families only because the figures for the 515 families include those who had studied in an old style school or in a People's School using the 1,000 character system. Without those two groups the figures were very similar. Of the 5,255 families, 16.4 per cent, and of the 515 families, 17.8 per cent of those who were five years of age or over were studying or had studied in a modern type school.

The average number of students per school was 37 for primary schools, about 100 for the higher primary schools, and 145 for the middle schools. For all the schools the average was 42 students per school and 32 students per teacher.

The number graduated in 1928 was reported as 2,228 or about one in eight of the student body. This was an unusually low number. The decrease undoubtedly was largely due to the disturbances and unrest connected with the arrival of the Nationalist forces from the south, the taking of Peking, and the unification of the country under the Nationalist government. In earlier years the schools generally reported at least 50 per cent more graduates.

The reported school income was $161,792; the expense $153,134. In view of all the educational needs it was surprising that there should have been a reported overall surplus of $8,658. The school income was derived from tuition, the rent of school land, interest on surplus funds, specially allocated tax income, hsien government subsidies, and the village funds collected by assessing all owners of land in the village area. The details on the division of income for all the schools were not available but the figures for the schools in the 62 villages of the Experimental District are given in Table 52.

Fifty-six per cent of the 438 lower primary schools reported their income as between $200 and $299 per year. Sixty-two schools received less than $200, while 14 received less than $125 a year. Only 18 had $500 or more a year. The average income was $227 per year, the average expense $197. The higher primaries spent an average of $3,000, the higher schools from $4,430 to $8,805.

The average expenditure for the 18,666 students in school in 1928 was $8.20. In the previous five years the average had varied from $6.50 to $9.05. For the boys the average in 1928 was $7.70, for the girls $10.50. Because of their smaller classes, the cost per student for the girls was regularly more than for the boys.

In the lower primary schools the average cost per student was only $5.35 in 1928. From 1923 to 1928 the average varied from $4.55 to $8.85. The general average was about $6.00 per student per year. In the higher primary schools the cost was about $30 per student. In the middle and vocational schools it was usually between $60 and $85 except that in 1928 the vocational school spent $221 per student. That year the enrolment was only 20 students, one-third of the figure for 1927.

The value of the property held by the schools was reported, in 1928, as $803,970. Of this, $135,405 (17 per cent) was held by the girls' schools. In 1926 the property total was $1,115,034. It is not clear why the boys' school property dropped $316,000 in two years.

The schools reported that the buildings they used varied from two to 227 chien. For the lower primary school buildings the range was from two to 34 chien but only 9 per cent had more than 10 chien. The average was six chien. The higher primary buidings varied from seven to 62 chien with the average 31 chien. One of the higher schools was very large with 227 chien. Two others had 46 and 91 chien.

A study of the number of the villages with graduates of higher pri-

mary, middle schools, and colleges and of the number of graduates
showed the following:

	Villages	Per Cent	Graduates	Average per Village
Higher primary	373	82.3	5,950	16
Middle school	300	66.2	1,588	5
College and technical schools	157	34.6	436	3
			7,974	

The total was only 2 per cent of the total population.

Seven villages reported over 100 higher primary graduates; one as
many as 600. Only five villages had more than 25 middle school graduates and only one had more than 35. That one reported 200. Seventeen
was the largest number of college graduates reported by any village.

The villages claimed 1,588 middle school and 436 college graduates
but they also reported that 583 of the middle school and 318 of the
college graduates were away from home. The number who could have
had any part in the life of Ting Hsien was, therefore, middle school
graduates 1,005, college and technical school graduates 118.

Adult Education

The public library, established in the city in 1917, had some 1,200
volumes on its shelves. It was open daily from nine to three. The daily
attendance was reported to be some 17 readers.

The newspaper reading room was first opened in 1912. In 1917 its
operation was made part of the program of the office of Social Education. Eight newspapers were subscribed for. The reading room was open
daily from eight to four.

The museum was organized in 1921 to preserve the relics dug up when
the roads were being repaired under the famine relief program. The
road excavations discovered relics of the T'ang and Sung dynasties
and carved figures from the Six Dynasties. Additional items were added
between 1921 and 1929. The budgeted expense for Social Education was
$628.

The Three Principles Lecture Hall was the successor of the Lecture
Hall for the Improvement of Social Customs that had been established
in 1912. Lectures were regularly given on the twelve city market days
per month. The topics were the Three Principles and the news of the

world. The average number of listeners was reported to be 30. The expenses of the lecture hall were given as $288 per year.

Chai Ch'eng had a Patriotic Lecture Hall and a library and newspaper reading room, organized as part of its model village program.

In 1934 seven "libraries" of the some 350 booklets that had been prepared by the Mass Education Movement were being circulated in the Ting Hsien villages. The booklets covered a wide variety of subjects, historical, scientific, biographical, plays, poems, stories, songs, and general information. They cost from 2.5 to five cents apiece.

Experimental District

As it was possible to make a much more complete and detailed study of the smaller number of schools in the Experimental District and sample numerous items that were not included in the hsien study, a separate report is given for the district. There were 63 village schools and 2,016 pupils in the 62 villages. The average was just over one school per village but there were 14 villages (23 per cent) that had no school. In the 2nd and 3rd Districts 21 per cent and in the hsien 28 per cent of the villages had no schools. Most of the villages without schools were small villages. Eight of the District villages (13 per cent) had less than 50 families, while 23 villages (37 per cent) had less than 100 families.

The following figures show the number of schools and students.

	Schools	Pupils
Boys' primary	43	1,369
Girls' primary	14	240
Boys' and girls' primary	2	102
Lower and higher primary, boys	3	268
Lower and higher primary, girls	1	37
	63	2,016[1]

[1] Girls, 15 per cent.

Twenty-seven per cent of the schools had girl pupils but only 15.5 per cent of the lower primary students and 7.9 per cent of the higher primary students were girls.

Modern schools were a fairly recent development in Ting Hsien. The first in the Experimental District was, apparently, the private school started by Mr. Mi Chien-san in Chai Ch'eng in 1894. The first village schools were opened in 1902, but progress was slow as the people were not yet convinced of the value of the new schools. Just under half of the schools, 48 per cent, were started during the first five years of the Republic, 1912–16. Only three schools had been organized after 1921, one in 1927, the year before our study. Two of the three were for girls. Only one school for girls was opened before 1912. Twelve of the 15 girls' schools were started in the decade from 1912 to 1921.

Two of the 18 schools opened before 1912 were for both boys and girls. Coeducation was tried but was not generally accepted and no additional coeducational schools were opened in the area or, if they were, they did not survive. In the hsien there were 16 coeducational lower primary schools and one higher primary. In both the 62 villages and in the hsien the coeducational schools were just over 3 per cent of the total.

The average number of students in the lower primary schools was 33 for the boys and 17 for the girls. In the higher primary schools it was 43 for the boys and 11 for the girls. As, until 1928, there were three classes in both the lower and higher primary schools, it would seem that the schools usually had small classes. The groups studying together, however, were fairly large as the average number of students per teacher was 26.

School attendance for the children of school age was far from being universally accepted in Ting Hsien even though the Nationalist government was attempting to make at least the first four years compulsory. In the 62 villages the attendance averaged only 0.2 pupils per family. Less than one in seven of the children between six and 14 years of age were in school.

School attendance apparently was not increasing at the time of our study. Only three schools said that the number of their students had increased during the previous five years. Those three were probably the three schools organized after 1922. Thirteen schools reported a decrease in pupils during the previous five years.

The ages of the pupils in the lower primary schools ranged from 5 to 18 years and in the higher primary from 10 to 19 years. In the rural areas the children who went to school were not regularly starting at the age of six. The largest groups in the lower primary schools were the 11 and 12 year olds. They apparently started school when they were eight or nine years old. The 152 boys over 14 years of age must have been 12 or over when they began studying. The wide range in ages

must have made for many problems, especially in the one teacher
schools.

The age range for the girls in the lower primary schools was from 6
to 16 years of age. Their median age was 10, one year less than the
median age of the boys.

The higher primary students were a much more uniform group. The
age range for the boys was only six years, from 11 to 16, and for the
girls four years, from 12 to 15, except for two individuals, 10 and 19
years of age. The median age was 13 for both the boys and the girls.

As would be expected in a farming area, 93.3 per cent of the children
came from families whose principal occupation was farming. The
families of 78 of the 2,016 children were engaged in commercial work,
30 in industry, and 27 in education.

The teaching staff of the 63 schools numbered 78. Ten were women.
The average number of students per teacher was 26. Fifty-two schools,
83 per cent, had only one teacher. The three boys' schools with both
lower and higher primary departments were the only ones that had
more than two teachers. Five was the largest number of teachers in
any school.

In age the teachers ranged from under 20 to over 70, but in general
they were a young group; 75 per cent were under 30 and 85 per cent
were under 40 years of age. All of the 14 men who were over 40 years
of age must have had their early training in the Chinese classics.

All the women teachers and all but five of the men were natives of
Ting Hsien. One-third of the men and two-thirds of the women were
natives of the village in which they were teaching. All but two of the
men teachers were married but only one-half of the women.

As indicated by their age, the group as a whole had not had long
teaching experience. Only 14 of the 78 had taught more than 10 years.
One man claimed to have taught between 35 and 39 years, while one,
possibly the one who was over 70 years of age, said he had taught between 40 and 45 years. The older teachers were evidently men who
earlier had taught the Chinese classics and then had found a place in
the modern system.

The teachers appeared to shift about a great deal. Only seven said
they had had as much as five years' service in the schools in which they
were teaching at the time of our study. Only two reported between 10
and 14 years' of service in the same school. In one village near Ting

Hsien the teacher was changed 11 times in 22 years.[3] Low salaries were undoubtedly responsible for much of the changing, especially during the time when salaries were still paid in rapidly depreciating copper coins. The shift from copper to silver was made about 1924.

The average annual salary of the lower primary teachers was $90 per year. It was $150 for the higher primary teachers. For the lower primary schools the minimum salaries were between $50 and $59 dollars. The maximum were in the $120–$139 group. For the higher primary teachers the lowest was in the $100–$119 group; the highest in the $160–$179 group. Almost half were in the highest group.

The number of women teachers, 10, was so small that it is difficult to draw any definite conclusions about their salaries, but the distribution figures seem to show that the salaries of the women teachers tended to be lower than those of the men.

Sixty-one per cent of the teachers had had normal school training; another 30 per cent were middle school graduates. Two had not gone beyond higher primary school. Two of the older men had won the hsiu t'sai degree, the first of the classical examination system. It would be difficult to judge the educational experience of students of a school for prison attendants, the society for the study of self-government, or a medical training school. They were each represented by one teacher in the 62 villages.

The usual teaching schedule called for the teacher to give from 8 to 10 different courses and to teach from 30 to 34 hours per week. Forty-seven per cent reported that number of courses while 52.6 per cent reported that many hours. Nine teachers said they taught less than five courses; another nine reported that they were giving from 11 to 13 courses. Nine were teaching less than 20 hours per week. Only one reported more than 34 hours per week.

Twelve of the 63 schools reported that they employed servants. Three-quarters of the 12 had only one servant but one school had five. Eight of the 19 servants were part-time workers. Wages ranged from $4.00 to $10.00 per year for the part-time workers and from $24 to $70 a year for those on full time.

A study of the families of the teachers, the amount of land the families owned, and the value of the family property showed that, as might be

3. Sidney D. Gamble, "Hsin Chuang", *Harvard Journal of Asiatic Studies*, vol. 8, no. 1 (1944).

expected, the teachers, in general, came from the larger and wealthier families. The median family had 10 members and some 50 mu of land worth about $5,000. Only one family had no land, while 82 per cent of the families had at least 20 mu. Fourteen per cent had 100 mu or more. For 18 per cent of the families the value of the family land was less than $2,000. For 10 per cent it was $10,000 or more.

Fifty-nine of the 71 married teachers reported that they had a total of 61 boys and 51 girls. Seven reported no children. Seventy-six per cent of those reporting had not more than two children. However, as 74 per cent of the teachers were under 30 years of age and 85 per cent under 40 years of age, their families probably were still incomplete.

All but two of the 63 village schools were housed in buildings owned by the village. In four villages the school buildings were also used for the office for village affairs.

The school buildings had an average of some seven chien for class rooms, offices, storage; 11 had less than five chien. Only five schools had more than 15 chien. They undoubtedly were the four schools with higher primary departments and probably one of the two schools for both boys and girls. Fifty-four per cent of the school buildings had from five to nine chien. This probably was adequate space as 52 of the schools had only one teacher.

The schools generally operated on a six day week. All of the schools closed for the New Year holidays, most of them for a full month. Some had even more than a month so that the pupils would be free to help with the preparation for the New Year and also have the full first month. Some had only about three weeks and began soon after the Feast of Lanterns on the 15th of the First Month.

All but one of the schools had vacation at the time of the spring wheat harvest. The date depended upon the season. For most of the schools that vacation period was about half a month. A few had as much as a month while a few others had less than ten days.

The schools that had a spring vacation also had vacation at the time of the fall harvest. Its dates also depended upon the season. Most of the schools were closed for a month or a month and a half. One school, however, reported its vacation as less than 20 days. Another had two months.

One village, Chai Ch'eng, closed its schools for a summer vacation. It probably was the one school that did not have the harvest time vacations. Most of the schools had a total of two and a half or three months' vacation during the year. The shortest time was just under two months. Evidently the vacation periods were set by the village school authorities rather than by the hsien Bureau of Education.

The 1928 income of the 63 schools totaled $16,700, an average of $265 per school and $8.30 per student. The income of the individual schools ranged from $100 to $2,200. Sixty-three per cent of the schools had incomes of less than $200 per year while 73 per cent had less than $250 per year. Seventeen per cent received from $250 to $399. Only six schools had $400 or over and only five had over $450. The four schools with the highest incomes were the four with both lower and higher primary departments. Their average income was $1,375 but the actual amounts ranged from $680 to $2,200.

The income of the schools came from a variety of sources, none of which were used by all the schools. Table 52 shows the income sources, the number of schools receiving income from each source, and the amounts received.

Almost half (47 per cent) of the school income came from school property, the rent of village land that had been assigned to the school, and interest on surplus school funds. The renting system varied from village to village. In some the village officers used the land in turn, paying a fixed rent for it. In others the land was rented to the highest bidder. In some villages the term was one year, in others as much as five years.

The available figures do not give the exact total of the land held by the schools but the middle figures of the groups with different sized holdings give a total of some 3,000 mu and the average rent $2.25 per mu. Judging from our study of rents (see Chapter X) this was a very low rent. The following figures give the reported land holdings of the schools.

Land	Schools	Per Cent
None	14	22.2
Under 25 mu	20	31.8
25–49	17	27.0
50–99	4	6.3
100–149	5	7.9
150 and over	3	4.8
	63	100.0

The three schools with more than 150 mu had 180, 216, and 384 mu respectively.

Most, if not all, of the villages assessed the farm land within the village limits for funds to meet the village expenses. Originally the assessment covered only the expenses of the Green Crop Society, Ch'ing Miao Hui, that undertook to watch the village crops at harvest time and protect them from theft. Later the assessment was increased to cover the amounts needed for the home guard, the village school, and the demands of the military forces. It varied from year to year and from village to village, but, judging from the few samples we secured, was usually about 10 or 15 cents per mu. The sum the schools received from that source amounted to only 1.7 cents per mu on all the farm land of the 62 villages or some 2.0 cents per mu on the land of the 46 villages raising school funds from that source.

Twenty-five per cent of the land transfer tax paid to the village by real estate buyers and sellers was allocated to the school budget in 50 villages. It is not clear why money was not received from this source by 13 schools unless, perhaps, sufficient amounts were received from other sources, or there were no land sales in their area.

The subsidy given to 14 schools by the hsien government was for special excellence and came from the $10,915 received from a special tax collected in eight centers. In 1931 the model village Chai Ch'eng received a subsidy of $300 from this fund for its schools. The hsien Bureau of Education also sent another $400.

Tuition brought in a relatively small amount, $1,021, an average of only 50 cents per student per year. The basis of the tuition and the amount varied from village to village but generally was not more than $1.00 a year for the lower primary and $2.00 for the higher primary. One school reported a charge of $4.00 for the higher primary. Fourteen schools had a straight tuition charge. Twenty-one villages varied the amount of the tuition according to the amount of land owned by the pupil's family; seven according to the class the child was in. As there were only four higher primary schools, at least three of the lower primary schools charged a higher tuition for the upper grades. Two schools charged extra for children who came from outside the village.

The five villages that used a total of $620 from the sales taxes collected on vegetables, cotton, and medicine must have needed extra funds for their schools and turned to this special source for them.

The total expenses of the 63 schools were reported as $13,920, an average of $221 per school and $6.90 per student. The amounts reported by the different schools varied from under $100 to $1,572. Seventy-three per cent of the schools spent less than $200. Only 11 per cent spent more than $25 per month, $300 per year.

According to the reports, the schools had a surplus of $2,780. The four schools with the highest incomes and expenses, evidently the higher primary schools, reported their combined surplus as $1,500. Two of the four had a surplus of more than $600. The highest was $628. We were not able to determine whether the surplus income was added to the school funds that were loaned at interest or whether it was used for other unreported expenditure. In spite of the reported overall surplus, 46 schools said their income was not sufficient to meet their budget.

The following table gives the distribution of the schools according to their income and expense.

Amount	Income	Per Cent	Expense	Per Cent
$ 50–99	4	6.4	5	7.9
100–149	17	26.9	21	33.3
150–199	19	30.1	20	31.7
200–249	6	9.5	4	6.4
250–299	5	7.9	6	9.5
300–349	3	4.8	2	3.2
350–399	3	4.8	–	–
400–449	2	3.2	1	1.6
Over 500	4	6.4	4	6.4
	63	100.0	63	100.0

The following figures show the distribution of the school expenses.

	Amount	Per Cent
Teachers' salaries	$7,760	55.8
Servants' wages	675	4.8
Books and apparatus	567	4.1
Other equipment	619	4.4
Miscellaneous	4,299	30.9
	$13,920	100.0

The average teacher's salary was just under $100 a year. Servants were hired by only 12 schools. Their largest possible average salary was $56 per year. For books, apparatus, and other equipment the average was

only $19 per school or about 55 cents per student. The salary and equip-
ment figures together give a picture of some of the problems of the Ting
Hsien village schools.

As none of the schools had had a history of more than 25 years, 20
was the largest number of classes graduated by any primary school.
That was one of the coeducational schools. But while 20 classes of boys
were graduated only six classes of girls had completed the course. The
other coeducational school had graduated 15 classes of boys but only
two of girls. Most of the boys' schools had graduated from 10 to 15
classes, but none of the girls' schools had graduated as many as 10
classes. Three girls' schools and one boys' school had graduated no
classes. One of the girls' schools was opened before 1922 but, as in the
coeducational schools, was evidently having difficulty in getting the
girls to complete the course. A similar story is told by the number of
students graduated. The figures for 1926 and 1927 were:

	Lower Primary Schools			
	1926		1927	
	Classes	Graduates	Classes	Graduates
Boys	44	279	42	233
Girls	7	22	6	21
	51	301	48	254
	Higher Primary Schools			
Boys	3	55	3	41
Girls	1	3	1	5
	4	58	4	46

Only six primary schools graduated 10 or more students in 1926 and
only four in 1927. None graduated as many as 20 students.

In the lower primary schools the graduation rate for the girls, 7.4
per cent, was less than half of that of the boys, 16.1 per cent. In the
higher primary schools the rates were almost the same: boys 37.5 per
cent, girls 36.5 per cent. Most of the girls who started the higher primary course went on to complete it.

The total number of graduates since the schools had opened was given
as:

	Lower Primary	Higher Primary
Boys	3,757	530
Girls	308	50
	4,065	580

The girls were 7.6 per cent of the lower primary and 8.6 per cent of the higher primary graduates. They were 14.6 per cent of the students in 1928.

The schools reported a total of 1,782 students—1,514 boys and 268 girls—who left school before graduating. Family finances were given as the cause of leaving for 1,601, "indifference to education" for 181. Thirty-two per cent of the girls were "indifferent to education" but only 6 per cent of the boys.

In 1926 there were 237 students who left before graduation—215 lower and 22 higher primary pupils. In 1927 the number was 208—203 lower primary but only five higher primary students. The average drop out rate was just over 10 per cent. The graduation rate was 16.4 per cent.

There were 304 persons, 272 males and 32 females, in the 62 villages who had graduated from a school higher than junior middle school. Seventy-three went no further than senior middle school, preparatory school, agricultural or technical high school. Two hundred and thirty-two had had work in normal school, college, or technical school. One hundred and fifty males and 25 females had graduated, nine men stopped before they finished their higher course, and 41 men and seven women were still in school in 1928. The graduates included 102 from normal and other teacher training schools and 39 from arts colleges or universities. Agriculture, law, medicine, military, and technical schools had from two to six graduates. We were interested to find that there were four returned students from Japan and one from France. One boy was studying in France and one in the United States. Our records do not show how many of this higher education group were living in Ting Hsien.

Normal school and other teacher training courses had been popular among the men graduates—82 of 150 had studied in that field—but, of the 41 men in college, only one was taking normal training.

The distribution of the higher education group, students and graduates, gave a very interesting picture of the 62 villages. There were 18 villages that had no one in the higher education group. Fourteen of these were small villages with less than 68 families. The other four had more than 155 families, the largest 293 families. In the Experimental District the average number of families per village was 168.

Only six villages had more than 10 men with higher education. Two of these, Chai Ch'eng and the neighboring market town of Tung T'ing, were the only ones with more than 15. Tung T'ing had 25 men. Chai Ch'eng, with 33, clearly showed the result of the long interest of the Mi family in education.

Only eight villages reported any women who had had any higher education. Eleven of the 32 women lived in Chai Ch'eng. The next largest number was five in Tung Wang. Fourteen of the 25 women graduates said they were employed in educational work but at the most only 10 of them could have been teaching in the schools in the 62 villages. One woman was a nurse. Ten were unemployed.

In only nine villages were there less than 20 families for each person with higher education. In three the ratio was less than 10 to one. We expected Chai Ch'eng to have the lowest ratio but it was third with 8.5. Hsi Chia Ying was second with a 5.5 ratio, 10 students and 55 families. Hsia Chi Cha Chuang was first with six students in 29 families, a ratio of only 4.8 families per student. Nothing that we can find in our records suggests why the two top villages should have such a low family-student ratio. The story of the model village Chai Ch'eng (see Chapter VIII) shows why it had such a high educational record.

Table 50. School Attendance, 5,255 Families

| | Attending | | Previously Attended | | Total | |
	Male	Female	Male	Female	Male	Female
Total number	1,267	102	2,931	116	4,198	218
Age	Per Cent		Per Cent		Per Cent	
5–9	30.0	3.1	7.4	0.2	37.4	3.3
10–14	34.7	2.6	24.3	2.7	59.0	5.3
15–19	10.1	1.0	34.5	3.4	44.6	4.4
20 and over	0.5	0.1	21.3	0.4	21.8	0.5
5 and over	9.1	0.8	21.2	0.9	30.3	1.7

TABLE 51. SCHOOL ATTENDANCE, 515 FAMILIES

	Attending		Previously Attended		Total	
	Male	Female	Male	Female	Male	Female
Primary school	135	24	203	22	338	46
Higher primary	21	1	69	6	90	7
Middle school	8	1	34	1	42	2
Above middle	9	–	3	–	12	–
People's school	16	3	4	–	20	3
Old style school	–	–	245	2	245	2
	189	29	558	31	747	60
Per cent of 5 years and over	11.9	2.0	35.2	2.2	47.1	4.2
Without people's and old style groups					30.4	3.8

Years Attended School

	Attending		Previously Attended		Total	
Years	Male	Female	Male	Female	Male	Female
Under 4	116	25	223	20	339	45
4–6	44	2	182	7	226	9
7–9	15	1	97	3	112	4
10–12	6	–	30	1	36	1
13–15	4	1	16	–	20	1
Over 15	4	–	10	–	14	–
	189	29	558	31	747	60

TABLE 52. SCHOOL INCOME IN EXPERIMENTAL DISTRICT

Source of Income	Schools	Amount	Per Cent
Land rent	49	$6,805	40.7
Village land assessment	46	3,916	23.5
Village land transfer tax	50	1,840	11.0
Hsien subsidy	14	1,451	8.7
Interest	16	1,047	6.3
Tuition	44	1,021	6.1
Sales tax	5	620	3.7
		$16,700	100.0

TABLE 53. SCHOOLS AND STUDENTS, 1928

| | Schools | | | Students | | | Students |
	Male	Female	Total	Male	Female	Total	per School
Kindergarten[1]	–	–	1	11	29	40	40
Lower primary	317	100	417	12,468	2,840	15,308	37
Higher and lower primary	19	2	21	2,437	105	2,542	121
Higher primary	2	1	3	244	52	296	99
Middle	1	1	2	120	170	290	145
Normal	1	1	2	77	93	170	85
Vocational	1	–	1	20	–	20	20
Total or average	342	105	447	15,377	3,289	18,666	42

[1] Coeducational.

TABLE 54. TEACHING AND NON-TEACHING STAFF, 1928

| | Teachers | | | Students per Teacher | Staff | | |
	Male	Female	Total		Male	Female	Total
Kindergarten	–	2	2	20	–	–	–
Lower primary	363	72	435	35	689	13	702
Higher and lower primary	77	6	83	31	51	–	51
Higher primary	10	2	12	25	7	–	7
Middle	20	4	24	12	4	2	6
Normal	13	2	15	11	6	–	6
Vocational	4	–	4	5	2	–	2
	487	88	575	32	759	15	774

TABLE 55. STUDENTS GRADUATED, 1928

	Male	Female	Total	Per Cent
Kindergarten	10	22	32	80.0
Lower primary	1,421	128	1,549	10.1
Higher and lower primary	412	50	462	18.2
Higher primary	31	20	51	17.2
Middle	55	–	55	19.0
Normal	40	19	59	32.4
Vocational	20	–	20	100.0
	1,989	239	2,228	
Per cent of students	12.9	7.3	12.0	

TABLE 56. SCHOOL PROPERTY VALUE AND EXPENDITURE, 1928

	Property			Expenditure		
	Male	Female	Total	Male	Female	Total
Kindergarten	$ 1,780	–	$ 1,780	$ 420	–	$ 420
Lower primary	373,285	$ 79,870	453,155	63,879	$18,303	82,182
Higher and lower primary	150,340	8,575	158,915	23,408	1,839	25,247
Higher primary	46,860	2,800	49,660	6,152	2,862	9,014
Middle	68,000	32,660	100,660	14,400	3,211	17,611
Normal	19,500	11,500	31,000	5,868	8,362	14,230
Vocational	8,800	–	8,800	4,430	–	4,430
	$668,565	$135,405	$803,970	$118,557	$34,577	$153,134

TABLE 57. SCHOOL PROPERTY VALUE AND EXPENDITURE PER STUDENT, 1928

	Property			Expenditure		
	Male	Female	Total	Male	Female	Total
Kindergarten	–	–	$ 45	–	–	$ 10.50
Lower primary	$ 30	$ 28	30	$ 5.10	$ 6.45	$ 5.35
Higher and lower primary	62	82	63	9.60	17.50	9.90
Higher primary	192	54	157	25.20	55.00	30.40
Middle	567	193	345	120.00	19.00	60.70
Normal	253	124	182	76.50	90.00	83.50
Vocational	440	–	440	221.00	–	221.00
Average	$44	$41	$43	$7.70	$10.50	$8.20

PART 3. AGRICULTURE

CHAPTER X

Farm Land: Ownership and Operation

OVER 92 PER CENT of the Ting Hsien families owned some farm land. Over 96 per cent farmed some land. All but 5,484 of the 70,034 families were land owners. All but 2,745 were farm operators. Only 1,361 families, 1.9 per cent, reported no farming connection. The average land holdings were: owners 21.9 mu, operators 21.2 mu, all families 20.4 mu. Just under 6 per cent of the land owning families rented land to others. Thirty per cent of the farming families rented land from others. Twelve per cent of the privately owned crop area was rented. Only 4.8 per cent of the farm operating families were full tenants. Only 1.3 per cent of the renters were share croppers. Only 0.7 per cent of the families were non-farming landlords. Twenty-eight per cent of the land was double cropped. The estimated value of the crops produced totaled some sixteen million dollars, an average of some $11.25 per mu and $40 per capita. These are the outstanding figures of our study, in 1931, of land ownership and farm operation.

Accurate figures on the area of Ting Hsien were not available as it had never been surveyed. The official land records were manifestly incomplete as it was generally recognized that there was a considerable amount of "black land" that was not on the books at the yamen and so escaped taxation. We were told that in not a few villages three sets of land books were kept, one to show the officials, one to show the villagers, one, the complete one, for the village elders. We were not able to verify this report but it is indicative of the difficulty of getting a complete land report.

In making our land study we did not attempt to secure the figures of the hsien land office but went instead to the village elders and got from them a report on the amount of land their village controlled. Any error in their figures undoubtedly would tend to be an under rather than an

209

over statement and so make our figures somewhat below the actual amount but still more accurate than the official figures. It has not been possible to measure or estimate the probable error.

Our land study was made in three sections, first of the Experimental District, second of the 1st District, and third of the rest of the hsien. The first two were more detailed than the third as it was felt that they were reasonable samples and it was not necessary to repeat all the detail in the larger study.

The total amount of arable land was reported as 1,424,931 mu, approximately 371 square miles. This was 76 per cent of the total reported area. In the Experimental District and the 1st District the non-farm area was reported as 11 and 18 per cent. A general inspection of the other districts showed that they had a considerably larger proportion of waste land. The proportion of non-farm land is not particularly significant in our study as the number of persons per square mile of gross area would be almost the only figure to be radically affected by any change in the percentage. It is of interest to note, however, that in the 1st District the village heads reported only 1.2 per cent of the district occupied by graves.

The crop area controlled by the different villages ranged from 245 to 32,500 mu. The average was 3,150 mu, 525 acres. Only one village had more than 13,000 mu, five had more than 12,000 mu (2,000 acres), 10 had 10,000 mu or more. Only 47, 10.4 per cent, had as much as 6,000 mu (1,000 acres). Fifty-four per cent of the villages had less than 2,500 mu and 19 per cent had less than 1,000 mu. (See Table 58.)

As the number of families in the villages varied from six to 1,200 the average amount of crop area per family was much more significant than the total amount of land held by the village. The per family average varied from seven to 76 mu. In 11 villages the average was less than 10 mu per family. It was less than 15 mu in 75 villages. These probably were the poorer villages of the hsien, though the lack of agricultural income may have been made up by industrial or other activity. In only 15 villages, 3.3 per cent, was the average 40 or more mu per family. Table 58 gives the averages for the villages in the 1st District, the Experimental District, and the hsien.

Grouping the villages according to the largest land holding of any of their families, we find that in seven villages the largest holding was less than 50 mu. In almost half the villages, 47.3 per cent, it was less than

150 mu, while in three-quarters of the villages it was less than 250 mu. In only 32 villages, 7.0 per cent, was the largest holding 400 or more mu. Only two villages reported their largest holding to be over 1,000 mu.

The largest amount of land owned by one family was 3,950 mu. That was a city family. The largest family holding in any village was 1,800 mu, 300 acres. Only three families owned more than 1,000 mu; only six more than 600 mu, 100 acres; only 11 more than 500 mu. There were only 132 families who owned 300 mu (50 acres) or more. They were only 0.2 per cent of the land owning families. Large land holdings were not a serious problem in Ting Hsien.

The 2.1 per cent of the families who owned 100 or more mu held 17.1 per cent of the farm land. The 9.0 per cent owning 50 or more mu owned 38.6 per cent of the crop area. At the lower end of the scale, 91 per cent of the land owning families had less than 50 mu, while 72 per cent had less than 25 mu each. The latter group owned 33.1 per cent of the crop area.

Our study did not subdivide the families with less than 25 mu, but in the study of a single village, located some miles south of Ting Hsien, 85.2 per cent of the families owned less than 50 mu, while 62.3 per cent had less than 20 mu. Fifteen per cent had less than five mu per family, 23.1 per cent had from 5.0 to 9.9 mu, and 24.2 per cent from 10.0 to 19.9 mu. The 15.0 per cent with less than five mu per family owned only 1.5 per cent of the land. Those with less than 20 mu owned some 22 per cent of the farm area. The 3.5 per cent of the families who owned 100 mu or more held 20.9 per cent of the land.[1]

Just over 10 per cent of the privately owned land was listed as worth less than $25 per mu. Just under one-quarter, 24.3 per cent, was worth from $25 to $49, while a little more than another quarter, 28.2 per cent, was valued between $50 and $74. Only 0.6 per cent was worth $150 or more per mu. (See Table 61.)

As might be expected, the distribution in the different price classifications varied considerably in the different districts. Forty-seven per cent of the land in the 3rd District was valued at under $50 per mu. In the city only 8.7 per cent was valued at less than $50 per mu and none at less than $25 per mu. At the upper end of the scale 48.5 per cent of the city land was worth $100 or more per mu. In the 2nd District the

1. Sidney D. Gamble, "Hsin Chuang", *Harvard Journal of Asiatic Studies*, vol. 8, no. 1 (1944).

proportion was 25.2 per cent, but it was only 8 per cent in the 4th District.

In 238 villages controlling 839,540 mu of land, of which 55.4 per cent was irrigated, 21.9 per cent of the unirrigated land was worth less than $25 and 66.2 per cent less than $50 per mu. Only 0.6 per cent was worth $100 or more. For the irrigated land the figures were practically reversed. Only 0.2 per cent was reported as worth less than $25 per mu, while 20.9 per cent was worth $100 or more. For the irrigated land the median value was between $75 and $99 per mu. For the unirrigated land it was between $25 and $49 per mu. (See Table 62.)

Only 3,826 families, 5.9 per cent of the land owning families, rented land to others. All but 514 of this number were owner-lessors and farmed part of the land they owned. The 514 non-farming landlords, who rented all the land they owned, were only 0.7 per cent of the Ting Hsien families. One-third of the non-farming landlords lived in the city and another one-sixth in the 1st District. Of the families living in the city, 7.8 per cent were listed as landlords. In the 1st District the figure was 1.5 per cent. In the other districts the non-farming landlords were not more than 0.7 per cent of the families. In the 4th District the figure was only 0.1 per cent.

The land rented to others by the owner-lessors and the landlords totaled 173,890 mu, 12.2 per cent of the privately owned crop area. (See Table 63.) Crop area, rather than farm area, figures are used as they do not include waste land, land used for houses, graves, and roads and so give a better basis for farming figures.

There was much more renting in the city and the 1st District around it than in the other districts. In this connection it must be remembered that 28,210 mu of land in the city and the three suburbs were classed as farm land and included in the crop area. In the 1st District and the city together 23.9 per cent of the crop area was rented, in the 2nd District 16.3 per cent, but in the 3rd District only 6.9 per cent. For the other districts the rental figures were all slightly more than 10 per cent.

Full tenants, those who rented all the land they farmed, numbered only 3,253. They were 4.7 per cent of all the families in the hsien and 4.8 per cent of the farm-operating families. The part-owners, who owned part and rented part of the land they farmed, were 24.2 per cent of all the families and 25.2 per cent of the farming families. If the part-owners are included in the tenant group the tenancy figure was 30 per cent of the farm operators, but then more than five out of six of the tenant group owned part of the land they farmed. If, on the other hand, the part-owners are included in the owning group the owner-farmers were 91.4 per cent of all the families and 95.1 per cent of the farming families. Tenancy could hardly be called a serious problem in Ting Hsien.

Renting part of a family's land holding was usually a matter of renting one or more separate fields. In a study of the land holdings of 1,136 families in four villages we found that the number of fields per family varied from one to 29; that 70 per cent of the families owned more than one field; that the total number of fields was 3,798; that the average was 3.3 fields per family. In one village the average was 5.2 fields per family. In another it was 2.9 fields. The highest average was in the smallest village of 103 families. The lowest average was in the largest village with 586 families. Just over two-thirds of the families, 67.4 per cent, had from one to three fields. Only 3.0 per cent had more than 10 fields.

In size the individual fields ranged from less than one mu to 78 mu. Twenty-five per cent were less than two mu, 70 per cent were under five mu, and 78.5 per cent were less than six mu, one acre. Only 8.8 per cent of the fields contained 10 or more mu while only 14 fields, 0.4 per cent, were as large as 30 mu, five acres. The average was just under five mu.

In the four villages 40 per cent of the fields were less than one li, one-third of a mile, from the owner's home in the village, while 87 per cent were within three li, one mile. In one village, however, almost one-quarter of the fields were reported to be more than one mile from the village. In two villages families reported that they had fields as much as two miles from their house. (See Table 64.)

The average family holding in the four villages was some 16 mu or six mu less than the hsien average. If allowance is made for this difference the average number of plots per land owning family in the hsien was probably at least four and possibly even slightly more.

The government's estimate of the average number of fields per family is shown by the minimum number of deeds the villages were required to submit in connection with the deed inspection program announced in August, 1927. At least 500 deeds were to be presented by villages with from 50 to 200 families, 1,500 by the 200 to 500 family villages, and 3,000 by those with from 500 to 1,000 families. With the minimum requirement three deeds per family and the maximum 10, the normal expectation evidently was between four and five deeds per family.

The division of the family land holdings, the relatively small size of the plots, the distances from the village, all would make for difficult farming, consume extra time in going to and from the fields, and require extra transportation of tools. At harvest time it would greatly complicate the supervision and protection of the crops and may very well have been one of the reasons for the Green Crop Society or the Agricultural Association taking over the general watching of the crops.

Only 271 families, 1.3 per cent of the 20,185 families who rented farm land, paid their rent by giving the landlord a share of the crop produced on the land. It had been our expectation that this would be a much higher figure. For over half the renters, 54.0 per cent, the rent was fixed in dollars. For 40.4 per cent it was stated in quantities of millet, cotton, wheat, or kaoliang per mu but usually it was paid in money, the amount being determined by the market value of the crop-rent at the time of payment. (See Table 65.) Millet was the most generally used unit for the cash-crop rent. It was reported by 7,947 families. Cotton was the unit for only 212 families. Wheat and kaoliang were used by only a few families.

Sample rent studies showed amounts ranging from 50 cents to $7.50 per mu and returns to the landlord of from 3.0 to 8.9 per cent of the value of the land. The average return apparently was not more than 6.0 per cent. There was considerable variation in the return on land of different value in a given area and on land of the same value in different parts of the hsien. Generally the middle value land appeared to be in greater demand than either the cheaper or the more expensive land and therefore to command a somewhat higher return.

Estimated rents in the 1st District were generally between 3.0 and 3.5 per cent of the value of the unirrigated land and from 4.0 to 4.6 per cent of the value of the irrigated land.

The rates were higher in two sample villages, one in the north part of the hsien, the other in the south. For the north village the average return was 5.9 per cent. For the south village it was 20 per cent higher, 7.1 per cent. (See Table 66.)

In six villages in the Experimental District the cash rent averaged 5.9, 6.3, and 5.2 per cent for the first, second, and third grades of land.

In our study of 400 farm families the average rent figure was $1.69 per mu for land worth less than $40 per mu, $3.63 for the middle grade of land worth from $40 to $79 per mu, and $4.20 for the land worth $80 or more per mu. The amounts were 6.2, 6.0, and 4.8 per cent of the average values of the three grades of land. For all the families the average was 5.25 per cent. (See Chapter III.)

Considering the high interest rates paid on loans we have been interested to find these relatively low returns on land values. Evidently the fact that land was the chief medium for investment in the rural areas had so increased the price that the rent produced only a relatively small yield on the land value.

The cash-crop rent paid in cotton was 35, 20, and 8 catties per mu for the first, second, and third grade land in one village of our six village group. In another village the rates were 40, 21.5, and 10 catties per mu. The millet rates were the same in both villages, 7.0 and 1.5 tou for first and third grade land. In two sample villages one tou of wheat was accepted as the equivalent of two tou of millet although at 1928 prices one tou of wheat was equal to 1.8 tou of millet and at 1931 prices to 1.6 tou.

In some villages, where the land was double cropped, from one-half to two-thirds of the rent was paid after the spring harvest.

In the six villages the cash rent, in 1928, was regularly higher than the cash-crop rent for the first and second grades of land, with values from $40 to $120 per mu, but it was lower for the third class land worth from $10 to $40 per mu. The more than 30 per cent drop in grain prices from 1928 to 1931 would greatly augment the difference for the higher priced lands and about equalize the rents for the third class land, if there was no change in the cash rents. However, it seems probable that the cash rents also went down unless the land was rented for more than one year.

Cotton rents were higher than grain rents in 1928 and the difference apparently was even larger in 1931 as the price of cotton went down some 11 per cent in three years while grain prices dropped more than 30 per cent.

The figures of our sample rent studies indicate that the cash and the cash-crop rent charge averaged between 35 and 40 per cent of the average gross income from the land. Share rent was regularly 50 per cent of the crop.

In one village the majority of the renters had their land on a year by year basis. In another village the landlords required a written rental contract, usually for a three year term. They also required an advance rent of $1.00 per mu. This was refunded at the end of the term, but was kept by the landlord in case the tenant gave up the land before the end of the rental contract. Another report said that the share rent contracts were generally on a one year basis, the cash-crop more often on a three year basis, while the cash contracts were often for five years.

One village rented its school land for a term of five years. The rent was paid in money, the amount being fixed by bidding at a town meeting when the previous renting contract expired. The successful bidder was required to have his contract guaranteed by one of his friends. Another village reported that the rent on its school land was set at $3.00 per mu per year.

There were 2,739 more farm-operating families than there were farm-owning families. The addition of 3,253 full tenant families and the subtraction of the 514 non-farming landlord families accounted for the difference. The crop area farmed by the operating families, 1,424,930 mu, was larger by some 8,070 mu than that held by the farm-owning families. The difference was the result of renting, to private operators, the lands owned by schools, temples, villages, or other public organizations. The average farm, per operating family, was 21.2 mu, only slightly less than the 21.9 mu average of the land-owning families. For an average family of 5.8 persons the average amount of land per person was 3.7 mu, about 0.6 of an acre.

The proportions of the operating families farming 50 or more mu and less than 25 mu were both less than the figures for the land owning families holding those amounts. The large land owners and the landlords reduced their holdings by renting, the tenants and the small land owners increased theirs. One hundred and thirty-two families owned 300 or more mu but only 15 families were farming that much land. The 840 families farming from 100 to 299 mu were almost one-third less than the families owning that much land. At least 141 and possibly considerably more of the 4,460 families owning from 50 to 99 mu rented out some of their land. After the land holding went above 60 mu, 10 acres, it apparently became more and more advantageous to rent part of the land rather than farm it with family or hired labor. The tenant shared the risk of the farm operation.

Detailed reports were secured on the area devoted to some 37 different crops. The list included nine grains, four legumes, six vegetables, three fruits, two oil seeds, cotton, tobacco, fruit trees, and trees grown for timber. The total number of crop mu was 1,830,140. This was 405,210 mu more than the crop area. The index of double cropping, therefore, was 128. If the index was determined only by the area planted to wheat and barley, the usual winter crops, it would be 126. In the six districts, the index varied from 114 in the 6th District to 144 in the 1st District. Differences in the type and quality of soil and in the amount of irrigation would account for most of the differences in the indices. The 6th District index was low because 44,114 mu, 14.5 per cent of the crop mu in the district, were planted to cotton. Almost one-third of the cotton area was in that district.

Wheat and barley, which are winter crops, were naturally first crops. Kaoliang, cotton, and watermelons were also listed as first crops. Cabbage and carrots were listed as second crops, grown after an earlier crop had been harvested. The other crops might be either first or second depending on the amount of double cropping. Corn or melons were sometimes harvested in time to permit the growing of a second crop.

The area used for the different crops varied from 493,500 mu for millet to 60 mu for apples. In determining the area used for the various crops it has been difficult to secure exact figures, as 12.4 per cent of the crop mu were reported as growing two crops simultaneously. On most of this area beans or turnips were grown between the rows of grain. The principal crops involved were millet and white beans with 146,740 mu, kaoliang and black beans with 68,030 mu, buckwheat and turnips with 10,580 mu. In all such instances the area has been equally divided between the jointly grown crops. (See Table 70.)

Sixty-three per cent of the crop mu were planted to grain, 79.2 per cent if we include all the land where grains and legumes were planted together. Sixteen per cent was used for beans and peas, 7.6 per cent for vegetables, and 6.6 per cent for cotton. Fruit, including melons and the orchard fruits—pears, dates, apricots, apples—had just under 0.5 per cent. Trees grown for timber—poplar, willow, elm—had 3.0 per cent of the crop mu. In per cent of crop area the figures were: grains 80 per cent, legumes 20.5 per cent, vegetables 9.7 per cent, cotton 8.5 per cent, and other crops 9.9 per cent. The total of these figures is over 100 because of the double cropping.

Millet was the most generally grown grain. If the panicled and glutinous varieties are both included, it was planted on almost 30 per cent of the crop mu and 37.8 per cent of the crop area. Wheat was second with 22 per cent of the crop area and kaoliang third with 8.2 per cent. Rice was grown on only 2,090 mu and only in the 6th District, where the springs in the Black Dragon Pool supplied the necessary water. The other grains were corn, barley, and buckwheat.

The legumes were black beans, white beans, green beans, and peas. Black beans were grown as the only crop on 187,090 mu and on 68,430 mu with either kaoliang or glutinous millet. White beans were grown with millet on 146,740 mu. Green beans and sesame were grown together on 1,550 mu.

Sweet potatoes were the principal vegetable. They were reported grown on 95,080 mu, or 6.7 per cent of the crop area. No other vegetable had as much as one per cent of the crop area. The estimated sweet potato crop was 190,217,000 catties, an average of 2,000 catties per mu, 2,700 catties per family, 470 catties per person. This agrees very closely with the 2,500 catties per family and 415 catties per person consumed by the families in our budget study (see Chapter V).

The oil seeds were peanuts and sesame. They were grown on 4.7 per cent of the crop area. Poplar and willow trees were the only other crops that had as much as one per cent of the crop area. They had approximately 2.0 and 1.7 per cent.

The estimated yield of each crop, when grown as a first or second crop on irrigated or unirrigated land, is shown in Table 69. Barley and millet, grown as the first crop on irrigated land, gave the largest return, 16 and 14 tou per mu. Unirrigated barley produced only eight tou per mu, while millet, grown as the first crop on unirrigated land, averaged only six tou. Wheat gave only half the return of barley, eight tou on irrigated and four tou on unirrigated land.

The sweet potato crop was estimated at 2,800 catties per mu, when grown as the first crop on irrigated land. The return was only 1,800 catties for a second crop on unirrigated land. Cabbage and carrots averaged 3,000 catties, two tons per mu, on irrigated land. The figures for cotton were 80 and 50 catties per mu. Generally, the figures in Table 69 are lower than the average yields shown by the prices and crop value figures in Table 70. The difference is due partly to the fact that Table 69 is for the 1st District while Table 70 is for the entire hsien, partly to the fact that the tables are for different years, partly to the estimates being made by different investigators.

An attempt was made to discover whether there was any generally adopted plan of crop rotation, but the best we could do was to secure a long list of three-year programs. On irrigated land some farmers were growing six crops in three years with wheat or barley as the winter crops and three years of millet or two years of millet and one year of beans as the summer crops. In another group of fields squash was planted between the rows of barley for two years and barley was grown alone the third year. The summer crops were millet one year and cabbage, carrots, and turnips two years. Another combination was one year of garlic and two of wheat with two years of millet and one of beans. More often the program called for five or four crops in three years. Usually, millet was the only crop one year.

On unirrigated land there was usually but little double cropping. At most four crops were raised in three years. Black beans were one of the crops in many of the dry land combinations. Millet was included in nearly all the combinations for both irrigated and unirrigated land. It naturally would be as it was planted on more than one-third of the crop area and just under 30 per cent of the crop mu.

The farmers made some interesting comments on their crop rotation programs. One said that it was possible to grow sweet potatoes two years in succession, but, while the potatoes would be larger the second year, the total weight of the crop would be less. Another stated that sesame could be grown on a plot only once in ten years. Cantaloupes could be grown for two years, but then it would be necessary to wait seven years as much of the crop would die if the interval between plantings was shorter.

One cotton farmer showed no rotation in his three-year program. He admitted it would be better to rotate, but said he could not do it as he had only one field.

The value of the Ting Hsien crops was estimated as just over $16,-000,000. Five crops were worth more than one million dollars each. Millet had the largest value, $3,550,000. Wheat was next with $2,690,-000. Sweet potatoes were third with $2,310,000. Cotton followed with $1,770,000 and black beans were fifth with $1,325,000. Peanuts and kaoliang were the only other crops valued at over $500,000.

The 1931 prices for the various crops are shown in Table 70. They ranged from less than one cent per catty for carrots and turnips to five cents a catty for peanuts and 14.7 cents per cotton. The highest price was the $1.60 per catty for onion seed, but that crop totaled less than 2,000 catties.

For the bulk grains the prices ranged from 40 cents a tou for barley to 88 cents for wheat and $1.16 for rice. Millet, kaoliang, corn, and buckwheat were all priced between 50 and 54 cents per tou.

The average gross return per mu for the grain crops ranged from $5.00 for kaoliang and $5.50 for barley to $8.60 for wheat and $11.80 for rice. The legumes averaged $6.00 per mu. The gross income from vegetables ranged from $20.00 per mu for carrots to $45.20 for cabbage. The figure for turnips was $53.30, but this probably is high, as most of the turnips were grown with buckwheat and the allocation of one-half the area to turnips is an arbitrary and possibly inexact division. The same situation may influence the figures for the legumes and, to a lesser extent, the figures for buckwheat, kaoliang, and millet.

For the oil seeds the figures were $8.00 per mu for sesame and $12.40 for peanuts. Cotton gave a gross return of $14.60 and tobacco $22.50 per mu.

The fruit trees returned amounts generally ranging from $30 to $62 per mu. Apricots and pears gave the highest return. Dates produced only $17 per mu. No return was reported from the timber trees that had 3.8 per cent of the crop area.

The average gross return from all crops was $8.75 per crop mu. It was $11.25 per mu of crop area. This was some $240 per farm family per year. The average crop value per capita was approximately $40 per year. These figures are basic in any picture of the economic life in an agricultural community and determine to a large degree the economic level of life in Ting Hsien.

Farm wages current in 1930 and the rates for 1912 and 1921 are shown in Table 71.

Room and board, three meals per day, were given to all workers. Four special meals with meat and wine were usually given during the year— at the end of the wheat harvest, at the middle of the summer crop season, at the end of fall harvest, and at the end of the work year.

It will be noted that, in general, the 1930 rates were about three times those for 1912. This 200 per cent increase in wages would seem to indicate an increase of some 70 per cent in the real wages of the workers, as the general index of wholesale prices in North China, compiled by the Nankai Institute of Economics, increased about 75 per cent from 1912 to 1930.[2]

Full time year round farm laborers were employed by 11 per cent of the 400 farm family group and by 10.1 per cent of the 515 family group. In the latter group the largest number employed by any one family was three. Only three families had that many helpers. Two per cent of the families with less than 50 mu, 30 per cent of the families with from 50 to 99 mu, and 72 per cent of the families with 100 or more mu of farm land employed full time workers. The average number of employees per family was 1.4 for the families with 100 mu or more and 0.5 for the 50–99 mu group, but only 0.02 for those with less than 50 mu. On that basis the number of full time hired farm workers in the hsien was some 6,300.

It was reported to be customary for the employers and their full time employees to discuss wages for the coming year at the time of the fall festival, the 15th of the 8th moon. When they and the middle man (conciliator) had had a good meal and had drunk wine together and while they were enjoying looking at the beauty of the full moon they would settle the rates for the coming year. Full time workers were generally paid in two instalments, at the beginning of their term and at the end of the year.

The monthly rates were usually the wages paid the seasonal workers, those who were taken on at the beginning of the growing season and laid off after the harvest. The seasonal workers were usually paid at Ch'ing Ming for the entire season. If, later on, they left or had to be let go their employer generally did not attempt to recover any unearned wages. The first of the tenth month or the first of the second month were the times when the full time workers hired by the year began their work. Some of the semi-permanent men worked from the 16th of the first month to the first of the 10th month.

For extra men, to work by the day at harvest time, spring and fall, the employers went to the "man market" which usually was held before sunrise at some central place in the village. The employers would circulate among the waiting workers quoting the price they would pay. The "condition of the market" would naturally push wages up to a peak at the height of the harvest and drop them rapidly thereafter. Our

2. National Tariff Commission, *The Shanghai Market Prices Report,* Shanghai, October–December, 1933.

daily rates are those paid under normal conditions rather than the harvest peak.

The holidays and festivals usually observed in the Experimental District were:

> First Days of the First Month: New Year Festival
> 15th of the First Month: Feast of Lanterns
> 2nd of the Second Month: The Dragon Raises His Head
> 21st of the Third Month: Pei Ch'i Temple Fair
> 5th of the Fifth Month: Spring Festival
> 13th of the Sixth Month: Kuan Kung Festival
> 15th of the Eighth Month: Fall Festival
> 9th of the Ninth Month: End of Work in the Fields
> Tung Chih: Beginning of Winter
> 8th of the Twelfth Month: La Pa

TABLE 58. CROP AREA PER FAMILY, VILLAGE AVERAGES

	1st District		Experimental District		Hsien	
Mu	Villages	Per Cent	Villages	Per Cent	Villages	Per Cent
Under 10	–	–	–	–	11	2.4
10–14	2	2.8	1	1.6	64	14.1
15–19	13	18.3	15	24.3	142	31.4
20–24	31	43.7	23	37.1	108	23.8
25–29	21	29.6	12	19.3	67	14.8
30–34	3	4.2	6	9.6	33	7.3
35–39	1	1.4	4	6.5	13	2.9
40–44	–	–	–	–	8	1.8
45–49	–	–	–	–	2	0.4
50 and over	–	–	1	1.6	5	1.1
	71	100.0	62	100.0	453	100.0

Table 59. Largest Farm Holding, 453 Villages[1]

Mu	Villages	Per Cent	Mu	Villages	Per Cent
Under 50	7	1.6	300–349	31	6.8
50–99	81	17.9	350–399	22	4.9
100–149	126	27.8	400–499	16	3.5
150–199	83	18.3	500–999	14	3.1
200–249	42	9.3	1,000–1,499	1[2]	0.2
250–299	29	6.4	1,500 and over	1[3]	0.2
				453	100.0

[1] Largest holding in city, 3,950 mu.   [2] 1,150.   [3] 1,800.

Table 60. Size of Farms Privately Owned

Area	Number	Per Cent	Mu	Per Cent	Average
Under 25 mu	46,447	72.0	468,940	33.1	10.1
25–49	12,288	19.0	401,230	28.3	32.7
50–99	4,460	6.9	304,830	21.5	68.1
100–299	1,223	1.9	180,280	12.7	147.0
300 and over	132	0.2	61,580	4.4	466.0
Total or average	64,550	100.0	1,416,860	100.0	22.0

Table 61. Value of Farm Land

Value per Mu	Total Mu	Per Cent
Under $25	149,160	10.5
25–49	344,320	24.3
50–74	399,340	28.2
75–99	307,190	21.7
100–124	169,010	11.9
125–149	39,580	2.8
150 and over	8,260	0.6
	1,416,860[1]	100.0

[1] Publicly owned land omitted.

TABLE 62. VALUE OF IRRIGATED AND UNIRRIGATED LAND, 238 VILLAGES

	Irrigated		Unirrigated	
Value per Mu	Mu	Per Cent	Mu	Per Cent
Under $25	1,080	0.2	81,910	21.9
25–49	65,040	14.0	166,000	44.3
50–74	152,600	32.8	102,060	27.3
75–99	149,030	32.1	21,950	5.9
100–124	77,840	16.7	2,210	0.6
125–149	16,900	3.6	–	–
150 and over	2,930	0.6	–	–
	465,420	100.0	374,130	100.0

Per cent irrigated, 55.5.

TABLE 63. LAND TENURE, 453 VILLAGES AND CITY

	Families	Per Cent
Owner	43,792	62.5
Owner lessor	3,312	4.7
Part-owner	16,932	24.2
Tenant	3,253	4.7
Landlord	514	0.7
Hired laborer	870	1.2
No farm	1,361	2.0
	70,034	100.0

	Number	Per Cent
Owners	64,550	92.1
Non-owners	5,484	7.9
	70,034	100.0

	Number	Per Cent
Operators	67,289	96.1
Non-operators	2,745	3.9
	70,034	100.0

	Mu	Per Cent
Land operated by owners	1,251,040	87.8
Land operated by renters	173,890	12.2

TABLE 64. FARM FIELDS IN FOUR VILLAGES

Fields per Family

Fields	Families	Per Cent	Fields	Families	Per Cent
1	337	29.6	9	11	1.0
2	269	23.6	10	10	0.9
3	162	14.2	11–15	25	2.0
4	108	9.5	16–20	8	0.7
5	72	6.3	Over 20	3	0.3
6	69	6.1	No data	3	0.3
7	34	3.0	Total	1,139	100.0
8	28	2.5			

Size of Fields

Size	Number	Per Cent	Size	Number	Per Cent
Under 1 mu	241	6.4	8–8.9	112	3.0
1–1.9	734	19.3	9–9.9	62	1.6
2–2.9	707	18.6	10–14.9	220	5.8
3–3.9	574	15.1	15–24.9	88	2.3
4–4.9	413	10.9	25–49.9	23	0.6
5–5.9	311	8.2	50 and over	3	0.1
6–6.9	176	4.6	No data	35	0.9
7–7.9	99	2.6	Total	3,798	100.0

Distance of Fields from Family Residence

Distance	Fields	Per Cent	Distance	Fields	Per Cent
Under 0.5 li	618	16.3	4.0–4.9	117	3.1
0.5–0.9	879	23.1	5.0–5.9	66	1.7
1.0–1.9	1,272	33.5	6 and over	6	0.2
2.0–2.9	528	13.9	Total	3,798	100.0
3.0–3.9	312	8.2			

TABLE 65. RENTING SYSTEM, 453 VILLAGES

	Part-owners	Tenants	Total	Per Cent
Cash	9,360	1,536	10,896	54.0
Cash crop millet	6,614	1,333	7,947	39.4
Cash crop cotton	188	24	212	1.0
Share	231	40	271	1.3
No data	539	320	859	4.3
	16,932	3,253	20,185	100.0

TABLE 66. PROPORTION OF LAND VALUE PAID AS RENT, TWO VILLAGES

| | Village No. 1 | | Village No. 2 | |
Land Value	Average Rent	Per Cent of Value	Average Rent	Per Cent of Value
Under $25	$1.10	5.5	$1.15	5.9
25–49	2.40	6.0	2.85	8.9
50–74	3.80	6.3	4.85	8.3
75–99	5.40	6.4	5.35	6.4
100–149	6.00	5.3	6.80	6.5
150 and over	7.50	5.0	–	–
Average	5.25	5.9	4.50	7.1

TABLE 67. CASH AND CROP RENT, SIX VILLAGES, 1928

| | Cash Rent | | Average Rent | |
Land Values	Rent	Per Cent	Cash	Kind
First class, $75–$120	$5.50–$7.00	5.0–7.3	$5.60	$4.90
Second class, $40–$80	$2.00–$4.00	5.0–7.8	$3.30	$2.60
Third class, $10–$40	$0.50–$1.00	5.0–6.0	$0.70	$1.20

| | Crop Rent, Amounts | | | |
	Cotton	Millet	Wheat	Kaoliang
First class	35–40 catties	5.5–7.0 tou	3.5 tou	–
Second class	20–25 "	2.0–4.0 "	1.4–2.0 "	4.0 tou
Third class	8–10 "	1.5 "	0.6–1.0 "	2.0 "

| | Crop Prices | | | |
	Cotton	Millet	Wheat	Kaoliang
1928	$0.145	$0.72	$1.30	$0.83
1931	0.128	0.50	0.88	0.543

TABLE 68. SIZE OF FARMS OPERATED

Area	Number	Per Cent	Mu	Per Cent	Average
Under 25 mu	47,105	70.1	539,310	37.9	11.4
25–49	15,010	22.3	482,950	33.9	32.2
50–99	4,319	6.4	286,960	20.1	66.5
100–299	840	1.2	109,760	7.7	130.7
300 and over	15	–	5,950	0.4	396.6
	67,289	100.0	1,424,930[1]	100.0	21.2

[1] Includes 8,070 mu of publicly owned land.

TABLE 69. AVERAGE CROP YIELD PER MU[1]

	Irrigated		Unirrigated	
	First	Second	First	Second
	(tou)			*(tou)*
Barley	16	–	8	–
Buckwheat	–	12	10	8
Corn	9	8	–	–
Kaoliang	–	–	7	–
Millet	14	10	9	6
Millet, glutinous	10	8	9	6
Millet, panicled	10	8	9	6
Wheat	8	–	4	–
Beans, black	8	6	5	3
Sesame	–	–	4	3
	(catties)			*(catties)*
Peanuts	350	300	–	–
Cabbage		3,000		
Carrots		3,000		
Garlic		600		
Onions	1,500	1,500		
Squash	2,500	2,500		
Sweet potatoes	2,800		2,000	1,800
Turnips		2,800		
Cotton	80	–	50	–

	(catties)
Dates	250
Pears	1,200
Willow shoots	1,500
	(plants)
Broom plants	300

---

[1] Estimate of field investigators for 1st District.

TABLE 70. CROP AREA, VALUE, AND PRICES, 1931

	Total Crop Mu	Per Cent of Crop Mu	Value (000)	Price (per tou)	Average Value per Crop Mu
Millet	493,560	27.0	$ 3,264	$0.50	$ 6.60
——, glutinous	23,240	1.3	145	.54	6.30
——, panicled	22,860	1.3	140	.53	6.10
Wheat	314,930	17.2	2,689	.88	8.60
Kaoliang	118,540	6.4	592	.54	5.00
Corn	60,960	3.3	407	.53	6.70
Barley	59,290	3.2	347	.40	5.50
Buckwheat	48,310	2.7	286	.50	6.00
Rice	2,090	0.1	25	1.16	11.80
Beans, black[1]	221,300	12.0			
——, white[2]	73,370	4.0	1,777	.77	6.00
——, green[3]	770	–			
Peas	350	–	–		
Sesamum	12,740	0.7	109	1.28	8.00
				(per catty)	
Peanuts	53,990	3.0	670	.05	12.40
Sweet potatoes	95,080	5.2	2,312	.012	24.30
Squash	12,470	0.7	278	.01	22.30
Cabbage	10,500	0.6	475	.015	45.20
Turnips[4]	6,140	0.3	45	.009	53.30
Carrots	2,140	0.1	43	.008	20.00
Onions	1,220	0.1	37	.014	30.60
Other vegetables	10,160	0.6	295		27.90
Cotton	121,190	6.6	1,770	.147	14.60
Watermelons	1,220	0.1	37	.10[5]	28.40
Muskmelons	1,190	0.1	34	.018	30.00
Rhubarb	140	–	4	.09	30.00
Pears	3,680	0.2	196	.027	54.50
Dates	1,870	0.1	32	.054	17.00
Apricots	150	–	9	.027	62.10
Apples	60	–	2	.023	39.00
Other fruit trees	440	–	13		30.70

(continued on next page)

(TABLE 70 CONTINUED)

	Total Crop Mu	Per Cent of Crop Mu	Value (000)	Price (per tou)	Average Value per Crop Mu
Medicine	250	–	3	–	12.75
Tobacco	700	–	16	.075	22.50
Broom plants	290	–	7	.0785	23.20
Onion seed	260	–	3	1.60	11.20
Other	330	–	1	–	3.95
Poplars	28,960	1.6	–	–	–
Willow trees	13,560	0.8	–	–	–
Willow shrubs	10,630	0.6	–	–	–
Elms	600	–	–	–	–
Other trees	160	–	–	–	–
Total	1,830,140		$16,063		$8.75
Crop area	1,424,930				$11.25
Per capita					$40.00

[1] 15 per cent grown with kaoliang and glutinous millet.
[2] Grown with millet.
[3] Grown with sesamum.
[4] 87 per cent grown with buckwheat.
[5] Per piece.

TABLE 71. FARM WAGES

	Annual Wage		
	1912	1921	1930
Head man	$20	$30	$60
Assistant head	15	25	50
Permanent worker	10	20	45
Beginner	5	10	20
	Monthly Wage		
1st class worker	$2.50	$3.50	$7.00
2nd " "	2.00	3.00	5.50
3rd " "	1.50	2.50	3.50
	Daily Wage, Busy Season		
1st " "	$0.10		$0.30–.40
2nd " "	.07		.25
3rd " "	.04		.13

CHAPTER XI

Wells and Irrigation

FORTY THOUSAND wells provided water for the irrigation of some 55 per cent of Ting Hsien's 1,425,000 mu of farm land. Another 20,000 wells inside the 453 villages furnished domestic water for the 67,865 village families. The average farm well irrigated some 20 mu. The average village well supplied water for 20 people.

Our well studies were sample and detailed surveys of the wells in the Experimental District in 1928 and the enumeration, in 1930, of all the wells in the hsien. The China International Famine Relief Commission also made a study of the Ting Hsien wells in 1930. This was part of a three hsien study made by the Commission at the request of General Hsü Yung-chang, then Governor of Hopei province. We have drawn on their Ting Hsien figures[1] to supplement our sample studies.

There was considerable difference between our detailed figures and theirs but there was general overall agreement. In the 62 villages in the Experimental District there were 25 villages where our count was larger, 36 where the Commission found more wells, and one village where their report was missing. The total difference for the area, however, was 140 wells and much of that difference might have been the result of additional wells dug during the two years between the two studies. There were similar differences in the figures for the six districts. In over half the districts our figures were the larger. The total difference for the hsien was 709 wells, 1.8 per cent. The Commission count was the larger.

The number of wells per village is shown in Table 72. Five villages had less than 10 wells for both irrigating and domestic use. One had 1,220 wells. The average was 131 wells per village. These were divided

1. China International Famine Relief Commission, Series B #49, *Well Irrigation in West Hopei,* Preliminary Report, December, 1931.

88 for irrigation and 43 for domestic use, or one domestic well for every two for irrigation. Counting both domestic and irrigating wells, there was an average of 0.87 wells per family.

Table 73 gives our count of the wells inside and outside the villages, the average number of mu of farm land per well, and the average number of families per well inside the villages. The average for the hsien was 35 mu per irrigating well and 3.5 families, or 20 persons, per domestic well. Only about half of the farm land was under irrigation. The number of mu watered by a sample of 471 wells in three villages is given in Table 74. The average was some 22 mu per well.

While the average number of persons per domestic well was 20, there was a wide range in the number actually served. Some supplied only a single family. Others furnished water for groups of families and supplied over 100 persons. The numbers using a sample of 183 wells are shown in Table 75.

In many courtyards either the space was not available or else no effort was made to separate the well and the latrine. In our sample of 183 domestic wells two-thirds of the wells were within 40 feet of the latrine and one in six was within 20 feet. However, because of the Chinese system of saving night soil and using it as fertilizer on the farm, there probably was little likelihood of contamination by seepage or surface drainage. (See Table 76.)

The average depth of the wells was some 21 feet. Some were less than 10 feet. None were over 45 feet deep. Fifty-nine per cent were between 15 and 25 feet, which meant moderate lift and moderate digging and operating costs.

The average depth of the water table was some 13 feet below the surface. In a few wells it was less than two feet below the ground. The deepest reported was between 38 and 40 feet. For two-thirds of the wells the depth of the water table was between six and 16 feet.

The average depth of water standing in the wells was some eight feet. While the measurements ranged from less than two feet to over 18 feet, in 80 per cent of the wells the water depth was between four and 10 feet.

The drought and famine of 1920–21 gave a great impetus to well digging. At that time the American Red Cross made a grant to assist in digging wells in Ting Hsien and five neighboring hsien. The Red Cross funds were for the labor cost. The workers had to be residents of the

village where the well was dug and in need of relief. The land owners
were to furnish the materials. The average labor cost was about $30.00
per well; the material cost about the same. Red Cross aid was given for
3,572 wells in the six hsien. Of these 463 were in Ting Hsien. Our investigators reported that, because families applying for aid had to be
investigated and a tablet had to be attached to the well showing that
it had been dug with Red Cross help, many families were unwilling to
accept the offered help. However, the offer of foreign aid stimulated the
Industrial Bureau of the hsien government to offer similar assistance to
those who wanted to dig wells. At that time the Industrial Bureau imported some well digging machines that expedited the work, after the
local workers had learned the necessary technique. Later Mr. Mi Chu-
wu, the village head of Chai Ch'eng, bought a machine for use in that
area and went to the neighboring villages to urge the farmers to dig
additional wells. Residents of Chai Ch'eng paid $7.00 for the use of the
machine. Other villages paid $12.00. In 1923 the Industrial Bureau sent
two of the Chai Ch'eng well diggers to Ts'ao Chou Fu in Shantung to
teach the people there the new technique.

How the impetus given to well digging by the drought of 1920–21
continued during the next decade is indicated by the C.I.F.R.C. figures
showing when the irrigating wells were dug.

	Number	Per Cent
Before 1915	13,876	34.7
1916–1920	5,778	14.5
1921–1925	9,771	24.4
1926–1930	10,554	26.8
	39,979	100.0

More than 50 per cent were dug after 1920.

In a study of the wells in three villages we found that 60 per cent of
the 471 irrigating wells were dug from 1921 to 1928 and another 23 per
cent from 1912 to 1920. Twenty-five wells, 5.2 per cent, were reported
to have been dug before 1894. The oldest one was said to date from the
reign of the Emperor Chia Ch'ing (1797–1820).

It was a very different story for the 183 domestic wells. Only 14 of
those, 7.7 per cent, had been dug after 1920. Forty-four, 24 per cent,
were dug between 1912 and 1920. Fifty-six, 31 per cent, were at least
thirty-five years old, dug before 1894. Five were said to have been dug
before 1796. The oldest was reported to be more than 265 years old, dug

during the reign of Shun Chih (1644–61). At least one well was reported to have been dug during the reign of each of the Ch'ing emperors except Yung Cheng (1723–1735).

Eighty-eight per cent of the Ting Hsien wells were curbed with brick, 8 per cent with earth, and 4 per cent with other material. When a new well that was to be brick curbed was some 10 feet deep, a circular willow wheel, several inches in width and up to 10 feet in diameter, depending on the size of the well, was hung by heavy ropes from timbers placed across the mouth of the well. The brick curbing was built up on this willow wheel. As the well was deepened the wheel and bricks were gradually lowered so that when the well was finished it was curbed from top to bottom.

Almost 55 per cent of the wells had a bottom diameter of from seven to ten feet; most of the others were between four and seven feet. There were a few smaller wells and a very few larger.

The top diameter of the wells, regularly considerably smaller than the bottom, was largely determined by whether the water was to be lifted by an animal driven Persian wheel or by a one, two, or three wheel hand windlass. Sixty-one per cent of the wells had a top diameter of from four to six feet. Almost all the others were between two and four feet. The wells were generally stone capped.

Our investigators reported that in 1928 it cost about $80 to dig a three wheel well, $55 for a two wheel well, and $38 for a one wheel well. For the three wheel well the expenses were $5.00 for the wooden wheel, $40 for some 3,500 bricks, $6.00 for the stone mouth, and other expenses about $30. The labor amounted to about 50 days' work. For the two wheel wells the wood wheel cost $3.50, the 2,800 bricks some $34. The one wheel well required only some 1,700 bricks. The C.I.F.R.C. study reported the average cost of the irrigating wells as $65.70, about $3.00 per foot of depth. Our study of 471 irrigation wells gave 54 days' work as the average digging time. For domestic wells inside the villages the average was 33 days' work.

A hand windlass, made of elm wood, cost from $1.50 to $2.00. The water baskets cost 55 cents each. The tripod for a one wheel well cost from $1.00 to $2.00, for a two wheel well from $1.20 to $2.00, and for a three wheel well from $2.00 to $3.00. A level pole, used on shallow wells, cost from $1.70 to $2.60. For the Persian wheels used to lift water by animal power we had a variety of quotations varying all the way from $50 to $150. The length of lift and the number of metal buckets in the lifting chain would naturally be a large factor.

Our field workers reported that a Persian wheel could irrigate from three to three and a half mu per day, three hand wheels from four to five mu, two hand wheels from three and a half to four mu, and one hand wheel from one to one and a half mu. The C.I.F.R.C. estimate was Persian wheel five mu per day, one windlass three mu, and level pole three mu per day.

The estimated daily operating cost was level pole 72 cents, windlass 59 cents, and Persian wheel $1.11. The average cost per mu was level pole 24 cents, windlass 19 cents, and Persian wheel 22 cents. Very little if any of these costs would represent cash outlay for the farmer as the level pole and windlass irrigating was regularly done by hand by members of the family and the family cow or donkey could run the Persian wheel without adding very much to the farm budget.

The C.I.F.R.C. engineers estimated that the standard well seven to eight feet in diameter with some six feet of water would produce enough water to irrigate more than 16 mu. The larger wells, if they were drawing from loose soil, could furnish enough water for from 30 to 40 mu, occasionally for more than 50 mu. The smaller wells would irrigate some 10 mu. In our study of 471 wells in three villages the average was 22 mu per well with one-quarter providing water for less than 15 mu and another quarter for from 30 to 55 mu. The details are given in Table 74.

If a standard well produced enough water to irrigate more than 16 mu of land, and the average size of the fields owned by a sample 200 families was 4.2 mu, and 68.9 per cent of the fields contained less than 5 mu and 92.8 per cent less than 10 mu, one wonders what arrangements, if any, were made for sharing the available water with the owners of adjacent fields. We know that in some instances the owners of small plots joined in digging community wells. Experience seemed to show, however, that this could lead to difficulties, for in some reports on the activities of the village government it was noted that one of the duties of the village elders was to see that the joint owners took their turns in looking after the wells and that the wells were properly protected against freezing and other winter damage. No figures were available giving any estimate of the amount of joint digging or the sharing of any surplus water.

It was estimated that the 40,000 irrigation wells could furnish water for some 55 per cent of the Ting Hsien farm area. To provide for the remaining acreage, if it were all suitable for irrigation, would require at least another 30,000 wells. Many of these apparently could be advantageously dug, for all the reports showed that irrigated land was generally worth more than twice the unirrigated land and that the added crop value from 16 mu would ordinarily be enough to pay for the well in about one year. Even so, most of the families would need help in financing a capital improvement of that size.

TABLE 72. WELLS PER VILLAGE, 1930

Wells	Villages	Per Cent	Wells	Villages	Per Cent
1–9	5	1.1	150–199	36	8.0
10–19	33	7.3	200–299	37	8.2
20–39	77	17.0	300–399	32	7.1
40–59	65	14.3	400–499	11	2.4
60–79	48	10.6	500–599	9	2.0
80–99	30	6.6	600 and over	5	1.1
100–149	65	14.3	Total	453	100.0

TABLE 73. WELLS PER DISTRICT

District	Inside Village	Families Per Well	Outside Village	Mu per Well	Total Wells
1	2,484	2.6	2,918	49	5,402
2	2,195	3.7	3,090	59	5,285
3	2,815	5.8	5,883	58	8,698
4	3,132	5.0	11,834	27	14,966
5	3,057	2.6	5,453	27	8,510
6	5,729	2.3	10,621	25	16,350
	19,412		39,799		59,211
Average	43	3.5	88	35	131

TABLE 74. AMOUNT OF LAND IRRIGATED BY 471 WELLS IN THREE VILLAGES

Mu	Wells	Per Cent	Mu	Wells	Per Cent
Under 5	23	4.9	30–39	108	22.9
5–9	50	10.6	40–49	15	3.2
10–19	114	24.2	50 and over	2	0.4
20–29	159	33.8	Total	471	100.0

TABLE 75. NUMBER OF PEOPLE DRAWING DOMESTIC WATER FROM WELLS

Persons	Wells	Persons	Wells
Under 10	21	50–59	6
10–19	52	60–69	2
20–29	47	100 and over	1
30–39	36	No data	6
40–49	12	Total	183

TABLE 76. DISTANCE OF WELLS FROM LATRINES

Distance	Wells	Distance	Wells
Under 10 ft.	7	60–69	12
10–19	22	70–79	3
20–29	41	80–89	3
30–39	40	100 and over	4
40–49	18	No data	18
50–59	15	Total	183

CHAPTER XII

Farm Operation—Costs and Returns

D EMONSTRATION farmers of the Mass Education Movement were enlisted to keep complete accounts for some of their fields during the crop year of 1930. From their records we have endeavored to secure cost and production figures on barley, buckwheat, corn, cotton, millet, and wheat in order to determine the approximate profit or reward of management accruing to Ting Hsien farmers. The demonstration farmers had been selected from the better graduates of the Movement's Peoples' Schools, had taken at least one of the short courses of the Movement's agricultural school, and had been appointed to demonstrate the approved methods of growing their special crop. They kept day by day records of their operations on their demonstration fields. Their records were totaled and then figured on a per mu basis. One series of reports was secured from farms in the Experimental District, a second from farms in the area around the city. The first series included reports on 28 plots of millet, 25 of wheat, 17 of buckwheat, 31 of barley, and 40 of cotton. In the second series were 44 fields of corn, 50 of barley, and two millet groups of 25 plots each. The total number of records studied was 285. The total area was 1,531.9 mu.

The individual fields varied in size from one to 55 mu, but only 36 were over nine mu, or one and one-half acres. One-half of the larger fields were in the third millet series. The average field had 5.4 mu, the median field 3.5 mu. For the different series the average fields were:

Barley 1	2.3 mu	Millet 1	5.5 mu
" 2	2.4	" 2	8.0
Buckwheat	4.3	" 3	17.5
Corn	4.3	Wheat	5.1
		Cotton	4.1

The cost items recorded included rent, seed, fertilizer, and labor. The rent was the amount paid for the use of the land if it was leased or the rent value if the land was owned by the farmer. The labor cost was sub-divided into the amounts used for plowing, seeding, applying fertilizer, irrigating, cultivating, and harvesting. Much of the labor used was naturally that of the farm family or the farm animals. For this it was necessary to set an arbitrary value, approximately the average of the current labor market. The amounts used per day were:

Man: 50 cents	Horse or mule: 60 cents
Woman or boy: 25 cents	Donkey or cow: 40 cents
Child: no charge	

In this study no attempt was made to set any cost for the use of the farm tools. A study of another group of families (see Chapter III) gave the average value of the tools as $1.25 per mu, and the cost of tool re-pair as three cents per mu. Depreciation of 10 per cent per year added to repairs would make the average tool cost amount to 16 cents per mu. This amount has been included as one of the cost items. Taxes have been entered as 10 cents per mu, the average amount of the hsien tax. No figures were available for village taxes.

It will be noted that most of the items listed as crop expense involve little if any expenditure of money by the farm family since they also can be listed as family income. This is particularly true of labor and rent. On the smaller farms no hired labor was used and land in Ting Hsien was 87.8 per cent owner operated.

The farms studied were samples of a fairly wide area for usually there were not more than one or two demonstration farmers for a crop in any village. The 40 cotton records came from 37 villages, the 50 barley rec-ords from 23 villages, the 28 millet records from 25 villages, the 17 buckwheat records from 15 villages.

As might be expected in a series of this sort, there was a wide vari-ation in the average amounts reported spent for the different items for the various crops. There was an even wider range in the amounts re-ported by the farmers growing the same crops. In some instances the largest amount reported for one particular item was as much as 10 or even 20 times the least amount reported. More generally the highest amount was three, four, or five times the lowest. Some of the differences were possibly due to some incomplete reporting. Others were definitely due to differences in the location and type of the soil, to different farm-ing methods, and to differences in the crop rotation system. The averages, however, seem to give a fair approximation of the total cost and gross and net returns for the different crops.

The averages given in Column 10 of Table 77 have been determined by weighting the averages for the different crops according to the hsien area planted to the six crops included in this study. Their area amounted to 60 per cent of the total crop mu in the hsien and almost 75 per cent of the total crop area. The weighting factors were millet 45, wheat 29, cotton 11, corn 6, barley 5, buckwheat 4.

The rent figures have been adjusted to reflect single or double cropping of the farm area. Fifty per cent was charged to each crop when there was double cropping, 100 per cent when there was single cropping. Barley and wheat are winter crops and are generally followed by a second crop. Cotton is regularly the only crop. Buckwheat is a second crop. Millet and corn may be the only crop or part of a double crop system. Rent for the cotton land ranged from $4.00 to $8.00 per mu. The year's rent for the land planted with buckwheat ranged from $3.00 to $5.50 per mu. For the wheat land it varied from $3.00 to $8.00 per mu. As the records were all for irrigated land, it seems evident that the usual rent, or rent value for such land, varied from $3.00 to $8.00 per mu per year, with the average about $4.80 or $5.00 per mu. From the rent figures, it seems probable that the index of double cropping for these farms was about 145. For the hsien it was 128.

Judging from the average cost of plowing, approximately 34 cents per mu, a man and a horse could plow a little more than three mu per day. From the records it would appear that the Ting Hsien farmers did extra plowing for cotton and buckwheat. We wonder if the 55 cents a mu reported by the millet farmers in the Experimental District was for deeper plowing, done as a result of longer contact with the Mass Education Movement's agricultural program. For the other millet groups the amounts were 20 and 39 cents per mu.

The value of the fertilizer used averaged $2.08 per mu. Barley, wheat, and cotton generally were given more than the other crops although the highest average for any one of the different crop groups was for the Experimental District millet. The cost of the labor for applying the fertilizer averaged 39 cents per mu, with the largest amounts reported for cotton and wheat.

The cost of the seed used showed a wide variation in the amounts planted. For most of the crops the heavy seeders used about twice as much as those who used the least amount. The average amount used was about one-tenth of a tou of millet, one-sixth of a tou of corn, one-fifth of a tou of buckwheat, six-tenths of a tou of wheat, and three-quarters of a tou of barley per mu. The average expenditure for seed was 28 cents per mu, but for millet it was only six cents, while for wheat it was 63 cents. The labor used to plant the seed averaged 32 cents per mu. The largest amount of labor was reported for barley, the smallest for corn and millet.

Irrigation from wells was used for all of the crops except buckwheat. The average cost was $1.06 per mu if the buckwheat area is omitted. The Experimental District millet farmers reported the smallest irrigation expenditure. We wonder whether this was related to the largest expenditure for plowing and for fertilizer. It was estimated that a man, working with a hand windlass, could irrigate about three mu per day at a cost of some 19 cents per mu. A Persian wheel, powered by an animal, could irrigate five mu at a cost of some 22 cents per mu.[1]

The mid-season cultivation cost of 63 cents per mu represented about one-half day's time of a man and an animal. Cotton required the most cultivation, corn and wheat the least.

Harvesting required an average of less than a day's labor per mu. A man could harvest some four mu of corn per day but only two of barley and one of cotton. It is difficult to see why harvesting should cost one millet group only 15 cents per mu and another 85 cents per mu and why one barley group should spend more than twice as much as the other. Differences in the distance the crops had to be hauled to the threshing floor would account for only a small part of the discrepancy.

The total average labor cost ($3.06 per mu) from plowing to harvesting represented some six man days of labor. Corn and buckwheat had the smallest labor cost, cotton and barley the largest.

The total production cost of the grains including rent, seed, fertilizer, and labor averaged, for these farms, $8.60 per mu. The corn and buckwheat farmers reported the smallest expense, the barley growers the largest. For cotton the expense was $12.35 per mu. Single crop rent and large use of fertilizer were mainly responsible for the extra expenditure for cotton.

1. China International Famine Relief Commission, Series B #49, *Well Irrigation in West Hopei,* Preliminary Report, December, 1931.

The production from the individual plots showed a wide range varying from 3.5 to 16 tou per mu for wheat and from 6 to 30 tou for corn. The averages for wheat, corn, barley, and millet were, however, similar. They all were between the 12 tou for wheat and the 13.6 tou for millet. Buckwheat averaged only 7.5 tou. Cotton production varied from 70 to 140 catties per mu, except for one farm that produced only 16 catties. Something very unusual must have happened to that plot. The cotton average was 95 catties per mu or approximately 750 pounds per acre.

The straw, stalks, and dried vines all had enough value to be counted as part of the farm production. The amounts reported varied from a minimum of 37 catties for one buckwheat farm to a maximum of 500 catties for a millet farm. For buckwheat the average was 105 catties. For wheat it was 145 catties. For barley and millet it was some 250 catties per mu. Beans grown on two millet plots and cabbage grown on five buckwheat plots were included in the by-products.

The prices quoted for the farm products varied to a considerable degree, possibly reflecting differences in quality and also possibly a market to market difference in price. The averages per tou were barley 63 cents, buckwheat 93 cents, corn 65 cents, millet 66 cents, and wheat $1.04. For cotton the average was 14.3 cents per catty. These prices were all considerably higher than the 1931 figures found in our hsien wide crop study. (See Chapter X, Table 70.) A weighted index number for the five grains showed a 20 per cent drop in 1931.

In Peking the 1931 weighted index number for the food items included in the working class family budgets was 17.3 per cent below the 1930 figure. In Tientsin the drop was 8.5 per cent.[2]

The average prices per 100 catties for the by-products were barley 46 cents, buckwheat 39 cents, corn 39 cents, wheat 42 cents, millet 65 cents, and cotton 95 cents. Beans were quoted at $1.00 and $1.20 per tou, cabbage at three, four, and five cents per catty.

The grains produced an average gross income of $9.50 per mu. Of this, $8.20 was for grain and $1.30 for straw and other products including a few beans and a little cabbage. The gross income from cotton was $14.85 per mu, considerably more than for any of the grains, but this was offset by the higher rent and cultivation costs.

Corn gave the largest average net return. Barley was the only crop

2. National Tariff Commission, *The Shanghai Market Prices Report*, Shanghai, October–December, 1933.

to show a loss but the profit from wheat was only three cents per mu. The best wheat farmer had a profit of $8.39 per mu. The poorest wheat crop showed a loss of $4.63 per mu. The largest loss reported by any farmer was $6.82 per mu for barley. The largest single gain was $14.57 per mu from corn.

The figures show that the average farm family received most of its income from the rent value of its land and the value of its labor. Its profits from its farming operations were relatively small. With the drop in prices in 1931 they would practically disappear.

TABLE 77. FARM COSTS AND CROP VALUE PER MU

	Barley 1	Barley 2	Buck-wheat	Corn	Millet 1	Millet 2	Millet 3	Wheat	Cotton	Weighted Average
Labor:										
Plowing	$0.29	$0.30	$0.46	$0.23	$ 0.55	$0.20	$ 0.39	$0.23	$ 0.46	$ 0.34
Seeding	.45	.66	.28	.14	.39	.10	.24	.36	.49	.32
Fertilizing	.43	.39	.59	.15	.40	.26	.19	.45	.71	.39
Irrigating	1.33	2.18	—	1.40	.80	1.05	1.22	.97	.91	1.01
Cultivating	.39	.94	.48	.31	.81	.70	.41	.33	1.05	.58
Harvesting	.52	.24	.71	.13	.85	.15	.21	.42	.51	.42
Total labor	3.41	4.71	2.52	2.36	3.80	2.46	2.66	2.76	4.13	3.06
Rent	2.23	1.85	2.17	1.83	2.33	3.22	4.46	3.03	5.25	3.23
Seed	.43	.49	.21	.10	.09	.06	.05	.63	.24	.28
Fertilizer	2.17	2.42	1.28	1.49	2.88	1.72	1.88	2.39	2.47	2.08
Implements and taxes	.26	.26	.26	.26	.26	.26	.26	.26	.26	.26
Total cost	8.50	9.73	6.44	6.04	9.36	7.72	9.31	9.07	12.35	8.91
Crop value	7.08	7.60	7.00	8.47	9.38	8.48	8.73	8.49	13.57	9.16
By-products	.63	1.68	1.07	.86	2.05	1.29	2.02	.61	1.28	1.28
Total products	7.71	9.28	8.07	9.33	11.73	9.77	10.76	9.10	14.85	10.44
Net return	(0.79)	(0.45)	1.63	3.29	2.37	2.05	1.44	0.33	2.50	1.53

PART 4. FINANCE, BUSINESS, AND INDUSTRY

CHAPTER XIII

Money, Exchange, and Credit

S ILVER AND COPPER coins and paper notes, representing silver and copper coins, were the money current in Ting Hsien at the time of our
study. The generally accepted standard of value was the minted silver
yüan (dollar), which, according to the law promulgated in 1910, contained seven mace and two candareens (0.72 Chinese ounces) of silver
890 fine. The Imperial or Dragon Dollars, coined before 1911, were 900
fine. The copper unit was the cash.

In earlier days retail transactions and the general economic activity
of the people was carried on in terms of copper cash with one tiao, 1,000
cash, the standard unit. For wholesale transactions the tael, ordinarily
defined as one Chinese ounce of silver bullion, was the monetary unit.
Actually there were several different kinds of taels of varying weight and
fineness. The more convenient dollar, of standard weight and quality,
gradually displaced the tael and silver gradually replaced copper as
the general standard of value because of the depreciation of the copper
coinage, especially after 1920 when the war lords were in control of the
North China mints. In 1923 the cotton gild changed its price for cotton cloth from copper to silver. In 1930 only the prices of the cheapest
farm products such as carrots, onions, and other vegetables, whose
prices were less than two cents per catty, were regularly quoted in copper.

Several different kinds of dollars were in circulation but they were
generally accepted as of equal value. The fractional silver coinage, 10-
cent, 20-cent, and 50-cent pieces, known as "little money", did not circulate at par but at a discount which, for some coins, was more than 15
per cent. The amount of the discount was not fixed, but depended on the
quality of the coins, the supply available, and the demand. The Imperial
fractional silver was discounted more than the Republican Yuan

Shih-kai fractional coins. Because of the difference the former was sometimes known as "little little money", the latter as "big little money".

The copper coins were the single cash, small cast coins with a square hole in the center, and minted 10-cash and 20-cash pieces. There were also some brass 50-cash and 100-cash coins, which had been minted in Szechuan.

The single cash coins, which weighed about 6.5 pounds per 1,000, had long been the standard copper coin, but because of their small value and the difficulty of counting, handling, and transporting them, they had generally been displaced by the other copper coins of higher value and had practically disappeared from Ting Hsien by 1930. During the earlier part of our study both the 10-cash "copper" and the 20-cash double "copper" were in general circulation, but by 1931 the 20-cash pieces were rapidly displacing the single "coppers". It was the old story of bad money driving out good. Even five years earlier the amount of copper in the large coins was seldom twice that in the smaller. In a chance collection of over four hundred "coppers" the 10-cash pieces ranged in weight from 97 to 112 grains and the 20-cash pieces from 155 to 199 grains. The majority of the single "coppers" weighed between 100 and 106 grains and the majority of the double "coppers" between 170 and 176 grains. In only one case was the weight of a double "copper" twice that of a single "copper". Generally they weighed 60 to 70 per cent more. The lightest double "copper" weighed only 20 per cent more than the heaviest single "copper".[1]

The paper notes in circulation represented copper cash, silver dollars, and fractional silver currency. They were issued by various banks. Some of these were foreign banks; some were Chinese owned; some were privately managed; some were under Chinese government control.

Exchange

One copper cash was supposed to be equal to one one-thousandth of a silver tael, but it seldom had that exact value. There was a constantly fluctuating tael-cash exchange rate that went up and down, sometimes as much as 20 per cent in one year's time. These variations in the silver-copper exchange could not help but be a factor in the

1. T. P. Meng and S. D. Gamble, "Prices, Wages and the Standard of Living in Peking", *Chinese Social and Political Science Review*, July, 1926.

economic life of Ting Hsien. They also made it possible for not a few people to earn their living changing money.

Old record books of the hsien government and the account books of stores in the city made it possible for us to trace the history of the silver-copper exchange rate for seventy-five years from 1857, the 7th year of Hsien Feng, through 1931, the 20th year of the Republic. The 1857–1928 figures, taken from the yamen account books, were secured during the early part of our study. Later the 1929–1931 rates were added from the records of a city exchange shop. For 1928 the yamen rate and the exchange shop rates differed by less than 1.5 per cent. To make sure that, through the years, the government rate was not a special official rate and different from that used in ordinary business transactions, we compared the yamen rates for some thirty years with those recorded in store account books. There was some difference between the rates but it was a small one. It is felt, therefore, that the changes in the official rate gave a good history of the silver-copper exchange rate and that the record was not materially altered by our using the more readily available exchange shop figures for the last three years, 1929–1931. Our figures are the average of the available quotations for each year.

From 1857 through 1913, the hsien accounts were all in terms of taels and cash. Dollars appeared in the accounts in 1914. For a time the two silver units, taels and dollars, were used, but later, by official order, the use of the tael was discontinued.

In order to give the record from 1857 through 1931 in terms of a single standard, the cash-tael rates have been converted into cash-dollar rates at 0.72. Figure 19 shows the changes in the cash-tael rates from 1857 to 1914 and in the cash-dollar rates for the entire 75 years from 1857 through 1931. Table 78 gives the figures for the cash-dollar rates.

In 1857 the average exchange rate was 1,518 cash per tael. The dollar equivalent was 1,093 cash. In 1931 the average was 4,090 cash per dollar, an increase of almost 275 per cent in 75 years. The highest rate, 4,400 cash per dollar, in the second month of 1929, was just over four times the average for 1857. In the first month of 1932 the rate was 3,870 cash per dollar.

During the last five years of the reign of Hsien Feng, 1857–1861, there was a 20 per cent increase in the exchange rate. It is rather sur-

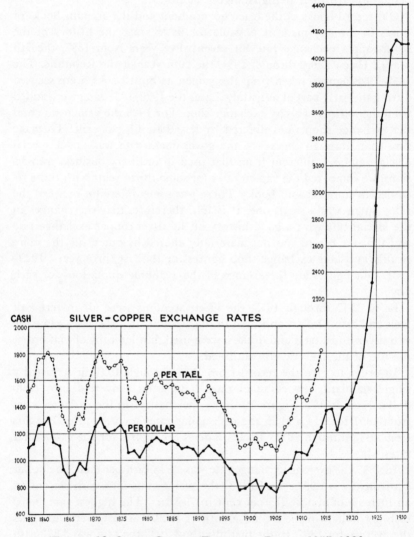

FIGURE 19. SILVER-COPPER EXCHANGE RATES, 1857–1930

prising that the Ting Hsien rate was not more seriously affected, for there was serious inflation in Peking. It was during those years that the Imperial forces were struggling with the T'ai P'ing rebels and with foreign invasion. Peking was captured by the foreign forces on September 21, 1860. The T'ai P'ing forces cut off Peking's supply of copper from the mines in Yunnan, so the capital had to make its coins from iron. That, plus the war expenditure, brought on the inflation.

Improvement of the copper coinage was evidently a high priority item on the program of the Emperor T'ung Chih when he came to the throne for the exchange rate dropped almost one-third, from 1,269 to 875 cash per dollar, in the first four years of his reign, 1862–1865. The improvement did not last, however, for by the end of his reign, 1874, the rate was back to 1,219 and had been up to 1,304 in 1871.

During the first five years of K'uang Hsü's reign, 1875–1879, the copper coinage again improved, for the exchange rate dropped almost 20 per cent. Most of this came, however, in 1877, which was a famine year in North China. During the next 15 years after 1879 there was little change in the rate. For only five of those years was the rate more than 3.5 per cent above or below the rate of the previous year. The 1894 rate was only nine cash more than the rate in 1879. From an intermediate peak in 1892 the rate dropped, with some fluctuation, until in 1905 it reached the lowest point in the 75 years, 757.8 cash per dollar. This was a drop of 33.3 per cent in 13 years. The 1905 rate was 42 per cent below the rates for 1861 and 1871 and 30.7 per cent below the 1857 rate. The fighting and disturbed conditions of Boxer year brought only a small increase, just over 2 per cent.

For the 24 years after 1905 the rate increased every year but three. Two of the three years were after Hsüan Tung ascended the throne in 1909. This was the third time in succession that the rate went down at the beginning of the reign of a new emperor. The third year with a decrease was 1917, when war conditions raised the price of copper to the point where the bullion value of the cash was above their monetary value. They were bought up in large quantities by the Japanese, melted down, and shipped out of the country. As a result the silver-copper rate went down 12.5 per cent. It went up again the next year and the average for 1918 was only five cash below that for 1916.

The political and economic difficulties of the Republic were reflected in the declining value of the copper coinage. It went down every

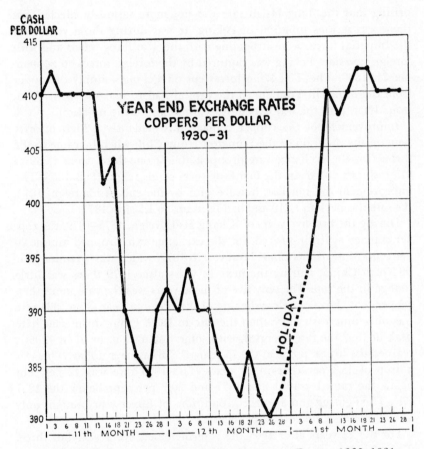

FIGURE 20. YEAR END SILVER-COPPER EXCHANGE RATES, 1930–1931

year but one from 1912 until after the Nationalist forces captured Peking in 1928 and unified the country. When the "war lords" had control of the local mints they profited by reducing the bullion content of the copper coins they issued. From 1920 to 1928 the exchange rate went up 180 per cent. After 1922 there were four successive years with increases of 16.5, 17.4, 25.0, and 22.3 per cent, an overall total of 109 per cent in four years.

The Nationalist government promptly moved to control the coinage for within seven months after the capture of Peking the exchange rate started to go down in Ting Hsien. It dropped 12 per cent in the next 35 months.

From the low point in 1905 to the peak in 1929 the exchange rate increased 469 per cent. From 1857 to 1929 the increase was 295 per cent. In 75 years, 1857–1931, the rate went up 275 per cent.

A comparison of the Ting Hsien and Peking exchange rates showed that from 1862 until 1877 the Ting Hsien rate was the higher. Peking did not have the 1876–1882 dip and rise. From 1882 to 1900 the two rates followed similar declining trends. The Peking rate reached its lowest point in 1900, Boxer year, five years before Ting Hsien. From 1900 to 1915 the Peking rate was higher. From 1918 to 1931 the Ting Hsien rate was regularly higher but both rates had practically the same rapid increase. In 1930 they were only 20 cash (two coppers) apart, 4,080 and 4,100. From 1915 through 1930 Ting Hsien's yearly rate ranged from 97 to 106 per cent of the Peking rate. Except for 1928 and 1929 the variation was not over 3.5 per cent, a very close agreement.

How the extra demand for money at Chinese New Year's time affected the exchange rate is shown in Figure 20. It gives the rates for the Ting-hsien market days of the 11th and 12th months of 1930 and the 1st month of 1931. The rate dropped 23 per cent from the first of the 11th month to the end of the 12th month, but by the eleventh of the 1st month it was back to the original rate, 410 coppers per dollar.

As the city markets were set according to the lunar calendar the exchange shops usually operated on the same basis. In 1930 they attempted to follow the solar calendar but it did not work out well and they went back to the lunar calendar in 1931.

Credit

Credit was provided in Ting Hsien by pawn shops, mutual savings societies, cooperative credit societies, and private lenders. There were no banks in the hsien at the time of our study. The pawn shops were found only in the towns. Mutual savings societies were, as their name implies, for regular savings over a long period of time rather than for short term loans. Cooperative credit societies could be organized under the Chinese law and some were very successful in providing credit at low rates of interest, but they were a new type of organization still largely in the promotion stage and so were not a large factor in the credit field. The village people who needed financial help had to depend, for the most part, on private money lenders.

To sample the extent of borrowing in Ting Hsien, the amount of credit needed, the interest rates, the terms of the loans, the security for the loans, and use of the money borrowed, we made a study in 1932 of the borrowing during the three years 1929, 1930, and 1931 of the 526 families living in five villages. They were relatively small villages; the largest had 145 families, the smallest 41. As the figures for the individual villages did not show any significant differences the five villages have been treated as a single group of families.

The number and the proportion of families borrowing, the number of times they borrowed, the amounts they borrowed, and the increase in borrowing in two years are shown by the following figures:

| | 1929 | | 1930 | | 1931 | |
	Number	Amount	Number	Amount	Number	Amount
Families borrowing	171	$21,026	230	$34,401	305	$48,944
Per cent borrowing	32.5		43.7		58.0	
Average amount		123		150		160
Per cent under $150	74.3		73.1		69.2	
Per cent over $250	13.5		16.1		18.0	
Number of loans	335		466		726	
Average amount		63		74		67

The large proportion of families borrowing in 1931, 58 per cent, the 78 per cent increase in two years in the number of families borrowing, the 116 per cent increase in the number of loans made, the 30 per cent increase in the average family indebtedness, and the 133 per cent increase in the total amount borrowed were evidently the result of falling prices and of the extra taxes and assessments that accompanied the disturbed political conditions that culminated in the fighting around Ting Hsien in 1931. In the two years from 1929 to 1931 the wholesale prices of farm crops in North China declined 10.3 per cent, wheat 14.5 per cent, millet 16.5 per cent, and kaoliang 23.5 per cent.[2]

In 1929 just over one-half, and in 1931 two-thirds, of the borrowing families found it necessary to borrow more than once during the year. In 1929 two families borrowed six times and one borrowed seven

2. Nankai Institute of Economics, *Nankai Index Numbers* (Nankai University, Tientsin, 1934).

times. In 1931 three families borrowed nine different times. In 1929 three families had more than five loans. In 1930 the number was seven. In 1931 it was 16. The average number of loans per family borrowing was 2.0 in 1929 and 2.4 in 1931. Loans that were not paid before Chinese New Year were refunded and so were counted in the next year's totals.

The individual loans varied in amount from $1.00 to $5,000. The borrowers must have figured their needs very closely, for in 1931 there were 24 different amounts in the $1.00 to $30 range, 38 different amounts under $50, and 35 in the $50 and over range.

Approximately one-third of the individual loans were for $25 or less, a little more than a quarter were for amounts of from $26 to $50, and another quarter from $51 to $100. Those for more than $100 were some 12.5 per cent of the total. Only a little more than one per cent of the loans were for amounts in excess of $300.

The total amounts borrowed by the individual families varied from $1.00 to $5,000, but for more than half of the families the amount was less than $100. The following figures show the proportion of the borrowing families whose total loans were less or more than certain given amounts.

	1929 Per Cent	1930 Per Cent	1931 Per Cent
Under $ 50	35	28	29
Under 100	62	53	54
Under 150	74	73	69
Under 250	87	84	82
Over 500	1.2	2.6	3.9

We cannot relate the amounts of the loans to the income or the property of these families but we know that $100 represented approximately one-third of a year's income for a group of farm families with from 21 to 30 mu of land, approximately the average land holding for Ting Hsien. (See Chapter X.) The repayment of such an amount would be a heavy burden on the family budget, especially when coupled with a high interest charge.

The term of practically all of the loans was for one year or less. In 1931 less than one per cent were reported as being made for an indefinite time. According to the Chinese custom outstanding obligations must be settled before New Year's, so the ordinary short term loan would not be for more than one year. As cash was available from the fall harvest by the 10th month many of the loans were arranged to come due at that time. When crops were poor many of these 10-month loans, undoubtedly, were carried over to the end of the year and then refunded, with any unpaid interest added to the amount of the new loan. In our study, from 27 to 20 per cent of the loans were for 12 months, while 54 or 55 per cent were made for 10 months. In 1929 and 1930 only some seven per cent of the loans were for six months or less. In 1931 the figure was 11.3 per cent, both because of the increased number of families who had to borrow more than once during the year and because the fighting with its attendant taxes and assessments came during the seventh month.

The figures for the amounts borrowed were almost the same. From 26 to 18 per cent was borrowed for the full year. Ten months was the term for from 57 to 49 per cent. Evidently some three-quarters of the borrowing was regularly done around New Year's time. Unpaid loans must be refunded then. Purchasers of land, animals, and other capital goods often borrowed in order to take advantage of the lower prices regularly current at New Year's. If the loans for an indefinite term are counted as being borrowed for one year the average time the money was on loan was 9.85 months.

It seems probable that in an average year less than 7 per cent of the money was borrowed during the last half of the year, with the time of the loan six months or less. In 1929 and 1930 the figure was 6.1 and 4.7 per cent. In 1931 it was 8.4 per cent, largely because of the increase in the number of families who borrowed more than once during the year.

Interest on the loans varied from nothing to 3 per cent per month. In 1931 only four loans had a rate of less than one per cent per month. The $5,000 loan paid only 0.8 per cent per month. Just over one-third of the loans carried a rate of 2 per cent per month. Just under 25 per cent paid more than 2 per cent. From 2.5 to 3.3 per cent paid 3 per cent per month. While we found no such loans in our study, we were told that on very poor risk loans the interest rate was sometimes as much as 5 or even 10 per cent per month.

The interest rate was figured closely, by tenths of a per cent per month. Twenty-two different rates were reported. Nine-tenths, 1.1 and 2.9 were the only tenths that were missing from 0.8 to 3.0 per cent. The rate was 2.0 per cent per month for 22 per cent of the money borrowed. It was over 2.0 per cent per month for some 11 per cent of the money. In 1931 it was 3.0 per cent per month for only $364, 0.75 per cent of the total amount borrowed that year. The 3 per cent loans evidently were made under pressure of extreme need for small amounts of cash. The 23 loans made at that rate averaged only $15.80.

The average interest rate in 1929 was 1.82 per cent per month, 21.8 per cent per year. In 1931 it was 1.75 per cent, 21.0 per cent per year. The 1931 average was the lower because of the $5,000 loan made at 0.8 per cent per month.

We were interested to find that for some loans the interest was set in terms of millet rather than money, so many tou of millet to be paid as interest on a given loan. In 1929 there were 12 such loans for a total of $1,360. In 1931 there were 20 loans for $1,980. Changes in the price of millet reduced the rate in 1930 but increased it in 1931. The annual interest on one loan outstanding through the three years was 19.9 per cent in 1929, 19.2 per cent in 1930, and 20.4 per cent in 1931. The other interest rates changed in the same ratio. The principal of the millet interest loans apparently was fixed in dollars rather than in grain. In times of rapid inflation and unstable currency, loans, both principal and interest, are often made in terms of grain rather than money.

The total annual interest charge for the borrowing families amounted to some $8,315, an average of $27.15 per borrowing family per year. This may not seem like a large amount but it becomes large when compared with the average family income.

Table 82 shows the number of loans and the amounts borrowed for different purposes. The 228 per cent increase from 1929 to 1931 in the amount borrowed to refund old debts is particularly outstanding. The large increase in both the amount and the proportion of borrowing necessary to refund matured loans clearly indicates the financial difficulties of 1930 and 1931. The 100 per cent increase in the amount borrowed for farm capital seems to indicate that the lower prices in 1930 and 1931 encouraged some families to borrow and invest. The three items of debt refunding, farm capital, and business capital included from 75 to 78 per cent of the loans and from 77 to 83 per cent of the amount borrowed.

While there was a 250 per cent increase in the number of loans for weddings and funerals, there was a 40 per cent decrease, from $101 to $61, in the average amount borrowed. The difficult times that made it necessary for more families to borrow for these occasions may have reduced somewhat the amounts spent.

We were interested to have four loans listed as providing funds for the smuggling of narcotics. Our investigators must have had the confidence of the families to secure that information. The fact that they were able to get it makes us feel more sure of the accuracy of the other information secured by our credit survey.

The three loans for village expenses were made by village vice-heads to secure money needed for village expenses. The amount probably was repaid after the next village assessment. The loans for education probably were for the expense of children attending school outside of Ting Hsien, possibly higher middle school or college. Loans for daily living were evidently small amounts borrowed to tide over emergencies. The average loan was only some $29.

Loans ordinarily were evidenced by notes, the form of which depended upon the security offered. Land, buildings, or land and buildings were pledged for about one-quarter of the loans. One family pledged its house; three their houses and courtyards. The loan value of property was about 40 per cent of its current market value. About three-quarters of the loans were secured only by the borrower's personal note. Many of these borrowers, of course, owned land and their credit was such that they did not have to pledge a definite piece of land for their loans. The following figures show the division between secured and unsecured loans.

	1929		1930		1931	
Secured	89	$ 8,668	115	$11,751	159	$15,441
Unsecured	246	12,358	351	22,650	567	33,503
	335	$21,026	466	$34,401	726	$48,944
Per cent secured	26.6	41.2	24.7	34.2	21.6	31.6

One form of note generally used for a loan without security was:

——————, being in need of money, borrows from ————— of ————— village with —————, a middle-man, as witness, the sum of ————— dollars principal and interest. This amount is to be repaid on [date]. Oral agreements cannot be depended upon, therefore this written contract is signed.

Middle-man   Borrower

Or the interest might be fixed at a given rate per month. In that case the interest usually was made payable when the note matured, as in an agricultural community cash is not ordinarily available until harvest time. In a few instances, however, the interest was made payable monthly.

When property was pledged as security for a loan the note often read:

_____ being in need of money pledges the following piece of land [description giving location, size, boundaries, character] by the agreement of the two parties and the middle-man to _____ of _____ village for the sum of $_____ with interest at the rate of _____ per cent a month. On [date] the principal and interest will be paid. Oral agreements cannot be depended upon, therefore this written contract is signed.

<table>
<tr><td>_____</td><td>_____</td></tr>
<tr><td>Middle-man</td><td>Borrower</td></tr>
</table>

If a borrower had no land to pledge and had so few assets that the lenders were not willing to give him a loan on his unsecured note, he could sometimes persuade the middle-man to act as his guarantor and sign the note in that capacity rather than simply as a witness.

If a creditor found himself in difficulty over the payment of his notes the matter was generally arranged between the borrower and creditor with the help of the middle-man who had negotiated the original loan. Even if a settlement had to be made, because the debtor's assets would not provide the cash needed to cover his indebtedness, the matter would usually be arranged by the creditors without recourse to the hsien court. It was generally stated that the court was used to enforce the collection of a loan only where the borrower had pledged his land as security for more than one loan. In such case the debtor's property would be sold and the proceeds either pro-rated among the creditors or in some cases priority would be given to the first creditor. The debtor would be liable to punishment for misrepresentation.

In order to avoid this complication lenders sometimes insisted that the deeds of the pledged property be deposited with them. Holding the deeds would assure the lender that in case of a default, the proceeds of any sale would be applied to the repayment of his loan.

When loans were wanted for more than a year and when the borrower wanted to avoid the necessity of securing the money needed to pay the interest charge, farm land was often mortgaged to secure the loan. In that case the mortgagee took over the land and farmed it during the term of the mortgage. The rent value of the land replaced the usual interest charge. The amount of the loan given on mortgaged property was usually less than 50 per cent of the value of the land. As the rent value of farm land averaged some 6 or 7 per cent of its value,[3] mortgagors were paying more than one per cent per month on their loans.

The mortgage contract, generally a very simply worded document, ordinarily provided for a minimum time during which the property could not be redeemed. In a group of 46 mortgagor families we found one mortgage for five years, the rest for three years. The 46 mortgages covered 269 mu of land. We were told that irrigated land was usually mortgaged for five years, unirrigated land for three years.

It apparently was not obligatory for the mortgagor to redeem his property at any particular time. There was a term during which he could not redeem it, but if he did not have the money to pay the loan, he could let the mortgages run on more or less indefinitely. The land, of course, would remain in the possession and use of the mortgagee. The right to redeem the land could be passed on to the mortgagor's heirs.

The regulations of the hsien government called for the payment of a tax of 5.3 per cent on all mortgages, but from the field reports it was apparent that a great many mortgages were held without being recorded in the yamen, and so escaped the tax.

A government study of credit made in December, 1933, found that in Hopei province the average annual interest on cash loans was 29 per cent. This was somewhat higher than our figures for Ting Hsien, but it undoubtedly was affected by the fact that the government figures covered 109 hsien, many of which would not be as well-to-do as Ting Hsien. Furthermore the demand for credit very evidently increased from 1931 to 1933 because the wholesale prices of farm crops in North China, which had declined 10.3 per cent from 1929 to 1931, dropped 23.5 per cent[4] from 1931 to 1933. Many farms would be operated at a loss and more than the usual proportion of loans would have to be refunded. It was estimated that the value of farm land in Hopei went down some 30 per cent from 1931 to 1933. The government study found

3. See Chapter X.   4. Nankai Institute of Economics, *op. cit.*

the average annual interest rate in Shansi to be 46 per cent and in Shensi 51 per cent.[5]

Besides the 305 families who were borrowers, our credit survey found 53 families, just over 10 per cent of 526 families in the five villages, who were lending money. These families reported making some 800 loans in 1929 and some 900 loans in 1931. The number cannot be exact as one family reported making "about 500 loans". Other families reported making up to 50 loans, but for over one-half of the lending families the number was five or less. Approximately one-third of the families loaned less than $100 each. Over one-half loaned less than $250 each. In 1930 and 1931 only nine families loaned more than $500 each. Six of these loaned more than $1,000 each, but only one loaned more than $3,500. That family, however, reported that it had made loans totaling $37,000 in 1929, $38,000 in 1930, and $39,000 in 1931. This one family loaned 75 per cent more than the total borrowed by all the families in the five villages in 1929, and some $3,500 more than the total for 1930.

We were interested to see that a family able to lend money in such amounts had kept its headquarters in the village in spite of the possible drawbacks of life in the country. While we found, in our five sample villages, one family that could lend $39,000, it hardly seems probable that that was typical of the rest of the hsien. It does indicate, however, that families living in small villages could amass considerable fortunes.

The total amount loaned by all the lending families was approximately $51,000 in 1929, $58,000 in 1930, and $59,000 in 1931. The amount loaned by the families in the five villages increased 16 per cent from 1929 to 1931, but the amount borrowed increased 133 per cent.

The lending families undoubtedly spread their loans over many villages, other than the five included in our study. The number of loans they made in 1929 was nearly two and a half times the number of loans given all the borrowing families in the five villages. Even in 1931, with its big increase in borrowing, there was a surplus of nearly 200 loans and $10,000. There was, of course, nothing except geography to indicate that these lending families monopolized the lending in the five villages.

If the amounts borrowed by the families in the five villages studied

5. Ministry of Industries, Committee for the Study of Silver Values and Commodity Prices, *Silver and Prices in China* (Commercial Press, Ltd., Shanghai, 1935).

were typical of the rest of the hsien, the credit needs of Ting Hsien, omitting the city, totaled some $2,750,000 in 1929 and $6,250,000 in 1931.

Mutual Savings Societies

When, in 1917, Mr. Chang found himself in need of money to meet some special business expenses he went to thirty of his friends and relatives, told them of his need for funds, and invited them to join a mutual savings society. Such societies were very numerous in North China. They were popular because the members provided the capital sums that they used in turn and so avoided the expensive services of the money lender.

The thirty members of Mr. Chang's society were asked to meet at his house on the 18th of the seventh month. As they were coming at his request and were going to help him with his need for funds, Mr. Chang provided a feast for his friends. A feast was served at all subsequent meetings of the society, but after the first meeting each member paid his share of the expense. The cost in 1927 was $3.20 per table for eight, or 40 cents per person.

After the feast the members discussed the organization of the society, the rules and regulations. First of all it was decided that the society would meet every four months and that it would continue for ten years, the time necessary to have the number of meetings equal the number of members. As Mr. Chang needed 120,000 cash, it was decided that the society should be a 4,000 cash society and that each member should contribute 4,000 cash each time the society met. Mr. Chang, as the organizer of the society, was to receive the amount collected at the first meeting. The sums collected at subsequent meetings were to go to the other members of the society in turn.

The members might have decided by lot who should have the fund collected at each meeting, but instead they arranged that the members who had not received money from the society might bid for the privilege of receiving the amount to be collected at the next or, in some instances, at the current meeting. Each member was assigned a number. It was written on one side of a piece of paper; on the other side he wrote an amount that he would be willing to receive from the other bidding members. The lowest bidder was given the fund at each meeting. The total money he received was determined by the amount of his bid, the number of other bidders who would each contribute that

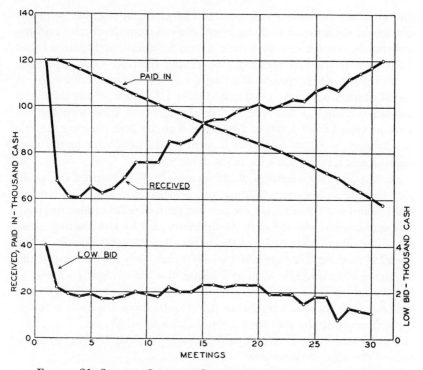

FIGURE 21. SAVINGS SOCIETY, COPPER VALUE OF AMOUNTS BID,
RECEIVED, AND PAID IN

amount, and the number of members who had previously had the fund, and therefore, paid 4,000 cash each.

Mr. Chang, as organizer and head of the society, opened the bids in the presence of the other members. The rules of the society provided that a member might change his bid at any time before the bids were opened, but once they were opened the bids had to stand. The bidding was evidently in units of one hundred cash (10 coppers). The rules did not say what was to be done in case there was a tie in the bidding, but we understand that the matter was decided by the drawing of lots. A member who was not present at a meeting could not receive the fund collected at that time, and he would have to arrange for someone to make his payment for him.

It was interesting to see how the amount of the bids changed through the ten years the society functioned. The changes, together with the changes in the amount each member received from the society and the amount he contributed to it, are shown in detail in Figure 21 and Table 84. At the first meeting, Mr. Chang received 4,000 cash from each member. At the second meeting the lowest bid was 2,200 cash. At the third meeting it was 1,900 cash. It was 1,700 cash for the sixth and seventh meetings. From the eighth through the 23rd meeting the amount varied from 1,800 to 2,300 cash. For the 24th meeting the low bid dropped to 1,500 cash, but it went up to 1,800 cash at the next meeting and was the same for the 26th meeting.

For the last four meetings of the society the bids dropped off, probably because so few were bidding and because the amount of the bid had less and less influence on the amount the successful bidder received. The amount bid affected only the amounts paid by the bidding members. The others, who had had the fund, all paid 4,000 cash each. For the 27th meeting the lowest bid was 800 cash, only 20 per cent of the original 4,000 cash. The member making that bid evidently wanted to be very sure that he would receive the fund at that meeting. This was the only time the bid went below 1,000 cash. From the 28th through the 30th meeting the bids were 1,300, 1,200, and 1,100 cash. At the 31st and final meeting the one unpaid member received 4,000 cash from each of the other 30 members.

The amounts received by the successful bidder at the different meetings showed a wide variation. The minimum was only 51.6 per cent of the maximum. Because the bidding determined the amount to be paid by a steadily declining number of members, and the number of 4,000 cash repayments increased at every meeting, the amount received varied much more than the bids. In fact, the size of the fund was different at every meeting. A bid of 1,900 cash brought a fund of 61,200 cash at the third meeting, but the same bid at the 23rd meeting made the fund 103,200 cash. Forty-two hundred cash more was received on a bid of 1,700 cash at the seventh meeting than on a bid of 1,800 cash at the fourth meeting. At the first meeting Mr. Chang received 120,000 cash, and the last member received 120,000 cash at the last meeting. Between those two meetings, the amounts varied from 60,600 cash, the amount secured at the fourth meeting with a bid of 1,800 cash, to 117,100 cash paid at the 30th meeting on a bid of 1,100 cash. Figure 21 and Table 84 show how the amount generally tended to increase meeting by meeting from the low point of the fourth meeting. Only six times in the next 27 meetings was the total less than the amount received by the successful bidder at the previous meeting.

From the way the amounts increased as the years went by, it would seem that a fairly set rate of discount was being figured on by the members. A special need for money such as a wedding or a funeral in the family might influence a member's bid and cause him to put in one lower than usual to insure his getting the fund at that particular meeting, but this apparently could be true in only one or two instances. The lowest bid at the 23rd meeting was 1,900 cash. At the next meeting it was 1,500 cash. For the 26th meeting the bid was 1,800 cash, but for the 27th meeting it was 800 cash.

Figure 21 and Table 84 also show the amounts each member paid in to the savings society over the ten years of its existence. The maximum was 120,000 cash, the minimum 57,800 cash. If the members are listed according to the meeting when they received their money from the society, the amount they paid in went down regularly after the second meeting. The later a member took the fund the less he contributed. The average decrease from one meeting to the next was 2,145 cash. The actual amounts were generally between 1,700 and 2,300 cash until the last four. Then the difference increased to 4,700, 2,500, 2,700, and 2,900 cash. The last man to take the fund paid in a total of 57,800 cash, or only 48.2 per cent of the 120,000 cash he received. He had a profit of 107.6 per cent on his investment.

The minimum return in per cent of the amount he contributed went to the man who took the fund at the third meeting. He received only 51.6 per cent of the sum he paid in. After that the per cent increased meeting by meeting. It was more than 72 per cent after the eighth, over 90 per cent for all the members who received the fund after the 13th meeting, and went above 100 per cent at the 16th meeting—the half-way point. The return was over 125 per cent after the 21st meeting, over 150 per cent after the 25th meeting, and over 180 per cent after the 28th meeting. It was over 200 per cent only for the last member.

Because of the varying amounts paid in at the meetings and the varying times at which the members took the fund, it is not easy to determine the average interest rate that the members apparently figured when they made their bids. The last man is the simplest to figure. His profit was 107.6 per cent on the 30 payments he had made during the

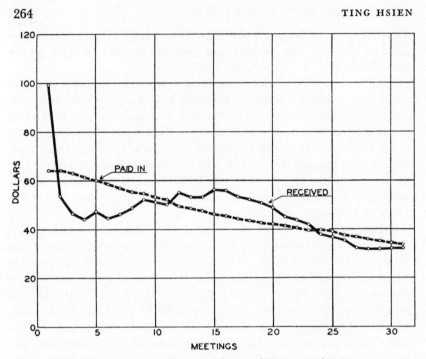

FIGURE 22. SAVINGS SOCIETY, SILVER VALUE OF AMOUNTS
RECEIVED AND PAID IN

10 years. At simple interest, his average return was 19.2 per cent per
year, or 1.6 per cent per month. At compound interest, compounded
every four months, the rate was just over 1.0 per cent per month. The
partial payments made by the second man work out at an interest rate
of just over 1.0 per cent per month with the interest being paid every
four months. The payments by the other members would probably
show similar rates, so it seems evident that even in a voluntary group
the people in this area in Ting Hsien felt that rates of 1.0 per cent per
month for compound interest and 1.5 per cent per month for simple
interest were not unduly high.

Prior to 1917 the silver-copper exchange rate was relatively stable
but after that the copper coinage depreciated so rapidly that the average
exchange rate went from 1,207.4 cash per dollar in 1917 to 3,750.7 cash
in 1927. All the savings society payments were made in terms of copper
cash, but as the change in the exchange rate could not help influencing

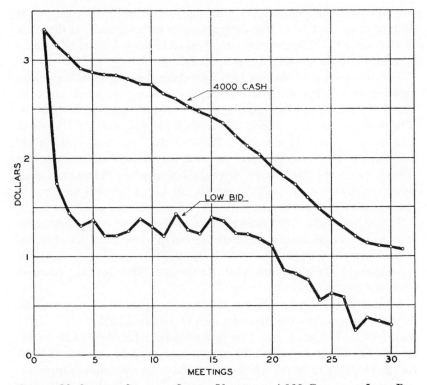

FIGURE 23. SAVINGS SOCIETY, SILVER VALUE OF 4,000 CASH AND LOW BID

the purchasing power of the sums the members paid to and received from the society, we have figured the silver equivalents of the copper figures. These are shown in Table 85 and Figures 22 and 23. Because of the rapid changes in the silver-copper exchange we have used interpolated figures for the spring and winter meetings and the annual averages for the fall meetings.

The 120,000 cash Mr. Chang received in 1917 was equivalent to $99.30. The 120,000 cash received by the last member in 1927 was worth only $32.00. In general the amounts paid to the successful bidders from the third to the ninth meetings ranged from $44.10 to $48.70. For the next eleven meetings the amounts were over $50.00, ranging from $50.50 to $56.00. Then the rapid depreciation of the copper currency caused a big drop in the value of the society's fund even though the number of cash increased at almost every meeting. From the $56.00 paid at the 15th meeting the silver value dropped every meeting until, at the 28th, it was only $31.60. Slight increases of 10 to 20 cents for the next three meetings brought the final value up to $32.00.

The silver value of the low bids followed a somewhat similar course (See Figure 23). The 4,000 cash of the first meeting were equivalent to $3.31. For the second meeting the 2,200 cash were equivalent to $1.74. The amount bid for the sixth and seventh meetings was equivalent to $1.21. For the 18th it was $1.22. Between these meetings the highest amount was $1.43, but that was the only time after the third meeting that the rate went above $1.40. After the 18th meeting the amount went down rapidly until, at the 27th meeting, the bid of 800 cash was equivalent to only 24 cents. For the 30th meeting the amount was 30 cents.

The value of the 4,000 cash paid at each meeting by the members who had received money from the society also declined steadily. In amount the decrease was from $3.31 for the first meeting to $2.91 for the fourth, $2.47 for the 14th, $1.91 for the 20th, $1.48 for the 24th, and $1.07 for the 31st meeting.

Because of the steady increase of the exchange rate, the silver value of the total amounts the different members contributed to the society also decreased steadily. Mr. Chang paid $64.21 for the $99.30 he received. The lowest bidder at the second meeting paid the most, $64.36 for the $53.60 he received. The later a member received money from the society the less he repaid in terms of both silver and copper. The 31st member invested $33.56 over the 10 years, just a little more than one-half the amount Mr. Chang contributed. He received, however, the equivalent of only $32.00, a loss of 4.5 per cent on his investment.

If we compare the silver value of the 30 payments made by each member with the value he received, we get some very interesting figures. Mr. Chang, who in terms of copper paid back the exact amount he received, returned in terms of silver only 64.7 per cent of the amount given him. If we invert the ratio, he received 155 per cent of the amount he paid. The member who took the fund at the fourth meeting received only 71.5 per cent of the amount he contributed. This was the lowest proportional return for the entire membership. After Mr. Chang, the man with the highest return was the one who was the successful bidder at the 16th meeting. He received 123.2 per cent of the amount he put in. After that, the ratio declined until the 23rd man received only 104 per cent of the amount he contributed over the 10 years. All of the last eight men received less than they paid. The lowest of this group was the 27th man. He received only 87.5 per cent of the amount he invested. He received a bit less on his investment than the man who took the fund at the eighth meeting and he got his money some six years later.

Because of the big change in the silver-copper exchange rate and its effect on the value of the funds that were received and repaid in copper, it is not possible to determine any interest factor in the silver figures. In fact, the last eight men had a definitely minus interest rate. The depreciation of the cash might have had some influence on the bidding of the later members, who may have felt that the sooner they took the fund the more it would be worth. However, this does not seem to be evident in the bidding except perhaps for the last four meetings, and there the small number bidding probably would have a larger influence.

Mr. Chang used the money he received from the savings society to meet some special business expenses. Three other members said they used the fund for the same purpose, four used it for family expenses, seven loaned the money to others, and one used it for the repayment of debt. Unfortunately there was no report from 15 members.

To insure the repayment of funds given to the members, the rules of the savings societies required that each member furnish two guarantors before he received money from the society. The member and his guarantors had to sign a receipt for the funds received. Some societies also required that the members pledge land as security for the amounts they received. Experience evidently had taught that more was needed than a member's promise to pay, especially when the period of repayment ran over several years. If a member was not present at a meeting the society looked to his guarantors for the payment of the amount due.

Mr. Chang's savings society was called a "Stationary Society" as all the meetings were held at his house. Another variety of society was known as a "Dry Stationary Society". This variety differed from a stationary society only in the fact that the head of the society made no repayment for the amount his fellow-members gave him at the first meeting. Instead, he paid all the expenses of the society including the cost of the feast served at each meeting. At 40 cents per member, which was apparently the current price in 1927, the cost of the feasts for 10 years would amount to some $372, or almost four times the value of the fund Mr. Chang received.

A third variety of savings society was known as a "Circulating Society" because it met in a different place each time. The place of meeting was decided by the bidding. The meeting was held in the home of the successful bidder. He not only was host, but he also paid the cost of the feast served the members when they met in his home. The rules of the society detailed the vegetables that should be served and the amount of meat and dried vegetables.

A fourth variety was called a "Dry Society". The members of a dry society generally met only twice and sometimes only once. Such a society was organized by an honest but poor farmer when he needed money. He asked his friends and relatives to organize a society and help him meet his debts. The amount the members paid depended on the need of the head of the society, the number of members, and sometimes on the member's relationship to the head of the society. The closer the relationship the more he might be asked to pay. The head of the society prepared a feast for the members attending the meeting and paid any other expenses. The society did not meet again until the head had enough money to pay back the amount he had received. In that happy event the society met, the head provided a feast for the members and paid off his debt.

The following are typical examples of the contracts and regulations for a stationary and a circulating society:

Stationary Savings Society Regulations

Mr. _____ has asked some relatives and friends to organize a savings society with _____ members. The society is to have _____ meetings every _____ months. The head of the society, Mr. _____, has received _____ dollars. At each meeting, bids shall be entered for the money to be received at the next meeting. Any member who takes money from the society must have two people to guarantee him. If a man who has had money from the society fails to pay an instalment, his guarantors must pay it for him. Any member who is not present at a meeting of the society cannot receive money from the society and should give his guarantors the money for his payment to the society. _____ dollars is to be paid for the feast at each meeting. If a man writes a wrong number in the bidding, there can be no argument over it, but a bid may be changed by word of mouth any time before the bids are opened. A member may not have his interest in the society apply on his debts to others. Oral agreements have no proof, so we have written this contract.

Amount Received: _____   _____ Head

Date: _____   _____ Guarantor

                                         _____ Guarantor

Circulating Savings Society Regulations

The following persons _____ have decided to form a circulating savings society and have adopted these regulations. The society shall have _____ meetings every year on the following dates: _____. At each meeting, bids shall be entered for the money to be collected at the following meeting. Any man receiving money from the society must have two guarantors. Anyone using the money must give land as security. If a man who has had money from the society is not present at a meeting, his guarantors must pay for him. If one who has not had money from the society is not present, he cannot receive money from the society. The year-round feast shall include vegetables, bean sprouts, green beans, cabbage, and egg plant. _____ catties of dried vegetables and _____ catties of meat shall be served. The bread and vegetables must be sufficient for the feast. All the members must obey the regulations. The one who receives the money will pay for the feast. Members must be present by noon when the feast will be served.

Amount Received: _____   _____ Head

Date: _____   _____ Guarantor

                                         _____ Guarantor

Three villages were studied in order to get an idea of the number of savings societies in the rural area where Mr. Chang lived. The number may not be complete, but we found 27 societies in the three villages. Seven were stationary societies, one was dry stationary, 18 were circulating, and one was a dry society. The total membership of the 27 societies was 1,093. The average membership was 32 for the stationary societies, and 38 for the circulating societies. The one dry society had 145 members, a surprisingly large group. The head of that society must have had large financial needs if he had to call on so many friends and relatives for help. The cost of a feast for that large a group would be a sizable item.

The number of male adults over 16 years of age living in the three villages was 1,650. The number of savings society members was, therefore, 60.6 per cent of the adult male population. This would not mean that 60.6 per cent of the males were members of a savings society, as some men were members of more than one society, but the figure is indicative of the popularity and prevalence of this cooperative method of providing capital funds for the rural people.

Some members summarized the good points of the savings societies as follows:

When it is difficult to get money in the village, the village people can help by organizing a society.

The societies provide funds at relatively low cost.

It is easy to pay in instalments.

Periodic payments encourage savings.

Money for debts or emergency needs can be secured through savings societies instead of by the sale of property.

The societies promote friendship among the men who come to the meetings and eat the feast together.

The guarantors insure the repayment of the sums given to the members.

The following bad points were mentioned by the members:

Some members cannot pay their instalments.

Sometimes members run away after they have had money from the society. (This seldom happens, however, because the society members are generally carefully chosen and are usually people of means and property.)

The feasts are relatively expensive and uneconomical.

The life of the society is usually so long that conditions are apt to change, members die or become poor.

Even if he would like to repay in advance the amount he received, a member cannot do so, but must continue to make periodic payments during the life of the society.

Cooperatives

To help bring financial relief to the farmers the Mass Education Movement encouraged the Alumni Association of the People's Schools to act as the nucleus for the organization of Self-Help Societies in the villages. It arranged with Bank of China and the Kincheng Bank to furnish credit, secured by the deposit of produce in centrally located warehouses, at a monthly interest rate of 0.85 per cent per month. The banks dealt directly with the societies and assisted in selling the former's produce when the market was favorable. It was reported that this arrangement brought the farmers a profit of some 25 per cent on the marketing of their 1933 wheat crop. In 1933–34 there were 295 Self-Help Societies.

It was intended that the Self-Help Societies should develop into Integrated Cooperative Societies that would provide for the purchasing, production, and marketing needs of the villages. In June, 1934, there were 22 Integrated Cooperative Societies.

It was proposed that the village cooperatives join in Cooperative Unions centered around the north and south business centers of the hsien and that the unions combine to form a Hsien Federation of Cooperatives. The northern union was operating in 1934 with a membership of 47 societies.

TABLE 78. SILVER-COPPER EXCHANGE RATE, 1857–1931[1]
(cash per dollar, annual average)

Year	Rate	Year	Rate	Year	Rate	Year	Rate
1857	1,093	1877	1,042	1897	889	1917	1,207
1858	1,136	1878	1,046	1898	785	1918	1,376
1859	1,257	1879	1,016	1899	792	1919	1,408
1860	1,265	1880	1,110	1900	812	1920	1,461
1861	1,303	1881	1,150	1901	840	1921	1,581
1862	1,269	1882	1,172	1902	774	1922	1,696
1863	1,107	1883	1,141	1903	807	1923	1,974
1864	958	1884	1,113	1904	793	1924	2,317
1865	875	1885	1,135	1905	758	1925	2,896
1866	884	1886	1,111	1906	829	1926	3,541
1867	983	1887	1,077	1907	890	1927	3,751
1868	938	1888	1,085	1908	937	1928	4,060
1869	1,136	1889	1,077	1909	1,056	1929	4,310
1870	1,246	1890	1,027	1910	1,052	1930	4,100
1871	1,305	1891	1,061	1911	1,034	1931	4,090
1872	1,240	1892	1,136	1912	1,100		
1873	1,208	1893	1,068	1913	1,205		
1874	1,219	1894	1,025	1914	1,236		
1875	1,253	1895	990	1915	1,372		
1876	1,209	1896	931	1916	1,382		

[1] Lunar years. 1857–1928 from hsien yamen accounts; 1929–1931 from exchange shop. 1857–1913 converted from cash-tael quotations at rate of $1 = 0.72 taels.

TABLE 79. LOANS OF 526 FAMILIES: AMOUNTS BORROWED, 1931

Amount	Total	Per Cent	Separate Loans	Per Cent
Under $25	41	13.4	249	34.2
25–49	47	15.4	142	19.5
50–99	77	25.3	164	22.6
100–149	46	15.1	108	14.9
150–199	24	7.9	21	2.9
200–249	15	4.9	20	2.8
250–299	12	3.9	6	0.8
300–349	9	3.0	7	1.0
350–399	5	1.6	–	–
400–449	12	3.9	5	0.7
450–499	4	1.3	–	–
500 and over	13	4.3	4	0.6
	305	100.0	726	100.0

TABLE 80. LOANS OF 526 FAMILIES: TERMS OF LOANS, 1931

	Loans	Per Cent	Amount	Per Cent
Under six months	45	6.2	$ 2,034	4.2
Six months	37	5.1	2,066	4.2
Seven months	48	6.6	2,938	6.0
Eight months	35	4.9	3,015	6.1
Nine months	9	1.2	523	1.1
Ten months	399	55.0	24,178	49.4
Eleven months	1	0.1	25	–
One year	146	20.1	8,975	18.4
Indefinite	6	0.8	5,190	10.6
	726	100.0	$48,944	100.0

TABLE 81. LOANS OF 526 FAMILIES: MONTHLY INTEREST RATES, 1929–1931

	Number of Loans			Average	Amount of Loans			Average
Per Cent	1929	1930	1931	Per Cent	1929	1930	1931	Per Cent
1.0 and under	2	4	5	0.7	$ 420	$ 5,480	$ 5,485	10.9
1.1–1.5	42	51	69	10.6	4,088	5,246	6,277	14.9
1.6–2.0	218	307	479	65.8	14,403	20,521	31,915	64.1
2.1–2.5	59	85	136	18.3	1,910	2,903	4,487	8.9
2.6–3.0	14	19	37	4.6	205	251	780	1.2
	335	466	726	100.0	$21,026	$34,401	$48,944	100.0

TABLE 82. LOANS OF 526 FAMILIES:
PURPOSE OF LOANS, NUMBER, AND AMOUNT

	Number of Loans			Amount		
	1929	1930	1931	1929	1930	1931
Old debts	124	225	328	$ 8,271	$20,089	$27,026
Farm capital	104	108	184	5,017	7,324	10,721
Business capital	31	18	56	3,055	1,054	4,005
Daily living	50	68	94	1,618	2,195	2,384
Funerals and weddings	15	37	53	1,515	2,544	3,256
Gambling and narcotics	4	1	6	380	70	242
Travel	1	2	1	40	65	30
Education	1	3	4	300	580	1,280
Narcotic smuggling	–	4	–	–	480	–
Village expenses	3	–	–	290	–	–
Lawsuits	2	–	–	540	–	–
	335	466	726	$21,026	$34,401	$48,944

TABLE 83. LENDING FAMILIES: LOANS MADE AND AMOUNTS LOANED, 1931

Loans	Families	Amount	Families	Per Cent
1–5	28	Under $50	10	18.9
6–10	12	50–99	8	15.1
11–15	7	100–199	5	9.5
16–25	2	200–299	10	18.9
26–50	3	300–399	6	11.3
500[1]	1	400–499	4	7.5
—		500–999	4	7.5
	53	1,000 and over	6	11.3
			53	100.0

Approximate totals: loans 913, amount $59,200.

[1] Estimated number.

TABLE 84. SAVINGS SOCIETY TRANSACTIONS, 1917–1927

Year	Meeting	Low Bid	Received	Paid In[1]	Amt. Recd. % Amt. Pd.	Cash Per Dollar
1917	1	4,000	120,000	120,000	100.0	1,207.4
	2	2,200	67,800	120,000	56.5	
1918	3	1,900	61,200	118,200	51.6	
	4	1,800	60,600	116,100	52.2	1,376.4
	5	1,900	65,400	113,900	57.5	
1919	6	1,700	62,500	111,800	56.0	
	7	1,700	64,800	109,500	59.2	1,407.9
	8	1,800	69,400	107,200	64.5	
1920	9	2,000	76,000	105,000	72.4	
	10	1,900	75,900	103,000	73.7	1,460.5
	11	1,800	76,000	100,900	75.3	
1921	12	2,200	85,800	98,700	86.9	
	13	2,000	84,000	96,900	86.7	1,580.7
	14	2,000	86,000	94,900	90.6	
1922	15	2,300	92,800	92,900	99.8	
	16	2,300	94,500	91,200	102.7	1,695.6
	17	2,200	94,800	89,500	104.8	
1923	18	2,300	97,900	87,700	111.5	
	19	2,300	99,600	86,000	116.0	1,973.9
	20	2,300	101,300	84,300	120.3	
1924	21	1,900	99,000	82,600	120.8	
	22	1,900	101,100	80,500	126.0	2,317.1
	23	1,900	103,200	78,400	131.5	
1925	24	1,500	102,500	76,300	134.3	
	25	1,800	106,800	73,800	144.5	2,895.9
	26	1,800	109,000	71,600	152.5	
1926	27	800	107,200	69,400	154.5	
	28	1,300	111,900	66,200	169.0	3,541.4
	29	1,200	114,400	63,500	181.4	
1927	30	1,100	117,100	60,700	192.9	
	31		120,000	57,800	207.6	3,750.7

[1] Members ranked according to the meeting at which they received money from the society.

TABLE 85. SAVINGS SOCIETY, SILVER EQUIVALENT OF COPPER PAYMENTS, 1917–1927

Year	Meeting	Low Bid	4,000 Cash	Received	Paid In[1]	Amt. Recd. % Amt. Pd.
1917	1	$3.31	$3.31	$99.30	$64.21	155.0
	2	1.74	3.16	53.60	64.36	83.3
1918	3	1.44	3.04	46.40	63.06	73.5
	4	1.31	2.91	44.10	61.59	71.5
	5	1.37	2.88	47.20	60.02	78.6
1919	6	1.21	2.86	44.60	58.53	76.2
	7	1.21	2.84	46.00	56.90	81.0
	8	1.26	2.81	48.70	55.30	88.1
1920	9	1.38	2.76	52.50	53.80	97.5
	10	1.30	2.74	52.00	52.44	99.2
	11	1.20	2.66	50.60	51.08	99.2
1921	12	1.43	2.60	55.70	49.68	112.1
	13	1.27	2.53	53.10	48.58	109.2
	14	1.23	2.47	53.10	47.38	112.1
1922	15	1.39	2.42	56.00	46.19	121.1
	16	1.36	2.36	55.70	45.22	123.2
	17	1.23	2.23	53.00	44.35	119.6
1923	18	1.22	2.12	52.00	43.46	120.0
	19	1.17	2.03	50.50	42.65	118.5
	20	1.10	1.91	48.50	41.91	115.7
1924	21	.86	1.81	44.80	41.20	108.5
	22	.82	1.73	43.70	40.33	108.5
	23	.76	1.59	41.10	39.56	104.0
1925	24	.55	1.48	37.90	38.84	97.6
	25	.62	1.38	36.85	38.01	97.0
	26	.58	1.29	35.10	37.34	94.0
1926	27	.24	1.20	32.10	36.72	87.5
	28	.37	1.13	31.60	35.83	88.5
	29	.33	1.11	31.70	35.09	90.5
1927	30	.30	1.09	31.80	34.33	92.7
	31	–	1.07	32.00	33.56	95.5

[1] Members ranked according to the meeting at which they received money from the society.

CHAPTER XIV

Buying and Selling

BUYING AND SELLING was carried on in Ting Hsien by 2,228 stores in the city and villages, by thousands of itinerant peddlers, in 83 periodic markets, usually held six days per month, and at 50 temple fairs, held once a year.

The main trading center of the hsien was naturally the city and its three suburbs. Its market was held 12 days a month instead of the usual six days of the village markets. It had eight temple fairs during the year.

A survey in 1930 of the stores in the city and its suburbs found 90 different kinds and a total of 654. Of these 467 were inside the city walls and 187 in the suburbs. Food shops totaled 104, restaurants and tea shops 81, and inns 32. Eighty-six stores carried stock that could be described only as miscellaneous. The complete list is given in Table 86. The 654 stores employed 2,761 workers, including 34 women, an average of 4.2 employees per store. About two-thirds of the men were natives of Ting Hsien.

The 1,985 workers employed by the 467 stores inside the walls included 292 apprentices, one apprentice to 5.8 other workers. Seventy-one per cent of the workers had had some formal education, but 561 were reported to have had none.

Some 60 per cent of the city stores had been open less than 10 years but there were 12 that claimed a history of more than 100 years. These included eye medicine stores, eye medicine makers, old style drug stores, tobacco, salt, and cloth shops. One family had been making eye medicine for more than seven generations.

Only 85 stores, 18.2 per cent, owned their buildings. Fifty-one per cent of the stores had no more than five chien of space. Only 19 had more than 20 chien. The largest store, which occupied several court yards, had 78 chien.

In the suburbs 21 per cent of the stores owned their premises. Three stores, two drug stores, and one warehouse were more than 100 years old.

There were 1,574 stores in the 453 villages. Thirty-four per cent of the villages had no stores and another 22 per cent had only one store. Only 25 villages had more than 10 stores and only four had more than 50 stores. The largest number was 160. If, as seems probable, the 10 highest numbers represented the 10 market towns, the number of stores in the towns ranged from 24 to 160.

In Tung T'ing, a market town of 362 families to the east of the city, there were 19 different kinds of stores. The total number was 51. Again the food shops, restaurants, and inns made up about one-third of the total number. The full list is given in Table 89.

Eighty-six per cent of the Tung T'ing stores owned their premises, more than four and a half times the city rate. Thirty-seven per cent of the stores had less than five chien, the largest 27 chien. Half the stores were less than five years old. The oldest was about 50 years old.

The capital of more than one-half of the shops was less than $300. Eleven had $1,000 or more. One, a money shop, had $20,000.

The profits of most of the stores were estimated to be below $300 a year. For 10 shops the amount was evidently over $1,000 per year but the exact amounts could not be determined.

The stores employed 146 men. Twelve of these were apprentices. This was one apprentice to 11 workers, almost one-half the rate in the city stores. The smaller size of the Tung T'ing stores—many were one man shops and the largest had only eight men—and the fact that, in many cases, the village stores were open only on market days would easily account for the smaller proportion of apprentices.

The origin of the workers was Tung T'ing 31 per cent, other villages in Ting Hsien 49 per cent, outside Ting Hsien 20 per cent. Thirteen came from Shansi. In the city about one-third of the workers came from other hsien. Seventy-one per cent of the employees were married.

Wages in the stores varied somewhat but the following figures give the general level: bookkeepers $50 per year; errand and counter boys $40; workers $30 to $40 per year plus meals. Presents and bonuses added some $30 for the bookkeepers, $20 for the counter boys, and $10 for the workers and apprentices.

Food for Tung T'ing workers cost about $4.00 a month, 50 cents less than in the city, where the workers regularly had wheat flour for at least one of their two meals.

Modern business influences were reaching the countryside for in Tung T'ing four of the stores were organized as limited corporations.

Some indication of the amount of peddling done by the villagers is given by the occupation figures of the 515 families in Table 14. Seven men were reported as full time peddlers. For 40 it was a part time occupation. If this sample was typical of other families in the hsien the number of peddlers was about 6,500.

The 83 periodic markets were where most of the people in Ting Hsien sold their farm produce and the output of their industry and where they bought the things they needed for the farm, the shop, or for personal use. Most of the trading was done out of doors. Many of the stores in the village or in neighboring villages sent their representatives with a stock of goods to the market. The map on page 5 shows how the markets were distributed in the hsien. Table 88 gives the number in each district and the dates on which the markets were held. The small number in the 1st District was undoubtedly due to proximity to the city market, which generally offered the best opportunity for trade. The Provincial Institute of Political and Social Reconstruction listed 9 village markets as first class, 17 as second class, and 36 as third class. The remaining 20 would be fourth class.

The markets were regularly held every five days, six times a month. The dates followed the lunar rather than the solar calendar. The dates for neighboring markets usually were arranged to avoid conflict. The hsien map shows the dates for the 15 markets in the Experimental District. The markets for farm produce were naturally most active in the fall. Those for horses, oxen, mules, and donkeys had their busiest time in the 2nd and 3rd months, when the animals were needed for the farm work, and in the 7th month when the farm season was over and the farmers were anxious to get rid of some of their stock. The pig markets were most active in the 8th and 12th months, before the fall and New Year festivals, when most families were buying meat for the festival feast. The thread markets had their busiest time in the fall and winter months.

In the Tung T'ing market, which drew traders from 50 neighboring villages and was one of the largest in Ting Hsien, there were special sections for grains, farm animals, pigs, ducks and chickens, cotton, vegetables, fuel, cotton cloth, peanut and cotton seed cake. In the watermelon and sweet melon markets the wares were not generally displayed. The buyer and seller met at the market and then went to the fields to select the melons and settle the details of price, transportation, etc. There were two sections for farm animals where, on some market days, as many as 500 animals were sold. The main street, two li in length, was regularly lined, on market day, with the stands and stalls of those offering different kinds of food, cigarettes, farming tools, wooden implements, mats, pottery, and fruit. Barbers, cobblers, and fortune-tellers set up their stands. There was a Dew Market early in the morning where the women came to sell the thread they had spun.

Many of the dealers apparently had regular places where they displayed their wares. Others set down their baskets or arranged their tables wherever they could find space when they arrived.

Middle-men and tax collectors, the functions usually combined in one person, were on hand in most of the markets. They introduced the buyers and sellers, helped them settle prices, acted as official measurers when needed, and guaranteed the buyer if payment was not made when the deal was closed. For this service the middle-men usually received 3 per cent of the value of the goods sold. In the grain market the fee was four coppers per tou for most grains, but it was eight coppers per tou for sesamum seed. The seller regularly paid the middle-men's fee, though the terms of a sale might determine who paid it. Where a 3 per cent sales tax was levied the buyer and seller usually divided the tax and middle-men's fees. Cotton cloth had to be stamped at the tax office before it was offered for sale.

On an average market day there were between two and three thousand visitors.

In Chai Ch'eng the market was much smaller than in Tung T'ing, not as many dealers came, and the goods offered were largely local farm products and food. There were only five sellers of miscellaneous goods.

In the grain market the middle-man assigned places where the sellers could arrange their wares—wheat, millet, panicled millet, corn, kaoliang, buckwheat, green, black, and white beans, sesamum, and peanuts. In the cotton market both the short staple native cotton and the longer staple grown from foreign (American) seed were on sale. Because its seed was larger and heavier the foreign seed cotton brought a lower price than the native cotton. The price in 1928 was between $15 and $16 per 100 catties.

On the 14th of the 8th moon of 1928 there were 262 sellers in the Chai Ch'eng food markets. This was a particularly busy day as it was the day before the fall festival. Table 90 gives the types and number of dealers, the prices, and the amounts of goods offered for sale. Eggplant, noodles, pears, and squash had the largest number of sellers. Even in this relatively small market over two and a half tons of pears were offered. It was pear season and everybody was buying food for the festival feast.

The festival was also undoubtedly responsible for the large amount of meat on sale, 175 pigs, 1,600 pounds of beef, and 200 pounds of mutton. There were 51 pork sellers. The beef and mutton sellers were all Mohammedans who came from another village.

The price figures give a good sample of the 1928 price level as they include the most generally used non-cereal foods. The cereal prices for 1930 are given in Chapter X.

Our study showed that the sellers of meat, fruit, cakes, and cooked food, who were not natives of Chai Ch'eng, paid a fee of 10 or 20 cents for the privilege of using market space. For some, at least, the fee also gave them the use of a board table. The field report said that there was no fee for vegetable sellers as the market did not last very long. In most cases the place fee went to the owner of the adjoining property and paid not only for a place to stand on market days, but also for a place to leave tables and other equipment between market days. In some villages a fee for the right to occupy a regular place on market days was paid to the village office. The system evidently varied from market to market. For the temple fairs the place fee went to the village government to help meet the cost of the fair.

In the Chai Ch'eng vegetable market the middle-man received the usual 3 per cent commission only on the larger sales. He generally was not involved in the small retail sales. Sales under 50 catties were regularly exempt.

The large number of roadside stalls was an outstanding feature of market day in the city. On non-market days our survey found 124 roadside stands. Except for the eleven barbers, cobblers, and cigarette sellers all of them were selling food. On market day the number of stands jumped to 434. Sixty-five different kinds were listed. The different kinds and the number of each are given in Table 91. On market days 94 of the stands were set up by city stores, 93 by city residents, and 247 by village residents who brought their wares into the city. We were interested to note that horse meat was offered on four stalls.

Most of the stalls were simply a table or stand that held a small amount of goods. On non-market days 31 per cent had less than 10 square feet of area and 88 per cent had less than 25 square feet. Only four per cent had 50 or more square feet. Larger stalls were set up to take care of the market day business. Then only 11 per cent had less than 10 square feet. Thirty per cent had 50 or more square feet. The largest had over 300 square feet.

The 50 temple fairs held in 35 different locations throughout the hsien gave a great opportunity for trade as they drew anywhere up to 10,000 people per day for the three, four, or more days of the fair. The free theatrical plays provided by the village holding the fair, the other entertainment, and the general excitement were very attractive. The shops, stalls, shows, and parking yard for carts in the largest fair at Pei Ch'i covered 150 mu, 25 acres. The map on page 5 shows where the fairs were held. The dates for the fairs, their connection with religion, and other details are given in Chapter XVIII.

Prices in the stores, markets, and fairs were not always easy to determine as there was no fixed price for many articles and usually there was no open bidding in the market. Sales were made between individuals and prices were often determined by signs rather than words, with the signs being made under cover of the buyer's and seller's sleeves. Their fingers on the other person's arm set one price while they might talk about an entirely different one. This, plus the lack of general intervillage communication, often made it difficult for the farmers to secure top or even fair prices for their produce. They kept a general check on current prices by visiting various markets in the neighborhood and getting reports from people who had visited the city and town markets.

TABLE 86. STORES IN CITY AND SUBURBS, 1930

Bamboo	2	Foreign goods	9	Paper	1
Barber	8	Fruit	7	Paper boxes	1
Bath house	5	Glass and frames	1	Pen and ink	1
Bicycle	5	Godown	7	Pewter	2
Biscuits and cakes	30	Gold plating	2	Photographer	3
Blacksmith	3	Grain and flour	15	Pottery	6
Bone collector	2	Hemp	5	Printer	4
Books	6	Iron	6	Restaurant, big	10
Bow and arrow	1	Inn	32	——, small	53
Boxes and furniture	8	Jewelry	14	Salt	4
Bread, steamed	11	Kerosene	2	Scroll maker	1
Camel stable	1	Laundry	1	Seal cutter	2
Candle	1	Leather tanning	1	Second hand clothes	3
Candy	5	Leather belts	2	Sedan chair	1
Cart	3	Lumber	2	Shoemaker	3
Cigarette agents	2	Meat	6	Shoes	9
Cloth, foreign	17	Meat, chicken	6	Sieve makers	3
——, native	6	Metal works	1	Tailor	8
Coal	13	Miscellaneous, big	18	Tea leaves	6
Coffin	1	——, small	68	Tea shop	18
Copper	3	Money	43	Tinsmith	3
Cotton	8	Money, government	7	Tobacco	3
Curio	1	Mules	4	Towels	2
Dentist	2	Noodles	7	Transportation	2
Doctors' office	7	Oil	7	Umbrella maker	1
Drugs	20	Oil cake	1	Uniform	1
Dyeing	10	Oiled containers	1	Watch repair	1
Eye medicine	18	Painting and		Wine	12
Felt	1	whitewash	2		—
Flour mills	11	Paintings and scrolls	2	Total	654

TABLE 87. VILLAGE STORES

Stores	Villages	Stores	Villages
0	155	11–15	14
1	100	16–20	1
2	59	21–25	1
3	36	26–30	3
4	20	31–50	2
5	21	51–100	3
6	13	160	1
7	8		453
8	5		
9	7	Total stores	1,574
10	4		

TABLE 88. VILLAGE MARKETS: NUMBER, DISTRIBUTION, AND DATES[1]

District	Number	Per Cent of Villages	Dates	Number
1	5	7	1, 5, 11, 15, 21, 25	1
2	10	16	1, 6, etc.	9
3	25	30	2, 7, etc.	18
4	19	26	3, 8, etc.	12
5	4	5	4, 9, etc.	20
6	19	21	5, 10, etc.	22
	82	18		82

[1] Dates follow the lunar calendar. City has two 5 day market series, 1, 6 . . ., and 3, 8 . . ., a total of 12 days per month.

TABLE 89. STORES IN TUNG T'ING

Bath house	1	Drug	3	Pork	1
Bellows	1	Dyeing	1	Restaurant, small	5
Bicycle	2	Inn	5	Rope	1
Cakes, wheat	4	Iron utensils	2	Salt	1
——, miscellaneous	1	Miscellaneous, big	10	Wine	1
Cloth, foreign	4	Money exchange	6	Total	51
Doctor	1	Oil	1		

TABLE 90. CHAI CH'ENG FOOD MARKETS
(8th month, 14th day, 1928)

	Sellers	Price per Catty[1]	Catties Offered	Stall Rent
Beans	18	9		
Beef	1	$0.142	1,200	$0.20
Cabbage	6	2		
Cakes	7	62–96	2,700	.20
Celery	1	5[2]		
Cucumbers	3	3[2]		
Eggplant	38	4		
Ginger	14	108		
Grapes	9	$0.18	280	.10
White beets	5	60		
Leeks	4	8		
Mutton	8	$0.167	150	.20
Noodles	29	$0.133		.20
Onions	6	4		
Pears	26	$0.16	3,900	.10
Persimmons	5	6[2]	76[3]	.10
Pomegranates	4	$0.14	160	.10
Pork	51	$0.20	175[4]	.10
Squash	23	2		
Cooked food	4			.20
	262			

[1] In coppers, except decimal figures, which are in cents.
[2] Each.
[3] Baskets.
[4] Pigs.

TABLE 91. ROADSIDE STALLS IN TINGHSIEN CITY, THIRD MONTH, 1930

	Market Day	Non Market Day		Market Day	Non Market Day
Barber	3	2	Leather belts	4	–
Baskets	2	–	Matches	1	–
Bean curd	3	1	Medicine	3	–
Beef	7	2	Metal utensils	19	–
Bowls	1	–	Noodles	18	2
Bread	38	15	Noodles, dried	4	–
Cakes and dumplings	52	13	Onions	15	–
Candy	16	11	Paper	6	–
Chicken, smoked	2	2	Pens	3	–
Cigarettes	11	6	Pork	4	3
Cloth, foreign	3	–	Quilts	1	–
——, native	2	–	Raisins	2	–
Cloth sacks	1	–	Rope	8	–
Cotton	5	–	Saddles	1	–
Cotton seed oil	1	–	Scales	2	–
Flint	1	–	Shoes, new	2	–
Fodder	1	–	——, used	4	–
Food, cooked	13	3	Shoe repair	4	3
——, miscellaneous	27	23	Shoes and stockings	1	–
Foreign goods	1	–	Socks	3	–
Fortune telling	4	–	Soup, meat	2	–
Fruit, dried	5	1	——, noodle	1	–
——, fresh	4	4	Sweet potatoes	2	3
Fuel	10	–	Tea and candy	1	2
Garlic	15	–	Thread	2	–
Ginger	1	–	Tin utensils	3	–
Grain	23	–	Tobacco leaves	2	–
Groceries	23	23	Towels	1	–
Honey	1	–	Vegetables	10	2
Horse meat	4	3	Vegetable seeds	11	–
Incense	8	–	Weaving supplies	1	–
Kerosene	1	–	Willow boxes	1	–
Lanterns	3	–	Total	434	124

CHAPTER XV

Industry

INDUSTRY in Ting Hsien was that of a non-mechanical, agricultural area. Power was almost entirely animal or human. The tools were mainly hand tools. The principal machines were the stone flour mill, the cotton gin, the cotton batting machine, the spinning wheel, the loom, and the Persian wheel for irrigation.

Because Ting Hsien was so predominately an agricultural area (96 per cent of its families farmed some land) only a small proportion of the industrial workers were engaged in year round industry. Most of them were farmers who turned to other occupations during the idle months on the farm. Because most of the industrial processes were relatively simple and required few tools and little capital, there was a large amount of home industry.

Industry, both home and shop,[1] engaged some 91,000 workers, about one in five of the total population and one in three of those over 14 years of age. The workers were divided approximately 24,500 males and 66,500 females. Approximately 12 per cent of all males and 34 per cent of all females were engaged in some form of industrial work. For those over 14 years of age the figures were males 18 per cent, females 50 per cent.

Every village had some form of home industry. Fifty-two per cent of the families in the hsien were engaged in some form of home industry. Fifty-seven per cent of the industrial output was produced by home industry. There were twenty times as many home industry families as there were industrial shops. There were ten times as many home workers as there were shop employees. Only 2.1 per cent of the population were shop workers.

Eighty-one per cent of the home workers were females, but only 4 per cent of the shop employees. Only one-quarter of one per cent of the females over 14 years of age were reported as shop workers. Two-

1. Shop is used for the non-family industrial workshop where production was the main activity. Store is used for the place where buying or selling, or both, was the primary business. See Chapter XIV.

thirds of the male workers and 99.5 per cent of the female workers were engaged in home industry. The widespread hand spinning and weaving of the locally grown cotton accounted for the very large proportion of female workers. Over 60,000 were spinning, weaving, or both. Another 6,000 were engaged in other kinds of work. Eighty-eight per cent of the home industry workers were engaged in spinning, weaving, or both. About one-third of all females in the villages and some 8 per cent of the males were engaged in some form of home industry.

Because some families and workers were engaged in more than one industry there was unavoidable duplication in the home industry figures for both families and workers. In determining the above figures we have made allowance, on the basis of the actual duplication in 1,220 home industry families (see Chapter IV), for the known but necessarily estimated duplication in our hsien totals. In the 1,220 families the duplication was 27.5 per cent for the families, 10.5 per cent for the female workers, but only 1.1 per cent for the male workers. Spinning and weaving covered all but 2 per cent of the workers' duplications. In our industry tables we have not attempted any adjustment in the totals as the duplication can only be estimated. It must, however, always be kept in mind when the family and worker totals are considered.

In some cases it was difficult to make a sharp distinction between home and shop industry. The payment or non-payment of wages to the workers has been the chief determining factor. Home industry generally did not involve paid workers though they might be hired occasionally during especially busy times. Home industry generally was carried on in winter or other leisure time, but might be year round. Shop industry was generally year round, but might be seasonal. Apprentices were employed in some of the shops. Cotton ginning, which in some instances was done in the homes, has been listed as a shop industry as most of the workers were paid on a piece rate basis. Weaving was classified as a home industry although a few weavers were paid according to their output.

The value of the industrial output in 1931 was estimated to be some $8,570,000. Fifty-seven per cent of this amount was produced by home industry. Cotton products were 56 per cent of the total. The village shops produced more than four times as much as the city shops but the city output per shop was almost twice that of the villages. The average annual output per worker was city shops $890, village shops

$400, and home industry workers $54. For the thread spinners production averaged only $13.80 per person per year.

The estimated profit of the shops totaled some $500,000. The gain from home industry was approximately $880,000. The profit per worker was city shops $260, village shops $36. The average gain for the home industry workers was only $10.70. For the thread spinners it was only $2.90. Without them the average was $15.45. The shop profit is figured after the payment of the workers' wages and other expenses, the home industry gain after the payment for raw materials, but before any wage allowance.

Table 92 shows the number of shops and workers and how the industrial work was divided between city and village shops and home industry. Because our production figures are based on estimates the tables give them only to the nearest $10.

Our industry figures are based on five studies:

(1) A survey of the primary and secondary occupations, farming, industrial, and professional, of all persons over 12 years of age in 515 families in the Experimental District. The results of this study are given in Chapter II.

(2) A detailed study of the 204 shops in the city and its three suburbs.

(3) A general study of home and shop industry in the 453 villages and towns.

(4) A house to house survey of the industrial activity of the 2,260 families living in six villages and a detailed study of 1,220 of the 1,740 families reporting some home industry. The findings of this study are reported in Chapter IV.

(5) A historical study of wages, prices, and other factors of cotton ginning and cloth weaving for various parts of the 52 years from 1882 through 1933.

The industrial information for the 515 families was secured as part of our detailed study of those families. The information on the shops in the city and the villages was secured, for the most part, by talking with the masters and workers of the shops. When definite information was unavailable, we endeavored to approximate it with help from neighboring shops or to make our own estimate. When there were only a few families in a particular type of home industry, we secured our figures from them. When large numbers of families were involved, as in spinning and weaving, we had to depend on the knowledge of the village elders or other representative persons to give us figures for the entire village. While our figures are, of necessity, based on the estimates of many different persons and there naturally were wide variations in the figures for the different villages, the proportion of families working, the average number of workers, the amount of output, and the totals and averages seem to give a reasonable approximation of the figures for the different types of industry and for the total industrial activity of the hsien.

Prices naturally varied from month to month and from market to market. With 83 different markets in the hsien there was opportunity for considerable divergence. The prices in our tables are based on figures from the main markets, secured at different times of the year. By averaging the quotations we have tried to show the general price level at the time of our industrial study, 1931.

In order to get at least a rough classification of the different industries we have divided them into seven groups: cotton ginning, spinning and weaving; weaving of non-cotton materials; food; wood and bamboo; metals; chemical goods and processes; miscellaneous. The second group. combining as it does the weaving of wool, hair, reeds, straw, and twigs, is a very heterogeneous group. Some of the other industries might have been otherwise classified but we have not attempted any rearrangement as it would not appreciably affect the principal items shown by the group figures, the generally low average output and gain per worker, the heavy concentration in cotton, and the very small proportion of metal work.

Fifty-six per cent of the total output and 61 per cent of the village shop and home industry output was in the cotton group. According to the tables, 89.7 per cent of the home industry families and 88.7 per cent of the home industry workers were working on cotton. These latter figures are higher than actual because of the large duplication in spinning and weaving, but even if allowance is made for this, on the basis of the duplication in the 1,220 home industry families, both figures are still over 86 per cent.

Almost three-quarters of the city shop output was either chemical goods or foods. It is indicative of general industrial activity in Ting Hsien that metal products were less than 2 per cent of the hsien output.

Only five of the 46 different city industries had reported outputs of more than $50,000. Eye medicine, for which Ting Hsien is famous throughout China and southeast Asia, had the largest total, $303,000, produced by 18 shops. This was 40 per cent of the city production. The other four large industries were cotton ginning, cakes and condiments, flour milling, and shoes. The five industries together accounted for 78 per cent of the city's total output.

Four of the 31 village industries, cotton ginning, timber, flour milling, and brick making, had totals of more than $150,000. Only one, cotton ginning, was over $300,000. Its total was $1,811,840. The four industries included 83 per cent of the village industry total.

Five of the 88 home industries—cotton cloth weaving, cotton thread spinning, pig bristle sorting, reed mat weaving, and bean curd making—had totals over $150,000. Three—spinning, weaving, and bristle sorting—were over $500,000. Cotton cloth weaving was the only one over $1,000,000. Its total was $2,307,000. The five industries accounted for 85 per cent of the home industry total.

In the detailed tables we have given an estimate of the rate of profit or gain as a percentage of the value of output of each industry. These can only be rough averages, for the proportion naturally varied from shop to shop and family to family, but the figures show what those in each industry thought was the general rate for their business. The range was from 3 per cent for the home industry vermicelli makers to 52 per cent for the eye medicine makers and 68 per cent for those making the screens used in making paper. The vermicelli makers were able to continue with a low profit because the residue from their operations was good food for pigs.

Four of the city industries reported profits of more than 30 per cent and four less than 10 per cent. Eye medicine was the highest. Vermicelli making was the lowest, with 8 per cent.

Six village industries had average profits over 30 per cent, three were under 10 per cent. Cotton ginning was the lowest with 6 per cent, pewter the highest with 47 per cent.

Because no wages were involved in the home industry figures their gain or profit rates ordinarily were higher than those of the shops. Six of the 86 reported rates were 60 per cent or more, 27 were over 30 per cent, seven were less than 15 per cent, but only one, vermicelli making, was less than 10 per cent. It was 3.0 per cent.

The average gain per worker per year for the different home industries ranged from $2.90 for the thread spinners to $427 for the wine makers. For eight industries the amount was over $100 but, except for bristle sorting, these were industries with few workers. Five of the eight industries had not more than 10 workers. For seven industries the amount was less than $5.00 per worker per year, for 14 it was less than $10.00. The seven industries with the lowest amount per worker included 46 per cent of the workers, the top eight industries only 0.6 per cent. The gain of each group was almost the same, 13.8 per cent of the total gain for the lowest group and 13.0 per cent for the top group. The industries with gains of not more than $10.00 per worker per year included 90.5 per cent of the workers, but only 59.3 per cent of the total gain.

Only seven of the 88 home industries—spinning, weaving, bean curd, vermicelli, noodle and soap making, and sesame oil pressing—were reported from all six districts of the hsien and could be said to be hsien wide. Sixty-one per cent were found in only one district.

Every village had at least one home industry, but none had more than eight. The average was 3.4. Spinning was the most widespread. It was reported by all but 16 of the 453 villages. Weaving was done in 378 villages. Bean curd was made in 249, vermicelli in 94, noodles in 77, and sesame oil in 51. These six industries were the only ones found in more than 10 per cent of the villages. Only five other industries were reported by 10 or more villages. Thirty-nine industries, 44 per cent, were reported by only one village; another 17 were found in only two villages.

Very little metal and woodworking was done as home industry. Together their output was only 2.1 per cent of the home industry total. All but one of the different types of metal work were reported by only one village. Only 26 families were doing metal work. Only one type of wood work, pitchfork making, was reported by more than three villages. It was carried on in seven villages. The output of the metal and wood working shops in the city and villages was some five times that of the home industry families. Itinerant blacksmiths and carpenters helped to meet the community need for metal and wood work. Not a few of the metal workers were Shansi men who came down to the coastal plain for work. They brought Shansi iron with them and added to it by accepting locally available scrap in part payment for their work.

Almost three-quarters, 72.5 per cent, of the 204 city shops were small businesses with less than five workers. Only one per cent had more than

14 workers. They were two large eye medicine shops, one with 25 workers, the other with 45.

The 824 workers in the city shops were divided:

	Number	Per Cent
Manager, accountants, clerks	119	14.4
Workmen	543	66.0
Apprentices	162	19.6
	824	100.0

The 162 apprentices were being trained in 117 of the shops, 58 per cent. The training period ordinarily was three years. In some cases it was three years plus a festival. In a few trades it was four or even five years. All the boys were given room and board. Some shops also provided their clothing. No regular wages were paid the apprentices but in most cases they were given presents of money at New Year's time. The amount was usually $5.00 or $10.00 depending on the time the boy had been with the shop. As so many of the shops had relatively few workers there were only 10 that had more than one or two apprentices. One large eye medicine shop reported 10. There was an average of one apprentice to 4.1 other employees and one apprentice to 3.4 other workmen.

The wages paid by some of the shops are shown in Table 94: daily from $0.45 to $1.00, monthly from $3.50 to $30, and yearly from $30 to $70—all plus board and tips.

The estimated value of the goods produced by the city shops totaled some $731,000. This was an average of just under $300 per shop per month. For one-third of the shops the amount was less than $85 per month. Only one-fifth of the shops produced as much as $250 per month.

The estimated profit of the city shops was some $216,000, almost 30 per cent of the value of the output. The high rate of profit of the eye medicine shops, 52 per cent, and their large proportion of the output, 42 per cent, were largely accountable for this high average. Only 10 industries reported a rate of more than 20 per cent and only five more than 25 per cent. Only 20 per cent of the shops were in the "more than 20 per cent" group.

Profits were less than $200 a year for 53 per cent of the shops. Only 14 per cent made as much as $50 a month. Three shops, evidently eye medicine shops, were in the $10,000 a year and over group.

The best reports and estimates we could get on the amount of capital invested in the city shops gave the total as $77,160, an average of only

$380 per shop. The individual amounts ranged from $30 to $5,500. For 52 per cent of the shops the amount was less than $300. For 81 per cent it was less than $500. The average investment per worker was only $95.

The relatively small amounts of capital shown may be partly due to under-reporting, as the shop keepers naturally were hesitant about giving complete answers to our questions. At the same time it must be remembered that a very large proportion of the shops were in rented quarters. (Eighty-two per cent of the stores in the city rented their buildings and the figure for the shops was probably about the same.) Almost no machinery was used; most of the equipment was inexpensive hand tools; only a small labor investment was required as wages were low and most of the manufacturing processes were simple and short; inventories of finished goods usually were not large. The reported value of the goods produced represented a capital turnover of 9.5 times. The estimated profit was 2.8 times the total capital. Any under-reporting of capital would make these figures larger than actual. It should also be noted that 72 per cent of the total profit was earned by the eye medicine stores, whose estimated profit rate was 52 per cent of their output.

Profit figures for the individual village shops, if available, would undoubtedly be smaller than for the city. The average shop output was only 52 per cent of the city average. The average output per worker was $400, less than half the city average. The total estimated profit for the 1,578 shops was only one-third larger than the total for the 204 city shops. Cotton ginning with a 6 per cent profit was the largest item rather than eye medicine making. The average rate was only 9.1 per cent. For the city shops it was 29.6 per cent.

If the rate of capital turnover was the same in the villages as in the city the average capital for the village shops was $180 and the profit 100 per cent per year.

If, after making allowance for possible under-reporting of capital, the profit rates still seem unduly high, it must be remembered that interest rates on secured personal loans averaged some 21 per cent per year in 1931 and many of the stores paid 18 and 24 per cent per year for money left on deposit with them.

Cotton Ginning and Batting

Cotton was the fifth Ting Hsien crop in value, $1,770,000. It was the largest money crop, as the other large crops, grains and sweet potatoes,

were largely consumed on the farms. Processing cotton was the chief
local industry. Cotton products were 56.4 per cent of the industrial output and more than four out of every five industrial workers worked on
cotton. The entire process was carried on with simple, usually locally
made, hand or foot powered machines. The machine spun thread generally used for the warp of the locally woven cloth came from Tientsin
or Shanghai.

Ginning was done on foot powered machines with which a man
could process about 80 catties of lint a day. Most of the work was done
on a piece work basis with the workers paid $1.10 per 100 catties in
1931, but only 75 cents in 1933. The ginning machines cost some $25.
The ginning shops ordinarily made no cash charge for their work, but
instead kept the seed from the ginned cotton. If the ginning was paid
for in cash the charge was three or four cents per catty.

A considerable portion of the ginned cotton was teased into batting
for use in bed quilts and padded winter clothing. This, too, was done on
a foot powered machine. Again the average output was some 80 catties
of lint per day. The price of the batting machines, according to one
report, was some $40. Another report gave the cost as $75.

The batting used to be done by hand by working a vibrating wire
through the cotton. The wire, stretched taut across a bow, was vibrated
by hitting it with a wooden stick. In some shops the bow was hung from
one end of a horizontal pole, the other end of which was fastened to the
ceiling. The bending of the pole allowed the bow to be lowered into and
worked across the cotton spread out on a flat table. In other shops the
bow was hung from the free end of a curved stick that a harness held
upright along the worker's back. The pole curved over the worker's
head so that the bow hung in front of him. By bending he lowered the
bow into the spread out cotton lint.

The 334 ginning and batting shops employed some 1,155 men and
144 women. They reported an output valued at $1,883,000. The esti-
mated profit was only some 6 per cent, the lowest rate for any shop industry.

Store records and the memory of the workers gave us a history of the
wages paid in the cotton ginning and batting shops for the 13 years
from 1921 through 1933. There were six different series of rates, three
different piece rates paid the men operating the ginning machines, the

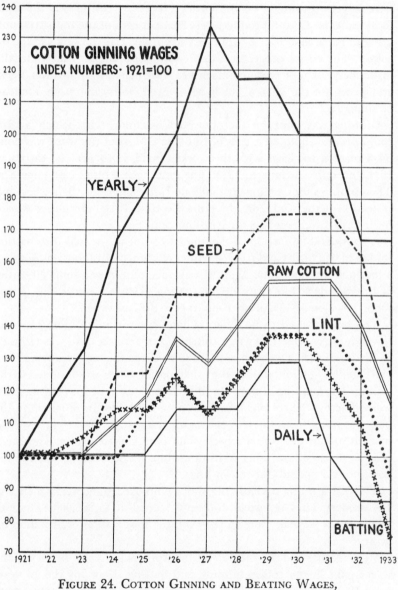

FIGURE 24. COTTON GINNING AND BEATING WAGES,
INDEX NUMBERS, 1921–1933

piece rate paid the batting machine operators, a day rate for temporary or seasonal workers, and a yearly rate for permanent employees.

The yearly rate varied from $30 to $70, the day rate from 30 to 45 cents. The average piece rate operator earned from 48 to 88 cents a day as an average day's work was processing 80 catties of lint and the piece rates varied from 60 cents to $1.10 per 100 catties of lint. Food was provided by the shop for the time workers but not for the piece workers.

The three ginning rates were based on processing 100 catties of raw cotton, producing 100 catties of ginned seed, and producing 100 catties of lint. The batting rate was for processing 100 catties of lint. There was a close relationship between the three ginning rates, for two-thirds of the seed rate plus one-third of the lint rate was regularly between one and two cents below the raw cotton rate. This would seem to indicate a general division of two-thirds seed and one-third lint for the Ting Hsien cotton.

The rates for ginning and batting 100 catties of lint were the same for eight of the 13 years. For some unexplained reason the batting rate was less than the lint ginning rate for the last three years of our study.

The index numbers of the six wage rates, with the 1921 rates equal to 100, are shown in Figure 24. The graphs for the piece rates show a fairly similar pattern, increases through the latter 1920s, a plateau for 1929–31, and then, as the depression reached Ting Hsien, a rapid decline to 1933. The decline was between 25 and 30 per cent for the ginning rates and 45 per cent for the batting rate. It will be noted from the graphs that the 1933 index number for ginning lint was 94, while that for batting lint was 75.

The fact that changes in the seed and lint rates were generally made in amounts of 10 cents per 100 catties accounted for most of the differences in the index numbers for the different piece rates.

The daily rate increased later than the piece rates, did not go as high proportionately, and started to decline a year earlier than the ginning piece rates. In 1933 the rate was 30 cents a day, or five cents (14 per cent) below the 1921 rate.

The yearly rate followed quite a different pattern. It increased every year for six years after 1921, reached a maximum in 1927 rather than in 1929, and showed two reductions before there was any decline in either the daily wage or the piece rate. The maximum, $70, was $2\frac{1}{3}$ times the 1921 rate of $30. In 1932 and 1933 the yearly rate was $50.

We could not find any reason that would explain why the 1933 index number was 167 for the annual wage, but only 86 for the daily wage; 125 for the highest ginning piece wage, but only 75 for the batting wage.

The yearly wage was 86 times the day rate in 1921, 175 times in 1927, and 167 times in 1933. During the 13 years covered by our figures there evidently was considerable improvement in the financial position of the yearly workers, at least when compared with that of the men who were paid by the day or on a piece rate basis.

Cotton Spinning

Most Ting Hsien families had a spinning wheel as part of their household equipment. Most of the girls and a few of the boys learned how to use it. The girls usually began spinning when they were 12 or 13 years old. Ordinarily it took them some four or five months to learn. During that time they practiced on "red" cotton. A new spinning wheel cost about 50 cents.

All but 16 of the 453 villages, 97.5 per cent, had at least one spinning family. One-third of the spinning villages had not more than 20. Just under two-thirds, 61 per cent, had not more than 50. Three had more than 300 and one had 360. The total number of spinning families was 28,367, an average of 65 per village. Forty-two per cent of all the village families had at least one member who was making thread.

The total number of spinners was 39,720. Almost 95 per cent of these were females, as only 2,106 male spinners were reported. Twenty-eight per cent of the females over 14 years of age were spinning. Only 55 villages reported any male spinners. All but six of those villages and all but 231 of the male spinners were in the 6th District. Three villages reported that all their spinners were males.

In most of the spinning families more than one person was doing some spinning. The average for the hsien was 1.4 per spinning family. In the 6th District it was 1.9. In eight villages, seven of which were in the 6th District, the average was over 2.5 per family while in three villages, all in the 6th District, it was three per family.

It was generally estimated that the women would spin one catty of thread in five days or from one market day to the next. This was borne out by the figures for the 67 spinning villages in the 1st District. There the village average per spinner ranged from 10 to 134 catties but for more than half the villages the average was between 20 and 30 catties per spinner or a little more than one catty per market day for the winter months.

The thread markets, usually called the Dew Market, were held early in the morning and lasted only a short time, ordinarily ending before 10 o'clock. One explanation of the market's name was that like the dew it disappeared early in the day. Another was that the thread came to market with dew on it, for on the eve of the market the finished thread was usually wrapped in a handkerchief that had been soaked in water and then was left over night on the ground in order that the dampness might add to its weight.

The different thread markets used different weight units. In some a catty of thread was only 3.5 ounces of the generally used 16 ounce catty. In others the thread catty was 4.5 or 5.5 ounces. All our price and weight figures have been adjusted to the 16 ounce catty base.

The estimated output of thread in 1931 was 962,300 catties, an average of 34 catties per spinning family and 24 catties per spinner. At 57 cents per catty, the average price for 1931, the value of the thread was just under $550,000. The average value per worker was $13.80.

The average gain from spinning was estimated to be 21 per cent of the market price or 12 cents per catty in 1931. At that rate the average gain per worker was $2.90 per year. In the 4th District the average was only 87 cents per worker but in the 4th, 5th, and 6th Districts it was $4.00 per year.

It was reported that, while in 1931 the average gain was 12 cents per catty, fluctuations in the price of thread sometimes reduced the gain to as little as 2.5 cents per catty. In 1932 the average price of thread in six sample villages ranged from 37 to 50 cents and averaged 45 cents per catty.

For the different villages the average gain per spinner ranged from 29 cents to $100 per year. The latter was for two men in one family who evidently were full time spinners. To make that much their average output would have to be some 2.5 catties per day. There were 58 villages in which the reported average gain per spinner was less than $1.00 per year. Fifty-two of these were in the 4th District. There were only six villages in which the reported average gain was over $10.00 per spinner per year.

In our group of 1,220 home industry families (see Chapter IV) it seems probable that even in the families with the largest farms (incomes) more than 25 per cent of all the females and more than 38 per cent of the females over 14 yars of age were spinning. Forty-five per cent of all the females in that group of families were doing some home industry. In the entire group of families 52 per cent of the working females were spinning and it seems probable that in the wealthier families the proportion would be even higher as the women would be less apt to do the heavier work of other occupations.

It was estimated that, when working, just over one-quarter of the spinners worked less than four hours per day, just under 50 per cent worked from four to eight hours, and just under a quarter worked over eight hours a day. It was not possible to estimate the total number of days worked by the entire group, but in one village the spinners estimated that the days when they did some spinning averaged 101 days per spinner per year. Four spinners said they worked at least 250 days per year. About one-third estimated their time between 50 and 100 days, another third between 100 and 150 days. For some it was full time work. Others worked only occasionally during the winter months. The estimated spinning time averaged five hours per worker per day. The total output was 7,340 catties or just over 23 catties per spinner. As the average price for that village was 50 cents per catty, the average spinner produced thread worth $11.60 and earned a profit of some $2.30 per year. From the time and production figures it appears that the average worker processed just under one-half a catty of thread in a 10 hour day. The average gain to the worker on that amount of thread was five cents.

The locally spun thread was largely used for weaving so after spinning it was reeled into skeins, then washed, sometimes dyed, starched, and dried. The thread was then wound onto shuttle bobbins, or, if it was to be used for warp, onto other bobbins that were placed on the upright spindles of a wooden "bed" so that some 360 threads could be drawn off together for the warp of the local looms. If the thread was dyed the charge was two cents per catty.

Cotton Weaving

Cotton cloth weaving was reported by 378 villages, 83 per cent. The weaving families numbered 13,385, 20 per cent, and the weavers 39,121, just under 10 per cent of the village population.

The average number of weaving families per weaving village was 35.

Almost one-quarter, 23 per cent, of the weaving villages had not more than five weaving families; 61 per cent had not more than 20; 79 per cent had not more than 50. Only four villages reported more than 200 weaving families. The largest number was 260.

Women were doing most of the weaving as 82 per cent of the weavers were females. They usually learned the art when they were 16 or 17 years of age. It generally took them about six months to acquire the skill necessary to produce salable cloth.

The value of the cloth produced totaled $2,307,000. This was 47 per cent of the total home industry output. Cloth and thread represented almost 60 per cent of the home industry total. The average cloth output was $6,100 per weaving village, $173 per family, and $59 per weaver. One village reported an output of just under $100,000. Thirty-four villages produced more than $10,000 each, 73 villages less than $1,000 each. For two villages the amount was only $81. In two villages the average per family was only $40. In three it was over $1,000. The highest average was $1,460 per family.

The gain to the workers was estimated as one-sixth of the market price. At that rate the average gain per family was $29.80, per worker $9.85.

The district figures show a very heavy concentration of cotton growing, spinning, and weaving in the 3rd and 6th Districts. Together the two districts accounted for the following per cents of the hsien totals; cotton production 83.5, ginning shops 70.4, ginning shop output 77.0, spinning families 45.2, spinners 51.9, spinning output 65.2, weaving families 36.2, weavers 31.7, and cloth output 65.

In one sample village the village elders told us that weaving had become increasingly popular with the village families during the 50 years from 1882 to 1932. The number of families living in the village increased 16 per cent during that time, but the number of weaving families increased 71 per cent, from 58 to 86 per cent of the total. Table 95 shows how the number of families and the number of weaving families changed during the 50 years.

Weaving was done on three different kinds of looms locally known as clumsy, pulling, and iron machines. The original "clumsy" loom was a wooden loom whose shuttle was thrown by hand; the "pulling" loom was an improved model in which the shuttle was thrown from shuttle boxes activated by pulling a string that hung in front of the operator.

The iron loom was an automatic model driven by foot power transmitted through pedals, chains, and gears. The pulling model was introduced about 1908, the iron loom about 1920. The prices of the looms were reported as "clumsy" $8.00–$10.00, improved $15–$20, iron $28. It was generally said that after the loom was set up a weaver could make one piece of cloth per day on the clumsy loom, two on the pulling loom, and four on the iron loom.

The report from one village (Table 96) showed how the number and type of looms had changed in the 20 years from 1912 to 1932. The "clumsy" looms fell from 260 to 48 but the "improved" wooden models rose from 20 to 122, and the iron looms from zero to 69. The total number had fallen some 15 per cent but there had been an increase in possible production of some 90 per cent due to the use of more efficient looms. The possible daily output had risen from 300 to 570 pieces.

In the 83 weaving villages in the 3rd District there were wooden looms in 2,021 homes in 75 villages and iron looms in 173 homes in 26 villages. The iron looms were 7.9 per cent of the looms but produced 15.7 per cent of the output. The average gain per family, for those with the iron loom, was more than twice that of the families with the wood looms, $86.55 compared with $39.70.

In the 6th District there were 69 weaving villages, 54 with wood looms and 64 with iron looms. Families with iron looms were 49 per cent of the 2,648 total, but they produced 77 per cent of the output. The average gain of the iron loom families was almost three and one-half times that of those with wood looms, $91.60 compared with $26.60.

With the average number of weavers almost three per family it is easy to see why a local proverb says "There is rest for the weaver but none for the loom". In many families the weaving was carried on in shifts with the men doing the night work.

In order to overcome the cold and low humidity of the winter days, in some villages several families joined together to dig, roof, and equip a cooperative weaving cellar. One about 28 feet long, 14 feet wide, and 10 feet high would be large enough for four looms. The cellars were lighted by three or four small two foot square windows set into the south wall of the cellar. The low, above ground walls were made from sun dried earthen bricks. In the spring the cellar usually was filled in, so that the area could be used for farming and also because, if not filled in, the cellar would not be as warm and damp the following winter.

Several different kinds of cloth were woven in Ting Hsien but two, "big" cloth for local use and "chuang" cloth for export from the hsien, accounted for most of the output. Size of the piece was the principal difference between the two types of cloth. Both were white, both were woven with Tientsin machine spun warp and locally spun woof. There was some variation in the size of the pieces but the big cloth was generally 42 feet long and from 1'2" to 1'3" in width. The export cloth was about 36 feet in length and 1'2" in width.

Other types of cloth were rough big, smooth big, and striped. Both the warp and woof of the rough big cloth were hand spun thread. For the smooth cloth they were both machine spun. A piece of rough cloth was usually 46' x 1'4", the smooth cloth 34' x 1'1". The striped cloth, striped blue and white, blue and yellow, or yellow and white, was usually 40' x 1'2". The yellow thread was spun from yellow cotton. The blue was locally dyed.

Prices varied from market to market but the average price per piece in 1931 was big cloth $1.80, export cloth $1.20, and striped cloth $2.30. The weaver's profit was estimated at 30 cents per piece for the big cloth and 20 cents per piece for the export cloth. Families who had big cloth woven for them supplied the thread and paid the weaver 30 cents per piece.

Big cloth was woven in 378 villages, export cloth in 203. Over 1,000,000 pieces of export cloth and 606,000 pieces of big cloth were produced in 1931. All of the export cloth was sold to the cloth stores and shipped out of Ting Hsien. Figures from the 3rd and 6th Districts indicate that about 23 per cent of the big cloth was used by the weaving families, the rest sold. Cotton cloth was a large cash item for the village families.

It was reported that there was a big decrease in spinning and weaving during the 1st month of the New Year, both because it was vacation and holiday time and because an old custom, followed in some villages, forbade the farmers' daughters to use needle and thread during the 1st moon.

Other materials woven from cotton thread were large and small gauze, waist bands, leg bands to tie trouser bottoms around the ankles, and bags of various sizes. The latter were generally woven from three or four ply thread.

Some of the old weavers said that the weaving of the waist bands began in the 6th year of Chia Ch'ing, 1801, when the floods of the T'ang river drove many families from their homes and they had to find some way to keep from starving. Tradition says that at that time someone made a narrow loom like the ordinary cloth loom and began the weaving of the waist bands, which were 4.5 feet long and one inch wide, and the leg bands, which were 3.5 feet long and 2 inches wide.

The waist and leg bands were still woven only on the banks of the T'ang. All of the leg band weavers lived in the 6th District and 90 per cent of the waist band weavers. The other 10 per cent lived across the river in the 5th District.

Waist band weaving was an especially prosperous occupation during the early years of the Republic for there was a large market for them in the northwest areas. Poor economic conditions in the northwest had later cut the export of waist bands by some 50 per cent. In 1931 some 70 or 80 per cent of the output was exported to other parts of China. The price of a waist band loom was only $2.50 or $3.00.

Some 90 per cent of the gauze was shipped to the northwest, where it was used for funeral clothes. The other 10 per cent was used in Ting Hsien in making bean curd.

The field reports noted that the heavy cloth woven from three or four ply thread could not be made in the weaving cellars as the dampness wrinkled the cloth.

Cotton Cloth Exports

Records of the cloth stores, figures from the shipping records of the railroads, and the reports of men who had been in the cloth business for many years made it possible to work out a history of the market prices of the chuang (export) cloth, the maximum prices set by the cloth gild, and the number of pieces exported from Ting Hsien to other parts of China during the 40 years from 1892 through 1931. The export and production figures were apparently identical as the cloth, woven in a special size, 36' x 1'2", was made exclusively for export to other parts of China and was handled through the cloth markets.

In 1892 the price of the chuang cloth was 700 cash per piece. It was the same for the next 10 years. In 16 years there was only one increase. That was 50 cash, 7 per cent. In the next 12 years, 1908–1919, there were six increases. The amounts were first 50 cash, then 100, then 150,

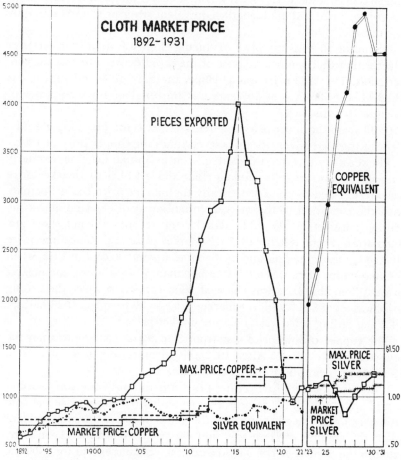

FIGURE 25. COTTON CLOTH, COPPER AND SILVER PRICES, EXPORTS

and finally 200 cash per piece. The seven increases totaled 700 cash. The copper price doubled in 28 years (see Figure 25).

The silver equivalent of the copper price of the cloth was 62 cents per piece in 1892. The decline in the silver-copper exchange rate,[2] plus the 1903 increase in the copper price, raised the silver equivalent to 99

2. See Chapter XIII.

cents per piece in 1905. From 1905 through 1922 it varied between 76 and 96 cents per piece. In 1922 it was 83 cents per piece. In 30 years, while the copper price had doubled, the equivalent silver price increased only one-third.

Beginning in 1923 the price of chuang cloth was quoted in terms of silver rather than copper, because of the rapid depreciation of the copper coins. The 1923 price was $1.00 per piece. In 1930 and 1931 it was $1.20. The difference of 20 cents was the total of three increases of five and 10 cents each.

In 40 years the silver price increased 94 per cent. The copper equivalent of the 1931 silver price was seven times the copper price of 1892.

The records show that the cloth gild, at its annual meeting, regularly set a maximum price for chuang cloth above which the market price was not allowed to go. Theoretically the market price could fluctuate with the condition of the market, providing it did not go above the ceiling price set by the gild. Actually the records did not show any fluctuation. From 1892 to 1927 the market price and the ceiling price changed at the same time and by the same amount, except in 1915, when the maximum price was set 100 rather than 50 cash above the market price. When the price was changed from copper to silver the ceiling price was set at $1.20 with the market price $1.00 per piece. In 1930 and 1931 the ceiling price was $1.42, the market price $1.20.

The copper ceiling price was from 5 to 9 per cent more than the reported market price. After 1922 the silver ceiling price was from 18 to 29 per cent above the market price.

While theoretically the ceiling price was the only one controlled it would appear, from the records, that actually the market price was controlled as well. The gild control of the market price is still more evident when the amount of cloth sold and exported from Ting Hsien is related to the quoted prices. The records showed that except for 1900 the number of pieces handled increased every year from 1892 to 1915, from 600,000 to 4,000,000 pieces. Six years later only 950,000 pieces were exported, a decrease of more than 75 per cent. From 1921 to 1930 the number was usually just over one million pieces. While the number of pieces exported more than doubled from 1903 to 1910, the copper price went up only 6.5 per cent, from 750 to 800 cash, and the silver equivalent went down 18.2 per cent, from 93 to 76 cents per piece. From 1910 to 1915 the number of pieces doubled again, from two to four million.

The copper price went up 37 per cent, from 800 to 1,100 cash per piece, but the silver equivalent rose only 5 per cent, from 76 to 80 cents.

During the six years from 1915 to 1921, the number of pieces sold went down 76.3 per cent, but during that time there were two increases in the copper price for a total of 300 cash, 27 per cent. The silver equivalent was nine cents, 11 per cent, higher in 1921 than it was in 1915. One wonders how it was that a community would see a 75 per cent decrease in demand and a sales loss of over $2,300,000 without attempting to save some of it by reducing rather than increasing prices. Even if it was spare time work the loss of the income from over a million and a half days of work could not help but be serious for any community.

Some of the loss undoubtedly was salvaged by shifting the looms to the weaving of other kinds of cloth. However, it does not seem probable that the local market could absorb any large additional amount. Unfortunately we were not able to get from the gild leaders their explanation of how it was that the price could go up in the face of a rapid decline in demand, or their estimate of the success of the weavers in shifting to other types of cloth when a large part of the market for chuang cloth disappeared. The price and output figures seem to indicate that the price of chuang cloth was very closely controlled by the cloth gild, a control made possible by the complete monopoly of the export market.

One wonders what were the influences that, after there had been a steadily increasing demand for almost a quarter century, cut the demand for chuang cloth by 50 per cent in four years and by more than 75 per cent in six years. Competition from Japanese cloth or from machine woven cloth from Tientsin might be a possible explanation, but in view of rapidly rising world prices and demand due to World War I, it hardly seems to be a probable one. We do not know of changed conditions in North China that would explain it. The floods of 1917 and the drought of 1920–21 do not seem to have been large factors. Poor economic conditions in the northwest provinces were given by one of our reports as the reason for the decline about that time of the market for waist bands.

The chuang cloth was shipped from six centers. Chuan Lu and Ch'ing Feng Tien, the two market towns in the 6th District, handled over 73 per cent of the shipments. Twenty-three per cent went from the hsien city. The business was handled by 45 cloth stores in the six centers. One had a history of 150 years. Twenty-five were less than 10 years old. The 45 stores had 350 employees, of whom 57 were apprentices. The apprentices were being trained by 33 stores. Three of the larger ones had three apprentices each. The capital of the stores ranged from $600 to some $12,000 with the average just under $4,000.

It was said that the cloth market in the city, where the city cloth stores regularly did their buying, was first opened in the 31st year of Ch'ien Lung, 1766. During the winter months, the busy season for the cloth weavers and merchants, the market was generally open from nine to 12 hours on market days. The usual amount of cloth handled was about 1,500 pieces. The smallest amount in 1931 was between 600 and 700 pieces, the largest about 4,000. The largest day's business in the previous 10 years was 17,000 pieces.

During the 10 years 1921–1930 over 10,600,000 pieces of chuang cloth worth over $11,000,000 were shipped from Ting Hsien. Over 70 per cent went to Chahar, with most of the remainder going to Shansi and Suiyuan. Less than one per cent was sent to Hopei.

The cloth going to Chahar and Shansi was shipped in 50 piece bundles except for Ta T'ung. There a bale was 45 pieces. For Suiyuan the cloth was packed in 40 piece bundles except for Hsing He, which used the 50 piece bale.

There was a tax of $1.20 per bale on all shipments except those for Suiyuan. For them the rate was $1.80 per bale. Railroad freight varied from $1.50 to $2.60 per package, the shipping commission from 50 to 90 cents. The total shipping charges amounted to from six to 10 cents per piece for the Chahar and Shansi shipments and from 14 to 16 cents per piece for those sent to Suiyuan.

Some locally grown wool was made into rugs. Rugs were also made from cow hair that had been ground with a stone to remove the lime with which it had been treated, teased with a bow, and spun on the ordinary spinning wheel. The cow hair rugs were being supplanted by factory woven rugs.

Food Industries

Bean curd making was a hsien wide activity reported by 249 villages, carried on by 735 families and 1,570 persons. It was a year round activity except for the hottest summer months. The curd was made from green or yellow beans, cotton seed oil, carbon (ashes), and brine. The beans were ground into small pieces, put to soak for five or six hours, then ground in a hand operated stone mill. A mixture of cotton seed oil and carbon, that had been boiled together, was added to the bean paste and the mixture brought to a boil. As the cooked bean paste rose to the top of the kettle it was dipped off and put into a cloth bag. The bag was put into a sieve and the liquid pressed out with a wooden paddle. The dried cake was fed to the pigs. The liquor was put into an iron kettle and boiled. The scum, known as "beancurd skin", was skimmed off once or twice. It could be used as food. Salt water was added to the boiled liquid to coagulate the curd. The amount of salt to be added had to be accurately gauged, for with too little the curd would not form, with too much it would be bitter. The curd was put into a mold that was about 2'7" long and 1'7" wide. A piece of cloth, then a bamboo cover, then several bricks were put on top of the mold and left for about two hours to press out any excess liquid. The weight of a finished mold of bean curd was about 37.5 catties. The mold was cut into from 50 to 80 pieces which retailed for two or three cents a piece, or a total of about $1.50.

Noodles were made from wheat flour, salt, and water. About 30 catties of flour were handled at one time. The mixture was first worked into a ball, then rolled out flat and thin with a rolling pin. It was then cut into four or five pieces that were brushed with peanut oil, rolled, and put into an earthen ware crock that was kept warm with a cotton padded cloth cover. After a time the pieces were taken out, spread out on a board, dusted with flour, and then rolled to about finger thickness. These were then rolled up and put back into the crock. When the dough had become soft it was taken out, unrolled, and fastened between two bamboo sticks. Dough and sticks were then put into a brick pit that was about 7 x 3 x 4 feet. One foot of its depth was usually below the ground level to give warmth in winter and coolness in summer. When the dough had reached the proper consistency it was taken out and the bamboo strips were pulled apart to make the strips of dough long and fine. One bamboo rod was then put on top of a frame that was about 10 feet high. The other was allowed to swing clear and by its weight gradually stretch the noodles. Sometimes two or three sticks were added if extra weight was needed. When the strips of dough had been stretched until they almost touched the ground they were allowed to dry. They were then taken down, put on a board, cut into pieces about eight inches long, and made into bundles that weighed about four ounces each. A man could make about 20 catties of noodles a day by hand.

Noodle making machines were introduced about 1920 and were used by some of the larger food shops. They were too expensive for home use as they cost $50 for a small machine and $70 for a large one. Their output was about 60 catties per worker per day.

Seventy-seven villages reported 165 families and 412 persons making noodles. The annual output was 573,300 catties worth 10 cents per catty. The reported gain was $27.85 per worker.

Another group of 351 families living in 94 villages had 1,206 members who were making fine noodles or vermicelli from beans, kaoliang, and sweet potatoes. Their output was 14,500 catties of bean noodles, 497,000 catties of kaoliang noodles, and 826,750 catties of sweet potato noodles, worth some $160,860. The prices of the noodles were bean 25 cents, kaoliang 15 cents, and sweet potato 10 cents per catty. The estimated gain was only 3.0 per cent, the gain per worker $4.20. This was the only home industry in which the gain was less than 10 per cent. Inquiry showed that the residuum of the noodle making process was used to feed pigs and that these families made most of their home industry gain from pork rather than from noodles. The vermicelli shops reported a profit rate of only 8 per cent.

In making bean noodles the beans, after being soaked in water until "bubbles came up from the bottom", were taken out and dried for two days, then ground in a small hand stone mill. The pulp was strained through a sieve into an earthen jar. Yin chiang and hsiao chiang, two kinds of sour paste made from green beans, were then added. The mixture was thoroughly stirred and allowed to settle. The "clean juice" was skimmed off the top and thrown away. The residue was strained again, mixed with more yin chiang and hsiao chiang and, after the "clean juice" had been removed a second time, was put into a cloth and hung up to dry. The white part of the bean flour was used for noodles, the black part was fed to the pigs.

Boiling water was added to the white bean flour to make a paste that was squeezed through small holes in the bottom of a dipper and dropped into a boiling kettle. When cooked the noodles were taken out, put into cold water, and then hung on a frame to dry. The noodles were generally bleached by adding alum to the flour paste. Kaoliang and sweet potato noodles were made by a similar process.

Other Industries

The equipment for making sesamum seed oil cost some $22.10, a stone mill $14.00, two big iron pots $1.50, an oil pot $4.00, a big willow basket $1.00, two willow twig scoops $1.00, and a long handled gourd dipper 60 cents. One tou of sesame seed made from 6.5 to 7.0 catties of oil, worth 30 cents a catty in 1931. The oil cake was used for fertilizer and was worth $4.50 per 100 catties.

Pig bristle sorting was the second largest home industry, with an estimated annual output of some $760,000 and a gain of $95,000. Unlike spinning and weaving, which were almost hsien wide, the bristle industry was concentrated in two villages near the southern border of the hsien, nearly 10 miles from the railroad. The work was carried on by 80 families and 445 workers. Most of the 90 men were engaged in the buying and selling. The women did most of the sorting. It was a business that required the use of considerable amounts of capital, for the bristles were purchased in Shantung, Honan, Shansi, and as far away as the Three Eastern Provinces, shipped to Ting Hsien for processing, and then sold to purchasers from Tientsin for export. Some of the families were able to provide the necessary capital. Others borrowed the needed funds from the money lenders.

The bristles were washed, combed, and sorted into three sizes, top quality with lengths of from five to seven inches, medium quality from three to four inches long and lowest grade from one to three inches long. The prices ranged from $1.00 to $6.00 per catty with the medium grade price about $2.00 per catty. The bristles too short for export were used locally to help make water baskets and buckets water tight, for bristle rope, or for fertilizer.

A worker ordinarily sorted some 20 catties per day. Some of the sorters were paid on a piece work basis which averaged about seven coppers, 1.75 cents, per catty or about 35 cents for a day's work. The estimated gain was some 24 cents per catty.

Mat weaving, the fourth largest home industry, with an output of $361,400, was not as concentrated as the bristle sorting but it was reported by only seven villages, five of which were in the 6th District. Seven hundred and seventy of the 1,012 families lived in one village (see Chapter IV). It, quite naturally, was the chief mat market of the hsien.

Mat weaving required almost no tools but did require considerable manual skill. The reeds, most of which came from outside Ting Hsien, were prepared for weaving by splitting, removing the bark, soaking in water, and pressing under a mill stone until flat. In winter time the weaving was done in a cellar in order to keep the reeds moist and soft. In the summer it was often done out under the trees. It was a moderately prosperous industry, for the estimated gain was $58 per worker per year. About 10 per cent of the families made it their year round occupation. For the others it was part time work, for they, like so many of the home industry families, were busy with farm work during the growing season.

TABLE 92. INDUSTRIAL SHOPS, FAMILIES, WORKERS,
OUTPUT, PROFIT OR GAIN

| | | Workers | | Output | | Profit or Gain | |
	Number	Total	Aver-age	Total	Per Shop	Amount	% of Output
City shops	204	824	4.0	$ 730,910	$3,580	$ 216,150[3]	29.6
Village shops	1,578	7,506	4.8	2,975,480	1,880	285,290[3]	9.1
Home industry families	47,400[1]	90,429[2]	1.9	4,865,500	105	878,340[4]	18.0
	49,182[1]	98,759[2]		$8,571,890		$1,379,780	16.1

[1] Includes some duplication because of multiple industries and families and workers engaged in more than one industry.

[2] Males 25,077, females 73,682.

[3] After paying workers' wages.

[4] No wages paid workers.

TABLE 93. TYPES OF INDUSTRY: SHOPS, FAMILIES, WORKERS, OUTPUT

	Number	Workers	Output	Output Per Worker	Per Cent of Total
Cotton Ginning, Spinning, and Weaving					
City shops	23	72	$ 76,380	$1,060	
Village shops	316	1,244	1,811,840	1,440	
Village families	42,518	80,212	2,948,960	40	
Total or average	42,857	81,528	4,837,180	60	56.4
Weaving Hair, Reeds, Straw, Twigs, and Wool					
City shops	1	7	2,590	370	
Village shops	–	–	–	–	
Village families	2,608	4,580	484,640	110	
Total or average	2,609	4,587	487,230	110	5.7
Food					
City shops	74	259	203,760	780	
Village shops	361	998	401,440	400	
Village families	1,353	3,441	425,420	120	
Total or average	1,788	4,698	1,030,620	220	12.0
Wood and Bamboo					
City shops	21	74	28,760	390	
Village shops	713	3,547	371,440	100	
Village families	336	642	77,900	120	
Total or average	1,070	4,263	478,100	110	5.6
Metal					
City shops	20	46	11,700	250	
Village shops	56	322	126,880	390	
Village families	26	51	26,770	520	
Total or average	102	419	165,350	400	1.9
Chemical					
City shops	40	245	341,110	1,390	
Village shops	116	1,334	239,200	180	
Village families	173	594	58,810	100	
Total or average	329	2,173	639,120	290	7.5
Miscellaneous					
City shops	25	121	66,610	550	
Village shops	16	51	24,680	500	
Village families	386	909	843,000	930	
Total or average	427	1,081	934,290	860	10.9

TABLE 94. INDUSTRIAL WAGES[1]

Per Day		(Per Month, cont.)	
Eye medicine	$0.40–1.00	Tailors	9.00
Sawyers	.50	Iron	7.00
Mat sheds	.45	Seal cutters	7.00
Per Month		Copper and tin	6.00
Leather:		Cart makers	5.00
Headman	30.00	Brick kiln	4.00
Trained worker	12.00	*Per Year*	
Graduate apprentice	10.00	Cotton ginning, laborers	60–70
Bookkeeper	10.00	Noodles	60
Foreman	5.00	Felt mats	40–50
Cook	4.00	Peanut oil	30–40
Laborer	3.50	Oil	30

1 Tips and presents generally added about $20 per year for workers and $10 for apprentices. Cost of meals was about $4.50 per month.

TABLE 95. INCREASE IN NUMBER OF FAMILIES AND FAMILIES WEAVING IN ONE VILLAGE, 1882–1932

Date	Total Families	Families Weaving	Per Cent Weaving
1882	155	90	58
1887	157	96	61
1892	158	110	70
1897	160	120	75
1902	162	125	77
1907	164	130	79
1912	165	130	79
1917	169	135	80
1922	172	140	81
1927	177	150	85
1932	180	154	86

TABLE 96. NUMBER AND KINDS OF LOOMS IN ONE VILLAGE, 1912–1932

Year	Iron	Wood		Total
		Improved	Original	
1912	–	20	260	280
1917	–	45	225	270
1922	15	72	168	255
1927	36	84	126	246
1932	69	122	48	239

TABLE 97. WORKSHOPS IN CITY AND SUBURBS, 1931

	Shops	Workers	Output	Per Cent Gain
Cotton Ginning, Spinning, and Weaving				
Ginning	18	55	$ 70,890	9
Rope	5	17	5,490	15
	23	72	76,380	
Wool Spinning				
Rugs	1	7	2,590	20
	1	7	2,590	
Food				
Cakes and condiments	9	69	85,350	21
Condiments	1	4	1,470	16
Candy	4	14	2,370	12
Flour mill	31	84	61,980	9
Flour, green bean and noodles	6	22	8,280	10
——, green bean	2	4	1,610	15
Noodles	5	10	6,400	17
Oil, cotton seed and peanut	4	17	12,550	19
——, sesame	7	16	4,950	18
Vermicelli	5	19	18,800	8
	74	259	203,760	
Wood and Bamboo				
Bamboo implements	2	11	6,620	10
Bellows	1	1	200	20
Boxes and wardrobes	5	22	6,810	14
Carts	2	5	2,400	13
Furniture	4	13	4,160	14
Sedan chairs	3	9	2,780	16
Sieves and steamers	2	6	2,380	15
Timber yard	1	3	820	13
Umbrellas	1	4	2,590	11
	21	74	28,760	

(continued on next page)

(TABLE 97 CONTINUED)

	Shops	Workers	Output	Per Cent Gain
Metal				
Blacksmith	2	7	3,900	13
Brass	3	6	1,450	38
Brass locks	1	3	1,100	24
Brass ornaments	1	1	480	39
Iron shop	5	17	2,040	21
Pewter	2	2	630	19
Tin	6	10	2,100	17
	20	46	11,700	
Chemical				
Cosmetics	1	2	4,800	7
Dyeing	9	41	10,110	21
Eye medicine	18	155	303,260	52
Paper	3	26	13,040	11
Soap, chicken fat	2	5	1,780	19
——, Chinese	2	2	250	32
——, foreign	2	6	2,890	16
Tanning	3	8	4,900	18
	40	245	341,110	
Miscellaneous				
Boxes, paper	2	7	1,300	25
Cigarettes	1	6	2,000	20
Flint	1	1	480	10
Heddles	1	1	120	28
Oil baskets	1	2	580	12
Oiled cloth	1	2	1,500	12
Pens	2	8	3,350	11
Shoes	14	86	51,400	12
Shoe parts	1	3	–	–
Uniforms	1	5	5,880	20
	25	121	66,610	
Total	204	824	730,910	
Average		4.0	3,590	
Average per worker			890	

Stores in city, 162; in suburbs, 42.

TABLE 98. WORKSHOPS IN 453 VILLAGES, 1931

	Shops	Workers	Output	Price[1]	Per Cent Gain
Cotton Ginning, Spinning, and Weaving					
Ginning[2]	316	1,244	$1,811,840		6
	316	1,244	1,811,840		
Food					
Flour mills[2]	251	599	215,150	$ 0.07[3]	14
Oil, cotton seed[2]	107	371	70,500	.11[3]	14
——, peanut	–	–	79,170	.16[3]	–
Wine	3	28	36,620	.17[3]	7
	361	998	401,440		
Wood and Bamboo					
Bamboo implements	1	5	3,000		17
Bellows	2	4	720	4.00	30
Boxes and wardrobes	34	120	21,380		26
Carts	61	207	55,080	62.00	13
Frames	1	6	640		37
Timber yards	614	3,205	290,620		17
	713	3,547	371,440		
Metal					
Blacksmith	20	62	6,590		32
Brass	1	2	700		30
Cotton batting machines	2	10	5,360	40.00	8
Iron goods	3	32	23,660		–
Iron parts of plows	1	11	500		33
Pewter	2	8	700		47
Tin	1	3	210		17
Water wheels	18	168	79,160	89.00	10
Water wheel buckets	8	26	10,000	1.10	18
	56	322	126,880		
Chemical					
Brick yards	73	1,105	154,060		11
Dyeing[2]	23	81	43,400		19
Earthen vessels	2	28	9,750		22
Paper	7	38	17,200		24
Tanning	7	19	4,860		24
Tiles	4	63	9,930		46
	116	1,334	239,200		

(continued on next page)

(TABLE 98 CONTINUED)

	Shops	Workers	Output	Price[1]	Per Cent Gain
		Miscellaneous			
Flint	1	5	700	.14	35
Hats	1	3	1,810		30
Rope	5	15	1,410		31
Shoes	5	22	6,360		15
Stockings	4	16	14,400	.25[4]	16
	16	61	24,680		
Total	1,578	7,506[2]	2,975,480		
Average per shop		4.7	1,890		
Average per worker			400		

[1] Each, except as indicated.

[2] Females in four industries: flour mills 156, cotton ginning 144, oils 14, dyeing 3, total 317.

[3] Per catty.

[4] Per pair.

TABLE 99. VILLAGE HOME INDUSTRY: COTTON SPINNING AND WEAVING

	Villages	Families	Males	Females	Output	Price[1]	Per Cent Gain
Cloth, export	203	13,385	7,029	32,092	$1,216,390	$1.20	17
——, big	378	–	–	–	1,090,630	1.80	–
{ Gauze, small[3]	1	2	2	–	1,280	1.00	13
{ ——, large	–	–	–	–	400	2.50	–
Leg bands	3	45	66	67	15,310	.08	19
Rope	2	48	40	15	3,780	.25[2]	31
Sacks, grain	8	285	251	369	32,150	1.45	33
——, money, big	1	10	10	29	1,000	2.00	25
——, money, small	1	5	5	12	200	.20	25
Spinning	437	28,367	2,106	37,613	548,560	.57[2]	21
Waistbands	5	371	301	205	39,260	.40	38
		42,518	9,810	70,402	$2,948,960		

[1] Per piece except as indicated.

[2] Per catty.

[3] Items bracketed were made by the same family.

TABLE 100. VILLAGE HOME INDUSTRY: HAIR, REED, STRAW, TWIG, AND WOOL WEAVING

	Villages	Families	Males	Females	Output	Price[1]	% Gain
Hair nets	1	1	–	4	$ 90	$0.02	50
Reed curtains	26	180	232	36	30,540	1.00	20
Reed mats	7	1,012	747	1,041	361,390	.70	29
Reed mat baskets	8	82	134	14	2,500	.15	47
Reed mat covers	9	106	186	4	7,490	.05	30
Straw hats	2	25	–	39	–	–	–
Straw pan covers	10	354	480	145	6,230	.25	60
Sage twig baskets	4	7	9	–	1,910	–[2]	31
Willow twig baskets	13	146	215	45	8,900	–[3]	–
Willow water baskets	12	466	654	232	54,280	.55	20
Willow winnowing and water baskets	2	165	220	10	–	–	–
Willow winnowing baskets	2	22	33	–	4,470	.50	14
Willow scoops	7	12	15	–	790	.07	42
Wool rugs	1	25	45	25	5,040	.80	25
Wool saddle quarter straps	–	5	10	5	1,010	.10	25
		2,608	2,980	1,600	$484,640		

[1] Each.

[2] Manure 10 cents, big 30, grain 80.

[3] Corn 10 cents, manure 20, cotton 30, big 40, open grain $1.00.

TABLE 101. VILLAGE HOME INDUSTRY: FOOD

	Villages	Families	Males	Females	Output	Price[1]	Per Cent Gain
Bean curd	249	735	922	648	$162,610	$1.50[2]	20
Bean sauce	1	3	9	–	1,130	.09	22
Candy	2	7	22	–	3,110	.14	10
Noodles	77	165	353	59	57,330	.10	20
Vermicelli, sweet potato	94	351	1,099	107	82,680	.10	3
——, kaoliang					74,560	.15	
——, green bean					3,620	.25	
Sesame candy	4	12	25	–	6,250	.15	13
Sesame oil	51	68	100	42	12,960	.30	17
Vinegar	4	8	29	1	1,670	.04	25
Wine, date	2	2	15	–	3,500	.10	30
——, yellow	2	2	10	–	16,000	.15	27
		1,353	2,584	857	$425,420		

[1] Per catty, except as indicated.   [2] Per mould.

TABLE 102. VILLAGE HOME INDUSTRY: WOOD AND BAMBOO

	Villages	Fami-lies	Males and Females	Output	Price[1]	Per Cent Gain
Bamboo rakes	1	1	1	$ 140	$ 0.10	–
Bellows	2	3	3	830	4.10	28
Benches, small	1	16	16	250	.05	20
{ Bread steamers[2]	1	1	3	400	1.10	30
{ Boxes	–	–	–	1,760	.05	–
Chairs	1	6	6	3,000	1.00	30
Ladles	2	64	90	9,690	.11	18
Looms	1	1	2	160	8.00	38
Pails	3	9	13	1,700	1.00	25
Peanut sieves	1	3	3	50	9.00	33
{ Pecks[2]	1	1	1	630	2.50	60
{ Pestles	–	–	–	6,600	.20	–
Pints	2	16	46	1,000	.05	–
Pitchforks	7	76	215	16,100	.50	27
{ Plows[2]	1	3	5	550	2.10	38
{ Poles	–	–	–	13,140	.20	–
{ ——, carrying[2]	1	1	2	240	.80	25
{ ——, spade handles	–	–	–	40	.20	28
Rolling pins	2	28	56	5,010	.10	40
Saddles	1	4	9	800	.25	40
Scales	2	2	5	440	–	33
Screens, for paper	2	2	2	150	1.25	68
——, for ko pai	1	1	1	50	.15	66
Seeders	1	1	2	150	3.00	16
Sieve hoops	1	1	3	–	–	20
Spindles	–	50	70	900	.09	28
Spinning wheels	–	2	4	140	.50	20
Thread reels	–	10	20	2,000	.80	25
{ Toys[2]	1	10	26	320	.04	–
{ Toy bowls	–	–	–	240	.02	–
{ Toy incense cases	–	–	–	230	.03	–
{ Toy lantern bottoms	–	–	–	40	.01	–
{ Toy penholders	–	–	–	2,700	.03	–
Water wheel handles	1	1	4	800	.10	–
Weaving reeds	–	2	4	700	.35	14
Well windlasses	–	15	16	5,870	2.50	20
Winnowing machines	2	6	12	1,080	12.00	33
		336	640	$77,900		

1 Each.   2 Items bracketed were made by the same family.

TABLE 103. VILLAGE HOME INDUSTRY: METALS

	Villages	Families	Males	Output	Price[1]	Per Cent Gain
Corn removers	1	1	2	$ 140	$ 0.01	30
Horse shoes	1	1	3	680	.15[2]	27
Kettles	1	1	1	200	–	40
Lanterns	1	1	1	200	–	30
Locks	1	2	4	1,010	.10	10
Looms	1	1	2	500	28.00	27
Rakes	1	1	1	20	.40	25
Razors	1	1	3	430	.18	22
Vegetable cutters	1	3	6	410	.12	25
Wire lanterns	1	2	3	70	.15	66
{ Wire scoops[3]	1	12	25	22,500	.125	17
Wire horse muzzles	–	–	–	210	.07	–
{ Wire mouse traps	–	–	–	400	.04	–
		26	51	$26,770		

[1] Each, except as indicated.   [2] Per set.
[3] Items bracketed were made by the same family.

TABLE 104. VILLAGE HOME INDUSTRY: CHEMICALS

	Villages	Families	Males	Females	Output	Price[1]	Per Cent Gain
Candles	2	4	21	–	$ 4,720	$0.18	44
Firecrackers	9	64	164	56	12,920		37
Glue	1	6	15	–	6,440	.33	15
Incense	2	19	75	30	9,370	.03[2]	17
Leather	3	3	12	–	4,860		19
Matches	1	7	9	5	280	.04	63
Paper, black	1	5	8	5	530	3.30[3]	38
——, ko pei	1	16	80	–	11,430	1.43[3]	11
{ ——, straw[4]	2	13	55	–	2,560	.05	50
{ ——, tinder	–	–	–	–	140	.41[3]	
Soap	9	28	32	9	3,360	.74	26
Toilet preparations	1	1	6	–	1,800[4]	–[5]	37
Face powder	2	7	12	–	400	1.10	49
		173	489	105	$58,810		

[1] Per catty, except as indicated.   [2] Per bundle.   [3] Per 1,000 pieces.
[4] Items bracketed were made by the same family.
[5] Toilet preparations:

Cosmetics	$ 500	$0.10 per bottle	Cologne	200	.20 per bottle
Pomatum	450	.15 " "	Tooth powder	80	.02 " bag
Perfume cream	330	.07 " "	Total	$1,800	
Talc powder	240	.16 " box			

TABLE 105. VILLAGE HOME INDUSTRY: MISCELLANEOUS

	Villages	Families	Males	Females	Output	Price[1]	Per Cent Gain
Bristles, pig	2	80	90	355	$760,000	$1.90[2]	13
Brooms	17	214	269	–	9,130	.10	30
Brushes	3	42	43	5	5,610	.02–.04	25
Heddles	3	18	43	12	1,970	.305	27
Horse collars	1	1	2	–	500	1.00	20
Rope, hemp	4	15	30	12	9,510	.33[2]	15
{ Sausage casings, pig[5]	1	15	30	15	43,200	.30[3]	17
{ ——, sheep	–	–	–	–	12,000	.40[3]	–
Shoes	1	1	3	–	1,080	1.50[4]	27
		386	510	399	$843,000		

[1] Each, except as indicated.   [3] Per piece.
[2] Per catty.   [4] Per pair.
[5] Items bracketed were made by the same family.

TABLE 106. NUMBER OF DIFFERENT HOME INDUSTRIES IN VILLAGES

Industries	Villages	Per Cent	Industries	Villages	Per Cent
1	28	6.2	5	56	12.4
2	96	21.2	6	26	5.7
3	135	29.8	7	10	2.2
4	101	22.3	8	1	0.2
				453	100.0

TABLE 107. CITY WORKSHOPS

Number	Workers Shops	Persons	Per Cent
Under 5	148	381	72.5
5–9	44	262	21.6
10–14	10	111	4.9
15–19	–	–	–
20 and over	2	70	1.0
	204	824	100.0

Number	Apprentices Shops	Per Cent	Apprentices
None	87	42.7	–
1	91	44.6	91
2	16	7.8	32
3	7	3.4	21
4	2	1.0	8
10	1	0.5	10
	204	100.0	162

Amount	Invested Capital Shops	Per Cent
Under $100	22	10.8
100–199	44	21.5
200–299	40	19.6
300–399	39	19.1
400–499	21	10.3
500–599	12	5.9
600–999	10	4.9
1,000–1,999	11	5.4
2,000 and over	5	2.5
	204	100.0

Minimum	$30	Average	$380
Maximum	$5,500	Capital per worker	$95
Total	$77,160		

(continued on next page)

(TABLE 107 CONTINUED)

Value of Goods Produced

Amount	Shops	Per Cent
Under $1,000	68	33.5
1,000–1,999	59	29.0
2,000–2,999	34	16.8
3,000–3,999	8	3.9
4,000–4,999	7	3.4
5,000–5,999	7	3.4
6,000–9,999	10	5.0
10,000–14,999	2	1.0
15,000–24,999	4	2.0
25,000–49,999	2	1.0
50,000 and over	2	1.0
	203[1]	100.0

Total $730,910.

[1] One shop omitted. Makes shoes for shoe store from material supplied by store. Income represents value of work done rather than of goods produced.

Annual Profit

Amount	Shops	Per Cent
Under $200	109	53.7
200–399	46	22.7
400–599	19	9.3
600–799	1	0.5
800–999	3	1.5
1,000–1,499	9	4.4
1,500–2,499	7	3.4
2,500–4,999	6	3.0
10,000 and over	3	1.5
	203	100.0

Total $216,150.

TABLE 108. WAGES, COTTON GINNING AND BATTING, 1921–1933

Date	Daily Wage	Yearly Wage	Piece Rates[1] Ginning[2] Raw Cotton	Seed	Batting Lint
1921	$0.35	$30	$0.55	S0.40	$0.80
1922	.35	35	.55	.40	.80
1923	.35	40	.55	.40	.85
1924	.35	50	.61	.50	.90
1925	.35	55	.65	.50	.90
1926	.40	60	.75	.60	1.00
1927	.40	70	.71	.60	.90
1928	.40	65	.78	.65	1.00
1929	.45	65	.85	.70	1.10
1930	.45	60	.85	.70	1.10
1931	.35	60	.85	.70	1.00
1932	.30	50	.78	.65	.80
1933	.30	50	.59	.50	.60

[1] Per 100 catties.

[2] Ginning rate per 100 catties of lint was generally the same as the batting rate. It varied from $0.75 to $1.10.

TABLE 109. EXPORT CLOTH: RETAIL PRICE, MAXIMUM GILD PRICE, AND EXPORTS, 1892–1931

Year	Average Price[1] Copper	Silver	Maximum Price Copper	Silver	Pieces Exported (000)
1892	700	$0.62	750	$0.66	600
1893		.66		.70	650
1894		.68		.73	740
1895		.71		.76	820
1896		.75		.81	830
1897		.79		.85	840
1898		.89		.96	920
1899		.88		.95	940
1900		.86		.92	850
1901		.83		.89	890
1902		.90		.97	950
1903	750	.93	800	.99	980
1904		.95		1.01	1,100
1905		.99		1.06	1,200
1906		.91		.97	1,250
1907		.84		.90	1,350
1908		.80		.85	1,450
1909	800	.76	850	.81	1,800
1910		.76		.81	2,000
1911	850	.82	900	.87	2,600
1912	950	.86	1,000	.91	2,900
1913		.79		.83	3,000
1914		.77		.81	3,500
1915	1,100	.80	1,200	.87	4,000
1916		.80		.87	3,400
1917		.91		.99	3,200
1918	1,200	.87	1,300	.94	2,500
1919		.85		.92	2,000
1920	1,400	.96	1,500	1.02	1,200
1921		.89		.95	950
1922		.83		.88	1,090
1923	1,974	1.00		1.20	1,080
1924	2,317	1.00		1.20	1,100
1925	2,896	1.00		1.20	1,172
1926	3,895	1.10		1.30	1,055
1927	4,125	1.10		1.42	810
1928	4,827	1.15		1.42	1,004
1929	4,959	1.15		1.42	1,121
1930	4,908	1.20		1.42	1,220
1931	4,908	1.20		1.42	–

59,062

[1] Market prices were quoted in copper from 1892 through 1922, in silver thereafter.

TABLE 110. COTTON CLOTH EXPORTS

Exports from Cloth Markets, 1921–1930

	Pieces	Value	Per Cent
Chuan Lu	4,188,000	$4,439,700	40.1
Ch'ing Feng Tien	3,535,000	3,666,000	33.1
City	2,492,900	2,550,300	23.1
Ta Hsing Chuang	278,000	284,700	2.6
Ta Hsi Chang	67,600	73,400	0.7
Hsiao Tsai T'un	41,000	47,800	0.4
	10,602,500	$11,061,900	100.0

Destination of Exports, 1921–1930

	Pieces	Value	Per Cent
Chahar	7,459,600	$7,782,400	70.4
Shansi	1,826,100	1,894,700	17.1
Suiyuan	1,280,500	1,344,400	12.1
Hopei	36,300	40,400	0.4
	10,602,500	$11,061,900	100.0

PART 5. SOCIAL AND RELIGIOUS ACTIVITIES

CHAPTER XVI

Yang Ke and Other Recreation

LOCAL TRADITION says that the poet Su Tung-p'o (1036–1101), when he was the magistrate in Ting Hsien, wrote songs for the farmers to sing while they were planting the rice fields watered by the Black and White Dragon Springs, in the northwest part of the hsien. The Chinese name for these songs is yang ke, green sprout or planting songs.

Local tradition does not say, nor does the memory of the oldest inhabitant recall, by what stages the yang ke moved from the rice fields onto the local stage, by what metamorphosis the original simple group songs became plays, with the dialogue generally sung and accompanied by music, nor how the singers changed from blue clad farmers into actors in costume performing for the pleasure and amusement of the people.

Nor does local tradition have an answer for another question: Why are the Ting Hsien yang ke different from those in other parts of the country? In some places they have kept their original character of simple folk songs. The Shanghai yang ke were street dances. In Peking the term was applied to the parade through the streets of actors on three or four foot stilts. There the chief actor, taking the part of a monk, led the procession and cleared a way through the crowd by swinging a long stick in front of him. The other characters were usually a regular fairly standardized group, a bearded man, a woman, a grandmother, a young man, a butterfly girl, a painted face, a stupid boy and his wife, military and civil attendants. The group sang short songs, played on the drums and gongs, made jokes and humorous remarks, and amused the crowd by their actions. In Shantung the yang ke stilt walkers used to be part of the entertainment at the temple fairs.

In the Experimental District we found five groups of yang ke players. On a proportional basis, this would indicate a total of some 36 groups in the hsien. Usually there were 15 or 16 men in a group. This number would include actors, musicians, make up and property men. Most of them were farmers during the growing season and gave the yang ke as amateurs or semi-amateurs for special village celebrations or in connection with the temple fairs. A few of the better actors apparently were paid a salary for their yang ke work. Some of the actors took boys as apprentices and taught them the singing and acting. There evidently was no fixed term for such an apprenticeship. The principal requirement for the boy was that he should be smart, have a good memory, and possess a reasonably good voice. As most of the yang ke players were illiterate, the roles were memorized and handed on from one actor to another. Female parts were all played by men. The costumes were of the type often used in the Chinese theater, but generally were not very elaborate.

New Year's time, especially at the time of the Lantern Festival, the spring and autumn festivals, the temple fairs, and after the harvest were the times when the yang ke were given. If the village had no permanent stage a temporary one was easily and cheaply erected. Sometimes a mat shed, costing about $15, was added to cover the audience, most of whom stood in the open space in front of the stage. No seats were provided, though sometimes carts would be ranked along the side of the mat shed to provide an advantageous position for some of the women spectators.

If the troupe were acting in its own village the cost of the plays was about $10 per day. This would cover the food for the actors and other incidentals. If they were playing in another village they were paid somewhat more. The money to pay for the yang ke was generally raised by assessing the entire village, usually according to the amount of farm land owned. As the plays were generally given for three or four days, sometimes for as long as 10 days, the actors needed a large repertoire.

Working with the yang ke groups in the Experimental District we were able to record, perhaps for the first time, the texts of 48 plays. These have been published as part of our Chinese report. At the end of the chapter we give the complete dialogue of four plays and the stories of seven more, as samples of the different kinds of plays.

One of the yang ke players was persuaded to make records of the singing of some of the characters in the plays. Samples of four different parts have been transcribed to give an idea of the tunes and tempos.

Ting Hsien Yang Ke

It must be remembered that they are sung in the falsetto voice regularly used in Chinese singing.

The stories of the plays can be generally divided into six different types. 1. Boy and girl. 2. Filial piety and chastity. 3. Husband and wife. 4. Mother-in-law and daughter-in-law. 5. Humorous. 6. Miscellaneous. Our 48 plays were divided boy and girl 11, filial piety and chastity 13, husband and wife 5, mother-in-law and daughter-in-law 4, humorous 6, and miscellaneous 9. The field reports did not say whether these 48 plays represented the entire repertoire of one group of players or whether they were in the repertoire of all the groups.

You do not have two saddles for a good horse; a good woman does not have two husbands; marriage is forever. This philosophy generally prevails in the boy and girl yang ke, but there are some with stories of romantic attachment and elopement. The plays show that the women like to marry men who are students, who will be scholars and can become officials.

Chinese life emphasizes filial piety as a primary obligation. Children must sacrifice themselves and the lives of their children to protect their parents. A filial daughter will sacrifice her honor, if necessary, to get an opportunity to avenge the death of her parents. True filial piety can move heaven and earth, God and the devil. One of the major sins against filial piety is to have no sons to carry on the family line and offer sacrifices to the spirits of the ancestors.

Between husband and wife, the husband is the master. His wife is his property and slave. He can send her away if she has no son, but she cannot leave of her own volition. If she is dismissed her loss of face will prevent her returning to her home, so she will rather persuade her husband to let her stay while he takes a concubine in order to have a son, or she will become a nun. In some cases the wife may be sent away, not by the wish of her husband, but at the order of her mother-in-law. The son sacrifices his wife rather than be unfilial. Some plays show the husband having the power to sell his wife.

When a girl marries she leaves her own family and becomes a member of her husband's family. His mother has complete power over her daughter-in-law. The daughter-in-law must listen to and submit to her mother-in-law, even before her husband. A daughter-in-law cannot have any freedom or any ideas of her own while her mother-in-law lives. The mother-in-law is inclined never to allow her daughter-in-law to do anything that she has never done or to enjoy anything she has never enjoyed. As a result a daughter-in-law is generally depicted as hoping that her mother-in-law will die very soon so that she may be mistress of the house. And she wants to treat her daughter-in-law in the same way that she has been treated.

When spirits take on human form and carry on work and romance, when a wife browbeats her husband and forces him to kneel with a brick or a lamp on his head as punishment for gambling, when a donkey driver and his woman passenger discuss affairs, the actors have an opportunity to insert plenty of slap-stick humor and broad jokes.

The miscellaneous group of yang ke included stories about Ting Hsien and stories borrowed from the regular Chinese stage.

The old people said that in the old days the yang ke were much more refined than they were when we studied them, that during the preceding 25 years the tunes, words, and acting had gradually become rougher and more boisterous and more and more popular. In fact, the year before our study the District Bureau of Education tried to suppress the plays on the grounds that they were a social and moral menace, but it could not enforce its prohibition.

Our investigators reported that while there was some vulgarity and considerable sex in the yang ke it was the sort to tickle the crowd and the plays were not, in their opinion, a harmful influence. The opposition to the plays apparently came from the old-fashioned people and the traditional attitudes of the countryside, where even a man and a woman shaking hands was considered to have a sex implication and where it was unheard of for a father to kiss his daughter in public.

The yang ke were very popular and had a large place in the recreational life of Ting Hsien. They were a people's literature, developed by local groups. Traditional stories had been subject to local editing and changes. They were simple enough for all to understand, but with literary quality. They pictured life in the country or life as the country people would like to have it. Life as depicted on the stage represented high society for many of the villagers. Love making on the stage was certainly an emotional release for the crowd.

The yang ke tunes were the popular music of the countryside. They were learned by young and old. We often heard them being sung at night by a belated villager walking through the fields. He would be singing for his own pleasure and to scare away any wandering spirits that might be about.

The reports spoke especially of the large numbers of women and girls who attended the yang ke plays. They were one of the big recreational events of the year and all the community made the most of them.

Theatrical performances were also given by troupes of professional actors engaged by some villages and by city organizations, such as the Lantern Association of the West Street, to give plays at New Year's time, for the temple fairs, and for other special occasions. The engagements were usually for a three or four day series of plays. The cost of this entertainment was about $130. The details of the expenditure are given in our report on the Temple Fairs in Chapter XVIII. The expenses of the plays given in the villages were usually paid by all the people in the village, generally by special graduated subscriptions rather than from general village funds. In some instances the amount of a family's subscription was determined by the amount of land the family held. In others the amount asked of each family was arbitrarily fixed, but it usually had some relation to the family's economic status. The subscription was practically obligatory, but we were told of some instances where families had refused to contribute. The collector threatened them with bodily harm if any member of the family went to the plays. In the city the cost was met by the members of the organization promoting the plays.

The spectators were not limited to the inhabitants of the village giving the plays, but came from the surrounding villages as well. It was an occasion for much local visiting and entertaining.

Worship of the gods was closely connected with most if not all of the plays given in 1929. A possible exception was those given for the Tung T'ing fairs, as it was reported that those fairs had no temple connection. If the stage was not set up in or near a temple courtyard where there was an altar, a shrine usually was built opposite the stage so that the gods might be worshiped and know that the plays were given as an offering to them. The people attending the plays combined worship and recreation. Theatrical plays were often given, as a special offering, when the community was seeking help from the gods, asking for rain, or wanting protection from locusts or other pests and disasters. The plays given at the temple fairs were naturally related to the temple worship.

In the shrine opposite the stage, in one of the villages, the tablet was that of All the Gods. On each side of the niche in which the tablet was stood was pasted a couplet printed on red paper. It read:

Be welcome Divine God
You are the Father who will soon give us blessing.
Be merry and happy
No locusts shall come morning or night.

The strip of red paper pasted above the shrine read:

Gratitude for Your Divine Kindness.

Three incense burners stood in front of the shrine. On the table in front of them there were three dishes of small loaves of Chinese bread, all colored red for the occasion, and five dishes of food. Each of the food dishes was decorated with a red flower. All day long people stopped before the altar to burn incense and paper money, to kotow and pray.

At one performance five plays were given in one evening. In another the program included eight plays.

One of the plays given by a professional troupe depicted in six scenes the story of Hsü-hsien, who fell in love with a young girl called White Serpent. They loved each other dearly and were quietly married. The fifth day of the fifth month was a time to dispel evil spirits and many people drank a specially potent wine that was said to be able to reveal a disguised spirit in its true form. On that day the couple drank to each other's health. Unbeknown to White Serpent, the special wine was used and as soon as it touched her lips her beautiful human form was changed into a white snake. Hsü-hsien fled to the Chin-shan Abbey, told his story to the abbot, and pled with him to save him. The white snake was very angry and went to her kinsman, the king of the water dragons, to ask his help against the abbot. He ordered his soldiers and subjects—the fish, turtles, lobsters, clams, oysters, and water insects—to lash the water into a tumult. The seas overflowed, the land was deluged, the Chin-shan Abbey was submerged. The white snake fought with the abbot, but was overcome by his great magic and the seas were returned to their bed. The white serpent was imprisoned in a tower by the abbot until she should repent of her evil ways and promise to be good. Hsü-hsien was saved by the power of the abbot.

The stage was usually about 30 feet square with the back third curtained off as a dressing room. The size of the mat shed put up for the audience varied from village to village. Some that we saw were 30 by 60 feet, others 40 by 80 feet with a ceiling of 20 feet or more. No scenery was used but the actors' costumes were very elaborate.

We did not attempt to determine how many villages gave plays during the year.

Some families engaged troupes of actors to perform for a specially elaborate funeral or birthday celebration.

The Dragon Lantern Show, the Ch'i Ch'iao Lantern Show, the Warrior Show, the Lion Show were among other New Year's entertainment provided by different community groups, usually during the Feast of Lanterns. The lantern shows were, of course, given at night. There was a musical accompaniment for all of the shows.

The gaily painted dragon, some 30 feet long, was carried through the streets by eight men. There were lanterns on the ends of the poles that the men carried so the light shone through the golden eyes, from the large red mouth, through the white beard of the papier mache head of the dragon, and through the translucent, scale-decorated cloth of the dragon's body. The carriers made the body twist and turn as the dragon made its way through the crowd. A pearl, a large round ball illuminated by an internal lantern, was carried in front of the dragon, always just out of its reach. To the people the illuminated dragon represented their "imagined, dignified, sublime, grand dragon". The men who carried the dragon kept together by following the tempo of the accompanying musicians.

The Ch'i Ch'iao Lantern Show was given by a group who must have done considerable rehearsing together, for their entertainment involved group maneuvers as well as individual dancing. Each of the performers carried a lighted lantern. They were of many different shapes and sizes and decorated with flowers, birds, butterflies, and characters. Some had popular poems written on them. The four large lanterns that led the procession each had a large carefully written character on it. Together they read "Ch'i Ch'iao Lantern Society". The dancers were dressed in figured clothes and hats. After various individual and group maneuvers, the men came together into two groups and, putting their lanterns together, made the illuminated figure of a fisherman and a farmer.

After finishing in one place the group moved on down the street and went through their dances and maneuvers again and again, keeping up the entertainment until about midnight. If the weather was clear the full moon added its light to that of the lanterns.

The Warrior Show was given from ten in the morning until six in the evening on the 15th of the first moon. Some 70 or 80 players took part, showing their prowess, agility, and muscular control with different kinds of weapons, spears, lances, tridents, knives, swords, daggers, and staves. Some were individual performances. Others were done in groups of two, three, or four. The latter showed very careful timing and much practice as in many instances the tempo was very fast and the weapons and dancers had to be at just the right place to avoid injury. Some of the individual posturing and muscle control is often called "Chinese boxing" by foreigners.

A flying star, a piece of iron tied to the end of a rope, was used to clear the spectators from the space the company needed for its show.

On the 14th of the first month the head of the Lion Society went from house to house and presented a red New Year's card that announced that the Lions would be entertaining the public on that day. It also probably intimated that a contribution would be greatly appreciated. The activities of the entertaining groups were regularly supported by contributions.

The beating of a drum and gong advertised the beginning of the show. It started with a group of clowns bringing out a wheelbarrow on which sat a man dressed in an old mandarin's robe and hat with black rings painted around his eyes. The wheelbarrow was pushed by a clown dressed as an old man and pulled by one dressed as an old woman.

Then came a boat made of willow twigs decorated with bright cloth. The passengers were a man dressed as a woman and one dressed as a sailor. The motion of the boat kept time with the drum and gong.

When the "boat" finished its voyage two "lions", one green, one red, came out to entertain the crowd with their capers and dances. Each had an embroidered ball with which it played. A man, with a club in his hand, played the part of the lion tamer and danced between the two lions. The show lasted for about an hour, after which the players were invited to go to the home of a well-to-do family for rest and refreshment.

The lion heads were bamboo frames covered with brightly decorated paper. Sometimes the lions were a one man variety, sometimes a two man species with the second man the hind legs and tail.

During the winter days, when there was little work on the farms,

LOTUS LANTERN

groups of men got together to make music with drums, gongs, and cymbals. The drummer stood in the center of the circle and set the tempo. The others followed his lead. As variations to the clashing of the cymbals and the ringing of the gongs, some groups added the posturing and gestures of Chinese "boxing", all done without interrupting the playing of the instruments.

Ice on the ditches and streams made skating possible for those who could fasten an iron bar to their shoes, but metal was usually so scarce that sliding had to be the way most of the young people used the ice.

Kicking the shuttlecock was a game that was popular with the boys and young men during the winter. The shuttlecock was made from chicken feathers and a flat round piece of metal. In earlier days the

TOP SPINNING

weight was usually several cash coins. The kicking was generally done with the side of the foot, but as the routine was extended and variations added the heel, toe, and instep were all used. Sometimes it was a group game with the shuttlecock kicked from one player to another, sometimes a contest between two players, sometimes simply individual practice and exercise.

Swinging on a rope swing fastened to a high wooden frame was very popular with both men and women. Bouncing balls and spinning tops were reported as women's recreation.

Board games were popular in the summertime. Figure 26 shows three different kinds of boards. Sometimes these are drawn on the ground and the pieces used are small stones picked up nearby. Sometimes the

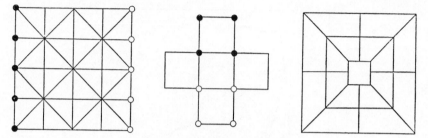

FIGURE 26. GAME BOARDS

boards are printed pieces of paper unfolded and put on a table at a tea shop or elsewhere, the men colored pieces of wood or stone.

Game number one, called sandwich and carrying pole, starts with five men lined up for each side. Moves are made one step at a time in either a vertical, diagonal, or horizontal direction. When a man is "surrounded" by two from the other side, he is removed from the board and replaced with one of his opponent's men. The game goes on until all the men of one side have been taken.

Game number two, called chicken feathers and garlic skin, starts with four men on each side. Ordinarily they are moved one step at a time but if it is possible to make four steps and land on an opponent's man that man is taken from the board. In making the four moves they must be counted "chicken, feathers, garlic, skin". The game ends when all the men of one side have been taken.

Game number three, called move into line, is apparently the same as the British game of Nine Man's Morris. Each player has twelve men and puts them on the board in turn. If a player can get three in a row he stops his opponent from entering one of his men. When all the men are on the board, less any that have been stopped, the players move in turn, trying to get three men in a row and the right to remove one of the opposition's men. The game continues until all the men of one side have been taken. In case all 24 men are entered without any stops each player removes one man to make a space into which to move.

Wine and tobacco were prominent items in the Ting Hsien recreation budget even though the average family expenditure for them was not large. In our family budgets (see Chapter V), the average expenditure was $1.02 per family for wine and $1.18 for tobacco.

The local tobacco crop was estimated to be some 210,000 catties. The dried leaf prepared for smoking cost from 20 to 25 cents per catty. Cigarettes were priced from 3.5 to 6.0 cents per box of 10. The wholesaler who handled all the cigarettes for Ting Hsien reported the monthly consumption as some five million cigarettes and the annual expenditure as some $200,000. This would be an average of some fifty cents per capita, a very much higher figure than the 6.5 cents per capita of our family budget study.

Date wine cost 16 cents, "tea" (white) wine 25 cents, and yellow wine more than 40 cents a catty. Bottled native wines were priced at more than 30 cents per bottle. The home industry report gives the family wine production as 35,000 catties of date wine and 106,670 catties of white or tea wine. The prices were given as 10 and 15 cents per catty.

Opium was used by only a very few families. Its cost was some $4.00 to $5.00 per ounce. The average user was said to spend from $7.00 to $8.00 per month.

Children, both boys and girls, had a large number of individual, team, and group games. Kites were flown by some of the boys, generally about the time of the Spring Festival. Hop-scotch and jacks, with the jack stones and "ball" made of stone or brick, were popular with the girls.

Small children, standing in a circle, played drop the handkerchief, the cat catching the mouse, the hawk chasing the sparrow. In a variation of this type of game the runner, if he is caught, is made to kneel down and kotow three times to the sun. If there were as many as 14 in the group the game might be "Eagle and Bird". One eagle and four birds are chosen. The others make three "nests" (circles), in which a "bird" can rest. The bird left outside the nest is pursued by the eagle. When tired or about to be caught a "bird" can run into any one of the nests. The "bird" then in the nest must run out immediately to be pursued by the eagle. When the eagle catches a "bird" the game is stopped and as punishment the "bird" is asked to bow to the eagle.

Sometimes the game is for a blindfolded hunter to chase a hare inside a circle. When the hunter says "one" the hare must say "two" so the hunter may locate him. In a similar game the blindfolded player is required to catch the player who has come up on tiptoe and touched or hit him. In another game a blindfolded player is required to recognize the other players from sounds they make and from the description given him of what they are doing, the gestures they are making.

Beating the Sticks was a group game popular in the autumn and winter. Each player had a stick from one to two feet long. These were lined up on the ground in front of a cross drawn some five or six feet from a long straight line. The first player, standing behind the cross, threw his stick at the other sticks in turn, trying to knock them across the line before his stick went over. After the player had thrown at each of the sticks, any that had not been knocked over the line were brought back and lined up on the level of the stick nearest the cross. The player continued throwing until he had knocked all the sticks across the line or until his stick went over.

For counting out, the players are seated so their feet can be counted. The counter uses a rhyme similar to eenie, meenie, minie, mo. The translation of one such rhyme, but without the accent and rhyme of the original, is:

"You have one, I have one, when we meet we bow
 You have two, I have two, there is grain in the unopened kaoliang
 You have three, I have three, when we weave we throw the shuttle
 You have four, I have four, when you eat the fish take out the bones
 You have gone over five passes, I have gone over five passes,[1] use the dipper
     to take out the rice
 You have six, I have six, we'll eat bread with meat."

The foot counted at the end of the rhyme is taken back. The first player with both feet counted out is the Big Officer. The next one is the Little Officer. The last one to be counted out is to be punished. The counter inquires of the Big and Little Officers how many eggs they would like to eat. The sum of their replies determines the number of blows the counter is to give the last man counted out.

Hide and seek is played by equal teams. All the seekers but one go out to hunt for those who have hidden. The one who stays behind is to protect home base, for a player who is found must be tagged before he gets back to home base. If he gets "home" without being tagged his side wins.

"Button, button, who has the button" is called "Guessing the Bean". The "bean" is a small piece of brick that the juggler leaves as he shakes hands with the players, who stand in a row with their hands tucked in

1. Kuan Yü had to fight his way through five passes.

their sleeves. If the bean guesser guesses correctly he becomes the juggler. If he fails he continues as the guesser.

A "Neighing Horse" is usually played on a moonlit night. The player who is the horse must neigh continuously as he stands near the peg or the corner of the wall that is home base. He tries, while neighing, to catch some of the other players. If he succeeds the caught player must run home. On the way he can be beaten by the other players. Then he must kotow to the moon. If the horse runs out of breath and stops his neighing he must run home and the other players can beat him as he runs.

In "A Crying Bird" a clever player from one side tries to make his opponents laugh by his strange cries and actions. In "Running on the Rope" a player tries to break through the line of players who stand with their arms linked together. In "Shooting An Arrow" a strong player tries to catch a named player on the other side.

A singing game is "Carrying the Singing Official". The official is carried in a rough sedan chair made from two poles. His servant walks by his side and carries a teapot and kettle. Four carriers carry the chair. The official sings first, the servant and carriers follow his lead. In a more acrobatic version the official stands on the two poles or sits on one and must stay on no matter how the carriers move. At the same time he must sing and make dancing gestures.

For a literate group the game may be to find Ts'ao Ts'ao, the traitor of the Three Kingdoms. The names of eight famous characters of that time —Liu Pei, Chu-ko Liang, Chang Fei, Kuan Yü, Chao Yun, Ma Ch'ao, Huang Chung, Ts'ao Ts'ao—are written on separate pieces of paper, mixed together, and drawn by the eight players. The one who draws Chu-ko Liang can order the generals Chao Yun or Chang Fei to guess which one of the players is Ts'ao Ts'ao. If Ts'ao Ts'ao is found, Liu Pei, the Emperor, is asked by Chu-ko Liang, the premier, to give orders for the punishment of Ts'ao Ts'ao and to set the amount of his punishment, the number of blows to be given him. Chao Yun, Chang Fei, or any one of the others may be appointed to administer the punishment. If Chao Yun or Chang Fei fail to find Ts'ao Ts'ao they may be punished for failing in their duty.

Yang Ke Plays

THE LUCKY PRINCE

(text)

MAN (*speaks*):

Little fish not yet become a dragon,
I have fallen in a muddy pool in the mountains.
Born in a family of kings,
I am now living in a thatch-roofed house.
When hungry I eat coarse corn;
When thirsty I drink tasteless tea.
Ah! such is my life, such is my fate!

MAN (*sings*):

I, a prince, am shedding tears, grieving,
Wishing that I'd never been born the son of a king.
I remember when I was very young
How once the king and queen
Conspired to kill me, as they desired
To give their throne to my younger brother, their favorite.
One day they tied me to a stake and were about to kill me
When a god came who was invisible to all but me;
He carried me away I knew not where.
Though I knew not how to walk before,
I had to walk then;
One li, another, another—
Though I knew not hardship before
I had to endure it then;
I climbed one mountain, another, another—
I wept and wailed;
I wailed and wept.
At last I arrived at a village.
There by the lake shore sat an old man.

344

As he had no sons or heirs he asked me to stay
And be his heir.
Here with this old man I lack nothing;
I have good food every day and suitable clothes for all the seasons.
I am now in school.
I began by learning the One Hundred Surnames;
Then the Three Character Classics;
Then the Four Books and the Five Classics.
My teacher asked me to write some compositions.
The first one I wrote was good;
The second one barely passed;
In the third I misspelled several words
For which I was rewarded with forty strokes of the rod.
Immediately afterward I fainted and dreamed dreams.
In the first dream I heard a god speak;
In the second I saw a flower-like maid;
In the third I went to hunt birds.
In rapture I awoke,
But now I am very sad
For all my dreams have vanished.
But let me see. What's this?
There are mud bullets in my pockets!
On my shoulder is a precious bow!
By the god's will my dreams are becoming real!
Slowly I walk outside the school, thinking:
"Today I will do nothing but hunt birds in the wild woods".

WOMAN (*enters and sings*):

I am flower-like Miao Mei;
I am happy in my heart.
Dressing up, beautifying myself,
I am going out to see the flowers.
With a comb of precious yellow wood,
I comb my cocoon-smooth black hair.
I step out of my embroidery room;[1]
And go to see the flowers in the garden.
Here blooms the Eternal Youth;
There the Good-Man Lotus;
All about are peonies and roses.

1. A young girl's bedroom. Having such a room indicates that her family is rich.

I come now to the fish pond;
Red fish, green fish, and gold fish;
In pairs they swim, merrily, merrily.
But, ah! I, Miao Mei, at sixteen,
I am alone.

MAN (*seeing the girl*):

What's there? A beauty! In the garden
She sits on the rock by the lake shore.
She looks about sixteen, cannot be more.
The hair on her head is ink-black;
It is tied by a silken red thread.
Her face is painted with the famous Chiang-nan powder;
Her lips are reddened with the rouge of Su-chou;
On her ears hang a pair of golden rings, lantern-like;
Her jacket is of red silk and her skirt black.
I want to attract her attention but how can I do it?
Ah, there a bird is calling. I stop.
From my pocket I take out a mud bullet,
And straightway shoot the bird.
Lo, the bird falls in the garden
Before the lovely maid!

WOMAN:

I was looking at the flowers and the fishes;
Suddenly from a tree a bird fell at my feet.
What omen does this foretell?
Poor bird, what can have caused your death?
There was no eagle in the air;
I saw no cat on the tree.
Unfortunate bird, let me bury you.
Oh, it is a large-beaked, white-necked mountain crow!
And yonder outside the garden hedge
Stands a handsome devil!
What shall I do?
If I should throw him the bird he killed,
He would laugh at me.
Let me pretend to be ignorant of the bird.
Slowly I walk by the little lake.

MAN:

My bird fell inside the garden;
I must have it; let me go in.

Now I have picked up the bird;
I must run out again. I run.

WOMAN:

Stop, young sir!
You are neither blind nor insane.
How dare you intrude into my garden?
If you have not come to steal the willow tree,
You have at least stolen a glimpse of me!
If you dare move one more step
I will call out and you will be caught
And be sent to court and locked up
After you have been rewarded with forty lashes.
But if you remain with me for a while,
I will be gentle with you; but I must know
What has made you intrude upon my solitude.
Your choice, young sir, a friend or a thief.

MAN:

Oh, to remain is my heart's desire.
But I say to her playfully:
"Noble young Lady, to the court
Let us go together, as you wish.
Surely not I alone am to be disgraced".

WOMAN:

You are no stupid fellow in your way of talking,
Though you do seem too handsome to be clever.
Now tell me about yourself and about your family.
In what district is your home, and in which province?
What is your father's name, and is your mother living?

MAN:

My home is not far; it is in Huang-kung-yuan.
My father is Squire Wang, and my mother is a philanthropist and
    a vegetarian.

WOMAN:

Tell me how many brothers you have,
And are you the youngest or which?

MAN:

I have neither an elder brother nor a younger one.
I am alone, the only son of my father.

WOMAN:

> You have married the daughter of which family?

MAN:

> Being born ugly and lone I am not yet married;
> No family wishes to give a daughter to an ugly man.

WOMAN:

> So you are not yet married,
> Nor am I yet betrothed.
> This year I am sixteen years old.
> I have something to say to you;
> You will not think me too bold?

MAN:

> Whatever you would say, pray say it without reserve;
> Your humble servant is most willing to listen.

WOMAN:

> I wish to marry you. Will you marry me?

MAN:

> Your wish is my desire.
> Let us ask a go-between to speak to our parents.

WOMAN:

> You are willing and I am willing;
> Pray where is the need of a go-between?

MAN:

> This open place is not suitable for intimate talk.

WOMAN:

> Let us go and sit in the bower.

MAN:

> Let me walk ahead.

WOMAN:

> Love is sweet; lovers know not shame;
> A maid of sixteen follows her beau.

MAN:

> Happy walk is swiftest.

WOMAN:

> Here we are in the bower.

MAN:

Out of the earth I make a calf for a sacrifice.

WOMAN:

Flowers take the place of incense.

MAN:

Having no paper we burn the flower petals.

WOMAN:

Having no music we chant our wedding hymn.

MAN:

Let us both kneel and ask heaven to bear witness.

WOMAN:

This year I am just sixteen.

MAN:

I am eighteen, two years older than you.

WOMAN:

As I am two years younger you will protect me.

MAN:

If I had known that hunting birds would give me a wife
I would not have been moping in the corner of the school.

WOMAN:

Had I known that looking at the flowers would bring me a husband
I would not have stayed in my chamber so long.

MAN:

Ah, I must go. Tomorrow I come again.

WOMAN:

May the plague take you if you do not come tomorrow.

MAN:

I kotow to you and bid you goodbye.

WOMAN:

I kotow to you and bid you farewell.

MAN (*speaks*):

Hurriedly I shall jump over the garden hedge.

WOMAN (*sings*):

    Happily I shall return to my embroidery chamber.

MAN (*speaks*):

    What if your parents ask you?

WOMAN (*speaks*):

    I will die before I confess.
    Farewell!

MAN (*speaks*):

    Goodbye!

THE MEETING AT THE BLUE BRIDGE[1]

(text)

MAN (*speaks*):

    Carrying my books I go to school;
    In the distance I see my home village;
    In my garden there is a wu-tung tree
    Waiting for the phoenix to build her nest.
    Behind the embroidered screen sit beautiful girls;
    From the school-room will come forth a Poet-Laureate.
    I am Wei Kuei-yan. Tired of studying I am going to take a walk.
      (*Exit.*)

Scene, Evening

MAN (*enters and sings*):

    Kuei-yuan is at home, when
    Suddenly something comes to his mind.
    Lazily he leaves his seat, and slowly walks out.

   1. Refers to the meeting of the Cow Boy and Weaving Girl on the 7th of the 7th moon.

Swiftly he passes through the streets,
And soon arrives at the school-house.
He enters the school-room. It is night.
He lights a lamp to study.
But he cannot study, thinking of a fair maid.
On every page he turns he reads only her name;
Ah, he had better go to sleep,
And meet her in dreamland. (*Exit.*)

Scene, Morning

WOMAN (*enters and sings*):
   I am Lan Jui-lien,
   Sent by my mother-in-law to fetch water.
   The pole on my shoulder is made of the rare box-wood.
   Hurriedly I hang a pail on each end
   And on my back I carry a rope twelve feet long.
   Slowly I walk out of the kitchen, out of the gate;
   I follow the highway leading toward the hill, toward the well.
   My husband's name is Chou Yü-tzu, and mine Lan Jui-lien.
   He is fifty-three years of age while I am but eighteen.
   He looks like a carbuncle;
   His nose is flat as a monkey's;
   His mouth is big as a crocodile's;
   He has an ear one-half of which is gone;
   He has only one leg and half of it is festering;
   And his short little queue is like sheep-wool.
   Standing he is like a ghost;
   Squatting he is like a mill-stone.
   Toward the well I go;
   One step, two steps—lotus steps,
   Three, four—chrysanthemum steps;
   Five, six—the tyrant's lash;
   Seven, eight—Pa Wang's whip
   Nine, ten—ten-colored flowers.
   Forward nine steps, backward three,
   I walk like a pearl-hanging-on-the-rolled-up-screen;
   I walk like the spread-of-the-bottle-gourd-vine;
   I walk to the north of the road;
   I walk to the south of the road.
   Around the well grow poplars and willow trees;
   Around the well stand the white-stone railings of the Han dynasty.

Slowly I ascend the steps to the well,
Laying aside my pole I take the rope in my hands.
Swiftly I let down the pail hanging on the hook;
Hurriedly I draw up the pail filled with water.
One pail of water being drawn up, I go on to get the other.
Both pails being filled with water, I grow tired;
My clothes are wet with sweat.
For a moment I sit down and rest before carrying the water home.

MAN (*enters and sings*):

From his school Kuei-yuan comes out, walking, thinking—
He thinks of the dream he had the night before:
He dreamed of a beautiful scene on the Blue Bridge:
In his dream he stood there and saw the fairest of women.
He has now come to this place.
He looks in front; he looks in back;
To the right; to the left;
But nowhere is she to be found.
There on the river bank an old man of eighty is fishing;
Here below a sweet maid of sixteen washing clothes—
These scenes are old, the same as last year,
But I am seeking a new scene, the scene of which I dreamed last
    night.
Ah, where shall I find my new scene?
Onward, onward I go.

(*He catches sight of the woman at the well*)

Who is there? Who is that?
A woman! a young woman! a beautiful young woman!
Her hair is cocoon-smooth and black as ink;
It is braided with red silk threads;
On each side of her head she wears a fresh flower
And a hairpin inlaid with kingfisher feathers;
She is dressed in flowered-cloth and crisp black skirt.
She is the very woman whom I saw in my dream last night!
Let me go near, bow to her, and speak to her.

WOMAN:

Having bowed to return your courtesy, I ask:
Has the young gentleman lost his way?
Or forgotten his home, being charmed by the natural beauty?

MAN:

> I have neither lost my way nor forgotten my home;
> I am merely made thirsty by the charm of natural beauty.
> Will the young lady give me a cup of her water?
> I am willing to pay her whatever price she may ask.

WOMAN:

> Here, young gentleman, I offer you water, free of charge.

MAN:

> The young gentleman rushes forward to embrace the wooden pail;
> He pretends to drink, but stealthily gazes closely at her feet.

WOMAN:

> Having discovered her gentle thief, the maid is irritated:
> You mean-hearted young man, you look at my feet
> And you tell me you are thirsty!

MAN:

> My thirst is of a kind different from that of common men.
> My fair one, may I know of your family, your home village?

WOMAN:

> Away! away! you mean-hearted young man;
> You have stolen a close glimpse of me
> And now you dare ask where my home is!
> My mother's home is in the rear of the Hua Shan mountains;
> My mother-in-law's in the front.

MAN:

> Your husband's name, my fair one, and your own?

WOMAN:

> My husband's name is Chou Yü-tzu and mine is Lan Jui-lien.

MAN:

> Will you tell me, my fair one,
> How old your husband is and how old you are?

WOMAN:

> My husband is fifty-three and I am eighteen.

MAN:

> Your husband is fifty-three while you are only eighteen!
> This is what you say, my fair one?

WOMAN:

    Yes; my husband is fifty-three and I am only eighteen.

MAN:

    A wife so young and a husband so old!
    How you must have suffered, my fair one!

WOMAN:

    I do not dislike my husband though he is old.

MAN:

    Looking around and seeing no one near,
    I venture to court the pretty maid:
    Do not be angry at me, my fair one,
    I wish to speak of you of a thing in my heart.

WOMAN:

    Speak out, young man;
    I take no offense at good and sincere talk.

MAN:

    I want to ask you to marry me, my fair one.
    Yes or no; but pray do not be angry at me.

WOMAN:

    Your impertinence makes me very angry;
    You had better ask your own sister to marry you!

MAN:

    Your scolding provokes me, my fair one;
    Pray listen to the story I tell you.

WOMAN:

    I shall listen if your story is good.

MAN:

    Once on a time Fan Li-hua the Beautiful
    Was given in marriage by her bad uncle to Ugly Yang.
    On the battlefield she fought with a young and handsome general;
    She fell so desperately in love with him that
    She killed her ugly old husband and married her beloved.

WOMAN:

    A good woman does not marry twice.

MAN:

> You are so very young, my fair one;
> Ah, how many days may a flower be blooming red?

WOMAN:

> Not being a stone, my heart is moved!
> Oh, what shall I think? What shall I do?

MAN:

> Let me tell you about my family, my fair one.
> I am a gentleman's son, living east of the river.
> My name is Wei Kuei-yuan, heir to
> An estate of several thousand mu of land
> And a mansion of several tens of rooms.
> In winter there is no lack of fur; in summer gauze.
> If you smoke there is a servant to light your pipe;
> When you drink, a maid always brings you hot water.
> Why would you not marry me?
> Why would you waste yourself on a disgusting old man?

WOMAN:

> Ah, I have been persuaded by him; I am convinced,
> Though I have been married by my parents to the ugly Chou,
> I cannot but love this young, handsome gentleman.
> Obey love I must; young sir, I will marry you.

MAN:

> How lovely! How delightful!
> Together we go yonder to the Blue Bridge.
> There to take our betrothal oath before Heaven.
> Let me lead.

WOMAN:

> And I follow you.

MAN:

> Here we are on the Blue Bridge.
> I, Wei Kuei-yuan, kneel down before Heaven.

WOMAN:

> I, Lan Jui-lien, kneel with my lover.

MAN:

> I shall love you forever, my fair one!

WOMAN:

Forever shall I love you, my young sir!

MAN:

We rise.

WOMAN:

I am going.

MAN:

Wait, give me a token to remember you by.

WOMAN:

I came out to fetch water, and brought nothing worth while.
But take this hairpin.
Hereafter when you come with this token,
Even though you are a beggar
I will not refuse you.

MAN:

Kuei-yuan is leaving.

WOMAN:

Wait, what will you give me to remember you by?

MAN:

I came out to enjoy the natural beauty, and have nothing.
Ah, let me tear a piece from my blue gown to give to you.
Hereafter when you come to me with this token,
Even though you are a servant-maid,
I will open my arms wide to receive you.

WOMAN:

Lan Jui-lien carefully takes her lover's token.

MAN:

Now I bid my lady good-bye.

WOMAN:

By the well is left Lan Jui-lien alone;
My young gentleman is gone.
I carry the two pails of water back,
Rejoicing that the new day of my life is to dawn.

CHAO MEI-JUNG ATTENDS THE FUNERAL
(text)

(A girl by the name of Chao Mei-jung goes to attend the funeral of Chang Pao-t'ung's grandmother. When she comes near Chang's home she is told that Pao-t'ung's father has left on business in another town and Pao-t'ung's mother, Lu Feng-ying, is alone at home. By nature mischievous, Mei-jung disguises herself as a man to test playfully the chasteness and devotion of this married woman. Imitating a man's voice, she calls Pao-t'ung's mother, Lu Feng-ying, to open the door.)

CHAO MEI-JUNG (*singing in a man's voice*):

Open the door, please.

LU FENG-YING (*alone inside the house*):

Who is it?

CHAO MEI-JUNG:

I am Er-hei of the South Street. The other day when I was on the way to school I saw you. You came out to throw away the ashes. But when you had emptied your ashes, you did not leave. You made eyes at me. And on another day while I was walking on the street I met your son, Pao-t'ung. He chased after me and asked me for a cake. Today I hear that Elder-brother [referring to her husband] is not at home, so I have come to keep you company before the coffin of your mother-in-law.

LU FENG-YING (*scolding*):

I, Lu Feng-ying, am as pure as the sound of a china tea-cup struck by a pair of chopsticks. You villain! Ask any one outside whether or not Mrs. Chang has ever done anything wrong. You sickly toad! You want to eat the flesh of the heavenly swan![1] Back in your own home you also have an elder sister and a younger sister! Go and marry one of them. In two or three years a bastard child will be born. Your mother will hold it to her bosom and will first call him *sun* [son's son] and then *wei sun* [daughter's son].[2]

CHAO MEI-JUNG:

Inside the house she is scolding with wide open mouth. Outside, her humble student kotows and begs. Please listen, pretty sister-

1. Thinking of the impossible.
2. Height of insult.

in-law Lu: I'll buy you good silk in Peking; I'll buy you silver bracelets in Nanking. Besides these I'll give you ten thousand big cash as a gift. Sister-in-law Lu, you are a fool if you don't open the door for these things.

LU FENG-YING:

Having heard the student say his say, I call to him, Dog, listen! You'd better tempt your own mother at home. Your mother has better looks than I. You'd better establish a Buddhist shrine, a round shrine, and then invite me, Feng-ying, to sit in it. Then every day you can bring me three meals and say your prayers to me while you burn incense.

CHAO MEI-JUNG:

Your student is bowing; please listen, sister-in-law Lu. If you don't open the door soon, your student will climb over the wall and jump down inside your courtyard. And then I'll carry you into the embroidery room.

LU FENG-YING:

Hearing this, Lu Feng-ying is frightened. If I say again "I won't open the door", the passers-by on the street will tell bad tales about me. If I do open the door, I'll bring shame and disgrace on my husband. With the two-horned pole I strengthen the door; I gather stones to reinforce the door; with nails I seal the door, now he can never open it! Now I go to the coffin of my mother-in-law. Having kotowed before it, I will hang myself.

CHAO MEI-JUNG:

These words frighten Chao Mei-jung. Although she has come to attend the funeral, she has said nothing about it. Why should she have made her sister-in-law Lu seek death? Thinking this, Chao Mei-jung hastens to change her costume. Taking off her man's hat, she appears with luxuriant black hair. Taking off her blue gown, she stands in her maiden dress. Slipping off the man's shoes, she walks on her golden-lotus feet. Hurriedly and loudly she shouts in her natural voice: "Sister-in-law Lu, open the door, please"!

LU FENG-YING:

Lu Feng-ying is just preparing to hang herself and suddenly hears a maiden call outside. It was a man who spoke, and now surely it is a maiden's voice. A lamp in hand, she peeps through the door-cleft; looking upward she sees the cloud of luxuriant, black hair; looking downward she sees a pair of golden-lotus feet. The one who

called was certainly a man and now stands outside a heavenly maid.
Can she be "Two-in-One?" Ah! now I have the explanation. I say:
"Younger-sister, you come to attend the funeral, why haven't you
spoken of it before? What tricks do you play? Fortunately I did not
open the door to you. If I had, you would have exposed me to
scandal! Let me remove the stones and open the door. Ah, little
wench, you have almost frightened me to death!"

CHAO MEI-JUNG:

   I only played a little trick on you and you scold me bitterly!

LU FENG-YING:

   Had you not frightened me so, would I have scolded you?

CHAO MEI-JUNG:

   If you hadn't scolded me, would I have frightened you?

A DAUGHTER-IN-LAW COMPLAINS

(text)

WANG SU-CHEN (*speaks*):

   Since my little sister came home
   I have not sent her to her mother-in-law's across the river.
   Seeking her I go,
   One li, two li, three li,
   Passing by four houses, five houses,
   Six pavilions, seven pavilions,
   Eight flowers, nine flowers, ten flowers—

   I am Wang Su-chen. Since I invited my little sister to spend a vacation with me, nine days have already elapsed. Let me ask her of
   the exact length of the leave of absence her mother-in-law had
   permitted her. Sister! Where are you? Lo! There she comes.

HIS SISTER:

>Hearing my brother's call,
>I go out to meet him, asking:
>"Elder Brother, pray,
>What are your orders?"

WANG:

>Be seated, Sister,
>I wish to talk to you.

SISTER:

>Thank you, Brother;
>I am listening.

WANG:

>How many days did your mother-in-law say you could stay here
>with me?

SISTER:

>Ten days, Brother.

WANG:

>How many days have you stayed with me already?

SISTER:

>Nine days already.

WANG:

>Little Sister, I am thinking of sending you back to your mother-in-
>law's home. What do you say?

SISTER:

>Really? No, Brother—no! Brother—

WANG:

>Sister, I am sorry. But I must.

SISTER:

>That is to kill your sister—Ah!
>(*Sings*):
>Hearing that Elder Brother must send me back to my mother-in-
>law, I cannot stop my tears that flow incessantly swift as shuttles—

WANG (*sings*):

>Little Sister, do not grieve,
>Do not shed tears,

Your Elder Brother is to go with you.
Now let me go and saddle the horse.

SISTER:

In the front parlor the little maiden is left alone.
Her Elder Brother has gone to saddle a horse.
She enters the embroidery chamber to change her dress.
The little maiden is changing her dress, preparatory to leaving
    for her mother-in-law's home.
Putting on her new dress;
Wrapping up her old dresses;
Carrying her bundles, she comes out again to the parlor.
There she meets her sister-in-law, her brother's wife.
She speaks to her brother's wife:
"Good-natured sister-in-law, pray listen.
Today my brother is to send me back to my mother-in-law,
To my dreadful mother-in-law.
When the next festival comes,
Please, please do not forget to invite me to your home."
Having thus begged her sister-in-law,
The maiden comes to the gate, waiting for her brother.

WANG:

With a saddled horse for my sister,
I have come toward the gate.
There I see my sister shedding tears,
Tears like the never-stopping swift shuttles.
Leading the horse, I call to her:
"Little Sister, please mount."

SISTER:

The little maiden has mounted the horse;
Her Elder Brother is carrying her packages.
The little maiden rides ahead, ahead—

WANG:

Her Elder Brother follows, follows—

SISTER:

The little maiden rides through the wilderness.

WANG:

Tell me, tell me, oh! Little Sister,
Tell me what lies heavy in your heart?

SISTER:

> Good Elder Brother, your sister will
> Unbosom her grief to you.
> Our father was Squire in this district.
> He promised a family in Chang-tse-p'o
> That they should have me as their daughter-in-law.
> But soon he died and a day was selected
> To marry me to the family of doom.
> I thought I was going to a rich house.
> But instead I got a very severe sister-in-law and a treacherous
> mother-in-law.
> Today I must return to their house again,
> I pray not to live, but to die soon.
> When your poor sister is dead, Elder Brother,
> You will see that they bury her body, well dressed, in a good coffin.
> If you do this I won't forget you even in the spirit world.
> If my corpse is dressed in poor clothes and put in a poor coffin,
> I shall be buried with endless griefs.

WANG:

> Do not weep so, Sister,
> Onward we must go.
> I blame the go-between woman who lied.
> I blame her. I hate her.
> Our parents died when you and I were very young.
> They believed all that the go-between said,
> And consented to give you to the family in Chang-tse-p'o.
> When you were eighteen years old, on a chosen lucky day,
> You were carried to the dreadful house of your husband, where
> you were married.
> Instead of a rich family with food, clothes, and a beautiful home,
> You were married to nothing but a severe sister-in-law and a cruel
> mother-in-law.
> This ill fortune was unexpected, Sister.
> Fortunately you are yet young, being now only nineteen.
> Your mother-in-law is over 60. She won't live another 60 years.
> Your sister-in-law is eighteen. Before long she will be married and
> go to another house.
> Those who should die will die and those who should marry will
> be married.
> Then, my sister, you will be left alone to enjoy life.

Then the narrow path of your life will be widened into a highway;
The little stream of your life will become a great river;
A small tender willow twig will grow to be a large tree, old and
  venerable.
After many years the daughter-in-law will become a mother-in-law.
Little Sister, you are not the first daughter-in-law;
Many others have had a fate more cruel than yours.
Listen to your brother's advice and do not think of death.
If you die a natural death I will see that you have good clothes and
  a good coffin.
If you die an unnatural death, your brother will do nothing for you.
Put up with what Heaven has assigned to you, Sister.
Onward, onward, let us go—

SISTER:

The little maiden whips the horse to cross the bridge;

WANG:

Elder Brother and Younger Sister have both crossed the bridge;

SISTER:

Sitting on horseback I look around.

WANG:

Yonder, not far, is Chang-tse-p'o, your mother-in-law's home.

SISTER:

The little maiden whips her horse to enter the village.

WANG:

Sister, here we are in front of your mother-in-law's house.
Let me help you to dismount.

SISTER:

I dismount.

WANG:

Here is your package, Sister. When you go in
You must ask after your mother-in-law's health,
Say "How-do-you-do" to your sister-in-law.
Though they are unkind to you, you must do what is right.

SISTER:

I want to ask my brother to come in and have some lunch,
But do not dare—

WANG:

> Thank you, but I am neither hungry nor thirsty.
>
> I ought, perhaps, to go in to wish your mother-in-law good health.
> Since I have so often disputed with her, she can have no desire to
> see me.
>
> I am going home directly. Goodbye—goodbye.

SISTER:

> Ah me! In front of this cruel gate I am left alone,
> And I must not stand here too long.
> The ugly daughter-in-law cannot avoid meeting her mother-in-law.
> Now I go to meet my fate.

THE DOUBLE LOCK CHEST

(synopsis)

ONCE THERE WAS a man by the name of Yü Lao-i who lived in Yü
Chia Tien. He had a younger sister who had been married to a
man by the name of Wang, and lived in Wang Chia Chai. These two
families were known as wealthy homes. Yü Lao-i and his younger sister
made an agreement that their children should marry each other. Not
long afterwards Yü Lao-i had a daughter named Yang Chieh and his
younger sister had a boy named Wang Chin-chui. These children were
later engaged to be married.

Not long afterward, there was a big fire in the home of Wang Chin-
chui. All their property and houses were burned and Wang Chin-chui
became poorer and poorer day by day. When Yü Lao-i heard the news,
he was greatly disappointed over his daughter's betrothal and contrived
to break the engagement. He made up a story that his daughter had
died and pretended to hold a funeral service for her. When this news
reached Wang Chin-chui's ear, he was deceived by it. He finally became
so poor that he had to become a beggar.

When he learned that Wang Chin-chui had become a beggar, Yü
Lao-i was very happy. Yü Lao-i then engaged his daughter to Chiang

Wu-chu, who lived on the east side of the village not far from his home. Chiang Wu-chu was also a wealthy man, and had a younger sister by the name of Lin Chieh. One day when Wang Chin-chui was walking along the lane asking for food at every door, he happened to come to Chiang Wu-chu's home. It happened that at that time Lin Chieh was standing at the door and saw him. She was surprised that such a splendid young man had become a beggar. For the sake of charity she secretly gave him ten taels of silver. Later a servant of Chiang Wu-chu's home came out and said to him, "Tomorrow is our master's wedding day. You can get plenty of food to eat if you come tomorrow."

Upon hearing this he felt very much pleased and thought that if a wedding ceremony was to be held in the bridegroom's home, a similar one would also be held in the bride's home. So he decided to go to the bridegroom's home on the next day and on the following day to the bride's home. When he went to ask who the bride was and where she was living, he learned it was Yü Lao-i's daughter who was about to be married. On hearing this he was very much surprised because he knew that his uncle, Yü Lao-i, had no other daughter than Yang Chieh. So he hurried back home and told the news to his mother. When she heard it she told Chin-chui the whole story of his past engagement.

As Wang Chin-chui was doubtful about this matter, he boldly went to his uncle's home to ask about it. It happened that, when Wang Chin-chui went to his uncle's home, both his uncle and his aunt were away on business and only their daughter, Yang Chieh, was at home. When the girl saw Chin-chui come in, she immediately got him something to eat. After a while, she heard her parents coming back. She was very much upset, and hurriedly told Chin-chui to hide in her wedding chest.

On the next day the chest was moved over to Chiang Wu-chu's home, but no one except Yang Chieh knew that Wang was in it. Lin Chieh, however, opened the chest and was greatly surprised to find Wang Chin-chui there. He whispered to her, "Please don't be afraid. I am Wang Chin-chui, to whom you gave ten taels of silver." Finding him to be that man, she put him into another chest.

Soon after the wedding ceremony, Yang Chieh remembered that Chin-chui was still in her chest. When there was no one in her room, she hurriedly opened the chest and was greatly surprised to find that he had disappeared. Just then, Lin Chieh happened to come in and saw what she was doing. She jokingly said to her, "Have you gone crazy over something you have lost from your chest?"

Knowing that Lin Chieh had discovered her secret, Yang Chieh told all the past story to her and asked her for aid. However, Lin Chieh had fallen in love with Chin-chui and asked Yang Chieh to help her. Finally the girls decided that they both would marry Chin-chui.

That night Wang Chin-chui and the two girls managed to escape from the home of Chiang Wu-chu and went to Lin Chieh's ancestral temple. No one was there, and the three knelt before the altar and made their vows. The village night watchman found them and reported Wang Chin-chui to the court. When the case was heard both Yü Lao-i and Wang Wu-chu were accused by the magistrate, one of breaking the engagement of his daughter and the other of attempting to marry a girl already engaged. They both pleaded guilty and were heavily fined. The fines were given as a dowry to Wang Chin-chui and his two wives, who lived happily together.

LIU YÜ-LAN

(synopsis)

A YOUNG WOMAN by the name of Liu Yü-lan was betrothed, when she was a child, to a Mr. Li Shao-hsien, who was doing business in a far-away town. One day Miss Liu was accidentally seen by a rich money-lender, Mr. Chang Ching-ch'uan, who came to her father to negotiate a loan. Her beauty so struck the rich man that he asked a distant relative of hers, Tang San, to act as go-between and arrange for her to be his wife. Knowing the advantage of serving a rich man, Tang San was willing to do what he could, but Miss Liu absolutely refused to listen to anything of the kind because her parents had already betrothed her to Mr. Li. The rich Mr. Chang was so deeply in love with the girl that he could not easily forget her. Thinking of her, he could neither sleep well nor enjoy his food. Finally he gave 50 taels of silver to Tang San and begged him to try again and to try very hard to get the girl for him. Moved by the money, Tang San made up a story that Mr. Li had died of sudden illness. He hoped that, because of this change of circumstance, Miss Liu would change her mind and marry the rich man. However, she wished to remain loyal to her betrothed, whether he was living or dead. In the meantime, Mr. Li, hearing of the scheme and his falsely reported death, hurried home and was married immediately.

CHANG MEI-YING GOES TO THE CAPITAL
TO FIND HER HUSBAND
(synopsis)

K AO WEN-CHU married Chang Mei-ying. Kao went to the capital to take the examination. He passed as "Chuang Yuan", the highest. The Premier, impressed by his success, forced him to marry his daughter. Kao could not send any word to his former wife and felt very sad. One day he was sitting all alone in his sitting room and saw a poem written in a handwriting very similar to his wife's. He was greatly surprised, for he knew she never went out and so could not have been in his home. He began to think about her. While he was sitting there thinking about his wife he heard a voice that he thought belonged to a ghost. At first he was afraid, then said that he was the top scholar, who did not need to be afraid of anything. Looking out, he saw a woman in the courtyard. He invited her in and later found that she was his first wife, who had finally managed to come to the capital after many hardships. There, in order to live, she managed to get a maid's position in the Premier's household and found her husband there. As she told her story it turned out that the Premier, imitating Kao's handwriting, had written her a letter divorcing her. She would not accept the divorce, as Kao owed a great deal of his success to her, so she came to the capital to see what she could do. When she found that the letter of divorce was a forgery she accused the Premier before the Emperor.

FINDING A SUBSTITUTE TO ATTEND
A MEMORIAL SERVICE
(synopsis)

O NCE THERE WAS a couple named Wang Chui-chung who had a very ugly daughter. Through the connivance of a skilled go-between they managed to have her engaged to the son of Chang Piao. Chang Piao's mother later learned of the deception, became very angry, and worried herself to death. Chang Piao wanted to use the opportunity of her death to see if his future daughter-in-law was as ugly as was rumored. He therefore invited the Wangs to bring their daughter to the funeral ceremonies. The Wangs became very worried and in order to cover up the matter, they persuaded Li Feng-ying, the beautiful daughter of a neighbor, to go with them to the funeral and impersonate their daughter. The Changs discovered the deception and, instead of having the funeral services, they insisted on the immediate marriage of Miss Li to their son.

FOUR QUARRELS

(synopsis)

THERE WAS once a woman by the name of Chang Szu-chieh, whose daughter was married to a fool. One day the woman went with her husband to see their daughter. When she saw her mother the daughter became exceedingly sad and, while they were talking together, she told her mother all about her bad conditions. During their conversation, however, her mother-in-law happened to come in and hear what they were talking about. She became very angry and began to quarrel with her daughter-in-law.

While they were quarreling, the girl's husband came in. Not knowing what to do, he immediately went to ask his wife about the matter, but she did not answer him. And his mother-in-law not only refused to answer him, but even scolded him seriously. When the boy's mother saw him scolded by his mother-in-law she got angry and quarreled with her. Thus a quarrel arose between these two families. Finally the trouble was peacefully settled by the fool himself.

THE DEATH OF LI WEN-CH'ENG

(synopsis)

ONCE THERE WAS a man by the name of Li Wen-ch'eng who was a soldier of General Ma. He was victorious in battle and was called by the Emperor to come and receive promotion and reward. The Emperor promoted him to a high rank but Li, hearing it was a low rank, was greatly disappointed.

As he had been away from home for about twelve years, he was very anxious to go back for a visit. When they heard that he was going, his master and his companion presented him with a horse and many taels of silver as a means of showing their good will.

On his way home, he came to a fork in the road. One road led to his father-in-law's village, Chen Chia-ying, the other to his home village, Ch'i Li-ying. He imagined that, as he had been away from home for several years, his wife, because of poverty, would probably be living in his father-in-law's home so he went to Chen Chia-ying to see her.

As he entered the village he saw his wife's brother, Chen Hu, out hunting. Li Wen-ch'eng had never seen him before so did not know him. He asked the boy, who was a fool, where Chen Liang, his father-in-law, lived. To his inquiry, the boy made many foolish answers which did not have anything to do with the question but finally he led Li Wen-ch'eng home.

His father-in-law, Chen Liang, gave him a hearty reception. Feeling very grateful for this kind of treatment, Li Wen-ch'eng presented his father-in-law with fifty taels of silver. But giving him this present was a fatal mistake for, believing that his son-in-law possessed a great deal of money, Chen Liang planned to commit murder in order that he might get all the money. During dinner he strongly urged Li Wen-ch'eng to drink many cups of wine. Finally, when Li Wen-ch'eng was intoxicated, his father-in-law killed him and buried him under the floor of the room.

The same night Li Wen-ch'eng's ghost went to his own home. At the door he was stopped by the gods who watch over the gate until he explained who he was. In a dream he told his wife about his death. At first she thought it was only a dream and did not believe it. But afterwords she began to wonder a great deal about it and the next day went to her father's home to see what had happened. As soon as she entered the door, Chen Hu, her younger brother, said to her, "Are you coming here on account of my brother-in-law?" After hearing these words she had no doubt that her dream was true. Thereupon she discovered her husband's corpse in the room.

Finding that his daughter had detected what he had done, Chen Liang asked Chen Hu to kill her, but his daughter understood their plot. She went to her brother and said: "Don't you want a bag to put your birds into? I have brought one for you. Would you like some sugar? I have brought you some." Her brother was a foolish boy and did not know that his sister was fooling him. When he opened his mouth for the sugar she threw dust in his face, filling his mouth and blinding his eyes. Then she immediately fled to the yamen and there brought suit against her father.

A JOKE IN LUNG-SHAN

(synopsis)

ONCE THERE WAS a poor scholar by the name of Wang. He wanted to go to the capital to take the examination for the degree of Chuang Yuan, but he had no money for his traveling expenses. He went to consult his wife and asked her for some financial help, but she refused his request. Thereupon he became very angry and quarreled with her. His wife finally said, "If you dare to go down to the valley without my permission, I will ask my men to chop off your legs and scratch out your eyes." To this he replied, "In this place I know it is the custom for a woman to be more powerful than a man, but down in the valley men rule, so I must go down even if you take my life."

After he said this he tried to kill himself. His wife immediately stopped him and said, "Why are you so angry and simple? How dare I stop you from going down to the valley?"

CHAPTER XVII

Festivals and Customs

MAJOR AND MINOR festivals, birthdays, weddings, funerals, all had special customs and practices. Some of these were carried on by varying sections of the community, some were observed by all the elements in the population. Wealth, education, conservatism, religious beliefs, all helped to determine whether and to what extent a family or group followed a particular custom. Since it was not possible to determine all the different customs that were observed by one or more groups, or the exact amount of observance of any one custom, we have endeavored to outline the principal ones followed in Ting Hsien. Basically they were very similar to the customs observed throughout North China, but many showed interesting local variations.

Festival Days

The dates of the various festivals were determined by the lunar calendar. The New Year, which comes in late January or early February, at the first new moon after the sun enters Aquarius, was the festival that all China celebrated. It was vacation time, a time of feasting, family reunions, recreation, and play. In many homes the departed ancestors were included in the feasting and festivities, and food and worship were offered to the gods.

The celebration began on New Year's eve, when new couplets were pasted on the door posts, and new pictures of the gate gods were put on the gates. The kitchen god returned from heaven and his picture was put up, with worshipful ceremony, on the wall near the stove. Lanterns were lighted in the courtyards and beside the main doorway. Banners were hung across the street. The banners often had characters on them and when hung in a proper row made sentences such as:

371

1. Yueh Wu-mu was a very faithful minister of the Sung Dynasty.
2. Shang Wang prayed for rain for his people.
3. Shun Wang, of the Yü Dynasty, had double pupils in his eyes.

Sesame stalks were spread in the courtyard to "pass the year away". They must be cleared away before the dawn of New Year's Day.

While the women were finishing the preparations for the evening feast, the men and the children went out to the family graveyard. Before the graves they lighted bundles of straw and invited the spirits of their ancestors to come home and eat New Year dumplings with the family. On the way back to their homes they kept the straw burning and kept repeating their invitation to their ancestors. Outside the doorway the last of the straw was burned except for one stick that was placed in front of the ancestral tablets.

The spirits of the ancestors were thought to stay for five days and offerings of food were set before their tablets three times a day during that time. In some families a special service was held at the end of five days to return the spirits of the ancestors to their tombs.

For New Year's eve all the family dressed up in their best clothes and, if possible, all wore something new. They had a family feast together and spent the night in celebration. Even the children stayed awake all night. Wine was generally served as part of the celebration. At midnight lanterns were lit and incense was burned to worship the God of Heaven and Earth, the God of Wealth, and the family's ancestors.

Before sunrise some families knelt and kotowed to the east, praying that they would not be stung by scorpions.

In the villages it was believed that it was very unlucky to awaken a person on New Year's by calling his name. To do so would subject him to bed-bugs and red eyes during the year.

On New Year's Day one of the first duties was to greet the spirits of the ancestors and to set a feast of bread, meat, vegetables, dumplings, and fruit before their tablets. The younger members of the family kotowed to the elders. The day was enlivened by shooting off firecrackers. Cash, woven with red string in the shape of a dragon, were hung around the children's necks to bring them wealth.

After a family dinner, family groups, except for the girls and the old people, went out to give their New Year's greetings to their relatives and neighbors. When a bride went to make her first New Year's call she was accompanied by other members of the family. She was expected to bow to the younger members of the family and kotow to the elder members. The bow was more and more taking the place of the kotow.

Everyone in China is one year older on New Year's Day.

On New Year's some families endeavored to foretell the weather for the coming year. On New Year's eve they put twelve white beans into small holes cut into a wheat stalk that had been split in half. The wheat straw was then tied together with a cord and put into the water jar, where it was left over night. When it was taken out, the next morning, it was opened and the beans were examined. If any of the beans were found to be soaked with water it was believed that the corresponding month of the year would have a heavy rainfall. Dry beans were thought to foretell months with little rainfall.

Following New Year's day was the time for visits with friends and relatives who lived at a distance. A bride was regularly invited to return then to her home for a visit that would last beyond the fifteenth of the month.

All sorts of games were enjoyed during the New Year season. In many villages, it was a time when there was a great deal of gambling. Officially, there was a law against gambling with the penalty running as high as a fine of $100 or $200. It generally had been customary for this restriction to be greatly relaxed, if not entirely removed, for all or part of the New Year's holiday. In some cases, the time of relaxation was fixed by the magistrate, sometimes by the village heads. One village might have ten days of freedom while another nearby village had only five days. In Chai Ch'eng no gambling was allowed at any time.

The New Year season ended with the Lantern Festival, which was celebrated on the 14th and 15th of the first month. The dragon lanterns were often brought out and carried through a series of dances for the enjoyment of the people. Athletic groups gave exhibitions and yang ke, planting songs, were often given on a stage.

On the 15th of the first month the women and girls wore cedar twigs in their hair to help them avoid lice.

On the 16th of the first month, the first working day of the year, it was customary for employers to provide a feast for their workers so that they might celebrate together.

Hair cutting was generally not done during the first month as, done at that time, it was thought to bring bad luck to one's maternal uncle.

In some families the girls were not allowed to use needle and thread during the first month.

On the second day of the second month the great dragon, ruler of the insects, lifted up his head after his winter sleep. Before sunrise the village people usually sat on their beds with pillows on their heads and said three times:

> "On the second day of the second moon
>   The dragon lifts up his head.
>   I lift up mine first so
>   No scorpion or earthworm will dare to crawl on my body."

If they did not put the pillows on their heads they would put something under or in their pillows to scare the dragon; red sulphur, cinnabar, green pepper. During the day new ashes were spread around the wells, as they were thought to be the home of the dragon, a water animal. Ashes from the wells were taken back to the family home and there spread around the walls and rooms to "guide the dragon".

Small chickens made from wheat straw were stuck into the outside walls of the houses so that the "chickens" could eat any scorpions coming into the house. The walls and rooms of the house were cleaned to keep away poisonous insects. Kaoliang seeds were planted so they would be free from disease at harvest time.

Ch'ing Ming, the spring festival, came on the third day of the third month. Originally it was the day when families went to the graves of their ancestors, repaired the graves, offered a feast to the spirits of the departed, and held a memorial service. More recently it had become also an Arbor Day. Many of the students in the villages went out into the country for a picnic or a walk in the fields as most of the flowers and trees were in bloom. Gourds were usually planted on this day as it was believed that it would protect them from injury by insects.

The fifth day of the fifth month was the summer festival and the Dragon Boat Festival. It was one of the three big festivals of the year and was generally a holiday. Most families hung artemesia and willow twigs over the doorway and pasted gourd-shaped, red papers on the walls. The children wore a five-colored "long life string". Many boys and girls and some women wore artemesia leaves in their hair and hung "tiger" characters on their clothes. This was to protect them from mishap or danger throughout the season. Three-cornered rice puddings, tsung tzu, were eaten by practically every family and wine was served. Wine and rice puddings were often sent as gifts to friends and relatives.

The sixth day of the sixth month was the time for airing books and clothes.

On the seventh day of the seventh month the women and the girls were asked to do sewing and knitting at home. On that night Cow Boy and Weaving Girl were believed to meet in heaven.

The 15th day of the seventh month was the Ghost Festival. Most families took offerings of fruit out to the family tombs. Paper money was often burned for the use of the departed spirits.

The mid-autumn festival, the 15th of the eighth month, was the third large festival of the year. In Ting Hsien it was generally celebrated by the village people with feasting and a three day holiday. Meat, fruit, noodles, rice puddings, and moon cakes were generally eaten. Pictures and images of the rabbit who lives in the moon were bought. Workers were invited to a feast by their employers. They were also given a basket containing ten pieces of bread, half a catty of sugared millet cakes, half a catty of moon cakes, a bunch of grapes, and a towel to take to their families. In the villages it was customary for the employers and employees to discuss, at this time, the wages that were to be paid during the coming year.

After the evening feast when the full moon had risen and was shining in all its splendor, many families set a table out in the courtyard and on it placed an incense burner with burning incense and several dishes of moon cakes, millet cakes, peaches, and grapes as an offering to the moon. After the family had worshiped the moon the food offerings were divided among the family.

On the 16th, the last day of the festival, it was customary for each family to eat meat dumplings and fruit for dinner.

On the ninth day of the ninth month many families went to the highest place in the neighborhood and enjoyed special wine and cakes made for the occasion.

On the first day of the 10th month, as on the third day of the third month, many families went out to the ancestral burying ground, repaired the graves, and offered sacrifices of food to the departed spirits. Paper clothes were often burned before the tombs to send winter clothes to the spirits.

On the 11th day of the 11th month students generally went to greet their teachers.

On the eighth day of the 12th month most families ate la pa chou, eight precious pudding. Dates, chestnuts, cereals, and jelly were mixed with rice gruel. After it had been put into bowls it was decorated with designs of birds and flowers made from red and white fruits. It was often sent as a present to relatives and intimate friends. Some was usually offered to the gods on the family altar.

On the 23rd of the 12th month Tsao Wang, the kitchen god, was worshiped, as that was the day he went up to heaven to report to the heavenly emperor on the family's conduct during the past year. His picture was taken down from the wall and burned. Sugar or a sweet syrup was often put on his lips so he could report only good things. On the table in front of the tablet of Tsao Wang was placed an offering of straw, black beans, yellow paper, and incense. After the worship ceremony the black beans were wrapped in small pieces of paper and then sewn into the belts worn by the family to help them avoid adversity.

During the following week the families were all very busy getting ready for the New Year. The house was cleaned, new clothes were made, special food was prepared for the New Year's feast, loans were collected, and debts were paid or refunded. By the 30th everything was ready for the New Year.

Other Customs

During the busy seasons the farmers had their dinner brought out to them and ate it in the fields. Before eating, they usually spread on the ground a small measure of grain as an offering to the god of the crops. It was believed that, if this was not done, the god would ruin the crop by beating the ears of grain with a small whip so that nothing would grow on the land of the offender.

Before going out to their fields to gather the harvest the farmers generally burned paper money and incense before the god of agriculture to insure a good crop. Firecrackers were often set off as part of the ceremony.

The farmers were upset if, at harvest time, anyone asked about their crops and when they would be harvested. Such questions were considered to be very unlucky.

It was believed that rain would fall whenever a snake's trail was seen on the road.

Hog cholera was avoided by attaching a small piece of red cloth to a stick and putting it at the gate of the pig sty.

If plague appeared in a village the farmers plucked peach twigs, made them into a bow, and tied them with five colored strings or thread. The bow with a piece of red cloth tied to it was hung on the family gateway.

Anyone who turned his bowl upside down on the table during a meal was sure to choke while eating.

Anyone who tore his clothing carelessly must not patch it himself when he was wearing it. He should get some member of his family or a friend to do it for him. While the mending was being done the owner of the garment should hold something in his mouth, like a chopstick or a piece of wheat straw. It was believed that if he did not do this, the owner would lose something.

If new paper was put on a window before the first of the 10th month, a small hole must be left in the corner until after the first of the 10th month. Ghosts and spirits were free to roam from the 15th of the seventh month until the first of the 10th month, when they were shut up for the winter by Ch'eng Huang, god of the city wall. If, when they were on their way back to the other world, the spirits should be unable to find a way out of a room they would bring disturbances and misfortune to the family living in the house.

To ward off evil spirits the farmers often erected a T'ai Shan stone at the corner of their house. This had a tiger's head at the top and five characters on the face of the stone. The geomancers said that the stone should be seven feet five inches in height and that it must be put up at the winter solstice.

The lions on top of the corner stones of the land along the road were regularly black with oil. Every carter that went by used his oil brush to feed the lion with oil and to brush his teeth. It was believed that those who did not feed the stone lions would have their axles broken.

Birth

When a child was born, news of the birth and presents were sent to the mother's family. Formerly a book was sent to announce the birth of a son and a bunch of flowers to announce the arrival of a daughter. At the time of our study, however, it was customary to send a book regardless of the sex of the baby. The mother's family gave the bearer of the good news a tip of about 100 coppers and sent, by him, a return gift that was usually a basket of eggs.

Three days after the birth of a child, friends and relatives came to bring their congratulations. Many brought presents, generally food. Members of the mother's family came and brought special food, such as eggs, wheat flour, or noodles for the mother and special clothes for the baby.

Nine days after the birth the father's family prepared a feast for their friends and relatives including the mother's mother, aunts, and other relatives. The guests brought gifts for the baby. Middle class families gave silver presents, bracelets, necklaces marked with the characters for good luck and long life, or silver coins. Workers' families generally gave money, about fifty coppers. This celebration on the ninth day apparently was the Ting Hsien equivalent of the first month celebration that was customary in other parts of China.

During the first month after birth no strangers or pregnant women were allowed to enter the mother's room, as it was believed that their presence would disturb the mother's milk. If a stranger or a pregnant woman should intrude, the danger could be avoided if the intruder immediately exchanged belts with the mother. Certain phrases were also reported to be tabu for the mother, as they were thought to make it difficult for her to nurse her child.

When a baby was one month old its maternal grandmother came to invite the mother and child to visit her family. According to custom the visit should be for one hundred days. On the way to her home the mother usually scattered a handful of grain, usually millet, or coins at each crossroads. This was to purchase the use of the road from the spirits, who, it was thought, must be placated lest they bring misfortune to the mother and child. Cash used to be used but as they gradually disappeared their place was taken by the ten cash coppers. One rich family was reported to have scattered silver dollars at the crossroads. This custom and belief appeared to be gradually losing their hold on the people.

When a child returned from this visit to its mother's home it was customary to shave its head.

When a child was one year old a tray with a book, a bunch of flowers, a piece of tile, and a small hoe, or a pair of scissors, if the child was a girl, were placed before the tablet of the God of Heaven and Earth. After the adults had worshiped the god the child was brought and allowed to choose from the articles on the tray. His choice was supposed to indicate his future. If the book was chosen the child would be a scholar. If the tile was selected he would be a useless man. If his first choice was the hoe he would be a good farmer. The choice of the scissors foretold that a girl would be a good knitter and seamstress.

Birthday anniversaries ordinarily were given but little recognition, though special foods were often prepared. Eggs and cakes for the boy carried with them the hope that he would continue to grow up in good health; "long-life" noodles for the family dinner expressed the wish for long life. The birthday of the oldest son was generally given more attention than the anniversaries of the other children.

When a man was 60 years old and had lived through a full cycle of the Chinese calendar his family generally held a special celebration. Relatives and friends called to offer their congratulations and present gifts, usually congratulatory scrolls. In some families the visitors kotowed to the man they were congratulating. A special feast was prepared for the family and friends. Wealthy families sometimes engaged bands of musicians and actors to provide entertainment on a stage erected in one of the family courtyards. In some cases the celebration might last three or four days.

What celebrations were held after the 60th anniversary would depend on the family. Some might have one every year. Others would pay special attention only to the 70th and 80th anniversaries. Others might celebrate every five years. The celebrations varied so much from family to family and depended so much on the financial situation of the family that no detailed study of them was attempted.

Marriage

Marriages were regularly arranged by the parents, generally through a match-maker. In some cases a marriage might even be arranged by two families before the birth of their children. If the children were of different sex they were engaged, if of the same sex they became sworn brothers or sisters.

When a marriage had been tentatively arranged the horoscopes of the boy and girl, the eight characters giving the year, month, day, and hour of their birth, were written out and sent to the fortune-teller for his consideration. If he decided that the two horoscopes were compatible the marriage would be definitely arranged. If they were incompatible the proposal was dropped.

After the fortune-teller had approved, the bridegroom's horoscope was written on red paper and sent to the bride's family, through the match-maker. If, after examining the horoscope, the bride's family approved, they returned a "card of consent" by the match-maker. This constituted the engagement.

The wedding day was fixed by the groom's family, who sent a card to the bride's family giving the proposed date. If it was approved by her family they returned an "answer of consent". This was the "exchange of papers" between the families.

One or two days before the wedding the groom's family prepared a cart load of presents to be sent to the bride's family. The presents included twenty-four pieces of bread, a box of noodles, salt, rice, and one-half of a pig. The match-maker went with the cart. All the presents were kept by the bride's family except the pig, which they cut in two, keeping one piece. The other piece, along with the red boxes containing the bride's dowry, was returned to the groom's family by the match-maker.

The day before the wedding a woman whose parents, husband, and children were all living, and who was, therefore, a person especially blessed with good fortune, was chosen from the groom's family or from a neighbor's family to prepare the bridal chamber for the new couple. While she was sweeping the bed she said various charms such as "Sweeping here and there, we pray for the birth of a boy and for a girl running around on the bed". While she arranged the bed quilts she repeated wishes such as "pushing here and there, we pray for the birth of plenty of babies". Dates and chestnuts were usually tucked into the bed quilts as the words for date and chestnut together have the same sound as "to have sons early".

On the wedding day the groom bowed three times before the tablet of the God of Heaven and Earth before he set out for the bride's home. He and his company made quite a procession, the length, of course, depending upon the economic position of his family. The procession was headed by two men with firecrackers that were shot off to welcome the bride and by two men carrying lanterns. Then, walking closely together, came men carrying banners and men beating drums and gongs. Next came a cart with a group of musicians, then a cart with two attendants of the groom. Finally came two sedan-chairs, one red and one green. Going for the bride the groom rode in the red chair. The green chair was empty.

On arriving at the bride's home the groom and his party were met by a man who brought out four dishes of food, a jug of wine, and three cups. After the wine was poured into the cups and offered to the groom and his two attendants, the groom was conducted to the family parlor and given tea. If the bride's family could afford it a feast was served to the groom and his attendants. The poorer families served only tea. After the reception the groom was presented with flowers made of paper or silk and with a piece of red cloth, cotton, or silk. The flowers were put on his hat, the red cloth on his sedan-chair or over his shoulders.

The bride, arrayed in her wedding finery, which usually was rented from the wedding shop, was escorted to the red sedan-chair. On the return trip to his home the groom rode in the green sedan-chair. A teapot full of water was usually hung on the back of the bride's chair so that the water would drip on the road between the home of the bride and the home of the groom and insure a long, happy relationship between the two families. The bride usually asked two of her friends to act as her attendants. Their cart was ordinarily followed by four carts for the representatives of her family going to the wedding celebration. Well-to-do families sometimes had an extra sedan-chair for the bride's principal attendant, who usually was a married woman. Two men were invited to ride on horseback ahead of the bride's chair and lead the way for her to her new home. A man carrying a jug of water walked along by the bride's chair, ready to give her a drink if she became thirsty, but a bride seldom stopped for a drink of water on the way to her wedding.

The bride usually carried a mirror inside her wedding dress to ward off any evil spirits who might be along the way. If they should see their reflection in the mirror they would be frightened away. The bride also carried some black beans hidden in her wedding robes. She would throw some of the beans on the guests in the groom's home and around her living room to protect her from any trouble that might be caused by the God of the Star of Misfortune.

The wedding procession regularly returned by a different route so as to be seen in as many villages as possible. When it arrived at the groom's home two bundles of wheat straw were burned outside the gate and one of the groom's attendants threw a small cake over the gate. These indicated that the family would be more fortunate and prosperous after the wedding.

When the bride walked from the sedan-chair to the house cloth was put down so that she did not step on the ground. A saddle was placed on the door so that the bride stepped over it as she entered the house. As the Chinese words for saddle and peace have the same sound, the bride brought peace to her husband's family. Flowers were put down the back of the bride's dress as the word combination ju i means to bring good fortune. Sometimes straw was used instead of flowers. Chenille flowers were given to the bride in order to bring her good fortune.

On her arrival at the groom's home the bride bowed before the tablet of the God of Heaven and Earth as the groom had done before he set out for her home.

Friends and relatives gathered for the wedding, to congratulate the bride and groom and to join in the celebration. A feast was served for all the visitors. After the feast the bride's matron of honor invited the groom's parents and grandparents to worship before the tablet of the God of Heaven and Earth. Three cups of wine were offered to the gods. Later another three cups of wine were offered to the family ancestors. Then the older members of both families bowed to each other, congratulated each other, and pledged the future friendship of the families. The matron of honor, representing the bride's family, then said to the older members of the groom's family "We congratulate you on the happy wedding of your son" or some similar phrase.

When this ceremony had been finished the older members of the two families went to the nuptial chamber to see the bride and groom and make sure that everything had been properly arranged. Then the guests and relatives all congratulated the groom's parents. When the bride and groom stepped into the nuptial chamber the musicians hired for the occasion commenced to play.

The younger relatives and friends teased the bride and groom, made jokes about them, and carried on the sport far into the night. The lamp in the wedding chamber was kept lighted throughout the wedding night, as putting it out would bring bad luck to the couple and it was believed that whichever one put out the lamp would be the first one to die.

Presents were given the bride and groom by friends and relatives. The close relatives of the bride usually gave clothing or jewelry. They sent their gifts a few days before the wedding so that they could go in the bride's chests when they were sent to the groom's home. For well-to-do families these presents might cost anywhere from four or five dollars up to 40 or 50 dollars.

Other relatives and friends usually brought their gifts when they came to the wedding. An "Account Book for the Wedding Gifts" was prepared and a man was asked to serve as secretary and enter in the book all the presents as they were received. The presents were generally scrolls, couplets, pictures, and money. Scrolls cost from $1.00 up to $10.00. Sometimes several friends joined together to give a specially fine one of silk or satin with gilt characters. Pictures cost from fifty cents up. A favorite picture, of a young mother holding a baby, carried with it the wish that a son might soon be born to the couple. Money presents usually ranged from fifty cents to $4.00. The money gifts all helped the family meet the expenses of the wedding.

The expenses of a wedding naturally varied with the financial status of the family, but almost always represented a relatively heavy expenditure. In Peking the cost of a group of weddings ranged from 1.5 to 9.0 times the monthly family income, but for one-half of them the expenditure was from 4.0 to 4.5 months income.[1]

A rough estimate made by our field workers of the total expense of a wedding in Ting Hsien was, for the groom's family, $200 for a wealthy family, $100 for a middle class family, and $50 for a lower class family. For the bride's family the expense would generally be about twice that of the groom's family, $400, $200, and $80. The average annual income of our 1,220 home industry families was $185. (See Chapter IV). For our 400 farm families the average was $247. (See Chapter III).

Food for the guests was four or five dollars per table of eight persons for a well-to-do family, two to three dollars per table for the poorer families. The dowry for the bride, which might cost from $15 to $100, usually included two pairs of boxes, a clock, a pair of jars, and a pair of mirrors. Often these conventional articles were rented from the sedan-chair shop, if the family could not afford them but wanted to make a proper showing when the bride's things were sent to her new home.

In some cases, where it was impossible for a family to finance a wed-

1. Sidney D. Gamble, *How Chinese Families Live in Peiping* (Funk and Wagnalls, New York, 1933).

ding, they went through the formalities of an engagement for their
daughter while she was still very young and with the understanding
that she should go to live in the home of her future husband. The wedding was held when she and her fiancé were older but without any dis-
play or special recognition. An engagement of this sort naturally meant
a great loss of face to the family and there seemed to be a general feeling
that a match made that way was not quite in the same class as one made
in the usual fashion. In 5,255 families in the 1st District there were only
two girls listed as future daughters-in-law.

The day after the wedding the bride and groom went to pay a visit
to her parents. A feast was served by her family in honor of the couple.
After the feast the groom was presented to all the members of her family.
The couple returned home in a cart provided by her family. The bride
was then presented to all the older members of her husband's family.
Later she was taken to visit the homes of her husband's relatives. Every
family that she visited gave her a present of "visiting money", which
might be from fifty cents up to one dollar but was never less than ten
coppers.

On the fourth day after the wedding the bride's family sent two carts
and invited the newly married couple to stay six days with them. On
the sixth day the couple returned home in a cart sent by the groom's
family.

Usually on the sixth or seventh day after New Year's following the
wedding the bride's family sent a cart for the bridal couple and invited
them to come for a visit that would last until the 16th of the month,
over the Feast of Lanterns. Ordinarily this invitation was given for
only the first New Year after the wedding, but enough well-to-do
families did it for three years for the Chinese to have a proverb that
says, "For the first three years a bride is not permitted to see the lanterns in the home of her mother-in-law".

After the wedding the bride was expected to make a pair of shoes
for every member of her husband's family and to do the housework
under the direction of her mother-in-law.

On the Dragon Festival, the fifth of the fifth month, after the wedding
the bride's family sent a present of fish, meat, fruit, millet, and other
foods to the groom's family. Again on the ninth of the ninth month the
women of the bride's family all helped to make a special cake, about
one foot long, to be sent to the groom's family. The cake contained

sugar, dates, chestnuts, etc., again making the date, chestnut wish for children.

Age at Marriage

Fourteen and 16 were the ages when the largest number of boys were married. Sixteen and 18 were the most popular ages for the girls. Some boys were married when they were only seven years old. Twelve was the youngest age for the girls. About 1.5 per cent of the women were over 25 when they married. Occasionally one was over 30, but in our study of 5,255 families there were only three unmarried females over 22 years of age. About one per cent of the men were over 40 when they married.

The average age at marriage, in two groups of families, was 17.2 and 18.7 for the males and 17.7 for both groups of females.

The size of the family income had a great influence on the age at which the sons were married. In a group of families with less than 50 mu of land, the average age of the husbands, at marriage, was 18.4 years. One-third were married before they were 15 years old. In the families with 100 mu or more the average age was only 13.2 years and 80.8 per cent were married before they were 15. There was not nearly as much difference for the girls. The average age for the poorer group was 17.8 years. It was 16.8 for the wealthier group. The figures are given in more detail in Chapter II.

Because so many more of the boys were married before they were 16 years old, it was natural that we should find a large proportion, 69.7 per cent, of the wives older than their husbands, in one instance as much as 11 years older. The husband was the older in 24.6 per cent of the couples. In those couples the maximum difference was 28 years. It was as much as 10 years for 6.1 per cent of the couples.

The average age at marriage appeared to be rising at the time of our study. Longer and more general school attendance, the efforts of reform groups, and outside ideas, were some of the influences helping to reduce the number of early marriages. One group was attempting to make 20 the minimum age for boys and 16 the minimum for girls.

Marriage after Death

Sometimes when a mature unmarried boy died his family would get a match-maker to arrange a wedding between the boy and a girl who had died unmarried. The couple might be buried in adjoining graves as was usual for a husband and wife. Their spirits could be together in the other world and they would not be lonely, as an heir could be picked who would carry on the ancestral worship and prevent their spirits wandering as orphans. If the wedding was arranged the chosen heir would go to the woman's home carrying in his hand a paper banner in which was written her name, age, etc. Accompanied by her family, he would bring her coffin to the boy's family graveyard. Sometimes it was the girl's family who took the initiative and called in the match-maker.

Death

When death occurred the first duty of the family was to dress the body in its grave clothes lest the spirit of the dead person make its entrance into the other world undressed. The clothes were usually purchased before death occurred so that they would be available for prompt use. A man was dressed in a big hat, a new pair of shoes, trousers, and a single cotton gown. A woman's head-dress was a piece of yellow cloth instead of a hat. The grave clothes had no buttons or buttonholes. The trousers of both men and women were fastened at the ankle with strings instead of the usual ankle bands. A small silver bell, with a string attached to it, was put into the dead person's mouth. The string hung outside the mouth. Poor families used a copper cash instead of a silver bell.

White papers folded and cut into three strips were hung outside the family gate to announce a death in the home. The papers were hung on the left side of the gate for a male, on the right side for a female. (Right and left are of a person looking out of the gate.) Later a large square of white paper was posted outside the gate. On it were written the deceased's name, age, and the date and time of his birth. The large square paper, too, was posted on the left of the gate for a male and on the right for a female. Still later mourning cards were sent to friends and relatives to announce the death and give the dates set for any special services, interment, etc.

When the body had been dressed in its funeral clothes it was taken from the k'ang and placed on a wooden board bed. On the bed was placed a mattress made of yellow-gold cloth, lined with blue cloth and filled with cotton. A wooden pillow was put under the corpse's head.

Its old pillow was put under the bed. The body was covered with a cotton or satin cloth instead of the usual bed quilt. A piece about one foot long was torn from this cover before the body was put into the coffin.

A paper screen was placed in front of the bed and later in front of the coffin to keep out the sunlight. The sun, belonging to the yang half of the universe, would be harmful to the spirit of the departed as it belonged to the yin half.

On the first evening after the death the sons of the deceased went to the Wu Tao temple to announce the death to the gods. Mourning papers and incense were burned before the altar and the gods were worshiped. On their way home the group all wept bitterly and continually until they returned to the bedside of the dead. While the sons went to the temple the rest of the family stayed at home in silence. If there was no Wu Tao temple in the area the death was announced to the gods at a nearby crossroads.

The body was usually placed in the coffin the day after death. Rich families often had the coffin especially made years before a person was expected to die. Families without money purchased a coffin with hastily borrowed money. Some poor families got the money for their coffins from friends or from charitable gifts of wealthier families.

A layer of ashes, covered with paper, was put in the coffin before it was placed by the wooden bed of the deceased. The face and eyes of the dead were carefully washed before the body was put into the coffin so that they could show their brightness after death. The sons and daughters of the deceased each took a handful of coins and spread them in the coffin. Sometimes close friends of the family would pick out some of the coins so they might be worn by their children. The wearing of such a coin was thought to hurry the child's development. As the body was placed in the coffin the family repeated, "Please listen, Father (Mother), we are going to put your body in the treasure chest". Seven dried stalks of grain, arranged in the form of a stick, were put into the hands of the body so that the spirit would not be bitten by a dog in the other world. When the body had been properly arranged the coffin was covered and nailed. The wooden bed was taken outside, washed, and dried and was not used for three days.

After death a final meal of rice was prepared for the dead, put into a bowl, and placed on the cover of the coffin. A table was placed at the head of the coffin. On it were a dish of fruit, a bowl of cooked rice, an incense burner, a lamp, and mourning papers. The oil lamp was kept lit day and night. Mourners who came to pay their respects to the dead lit the mourning papers from the lamp and burned them to illuminate the way for the dead and so keep him from going astray.

On the night after the body was put into the coffin, usually the second night after death, the members of the family, except the sons who stayed at home to mourn, went to the T'u Ti temple to worship. They carried with them a broom, a stick, and a gown belonging to the dead person. The broom, with the stick tied across it, was placed before the altar of the god and later was covered with the gown. The family carried the broom back home saying "Father (Mother), please dress yourself and have something to eat. We are going to send you away to heaven in a cart".

When they got home they set up a table on the roadside outside the gate. On the table were placed three bowls of meat dumplings, a mirror, a handkerchief, and a basin (a feast and toilet equipment for the dead). A circle of ashes was spread in the road and into this was put a horse and cart made of paper and kaoliang stalks. Sometimes a paper image of a cart driver was added. The horse, cart, and driver were set facing the east. Then they were burned in order to provide transportation for the spirit to the Western Heaven and to keep it from becoming too tired from walking. The ashes were put around the paper horse and cart to insure their use by the deceased, and to prevent any wandering orphaned spirits from coming near and taking the cart as it burned.

Some families made special flour cakes to be burned with the horse and cart. The number of cakes was equal to the age of the deceased. It was said that if, the next morning, a boy picked up a cake and ate it he would grow up to be brave and strong.

When a death occurred neighbors often spread ashes in front of their doorways to keep the departed spirit from entering. The spirits avoided the ashes lest they show their presence by leaving a footprint in them. Spirits also feared ashes as fire, which ashes represent, is a yang element while ghosts belong to the yin part of the universe. Ashes were put before the family gate when a man went to pay his respects to the dead in a neighbor's family, so that when he returned the spirit of the departed could not come back with him.

If the funeral was for a member of a wealthy family a mat shed was built over the courtyard, furniture was rented, and a feast was provided for the friends and relatives who came for the memorial service; paper houses, paper servants, paper rolls of cloth, paper flowers, paper models of any article of which the dead was particularly fond were purchased; bands were hired to furnish music; sometimes troupes of actors were engaged to give plays; Taoist or Buddhist monks (or both) were called in to hold services for the soul of the departed. These services were generally held both before and on the day of the funeral.

When the father or mother of a family died every one in the family, men, women, and children, put on mourning clothes of white coarse cloth, and a white sash, a white cap, and white shoes. Near male relatives wore white caps and shoes. Near female relatives wrapped a white cloth around their head. Friends or distant relatives wore a piece of white cloth pinned to their coat. Full mourning clothes were worn until after the funeral, but some sign of mourning, usually white shoes and sometimes a white button on a hat, was worn for two and a half years for a father and three years for a mother.

Friends and relatives who came to pay their respects to the dead and condole with the family usually burned some mourning papers and bowed or kotowed four times before the coffin. The sons of the family knelt at the left side of the coffin and returned the bows or kotows. Along with the mourning papers some visitors burned paper money to help provide funds for the spirit of the deceased. This cost about 20 cents.

Relatives and friends generally brought or sent some gifts. Meat, wheat cakes, fruit, and other food were often sent to help furnish the food for the visitors. Other presents were white scrolls, cloth curtains with gilt paper characters pinned to them expressing laudatory statements concerning the deceased or expressions of condolence, and money, usually from 100 coppers up to $1.00.

On the day of the funeral, before the coffin was carried out, the chief monk stood before the tablet of the dead and with the other monks read the Buddhist scriptures. A member of the family took a broom and a winnowing basket and swept the coffin to make sure that money would come into the house instead of being left outside. The sons knelt before the coffin and burned yellow papers, putting them in a small basin that had stood at the head of the coffin. As the coffin moved from the house this bowl was broken to signify that the mourning services were over. This bowl usually had a hole in the bottom as it was be-

lieved that the spirit of the deceased would be required to use the
bowl to drink the water it had wasted in this world. The hole in the
bottom would allow much of the water to run away and so save the
spirit a large part of its task.

The catafalque most generally used in Ting Hsien was hung from
a long pole the front of which was a dragon's head and the end a
phoenix's tail. The catafalque was carried by 16, 32, or 36 men. There
was a coffin cart that was pulled by 30 men. In very fine funerals the
coffin was carried on a platform placed on two large red lacquered poles
and surmounted with a high framework hung with red curtains, similar
to the big catafalque often used in Peking.

The musicians and priests preceded the coffin. The sons of the deceased walked immediately in front of the catafalque. The oldest son
usually carried a special soul flag, carrying it in his left or right hand
depending on the sex of the deceased. Other sons carried mourning
sticks, wrapped in white. The women of the family rode in carts and
followed the coffin.

Friends or relatives sometimes set a small table at the side of the
road to show their respect for the person being buried and their sym-
pathy for the family. On the table they put wine, pork, chicken, fruit,
paper money, and incense. When the procession came to the table the
catafalque would stop, the friends and relatives would kotow to the
coffin and the sons would kneel and return the kotow. This was the
"libation in the road".

Paper money, shaped like large cash, was often thrown into the air
as the funeral procession went along the road. This was "money to
buy the use of the road" and was to placate the wandering spirits and
keep them from doing harm to the spirit of the deceased or his family.
These papers were quickly picked up by spectators as they were thought
to be very beneficial for scabies.

The time between death and burial varied greatly, depending on the
status of the family and the will of the geomancer. He was usually
called upon to locate a suitable grave, to set the day when the feng
shui would be propitious, and to use his compass to see that the coffin
was located in the grave so that it would be in line with the strongest
influences and forces of the spirit world. If graveyard and graves were
properly located it was believed that it would help the family become
rich and prosperous. The seventh day after death was the usual time for

burial among the better-off families. Poorer families, who had fewer arrangements to make and were less able to give time to mourning, usually waited only three days. Wealthy families often had special memorial services on the seventh day after death and might delay the actual burial beyond that time.

At the grave the coffin was lowered into the earth and then its axis was carefully located according to the geomancer's compass. A small jar containing food was generally placed at the head of the coffin to provide sustenance for the departed. The sons walked around the tomb three times after the coffin was in place and before the grave was filled. The paper houses, servants, and cloth were burned. The women of the family generally carried home with them some of the earth from the grave in order to bring riches to the family.

After the burial the funeral party returned home along the same road by which they came and after leaving the grave they were not to look back until they had reached home.

On the third day after the burial the descendants of the deceased went to visit the tomb. They took paper money, fruit, and cakes with them and they wept before the grave.

The 21st and 35th days after death were generally two special memorial days for the departed. The family, men and women, burned mourning papers and incense and wept before the tomb. After those special days the deceased were remembered at Ch'ing Ming and on the first of the 10th moon, along with all the ancestors. Then the graves were repaired, food was offered, and incense was burned. Sometimes paper clothes, paper money, and other paper items were burned before the grave mounds to keep evil spirits away. On the 30th of the 12th moon the ancestral spirits were invited to spend the first five days of the New Year with their descendants.

Funeral expenses varied with the financial condition of the family, but almost always were a heavy drain on the family finances. Coffins for adults cost anywhere from $7.00 to $300 or more. Grave clothes for a parent of a wealthy family cost from $80 to $150 and from $30 to $60 for a middle-class family. From $150 to $300 might be spent on food and music, while another $200 to $300 might be needed to cover the cost of mourning clothes, paper images, and priests. The average total funeral expense for different class families was approximately $600, $360, $70, and $40.

The ceremonies and costs were highest for parents and those in the older generation. Infants and small children were buried with practically no ceremony. Older unmarried children had but little more ceremony as they generally could not be buried in the regular family graveyard. Sometimes the marriage match-maker was called in to arrange a wedding for the deceased child with an unmarried person of the opposite sex who died about the same time. In some cases the couple could then be buried in the main graveyard; in others they would have to be interred in a separate plot.

A man and wife were buried side by side in the same grave from three to four feet apart. Too great a distance might mean misfortune for the family.

In many of the villages some land was set aside for a public graveyard for poor families who could not afford to buy a grave plot.

For some of the large families who had been long in Ting Hsien the maintenance of the family graveyard was a matter for the entire clan and involved many related families and many people. A notice was sent out to each family of the clan, by the chairman for the year, giving the time of the memorial service on Ch'ing Ming and the first of the 10th moon. A fine of one or two catties of wine was imposed on anyone who was intentionally absent. The families met at the home of the chairman and went together to the family graveyard to repair the graves and worship the ancestors with offerings, paper money, and incense.

After the worship service the group often ate and drank together and discussed the repairing of the tombs, the planting of trees, the leasing of the clan property, and any other clan problems. The chairman, collectors, business manager, and clerk were elected by the members. The chairman served for one year. If no cooks were secured the collectors were responsible for preparing the feast. In some cases only the elders "of a suitable age" attended the "eating meeting". In others any one belonging to the clan was qualified to participate in the meeting, but it was generally customary for no women or children to attend.

The expenses for the care of the tombs and the "eating meeting" were met from the income from the clan property, or, if there was no property or the income was not sufficient to cover the expenses, by contributions from those who attended.

The clan property was usually land that had been given or left as a legacy to the clan by some of its prosperous members. The land was regularly rented. Any money included in the clan property was usually loaned at interest, ordinarily at 1.5 per cent per month. The clan property was looked after in turn by the different families. The details on some clan property, income, and expenses are given in Chapter II.

It was said that the geomancers who helped locate suitable graves must spend 10 years before they could properly recognize the footprints of the dragon and 20 years before they could master the art of locating peaceful graves. Also that, as the dragon is an animal that walks near the water, it is proper to locate graves near the water.

When a family graveyard had been filled the geomancer was called in to find a new burial plot with auspicious influences that would add to the family welfare. This might be one plot for the large family or, if there were several families whose ancestors were buried in the original graveyard, each family might establish a separate plot in the same way that a family was often divided after the death of the father, with the sons setting up separate households.

In order to maintain the continuity of the generations some families exhumed their parents' bones and buried them in the position of honor at the top of the new graveyard. Whether this was done or not depended on the will of the clan and the decision of the geomancer. Neither would allow anything that would break the auspicious influence of the old graveyard.

If the decision was against moving the parents' bones a small symbolic coffin was often buried in the new graveyard. Then the current head of the family and his wife would be buried at the top of the plot, his sons and their wives in the next row and his grandsons and their wives in the third row.

If the geomancer approved of moving the parents' bones from the old to the new graveyard, the grave was opened at night or a mat-shed was built over the grave to keep out the sunlight lest it harm the spirits of the dead. A small coffin would still be used to hold the bones that were moved from the old to the new graveyard.

Proverbs

Proverbs, customary sayings, and rhymes were very numerous in the Ting Hsien villages. A few samples, selected by our Chinese associates, are given to show how they comment on family life, farming, and village life.

Feeling hungry and cold, a child goes to his mother.
He knows nothing but how to play and be happy.
If his mother is away for a day,
He cries and cries for her.
Seeing his mother's sorrow, he, too, becomes sad;
That is the real love for his mother.
After he grows up and gets married, then
He forgets his mother entirely.
He seeks happiness with his wife every day.
One day's separation from her is like ten to him.
In his childhood, he loves his mother best;
But after he gets married, there is a change in his affection.
Then he no longer loves his mother the most, but his wife.
He forgets his filial duty to his mother
And so cannot be regarded as a man.

A jay is a long-tailed bird.
Finding a mate, he forgets his mother.
He takes his mother away to the desolate valley,
But keeps his wife at home.
He cooks rice and soup for her.
Although she dislikes it,
He begs her to eat it.

A small girl,
Climbing up a ladder to play,
Has her eyeball pecked by a crow.
Her parents scold the crow,
But her sister-in-law comes out and says:
"What, are you pecked?"

The bean-sticks are full of beans.
A daughter goes to see her mother.
When they see their daughter arrive,
Her father goes to fetch her bag,
Her mother goes to get the baby,
But her sister-in-law turns her head
And shows an angry face.

The daughter says, "Don't look at me that way,
I won't stay long.
While my parents are alive
I will come occasionally to see them.
When they are gone, we will separate forever".

Here is a man who had many wives.
Within a year he was married fifteen times.
But all his beautiful wives have been sold,
And only an ugly woman remains.
Not obeying the command to brush the pan,
She stands on the pan scolding her mother-in-law.
Not obeying the command to brush the jar,
She stands on the jar scolding her father-in-law.
Not obeying the command to brush the bowl,
She uses the bowl to wash her face.
Not obeying the command to brush the ladle,
She uses the ladle to wash her feet.
Not obeying the command to water the garden,
She uses the water-wheel as her plaything.
Not obeying the command to dig the ditch,
She stands by the side of the ditch scolding her uncle.

A lady is spinning with a spinning wheel;
It makes a noise like tra la la.
After her mother-in-law's death,
She takes charge of the family.
She bakes many cakes and fries cucumbers.
Then she shuts the door and begins to eat.
Presently she has eaten too much.
Surrounded by people,
She cannot walk or move,
But cries to her neighbors for help.

Stale food can not be easily warmed.
A second wife can not be easily controlled.

Beat a lamp-stand with a stick.
The grandfather has married a woman
With two big feet and a slanting mouth.
She looks so much like a crocodile,

That the old man is greatly disappointed with her ugly face.
Then the old man's grandson said:
"Please leave our home a while,
At least until my grandfather has recovered".
Beat a lamp-stand with a stick.
This old man has married a beautiful young lady.
She powders her face and puts flowers in her hair.
Grandpa is tickled to death.

The cotton has grown from the ground.
A grandmother loves her daughter's child.
Seeing this, the child's aunt is displeased.
"Aunt! aunt! don't frown at me,
It does not help matters".

If you have money
Don't marry a woman who has a husband;
Don't buy a field along the road.

On the second day of the Second Moon,
The dragon raises his head.
The Emperor plows the fields
And the ministers help him drive the cows.
The Empress, the National Mother,
Makes the porridge herself and sends it
To the Emperor and the ministers working in the fields.
All pray for a rich harvest throughout the year.

The farmer is always busy with his work.
Wherever he goes, he carries a manure-basket.
Within a year he gathers several piculs of fertilizer
And with this he cultivates his field.

Don't blame Heaven if you haven't
Dug your cabbage before the winter solstice.
Don't be sorry for yourself if you haven't
Protected your onions before the coming of the first frost.

Cultivate a field without enough capital,
And you cannot expect much return;
Cultivate a field without fertilizer,
And you do not get a good crop any year.

Rain at night, clear skies and sunshine during the day.
The crops will burst the barn.

The farm hand says:
"Through a sieve the flour is sifted.
The quality of work depends upon the quality of food.
If you don't give me good food I will dilly-dally in the field,
Then you will see who is the one to lose".

Men seek men;
The birds seek the forest.
Monks seek the priests;
While vagabonds stay with scoundrels.

Here is a lady with two big feet.
She walks with a big noise.
But having big feet
She will not suffer in her mother-in-law's home.[2]

A blind fortune-teller's mouth
Is like a bottomless dipper.
Whatever question you ask, he can answer.

To the hungry everything is sweet;
To the well-fed even sugar is tasteless.

2. I.e., she will be able to work.

CHAPTER XVIII

Religion

RELIGION in Ting Hsien finds its outward expression in the Buddhist, Taoist, and Official temples, in the Mohammedan mosques and Christian churches. Just when these various religions first came to Ting Hsien cannot now be determined. Some of the gods belong to China's earliest history, others have arisen or become prominent in the more recent past. Some are pure spirits, others are heroes and famous men of an earlier time who have been deified by the Emperor and given rank and title in the spirit world. It is said that Emperor Yao was the first one to offer sacrifices to Ch'eng Huang, the god of the city walls and moat. Yueh Fei, who lived from 1103 to 1141 in the later part of the Sung dynasty, is one of the gods of war, a god of filial piety and gives help to those seeking to settle disputes. Lao Tzu, the reputed founder of Taoism, is said by some to have been born in Honan in 604 B.C. Confucius, the most prominent of the worthies worshiped in the Official temples, lived from 551 to 479 B.C. Sakyamuni, the founder of Buddhism, was born in 624 B.C., but it was probably the first century A.D. before Buddhism was introduced into China. Mohammedans first settled in China early in the seventh century. A Nestorian monk arrived in 635 A.D. Giovanni Di Monte Corvino, the first Christian missionary who is known to have come to Peking, arrived in 1293. During the reign of K'ang Hsi, 1662–1722, Catholic converts came from Peking to at least one of the hsien near Ting Hsien. Protestant Christian missions first began work in Peking in 1861.

In our study of religion in Ting Hsien we have concerned ourselves primarily with its outward expression, the number of the temples, mosques, and churches, the temple fairs, and various religious organizations. The beliefs, ceremonies, and rituals of the various religions and cults were for the most part the same as those found in other parts of North China and have been studied and described by others.

Two studies were made of the temples. The first and more complete study was made in 1928 of the temples in the 62 villages of the Experimental District. A more general study of the entire hsien was made in 1930. There were 855 temples in the 453 villages and market towns of the hsien, an average of 1.9 temples per village. Tinghsien city had 22 temples. For the Experimental District, the figure was 104 temples, an average of 1.7 temples per village. Some villages had no temples. Others had as many as 11. In the Experimental District 31, or one-half of the villages, had no temples; eight had only one temple. Eleven villages, 18 per cent, had more than three temples, but only four villages, 6 per cent, had more than five temples.

There were three Mohammedan mosques in the hsien, two in the villages and one in the city.

The Catholics had a large city church, six village churches, and 36 other places of meeting, the Protestants a city church, 14 village congregations, but no village churches.

The list of the principal gods in the temples showed that there were four kinds or groups of temples, Buddhist, Taoist, Official, and Individual.

The outstanding deities of the different cults are, of course, quite clear. The various Buddhas and Bodhisattvas, and Kuan Yin, the goddess of mercy, are unmistakably Buddhist. Yü Huang, the San Ching, the San Kuan, Chen Wu, Erh Lang, Lao Tzu, and the Stellar Deities are the chief Taoist gods. The Niang Niangs, a group of some nine goddesses, are included in this group even though their origin is probably pre-Taoist and may trace back to a very early goddess of fecundity. National heroes who have gradually been deified and given a place in the Official temples are Confucius; China's three mythical emperors, Fu Hsi, Shen Nung, and Huang Ti; the three heroes of San Kuo times, Kuan Yü, Liu Pei, and Chang Fei; and Yüeh Fei, a Sung dynasty warrior. Besides these heroes the Official list includes the Ch'eng Huang and the T'u Ti, the gods of the particular locality. Ch'eng Huang, the protector of the city, had the same rank in the spirit world as the local official had in the temporal world. The T'u Ti is the local constable. The dragons are included in the official list as they controlled the rain, and it was part of the officials' duty to offer prayers for propitious weather.

Another group of gods who are neither Buddhist, Taoist, nor Official can best be classified as the gods of individual cults. They are generally polytheistic in nature. Such gods are the Ch'ung Wang, god of the insects, Ma Wang, god of the horses, Ho Shen, god of the river, and others of a similar nature.

When a temple is classified as Buddhist, Taoist, Official, or as belonging to one of the individual cults, it means that the principal deity belongs to that group. The lesser gods of the temple may, and often do, belong to one of the other groups. The Buddhist Kuan Yin and the Official Kuan Ti are found on the side altars of many temples dedicated to other deities.

Through the years Buddhism, Taoism, and the Official and individual cults have influenced each other, borrowed from each other, and imitated each other as one or the other has gained in popularity, prestige, and power until now, in some cases, it is difficult to decide the group to which some of the temples belong.

Several examples will perhaps illustrate how the different groups have intermingled and influenced each other. The origin of the dragon is pre-Buddhist as it goes back to very early days, but it is the Buddhists who have personalized the dragons and the dragon mother. We have included the dragons in the Official list because of their official function in controlling the rain. The Ch'eng Huang has long been the official protector of the city walls, but under the Manchu dynasty the deceased official whose spirit was to occupy that position for three years was nominated by the Taoist pope. At the end of his term the Ch'eng Huang might be renominated or replaced. The Buddhists claim that Yü Huang, the chief god of the Taoist trinity, is their god Yü Ti, stolen by the Taoists. The head Taoist priest in Ting Hsien lived in the city Ch'eng Huang temple. There used to be one temple, T'ien Chen Szu, that combined Buddhism, Taoism, Confucianism, and Mohammedanism so that any sect could come there to worship.

The Buddhist and Taoist temples did not appear to have any close connection with a central organization or governing body as is true of religious sects in most Western countries. The temples seemed to be relatively independent units. Most of them had been erected by the people living in the village. The building was financed sometimes by popular subscription, sometimes from official village funds, occasionally by an individual who had acquired wealth and wanted to do something for his native village. When built, the temple was dedicated to the deity who offered the type of protection the people felt they needed or who personified the characteristics they honored and revered. Most of the temples were looked after by the village people. Priests were in attendance only for special services. These priests had had, of course, the official Buddhist or Taoist training.

It must also be remembered that generally most of the Chinese do not feel the exclusiveness about their religion that often is felt by those trained in the traditions of Western countries. They can believe in both Buddhist and Taoist teachings and can worship in any of the temples if the deities have the attributes they desire to worship or are able to give the sort of help they need. One writer says that this is due to the fact that a popular religion has developed that has borrowed from Buddhism, Taoism, and the Official cult but is distinct from them and must be regarded as a separate system.

If the 855 village temples are grouped according to the connection of the principal deity, there were 345 Taoist, 223 Official, 215 Buddhist, 54 belonging to individual cults, and 18 that must be classed as miscellaneous as they were dedicated to all the gods or else their name, such as Big Temple, did not indicate their connection. The percentage division was 41 per cent Taoist, 26 per cent Official, 25 per cent Buddhist, 6 per cent Individual, and 2 per cent miscellaneous. In the Experimental District the division was very similar—45 per cent Taoist, 24 per cent Official, 23 per cent Buddhist, and 8 per cent Individual.

The principal Taoist deities, judging from the number of temples dedicated to them, were the Wu Tao, gods of the five elements, with 157 temples; the San Kuan, the three rulers of heaven, earth, and water; the Niang Niangs, a group of female deities who grant children, protect the eyes, etc.; Chen Wu, who alone among men is perfection itself; Yü Huang, the Jade or Pearly Emperor, the supreme god of the Taoist pantheon. Forty-five per cent of the Taoist temples were Wu Tao Miao; 91 per cent were dedicated to the above five groups of deities.

Kuan Yü, the Chinese god of war and also one of the gods of literature, was by far the most popular of the Official gods. He was the chief or one of the chief gods in 148, two-thirds, of the Official Temples. The dragons had 45 temples dedicated to them in Ting Hsien. These two groups included 86 per cent of the Official temples.

In 91 per cent of the Buddhist temples the chief deity was one of the manifestations of Kuan Yin, the Buddhist Goddess of Mercy. In some temples she was known as the Nan Hai Ta Shih, South Sea Grand Goddess, in others as Lao Mu, old mother.

Three quarters of the individual cult temples were dedicated to the king of the horses or the king of the insects. The Huo Shen, fire god, did not have any temple in Ting Hsien, but was one of the secondary gods in some of the other temples.

In size the temples varied from one to 30 chien. There were 1,397 chien in the 855 temples, or an average of 1.6 chien per temple. For the Experimental District, 83 per cent of the temples had only one chien. Eleven per cent had three chien and only 3 per cent had more than three.

Three was the average number of temple chien per village for the entire hsien. For the six Districts the averages ranged from 2.2 in the 4th District to 3.4 in the 6th District. In the Experimental District the average was 2.8 chien per village. It has been difficult to find any reason for this difference in the averages. A difference in wealth might account for it, but the cost of erecting a one-chien temple was relatively small. The religious beliefs of the past may have made a deeper and more lasting impression on those living in the northern part of the hsien so that they built more and larger temples, or they may have been more conservative and so have preserved more of their temples. In the 4th District, there were many more villages where some of the people had been willing to accept the newer ideas presented by Christianity.

The operating expenses of a temple ordinarily were very small. Except for special services and occasional repairs only a few dollars a year would be needed for incense and paper money. Very few of the temples had any priest connected with them, so the support of a priest was seldom an item in the temple budget. One or more of the villagers was appointed to look after the temple and light the incense in front of the altar.

There were 24 Buddhist and 15 Taoist priests in Ting Hsien. Eight of the Buddhists and seven of the Taoists lived in the city. The others were in the 1st, 3rd, and 5th Districts. Twelve of the 15 Taoist priests were married. They belonged to a class that did not take the vow of celibacy.

Many of the priests were paid only when they took part in some special service, such as those held during a temple fair; during the temples' special pilgrimage time; when the gods were asked for special help or protection; or for a funeral. This means they had only a limited amount of support from their religious position and many of the priests and monks had to earn a large part of their living by other means, usually by farming.

One report says the priests charged $1.00 a night per man for their part in funeral services, another that the charge was $4 for six men with an extra charge of $1.20 for music. The usual number of priests called in for the funeral services was four, six, or 12. In not a few instances men who were not priests put on the priests' robes and took part in the funeral service.

When the village elders of the Experimental District were asked about the number of temples, the religious societies, and religious observances in their village, they also were asked how much had been spent for special religious observances during the five years from 1922 through 1926. They reported a total expenditure of $5,455 for seven different causes: praying for rain, praying for protection from insects, hail, flood, sickness, and looting, and celebrating the reappearance of a god. The largest number of villages, 15, reported services praying for protection from insects. The total expediture was $996, an average of $66 per village. There was only one Ch'ung Wang Miao, Insect King Temple, in the Experimental District. The prayers, therefore, were offered in other temples where the Ch'ung Wang was a secondary deity or else before an altar specially set up for the occasion. Probably most of these services were held when the locusts came in 1922.

Fourteen villages reported praying for rain. Their total expenditure was $1,550, an average of $111 per village. The services probably were held in the spring of 1924 and the spring of 1925, for in both those years the lack of spring rain was serious enough to be noted in the list of calamities. The dragon would be the god prayed to as he controls the waters and therefore the rain. There were only five temples dedicated to the dragon king or his mother, but it was not difficult to arrange an altar for special services.

Ten villages offered special prayers for protection from looting. The average expenditure was $65 per village. Most of this expediture would be in 1926, when there was fighting in Ting Hsien between the Fengtien and Shansi forces. The Shansi forces first drove the Fengtien army from Shih Chia Chuang almost to Paoting, and then they themselves were driven south of Ting Hsien. There was looting when the Fengtien forces left Ting Hsien, and more when they returned and re-captured the area after fighting inside the city walls. This is said to be one of the worst times in Ting Hsien in recent years. After they had one experience with the looting of the Fengtien troops, it is not to be wondered at that the people turned to their gods for protection against a repetition of that experience. The year 1928 was not included in the period of our study of special religious expenditure, so we have no re-port concerning special services that may have been held because of the fighting and looting of that year.

Three villages spent $440 praying for protection from sickness, an average of $147 per village. One village reported spending $600 during five years for services seeking protection from hail. This total probably included a large amount spent for some special item such as the renova-tion of the temple. Perhaps an annual service was held in anticipation of possible damage. Hail damaged the crops in both 1923 and 1926.

There was damage from floods every year from 1922 to 1926, but only one village in the Experimental District reported holding special serv-ices to ask for divine protection from that sort of damage. The expen-diture was only $70, so probably only one, or not more than two, serv-ices were held during the five years.

The largest average expenditure was made in connection with re-appearances of the gods. Three villages reported a total expenditure of $1,150, or an average of $385 per village, for such services. This amount probably included some expenditure for the renovation of the temples as well as the cost of the celebration services.

During the 12 years from 1915 to 1926, the record of calamities shows seven years with flood, three with drought, five with hail, seven with locusts, three with sickness, cholera or plague, one with frost, and three with looting.

The families in our budget study (see Chapter V) spent an average of 75 cents when they went to the temple fair, but most of that was for entertainment rather than for any religious items. Their expenditure for religion averaged 70 cents for the year, most of it for paper money and incense.

One wishes the records were available to show what special events or particular influences were connected with the erection of the various temples and what were the special periods of temple building and rebuilding. We know that the history of some temples goes back to Ming, Yuan, and even Sung times, but, for the present at least, the other questions cannot be answered for Ting Hsien. In order to determine how much of a change there had been in recent years, the village elders of the Experimental District were asked what temples they had in their villages, what temples they used to have, and when any discontinued temples had been given up. The comparison of the two lists showed a tremendous decrease. The fifty years from 1882 to 1932 were a period of temple destruction rather than of temple building or rebuilding. Increasing contacts with the outside world, modern education, and many other influences had apparently weakened the hold of the gods on the people, and through the years a large proportion of the temples had been given up, converted to other uses, sold, or torn down.

Before 1882 there were 435 temples in the 62 villages of the Experimental District, but in 1928 the number was only 104. Three hundred and thirty-one temples, 76 per cent of the original list, had been given up. Before 1899 only two temples were reported as being discontinued, one in 1882 and one in 1889. From 1899 through 1917 there were only two years when at least one temple was not given up. Those years were 1901 and 1903. Between 1917 and 1928 only two were discontinued, one in 1926 and one in 1928. Eighty-two per cent of the discontinued temples were given up during three years 1900, 1914, and 1915. Twenty-seven were destroyed in 1900, Boxer year, largely as a result of the foreign troops coming to Ting Hsien after the capture of Peking. Two hundred were discontinued in 1914 and another 45 were given up in 1915. The influence of the Revolution and of the magistrate Sun Fa Hsü seems to have been responsible for this big decrease. Taking office in May, 1914, Sun came to Ting Hsien with the idea of getting rid of many of the old customs and promoting modern education throughout the entire hsien. He put pressure on the village elders to get them to give up the temples and to open schools. This program was opposed by many of the villages. In one part of the hsien some 10,000 people joined the Catholic church hoping that thereby they might avoid the additional taxes that would be necessary to provide for the school budget. In this they were unsuccessful. Magistrate Sun was in office less than two and a half years, but during that time 68 per cent of the existing temples were discontinued. Forty-eight per cent of the schools of the Experimental District were opened during the five years from 1912 to 1916, practically all of them during the last two years of that period.

As money was not readily available for the erection of any considerable number of school buildings, the elders of not a few villages were willing to accept the suggestion of the magistrate that they turn some of the available and relatively little used temples into schoolrooms. Most of them had been built by popular subscription, so it was not difficult to turn them over to other uses if the village elders could be persuaded that the new uses were a public benefit. It is rather surprising, however, to find that even as early as 1914 the old beliefs had been so undermined that the people were able to see so many temples given up without too much fear of the wrath of the gods.

The rent of land that had been given to some of the temples was, in several cases at least, transferred from the temple to the village school as the popularity of the temple waned and the village was required to expand its educational program.

If the change in the number of temples in the Experimental District can be taken as typical of the entire hsien, there used to be some 3,575 temples in the 453 villages and some 2,000 of these were given up during 1914 and 1915 while Sun Fa-hsü was in office. This seems to be an almost impossible number, but there does not seem to be any reason why a larger proportion should be given up in the Experimental District than in the rest of the hsien. Even if the temples discontinued during those years were only one-half the estimated number, it still would show that new ideas brought in by the Revolution of 1911 and by Magistrate Sun had a tremendous influence on the external expression of the religious life of the hsien. As only two temples were given up between 1917 and 1928, the wave of anti-religious feeling that started as anti-Christian about 1921, but gradually became anti-all-religion as it reached its height in 1927–1928, seems to have had but little influence on the religious life of Ting Hsien. The movement centered in South and Central China and in the cities and, as far as we can see, did not greatly affect the rural areas of North China.

The 1882 list of temples in the Experimental District shows that all but one of the villages had one or more temples. The single exception was a village in which, in 1928, 72 per cent of the families were Mohammedans. Thirty-six per cent of the villages had from one to five temples, 48 per cent from six to 10, and 15 per cent had more than 10 temples. Only one village had more than 17. For it the number was 22. The average was seven temples per village.

On the 1928 list 50 per cent of the Experimental District villages had no temples and only 6.4 per cent instead of 63 per cent had more than five temples. The maximum was 11. The average for all the villages was 1.7 or 3.4 for the villages that had temples.

While 30 villages had given up all their temples, seven still had the same number. One wishes it were possible to determine what were the differences in belief, experience, and contact with new ideas that led one village with 22 temples and another with 17 to give up all of them and one with 17 and another with 15 temples to discontinue all but one each while one village with 12 temples kept all but one and one village with seven temples and another with eight gave up none.

If we assume that the number of families in each village remained constant from 1882 to 1928, one village had, in 1882, one temple for every four families and there were six villages where there were less than 10 families per temple. In two of these six villages the number was still under 10 in 1928. In 1882 40 per cent of the villages had less than 20 families and 92 per cent had less than 50 families per temple. The maximum was 90, the average 24. In 1928 only 8 per cent of the villages had less than 20 families per temple. In only 13 per cent, instead of 92 per cent, was the number less than 50 families per temple. In six villages it was over 100 and in two it was over 345. The maximum was 362. One-half the villages had no temples. For the 62 villages the average number of families per temple was 100 or 10 more than the earlier maximum. For the entire hsien the 1930 average was 78 families per temple.

The village elders reported the 1928 use of 135, 41 per cent, of the discontinued temples. Fifty-seven were used for school buildings; another 25 were being used for other public purposes, such as village offices and public storehouses; 47 had been sold to private owners and probably had been torn down for the material in them; two were being rented out, the rent going to the public funds of the village; three had been torn down and the land added to the village public land; one had been turned over to some monks and was used by them as their residence.

More than a proportionate number of the larger temples were given up, possibly because they would provide better school accommodations, perhaps because of the cost involved in repairing them if they had fallen into disrepair. In 1928 83 per cent of the Experimental District temples had only one chien and only 3 per cent had more than three chien. In the 1882 list the corresponding figures were 70 per cent and 9 per cent. According to the earlier list the average number of temple chien per village was 15. In 1928 it was 2.8.

In 396 temples of the earlier list the gods were represented by images, in 31 by pictures painted on the walls. There were 2,157 images in the 396 temples, an average for the temples with images of 5.4. One-half of the temples had three images and another 14 per cent had only one image. Forty-eight temples, 12 per cent, had 10 or more images. The maximum was 116. Of these 48 larger temples, only six were maintained in 1928.

In 1928 there were 78 temples with images and 26 with pictures. The number of images was 404 or an average of 5.2. This was only slightly lower than the 1882 average. There was not more difference because one temple with 116 images was included in both lists. If that temple is omitted, the 1928 average was 3.7 images per temple. One would naturally expect a low average as 83 per cent of the temples on the 1928 list had only one chien and on a single altar there is hardly room for more than one large image or three smaller ones.

A comparison of the 1928 and 1882 lists shows that while 76 per cent of all the temples had been given up, 85 per cent of those with five or more images had been discontinued, 91 per cent of those with 15 or more, and 94 per cent of those with 20 or more images.

Because there are some 18 different names of Buddhist temples on the earlier list, but only five on the 1928 list, our first impression was that the non-Buddhist gods had the stronger hold on the people and that a larger proportion of the Buddhist temples had been given up than was true of the other groups. Further analysis of the figures showed that the opposite was true. The Taoist, Official, and Individual groups lost from 75 to 78 per cent of their temples but only 70 per cent of the Buddhist temples were discontinued. The difference is not large, but it would seem to suggest that the Buddhist gods or more especially Kuan Yin, to whom in her various manifestations some 91 per cent of the Buddhist temples are dedicated, had a stronger hold on the hearts of the people than most of the other gods.

Two-thirds of the temples dedicated to Kuan Yin had been given up but of the more popular deities, those with four or more temples, she was the only one that, in 1928, had more than 30 per cent of the number in 1882. Yü Huang, the Pearly Emperor, had only one left out of 22, a 95 per cent loss. The decrease in the temples dedicated to the other female deities was 77 per cent or just about the average loss. For all of the goddesses together, the decrease was 70 per cent. Their temples were 21 per cent of the earlier list but were 27 per cent of the 1928 list.

Some new temples were built after 1928 and others were renovated. We have not attempted a study of the reasons for this activity, but it seems to indicate that some of the people were turning again to the old gods. Considering the events of the years immediately following 1925, this is hardly surprising. Chinese armies marched through and occupied the district. There was fighting, bombing from airplanes, looting, heavier taxes, and extraordinary demands for money, supplies, and men. Unable to get help and protection from the forces of this world, it is not surprising that some of the people came to feel that their only hope was in the forces of the spirit world and that their help should be sought through special services, the rebuilding of temples fallen into disrepair, and the erection of new shrines.

Soon after the uniting of the country in 1928 the Nationalist government issued a decree concerning the temples. Those dedicated to the sages and worthies of preceding ages were to be kept up. This list included the three mythical emperors, Fu Hsi, Shen Nung, Huang Ti, Lei Ts'u (who first reared silk worms), Ts'ang Chieh (the inventor of writing), Hou Chi (the Harvest Patron), Emperor Yü, Confucius, Mencius, Kung Shu Pan, Kuan Yü, and Yueh Fei. The temples and churches of the religious sect teaching theism with a pure and right intention were to be continued. These included the followers of Sakyamuni and Lao Tzu, Mohammedanism and Christianity.

The temples to be suppressed were those in which purely legendary personages were worshiped with no practical utility. These included the temples of the stellar spirits, the sun, the moon, etc., of Huo Shen the fire god, of K'uei Hsing the god of literature, of Wen Ch'ang (the cult of the battleflag), of the genii of the mountains, rivers, and earth, of the five holy peaks, the four rivers, the river spirits, the Dragon Kings, the Ministry of Thunder, of T'ai Shan, Tung Yueh, Ch'eng Huang, and T'u Ti; also the temples offending against public morality by playing on the credulity of people for gain, the temples of Chang

Hsien, Sung Tzu, Niang Niang, Ts'ai Shen, Erh Lang, Sun Hou Tzu the monkey god, Wen Shen, Hsüan T'an the god of riches, Shih Ch'ien, and Hu Hsien the fox spirit.

The decree marked for suppression a large part of the Ting Hsien temples, but, up to 1935, there seems to have been no serious effort to enforce it in North China. It seemed then that, lacking governmental pressure, the number of temples would probably diminish very gradually, that as the less popular temples fell into disrepair they would be given up, but that the belief in the more popular deities was so widespread and so deeply imbedded in the life of the people that it would continue for a long time. What influence the war with Japan and the Japanese occupation had on the religious life of Ting Hsien is unknown.

Freedom of religion is part of the constitution of the new Central People's Government, but it is reported that when the Communists were in control of parts of Kiangsi province they destroyed all the temples and shrines in the area. How many temples will survive in Ting Hsien?

Temple Fairs

Fairs held to honor the gods and to present them with incense, feasts, and entertainment combined religious worship, amusement, recreation, business, and sociability. They were the largest public activities associated with any of the temples. Thousands of people came from neighboring villages and even farther afield and there was great activity during the three, four, or more days of the fair. Free theatrical performances were regularly part of the program and were very popular.

Many of the fairs have a long history but we also found that new ones were being organized at the time of our study.

While the fairs usually were held to honor one of the more popular gods and worship was regularly part of the program, in at least one town there were two annual fairs that had no religious connection.

Not every temple or every village or even every market village had a fair. The city, two of its three suburbs, and 35 of the 453 towns and villages held fairs. How they were distributed throughout the hsien is shown on the hsien map on page 5. The map also shows the month when the fairs were held. Fifty was the total number reported. Six fairs were listed in the city, four in one town, three in another, and two in another. Only one village had two fairs and they were both in the same month.

The third lunar month with 14 fairs and the second month with 12 were the most popular times for fairs. Sixty-two per cent were held in the first quarter of the year but only 4 per cent in the last quarter. There were no fairs in the 11th and 12th months. The sixth, seventh, and eighth month had only one fair each.

A fair was usually an all village activity with various committees taking charge of the necessary arrangements for the worship, for the theatricals, for the erection of the stage for the players and the mat shed for the spectators, for the selling booths, for the grouping of the various kinds of products offered for sale, for the collection of the necessary funds. For some fairs the money was collected from everyone in the village on the basis of their estimated wealth or the amount of land they owned. In others the money was collected from the shops and stores in the village and from the merchants coming for the fair. In still others an attempt was made to collect the cost of the fair from the visiting merchants and those who set up temporary booths. Only if these contributions left a deficit were the residents of the village asked to subscribe. If there was any surplus in the fair account it usually was added to the general fund of the village.

In most villages the fair was run by the group in charge of the village government, but in some it was in the hands of an entirely different group.

The cost of a fair lasting four days ordinarily varied from $100 to $150. The theatricals given for the entertainment of the gods and the visitors, except one or two caretakers who had to be left in each $114, the main items were:

Theatrical troupe	$60.00	Light and fuel	$6.50
Tip for head of troupe	4.00	Entertainment of soldiers	8.00
Mat shed	17.00	Tax for entertainment	4.00
Stage	10.00	Miscellaneous	4.50

The Pei Ch'i fair was given to honor Han Tsu (see pages 420–21). His worship was the high point of the fair. On the evening of the 20th of the 3rd month practically the entire village of 326 families and their many visitors, except for one or two caretakers who had to be left in each house, went to the temple. Many devout worshippers kotowed every ten steps from their home to the temple. They all spent the night in the temple sitting on the floor in front of the altar. The nearer one sat to the altar the better chance he would have to get a blessing from the god early in the morning.

In the morning a new robe was put on the god, he was fanned, incense was burned, and feasts were offered on the altar. Oil money was given for the god. Other contributions were put into the money box.

It was estimated that the shops and stalls and displays of goods for this fair covered 150 mu, 25 acres, and that the attendance was some 10,000 persons per day for four days. In the animal market some 2,400 head were sold. The shops and dealers at the 1927 fair were listed as:

Cloth	80	Bamboo articles	7	Tea shops	10
Silk	6	Reed curtains	7	Wine	5
Jewelry	30	Willow baskets	7	Miscellaneous food	30
Furs	15	Stone articles	3	Barbers	20
Imported goods	6	Winnowing		Fortune tellers	10
Brooms and dusters	50	machines	3	Peep shows	6
Iron goods	35	Rolls	15	Story tellers	5
Baskets	10	Noodles	12	Chinese boxers	3
Fertilizer	10	Bread	7		
Drug shops	8	Meat	14		

Lumber and wood sellers covered an area of 10 mu. No count was made of dealers in agricultural implements.

Tung Wang, a village of 319 families, held its fair on the 15th–19th of the third month to honor the god Ch'eng Huang (see page 400). He was noted for his ability to cure disease and settle problems for his worshipers. The activities of the fair covered some 30 mu. The attendance was some 4,000 per day.

The fair in Yao Lu Chuang, a small village with only 51 families, was started in 1927, because so many people came to worship the spirit of a willow tree that stood at the edge of the village. The village head had wanted to cut the tree down to get some money for the village school but before it was done a man came and said that a god had appeared to him in a dream and had told him that the willow tree was about to be deified and that pieces of the tree would cure sickness. The news spread around. People came to worship. A man was cured. Then so many people came that the village organized a four day fair from the 2nd to the 5th of the 3rd month.

The reputation of the tree was increased when a man who never believed in the willow tree god was struck with paralysis as he passed the tree, stayed there a day and had to be carried home. A sick man on a journey was impressed by the size of the tree. He stopped, kotowed, and prayed for help. The spirit of the tree cured him.

There was no temple near the tree so the village put up, for the fair days, a mat shed where the visitors could rest and an altar where they could pray. The names of those who contributed were written on yellow paper and pasted on the walls of the mat shed. The worshipers took pieces of the tree away with them. If the tree cured them they presented a board or a cloth scroll that was hung on the tree.

The fair covered some 30 mu of land and had an estimated attendance of some 4,000 a day. The shops listed were:

Cloth	5	Bread	3	Miscellaneous food	14
Jewelry	3	Noodles	3	Cigarettes	11
Paper flowers	3	Meat	3		
Toys	6	Tea	3	Barbers	2
Miscellaneous goods	6	Wine	3	Gambling	11

The Tung T'ing fall fair was first organized about 1921. It was held in the 9th month to supplement the spring fair held in the 1st month. There was no temple connected with the fair and no altar was set up for worship by the visitors.

This fair was next to the Pei Ch'i fair in size. It covered some 50 mu and drew some 5,000 visitors per day. About 1,000 animals were sold during the four days. There were 22 games of chance on the fair grounds, fish bowls from which to draw numbers, bamboo sticks to be shaken until one came out, and shell games. The report stated that there was not as much entertainment at Tung T'ing as at Pei Chi.

The shops at the fall fair were:

Cotton cloth	30	Carts	6	Tea	6
Silk	5	Willow twigs	6	Miscellaneous food	25
Fur lined coats	12	Boxes	5		
Jewelry	9	Paper flowers	5	Barbers	15
Imported goods	5			Fortune tellers	5
Iron	10	Rolls	8	Chinese boxers	3
Leather	7	Bread	3	Story tellers	3
Rugs	7	Meat	5	Gambling	22
Toys	7	Wine	3		

One wonders whether the omission of worship by this lately organized fair points toward the gradual elimination of worship from the other fairs. It seems probable that the worship feature will continue, but with fewer and fewer worshipers. Even now by no means all of the people stop to burn a bundle of incense and bow in front of the altar before they enjoy the fair.

The fairs were a great opportunity for entertainment and recreation. They were also the occasion for the local people to sell their products and buy things brought in by itinerant merchants. They also brought considerable income to those who could rent quarters to visitors. It will be noted that farm products such as grain and vegetables were not listed as on sale at the fairs. The taxes collected on animals, wood, and other local products sold during the fair were a big item, but, as the tax collection privilege had been bought from the hsien, the amount collected at the fairs went to the tax collector rather than to the government tax office.

Some people complained that the expense of entertaining visiting friends and relatives who came for the fair was a heavy financial burden and was an annual item; also that there was a great temptation to spend more at the fair than the family budget could afford. The fairs also attracted thieves, pickpockets, confidence men, and gamblers.

The fairs were one of few occasions during the year when the entire family came out for recreation and entertainment and so were one of the few times that large numbers of women were seen abroad.

Religious Societies

Besides the temples to which anyone could go for worship there were special Buddhist and Taoist societies with a limited membership. Only members were admitted to their meetings; there were special rules of conduct and abstinence for their members. Most of these organizations, especially the Taoist ones, had many of the characteristics of secret societies, with a ritual, dogma, and practice known only to their members. Consequently we have been able to secure only general information about them. As far as we could learn several societies may be represented in a given village, but a person can be a member of only one. In the 62 villages of the Experimental District we found one Buddhist and nine Taoist societies. At least six of the Taoist societies had both men and women members.

The Buddhist society was called the Universal Salvation Buddhist Society. It was named for the monk Pu Chi, whose doctrines it was formed to perpetuate after his death at Wu T'ai Shan. Joining the society involved the payment of an initiation fee, a contribution that was said to bring blessing and benefit to departed parents and relatives. It was reported that there were 854 members in 13 villages.

The Taoist societies in the order of size were The Grain Carrying, Pei Liang Tao; The Sage and Virtuous, Sheng Hsien Tao; The Nine Functions, Chiu Kung Tao; The Teachers' Society, Lao Shih Tao; The Li Men, doctrine sect; The Hsiang Men Tao, incense sect; The Sitting and Practising, Tso Kung Tao; The Quiet Heart, Ching Hsin Tao; The Gold Incense, Chin Hsiang Tao.

The Pei Liang Tao got its name from the fact that on the 15th of the month certain of the women and on the 16th certain of the men put a package of grain on their backs and went out to call on their fellow members and to try to convert others. On the 1st of the month the members met at the home of the head of the group. The grain they carried on their backs was used for food at the meeting or while on the road. At their meeting the members sang songs together and practiced contemplation. They said that with practice magic rays came from their eyes and that they were able to see the spirits of the dead. There were 570 members in six villages.

The Sheng Hsien Tao was started in Ting Hsien on the 24th of the 8th month of 1898 by a man named Wang Tang Chia who said he came from San Tsun Fo Shan or the Three Buddha Hill. Meetings were held every three months, at which time one of the older members was invited to preach the doctrine of the society. The rules required that the members abstain from dog meat, pigeons, and wild geese. In order that they might receive a blessing the members sang songs and practiced contemplation. The Sheng Hsien Tao had 243 members in 22 villages.

The Chiu Kung Tao came from T'ai Shan in Shantung, where it was started in 1852. It first reached Ting Hsien in 1854, coming by way of T'ang Hsien. The members of this society were not allowed to eat meat, garlic, or onions, to drink wine, or to use tobacco. It was said that they could predict future danger and happiness, could cure people, and with practice could learn to see the spirits of the dead. No regular meetings were held but when a member effected a cure the family of the patient arranged for a meeting. Some families asked the members not only to work cures but also to bring a blessing to their deceased parents and relatives. This society had 109 members in five villages.

The Lao Shih Tao, Teachers' Society, was started during the reign of Shun Chih, 1644–1661, by a man called Tung Szu Feng Tzu who lived in Shantung. The Emperor sent for him, liked him, and encouraged him to preach his doctrine. He accompanied the Emperor on a trip to T'ai Shan. The society first came to Ting Hsien in 1822. It got its name from the fact that its members addressed each other as Lao Shih, teacher, whenever they met on the street. The rules of the society prohibited the use of meat. The members were said to be able to predict the future. There were 106 members in 13 villages.

The Li Men, doctrine sect, was founded by Yang Tzu during the reign of K'ang Hsi, 1662–1722. He originally taught how to control the mind and body and how to practice self denial. His followers, who had given up many of the original beliefs and practices, worshiped the fox, snake, and weasel and abstained from wine and tobacco. The society held a meeting once a year. New members were initiated at that time. The charge for the meeting was some 70 cents and a meal was served those who attended. This society seems to have had more organization than most of the others, with a head man, a business manager, a supervisor, and a number of preachers. The head office of the society was near Yenchiang in Kua Chia T'un. There were 90 members in 16 villages.

Members of the Hsiang Men Tao, incense sect, were said to burn incense and kotow 800 times after midnight on the 1st and 15th of the month. The society held no regular meetings but came together occasionally when one of the members had worked a cure and the cured man provided for the meeting. At such meetings the general beliefs of the group were set forth. The society was said also to have considerable secret material known only to the members. There were 28 members in three villages.

The Tso Kung Tao, founded on the shores of the Hsi Hu, or Western Lake, came to T'ang Hsien in 1650 and to Ting Hsien in 1661. As far as we could learn the chief duty of the members was to practice contemplation and the development of the quiet mind, thereby bringing longevity to the body and harmony to the soul. They sat down and meditated three times a day, early morning, noon, and midnight. They believed that if they practiced well their souls could leave their bodies and travel around the world. They also believed that this freedom of the soul made it possible for them to communicate with the spirits and that from them they could get the power to cure sickness.

The members of this Tao met in the home of the head of the society on the 15th day of the 1st, 5th, and 9th months. They all contributed money to cover the cost of the meeting but the largest item was always the meal served to the members. Any surplus was used for the good of the group. The society had only nine members in one village.

The Ching Hsin Tao and Chin Hsiang Tao were, to the outsider, very similar to the Tso Kung Tao in their practices of contemplation and the quiet mind. It was not possible to discover just how the societies differed from each other in belief and teaching. The Ching Hsin Tao had only seven members in one village. The Ching Hsiang Tao had but five members.

The total membership in the nine Taoist societies was 1,167. It was not possible to determine from the field reports how many of the 62 villages of the Experimental District had one or more Taoist societies, but as the nine societies reported 68 village organizations and the Sheng Hsien Tao was represented in 22 villages, it seems probable that at least half and possibly two-thirds of the villages had one or more of the Taoist groups represented among their inhabitants.

It will be noted that contemplation was used by the members of most of these Taoist organizations in order to gain peace of mind, freedom of the soul, and contact with the spirit world and in some instances to develop the power of healing. Some, but not all, of the societies required their members to abstain from the use of all or special kinds of meat, wine, and tobacco. It would seem probable, therefore, that the membership would include the more devout Taoists and would be made up largely of older men and women. One investigator reported that the members were largely old type schoolmasters, men without regular occupations, and obstinate men, that some of the members joined because they were old and had no sons or no children. He also reported that the women members were well along in years and that not a few of them were widows.

Besides the societies directly connected with Buddhism and Taoism there were others that had no religious connection but appealed to the people on the basis of morality and good works. The Wan Kuo Tao Te Hui, International Moral Society, founded in 1921 in Shantung, first came to Ting Hsien in 1923. Many people joined at that time, especially those with some education. Since then the membership had fallen off. The society had some secret rules and regulations and was very strict on keeping them secret. The group held no regular meetings. In the Experimental District there were members in only one village.

The Hao Shih Hui, Good Deeds Society, came to Ting Hsien from An Kuo Hsien in 1906. All that we could learn about this society was that it held a three day meeting beginning on the 19th of the first month. The amusements provided included theatricals, acrobats, and performing monkeys. The expense of the meeting was met by contributions from the members. Only a few families in one village in the Experimental District were members.

We did not attempt a study of the powers, attributes, and history of the gods of Ting Hsien, as they generally were the same as the gods worshiped in other parts of China and have been studied and described by others. A list of the gods represented in the Ting Hsien temples will, however, give an idea of the spirits worshiped in that area.[1]

Chang Fei, companion of Kuan Ti.
Ch'eng Huang, god of the city walls and moat.
Ch'i Shen, seven spirits of seven stars of the Big Dipper.
Chiang T'ai Kung, hero of 12th century B.C., reincarnated as advisor of first
    Chou Emperor.
Chiu Shen, nine gods in charge of nine levels of heaven.
Ch'ung Wang, god of the insects.
Confucius, China's great teacher, philosopher, and sage.
Dragons, gods of rain, rivers, and streams.
Erh Lang, nephew of Yü Huang, with power over ghosts and evil spirits.
Fox spirits.
Han Tsu, distributor of buckwheat seed.
Ho Shen, river god.
Kuan Yin, Buddhist goddess of mercy.
Kuan Yü, also known as Kuan Ti or Kuang Kung, hero of Three Kingdoms,
    god of war, literature, and the theatre.
Lao Tzu, reputed founder of Taoism.
Liu Pei, god of carpenters, hero of Three Kingdoms.
Ma Mien, horse face, attendant of Ch'eng Huang.
Ma Wang, King of the horses.
Niang Niangs, group of female deities.

1. We are indebted to Mrs. L. Carrington Goodrich for her help in securing information on the character, history, and classification of the gods.

Niu T'ou, cow head, attendant of Ch'eng Huang.

Pei Tou, Big Dipper.

San Ch'ing, three pure ones, inhabitants of three heavens.

San Huang, China's three mythical emperors.

San Kuan, Three Causes or Agents, Taoist rulers of heaven, earth, and water, personified by various groups of three heroes.

Shan Shen, god of the mountains.

Szu Ta T'ien Wang, Four Diamond Kings of Heaven, rulers of the four quarters of the universe and of the four seas.

Tsang Ku, maiden of the time of Confucius, an expert in needle work.

T'u Ti, subordinate of Ch'eng Huang, constable of spirits in the district.

Tung Yueh Ta Ti, ruler of the Eastern Hell, helper of Chou Wang of the Shang dynasty.

Wen Shen, god of epidemics.

Wu Tao, gods of the five elements, five points of the compass, five grains.

Wu Tou, five stars, representing the five points of the compass.

Yao Wang, god of medicine.

Yü Huang, Jade or Pearly Emperor, ruler of heaven.

Yüeh Fei, a general of the Sung dynasty.

The story of Kuan Yü, who was also known as Kuan Ti or Kuan Kung, will show how one of the most popular of the gods increased in influence and popularity, and was given increasingly exalted titles by the Emperor.

Kuan Yü was known as the god of war, and his temples were often called military temples. He was the patron saint of all soldiers, but was also worshiped by many other groups because of his sincerity, loyalty, bravery, righteousness, generosity, and honesty. He had power over demons, and was sometimes known as a god of literature and of the theatre. A picture showing him presenting sons wearing official head-dress was often hung on the wall of the bridal chamber. It was believed that he granted immunity from disease, success to the scholar, old age for parents, a quick passage through hell, and a speedy rebirth for departed spirits. He was one of the gods whose pictures were burned at New Year's time. He was specially worshiped on the 15th of the second moon and the 13th of the fifth moon. He was on the rabbit pictures used for the Moon Festival on the 15th of the eighth moon.

According to tradition he died in 220, executed by his enemy Sun Ch'üan. In 260 the son of his friend Liu Pei gave him the title of "Brave Western Marquis". In 583 the Sui Emperor added the title, "Sincere and Merciful Duke". In 676 he was made the tutelary god of a monastery built near his grave by the T'ang Emperor to the memory of the six Buddhist Patriarchs. The Taoist pope and the people soon recognized his power over demons. In 1096 a tablet with the title "Prayer Answering Illustrious King" was placed in his temple. In 1108 was added the title "Brave Peace Bringing King". He was also called "Faithful and Loyal Duke", "Magnificent Prince and Pacificator", and "Warrior Prince and Civilizer". In 1129 the Sung Emperor ordered that regular official sacrifices be made to him. In 1614 he was granted the title "Great Emperor, subduing the demons of the three regions, Heaven Exalted One whose powerful authority makes the most remote stand in awe of him, Kuan, the Holy Ruler". In 1856, because of his help during the Taiping rebellion, he was made the "Protector of the Dynasty" and the equal of Confucius. In 1914 the Republican government ordered that sacrifices be made to him in all the military temples, and generals and soldiers took their oath of allegiance before his image.

Kuan Ti was reported to have appeared in Peking during the reign of Hsün Chih (1644–1661). He was said to have given stomach trouble to any of the foreign troops that attempted to stay in the Tung Yueh Miao in 1900, and, as a cloud of yellow dust, to have protected the Empress Dowager when she fled from Peking.

If rain fell on the 13th of the fifth moon it was because Kuan Ti was sharpening his sword and the water dripped from his grindstone; if on the 24th of the sixth moon, he was celebrating his birthday and was drunk. His birthday was the date when usually, in North China, the Green Crop Associations, Ch'ing Miao Hui, held their first fall meeting and the crop watchmen started their protection of the fall harvest.

Kuan Ti was associated with Chang Fei and Liu Pei in the 13 San I Miao in Ting Hsien. These three were specially noted for ther unsurpassed loyalty. They were worshiped by those swearing brotherhood. Together they protected the district and kept it peaceful as Kuan Ti's big sword chased away the demons, Liu Pei's two edged sword had power over poisonous insects, and Chang Fei's spear gave prosperity. Kuan Ti was known as one of the emperors of heaven, Liu Pei represented men or earth, and Chang Fei the underworld. Liu Pei had a white face like the moon, Chang Fei a black face with big eyes like the stars, and Kuan Ti a red face like the sun.

We found one god, Han Tsu, who was especially connected with Ting

Hsien. In some areas he was known as the god of silk worms, but in Ting Hsien it was believed that he was responsible for the miraculous distribution of greatly needed buckwheat seed. The story is that some time ago when there was drought in Shen Chow Hsien and Yao Yang Hsien, the rain came just at the time for the sowing of buckwheat, but the people had no seed left. An old man appeared with a large supply of seed and sold it to the farmers. Instead of asking for money he said, "I know you have no money so I do not want any now. Give it to me after the harvest". He said his name was Han and his home Pei Ch'i in Ting Hsien. That year there was an unusually large buckwheat harvest and the farmers were very grateful to the old man who had sold them the seed. When, long after the harvest, he had not come for his money, the people met to discuss the matter. They finally collected the money that was due and delegated one of their number to take it to Pei Ch'i. He could find no family there with the surname of Han, only a small broken-down temple dedicated to Han Tsu. The people, consequently, believed that it was Han Tsu who gave them the buckwheat. Out of gratitude they rebuilt the temple and organized a temple fair that was held from the 21st to the 24th of the third moon. It was the largest of the temple fairs in Ting Hsien. People came to it from all the surrounding hsien as well as from many of the villages in Ting Hsien. The first day of the fair was a general holiday for the area.

Mohammedanism

Mohammedanism has had a place in the religious life of Ting Hsien for more than three hundred years, possibly much longer, for Mohammedans came to Peking as residents during the Sung dynasty (960–1278). Mosques, Ch'ing Chen Szu, had been built in two villages and in the hsien city. The ahongs and their assistants carried on worship the usual five times a day. Meetings for members were held on Friday. All were required to bathe before attending service.

In the two villages with mosques there were 1,400 Mohammedans, 1,210 in one village and 190 in the other. Three other nearby villages had five Mohammedans each. The number of families represented was 255 or an average of 5.5 persons per family. In one village 72 per cent and in another 36 per cent of the families were Mohammedans. Food requirements and other customs are more conveniently observed if the adherents live fairly close together.

Undoubtedly there were some Mohammedans living in other villages throughout the hsien, but, except for those connected with the city mosque, their number was probably small. In the Experimental District, which includes the five villages mentioned above, 2.4 per cent of the families were Mohammedan. Corresponding figures for the entire hsien are not available as no attempt was made to determine religious affiliations throughout the hsien.

The elders of T'ang Chia Chuang, the village in which 72 per cent of the families were Mohammedan, told us that during the last 45 years there had not been any temple in their village. All the other villages of the Experimental District had had one or more temples even though one-half of the villages did not have any in 1928. Evidently the Mohammedans had been in the majority and in control of the affairs of T'ang Chia Chuang for many years.

Christianity

Christianity came to Ting Hsien from Ning Chin Hsien, where it had been preached by converts from the time of K'ang Hsi (1662–1723). The most prominent of these men had been officials in Peking, where they had been converted by the teaching of Catholic priests. During the years from 1820 to 1840 there was one village where the people were almost all Catholics. Many of the people of this village were killed in later persecutions. There were no Christian believers in that particular village in 1930, but the people did not worship the usual Chinese deities.

A French priest was resident in Ting Hsien in 1858 but had to leave because of the troubles that came soon thereafter. He was able to return soon after 1860, as a priest had acted as interpreter for Prince Kung in the negotiations that ended the war with France and England. The Prince persuaded the Emperor to give orders that the Catholic priests might work in North China. It is reported that when the priest came back to Ting Hsien, after 1860, there were only some 8,000 adherents in the 32 hsien included in the entire Cheng Ting area, of which Ting Hsien is a part. In 1930 the Catholic churches in Ting Hsien had some 5,800 members scattered in 58 villages and belonging to some 1,100 families. This was about 1.5 per cent of the population. In the city there were some 36 Catholic families with 130 persons. A French priest was in charge of the large church in the city. There were also one Chinese priest, three assistants, and one Chinese nun. The church school had 40 students. The church was built in 1929. In the villages there were six churches and 36 other places of meeting. The church in Nan Ch'e Chi was built in 1904. The value of the church property, including the church buildings, was estimated at $200,000.

When the magistrate Sun Fa-hsü, in 1914–1915, attempted to make every village in the hsien maintain a primary school, many of the people thought that the village schools were foreign organizations and did not want to support them. In the east part of the hsien some 10,000 people quickly joined the Catholic church, thinking that thereby they could escape the taxation levied for the schools. The magistrate took the matter up with the priest, who told the church members they would have to obey the government's orders. One report also says that many families were fined because of their disregard of the magistrate's orders. When they could get no help from the church, most of the "converts" left and by the next year not more than 500 remained.

Protestant Christianity was represented in Ting Hsien by the Kung Li Hui, Congregational Church, and by the Salvation Army. The church was part of the field that had its center at Paotingfu. According to the church figures there were 525 members in 256 families. In only some 30 per cent of the families was the entire family Christian. In 1928 there were families with one or more church members in 59 villages and towns scattered throughout the hsien. Twenty-six of the villages were in the 4th District, in the southern part of the hsien. Another 10 villages were in the southern end of the 2nd and 3rd Districts just across the Sha River from the 4th District. Only two of the 62 villages of the Experimental District had any church members.

Ordinarily a church was organized wherever there were 10 or more members in a village. The 1928 map showed 14 of these congregations. They regularly met in the homes of the members as the only church building was in the city, on the main south street. That congregation had 48 members. The Chinese pastor, who lived in the city, was in charge of the city church, but was also related to the work of the entire hsien. In view of the figures secured from some other countries, it is of interest to note that 60 per cent of the Protestants in Ting Hsien were males. This might be expected because of the greater ease with which the men can be approached.

The church groups consistently stressed the need of education for the church members. When the Mass Education program was concentrating its work on the villages of the Experimental District, the church groups had seven Mass Education schools of their own. The report showed approximately 75 per cent literacy in the Christian families. In an effort to start a home industry that would enable the women to add a little to the family income, some of the church groups had classes in knitting.

The Salvation Army first came to Ting Hsien in 1918. It had a meeting hall on the main north street of the city, sub-headquarters, with Chinese officers in charge, in two towns and one village, and centers in eight villages, where work was carried on by the officers from the nearby headquarters. There was one foreign officer living in the city. He reported, in 1930, a membership of 500 in all the different centers, with 268 of these in the city. Besides these there were a number of inquirers not yet admitted to membership. Plans had been prepared for the building of a hospital in the west suburb.

TABLE 111. TEMPLES, 1930

Wu Tao Miao	157	Ho Shen Miao	5	Mu T'a Szu	1
Kuan Ti Miao	123	K'ung Tzu Miao	5	Pa En Szu	1
Lao Mu Miao	102	T'ai Kung Miao	5	Pai T'a Szu	1
Nan Hai Ta Shih		Ch'uan Shen Miao	4	Pei Tou Miao	1
Miao	80	San Huang Miao	4	San Ch'ing Kuan	1
San Kuan Miao	48	Yueh Wang Miao	4	Szu Chieh Miao	1
Nai Nai Miao	45	Ch'eng Huang Miao	3	Ta Wang Miao	1
Chen Wu Miao	41	Ch'i Shen Miao	3	T'ien Ch'i Miao	1
Lung Wang Miao	32	Hsien Ku Miao	3	T'ien T'ai Szu	1
Yü Huang Miao	22	Fo Szu	2	T'ien Ti Miao	1
Ma Wang Miao	21	Fo Yeh Szu	2	Ts'ang Ku Miao	1
Ch'ung Wang Miao	20	Hu Hsien Miao	2	Ts'ang Shan Yüan	1
Yao Wang Miao	14	Kuan Yüeh Miao	2	Tz'u Yün Szu	1
Kuan Yin Miao	13	T'ien Hsien Sheng		Wen Shen Miao	1
San I Miao	13	Mu Miao	2	Wu Chiang Miao	1
Ta Szu	13	Chiu Shen Miao	1	Wu Ling Miao	1
Lung Mu Miao	12	Fo Tsu Szu	1	Yen Wang Miao	1
P'u Sa Miao	9	Han Tsu Miao	1	Yü Wang Miao	1
Erh Lang Miao	7	Hsien Hsing Szu	1		—
T'u Ti Miao	7	Kao Ke Miao	1	Total	855
Lao Chün Miao	6	Mi Le An	1		

TABLE 112. TEMPLES IN EXPERIMENTAL DISTRICT VILLAGES,
BEFORE 1882 AND IN 1928

	Before 1882	1928		Before 1882	1928
Wu Tao Miao	68	17	San Huang Miao	3	1
Lao Mu Miao	54	19	Ho Shen Miao	2	1
Kuan Ti Miao	40	10	Wu Sheng Lao Mu Miao	2	1
Chen Wu Miao	37	11	Ch'eng Huang Miao	1	1
San Kuan Miao	32	9	Ch'i T'ien Ta Sheng Miao	1	1
Nai Nai Miao	22	5	Chou Kung Miao	1	1
Yü Huang Miao	22	1	Fo Yeh Miao	1	1
Lung Wang Miao	21	4	Han Tsu Miao	1	1
Yao Wang Miao	18	5	Li Ching Miao	1	1
Ma Wang Miao	17	3	Lo Han Miao	1	1
Ch'ung Wang Miao	9	1	Lung Mu Miao	1	1
Kuan Yin Miao	7	2	San Ch'ing Kuan	1	1
Erh Lang Miao	6	1	Ts'ai Shen Miao	1	1
T'ai Kung Miao	4	1	Wen Miao	1	1
T'u Ti Miao	4	1			

All Given Up by 1928

Ta Szu	12	Lao Chang Miao	1
San I Miao	5	Lao Chün Miao	1
Ch'i Shen Miao	3	Liu Hsiu Miao	1
Wu Lung Sheng Mu Miao	3	Lung Ch'üan Szu	1
Ch'ung Ning Szu	2	Mi Le Szu	1
Fo Kuang Szu	2	Ni Ku An	1
Wen Shen Miao	2	Pa Ch'a Miao	1
Yung Ning Szu	2	Pai Ma Szu	1
An Le Szu	1	Pei Yüeh Miao	1
Ching Yeh Szu	1	Ta Fo Szu	1
Feng Huang Szu	1	Ti Tsang An	1
Fu Ch'ang Szu	1	T'ien Chen Szu	1
Hsiao Szu	1	T'ien Hsien Ling Mu Miao	1
Hsing Fu Szu	1	Ts'ang Ku Miao	1
Hsing Yuan Szu	1	Tso Fo Szu	1
Hung Men Szu	1	Wu Shen Miao	1
K'ai Ming Szu	1		

PART 6. HISTORICAL AND GEOGRAPHICAL BACKGROUND

CHAPTER XIX

Myths, Legends, and History

THE TING HSIEN histories and other sources trace the story of the Ting Hsien area back to the time of China's early Emperors Huang Ti and his grandson Chuan Hsü. Some authorities even give dates for those rulers and the outstanding events of their reigns. The great flood from which Emperor Yü saved the land has been dated as occurring in 2297 B.C. Beyond recognizing that such accuracy is hardly possible and that much of China's early history is largely myth and many of her early heroes are probably legendary rather than real, we have not attempted to determine where myth and legend end and history begins. Our story of Ting Hsien through the centuries is a combination of myth, legend, and history as recorded by the local and other historians. Whether or not it is actual history makes little difference in our study for the story as told depicts the accepted cultural and social background of the people, the emperors, the heroes, the demi-gods that they think of as belonging to their heritage, and so has a very definite place in a social study of the area.

It is said that the Emperor Huang Ti conquered the aborigines and invented the Chinese calendar and the cycle of sixty years. His kingdom included the area south of the present Paoting, so from earliest times Ting Hsien has been part of China and has shared in its political history, the invasions from the north, and the big dynastic changes. It has also had its own political history, belonging first to one and then to another of the small states or other political divisions of the country. The Ting Hsien chih,[1] or county histories, begin their story at the time

1. The Harvard Yenching Index of Hsien Chih lists the editions of the Ting Hsien History as K'ang Hsi 11th year (1672), Yung Cheng 11th year (1733), Ch'ien Lung 10th year (1745), Tao Kuang 29th year (1849), Hsien Feng 19th year (1860). A new edition, published in 1934, was in preparation at the time of our study, and its material was made available to us.

when Emperor Chuan Hsü, the grandson of Huang Ti, divided the
nation into nine parts. Ting Hsien belonged then to Chi Chou, one of
the nine divisions.

In the fifth year of Ti Chih, the future Emperor Yao was made Marquis of T'ang, an area that is said to lie between the T'ang River, which
runs across the northern part of Ting Hsien, and the present Hsin Lu,
which is some 60 li west of Tinghsien city.[2] T'ang Ch'eng Ts'un, a
village nine li north of Tinghsien, is said to have been the capital of
the Marquis of T'ang.

Tradition has it that Emperor Yü built the pagoda in Ku Ch'eng
Ts'un so that he could watch the flood. While that was hardly possible,
it is interesting as an example of how attempts have been made to con-
nect the locality with outstanding early events. The maps of ancient
China show the Yellow River flowing not far east of the present Ting
Hsien[3] and emptying into the Yellow Sea near the present Tientsin.

Ting Hsien was part of Chi Chou during the Hsia and Shang dynasties, but belonged to P'ing Chou during the Chou dynasty. At the time
of the Spring and Autumn Annals it was part of Chin, one of the large
feudal states that made up the empire. At this time, 530 B.C., the name
given to the area apparently was Hsien Yu Kuo. About 500 B.C. it was
changed to Chung Shan Kuo, Middle Hill Kingdom. The name Chung
Shan was connected with the area, off and on, for the next 1,800 years.
It finally disappeared in 1368 when Hung Wu, the first Ming Emperor,
changed Chung Shan Fu to Ting Chou.

In 408 B.C., during the Chan Kuo or Age of the Contending States,
when the Chou Emperor was largely a figurehead and the wars between
the feudal states were generally wars of annihilation, Chung Shan was
overcome by Wei Wen Ho, the King of the State of Wei. He occupied
it, but continued it as a state.

In 308 B.C. Wu Ling Wang of Chao, one of the Chih States, went to
the village of Chiu Men to contemplate, at his ease, the frontiers of Ch'i
and Chung Shan, two countries that he coveted. In 307 B.C. he launched
an expedition against the principality of Chung Shan and took part of
it, up to the city of Fang-tse. The next year he returned to the attack

2. Ting Hsien indicates the county, Tinghsien the hsien city.
3. George B. Cressey, *China's Geographic Foundations* (McGraw Hill Book Co.,
New York, 1934).

and penetrated to the city of Ning Chia. In 300 B.C. he secured control of three quarters of the country and the Tartar Prince of Chung Shan took refuge at the court of Ch'i. The annexed territory extended north to the province of Tai and the Kingdom of Yen. In 295 B.C., with the help of the Kings of Ch'i and Yen, Wu Ling Wang completed the annexation of Chung Shan.

In 221 B.C. Cheng, the Prince of Ch'in, conquered Ch'u and completed the unification of the country. He took the imperial title of Ch'in Shih Huang Ti. He had such complete control of the country that he was able to abolish the old feudal states. For administrative purposes he divided the country into 36 chün, districts. Ting Hsien was part of the district named Chü Lu.

Han Kao Tsu (206–195 B.C.), the first Emperor of the next dynasty, divided the country into 62 districts. One of these was Chung Shan Chün. It included 14 hsien. A half century later, 154 B.C., the Emperor Ching Ti appointed his ninth son, Liu Sheng, King of the country of Chung Shan. His capital, Lu Nu, is said to have occupied the site of the present city of Tinghsien. He died in 113 B.C. and was buried in a big tomb that is still one of the sights of the city. A biographical note says that he was fond of wine, loved women, and was the father of more than 120 sons.

In 106 B.C. many of the states and districts were consolidated when the Emperor Yuan Feng appointed 13 rulers who should divide the administration of the country. Chung Shan was then part of Chi Chou.

Tradition has it that Kuang Wu Ti had a narrow escape in Ting Hsien during the fighting preceding the establishment of the Later Han dynasty. Being closely pursued by the troops of his enemy, the usurper Wang Mang, he sought help from a farmer he found plowing in the field. The farmer buried him in a furrow and so enabled him to escape. The big tomb near Chou Ts'un, some 30 li from Tinghsien, is said by some to be the grave of this farmer; because of his help to the Emperor he was buried in an almost imperial tomb. A temple built on the slope of the hill covering the grave is dedicated to Han Kao Tsu.

Another story says that Han Kuang Wu, after his escape from Wang Mang, could not decide which way he should go. He sought advice from the ants and they formed the character Tung for east. Going in that direction he not only escaped further pursuit but was able to raise the forces with which to defeat Wang Mang and gain the Imperial throne.

The country of Chung Shan was reestablished soon after the beginning of the Later Han dynasty when the Emperor Kuang Wu appointed his uncle Mao as the ruler. The succession lapsed 140 years later when, in A.D. 195, the King of Chung Shan died leaving no heirs.

During the period of the San Kuo, or Three Kingdoms (221–265), Ting Hsien was part of the Kingdom of Wei which was ruled by Ts'ao Ts'ao, who is known as one of the great traitors of Chinese history. The western Kingdom of Shu was ruled by the famous prince Liu Pei who was assisted by the two generals Chang Fei and Kuan Yü and his famous Prime Minister Chu-Ko Liang. There was fighting between the Three Kingdoms, but it was in the west so did not disturb Chung Shan.

The country was united once more under Szu-ma Yen, who established the Chin dynasty in 265. He appointed Szu-ma Mu the King of Chung Shan. The records say that 5,200 families were taxed and that the country was divided into eight hsien.

In 309 Shih Lo ordered his generals to attack Chung Shan, Po Ling, and Kao Yang. Several tens of thousands of the enemy surrendered. Chung Shan was captured and made a part of the Hsiung Mi state of Chao. Some years later Jan Min overcame Chao and added Chung Shan to the State of Wei. In 351 Chung Shan was conquered by the State of Yen, generally known as Ch'ien Yen or Earlier Yen. Yen was ruled by the members of the Mu-jung family, descendants of the Khan of the Turkic tribe of Hsien Pei which had come in and settled north of the present Peking, then known as Yu Chou.

The story of the rise and fall of the Mu-jung family during 160 years gives a picture of the disturbed conditions of that time and indicates at least some of the difficulties of the inhabitants of the area that is now Ting Hsien.

Mu-jung Hui (268–333) is looked on as the founder of the Yen imperial family and has been canonized as a military genius of the Earlier State of Yen. Part of his prowess came from his immense size. The records state that he was eight feet tall.[4] When a younger brother usurped his rights, Mu-jung Hui joined forces with the Chün Emperor, who had made himself the ruler of the State of Wei. His capital was located at Loyang.

Mu-jung Huang, the third son of Mu-jung Hui, is described as hav-

4. About 6′ 8″ by present standards. The Chinese foot of that period was equal to about 10 inches.

ing a dragon countenance and is said to have been seven feet eight inches tall. He proclaimed himself the Prince of Yen in 337.

Mu-jung Ts'un (319–360?), the second son of Mu-jung Huang, was the giant of the family. He was eight feet two inches in height, six inches taller than his father and two inches taller than his grandfather. He succeeded his father as the Prince of Yen in 348 and assumed the imperial title in 352. It was his army, under the leadership of Mu-jung Ke, that captured Chung Shan in 351. In 354 he appointed his son, Mu-jung Wei, as King of Chung Shan. Another son, Mu-jung Ch'ung, was made King of Chung Shan in 359.

Mu-jung Ts'un's principal opponent in his struggle for power and the control of territory was Fu Chien (337–384), the Earlier Ch'in Emperor. Mu-jung Ts'un was able to maintain his position for a time but finally was captured by Fu Chien in 360. His third son, Mu-jung Wei (350–385), succeeded him but could not hold out against Fu Chien and was captured by the army led by Wang Meng. The next Prince of Yen was Mu-jung Ke, but his death in 370 enabled Wang Meng to annex the State of Yen to the Kingdom of Wei.

Mu-jung Ts'un was accompanied in his captivity by his youngest brother, Mu-jung Te (336–405), another eight foot two giant. He also found there his younger brother, Mu-jung Ch'ui, who had sought refuge from his brother with Fu Chien. He was the small member of the family, only seven feet four inches tall. Mu-jung Ch'ui was given official position by Fu Chien, but conspired with Mu-jung Wei to set up an independent kingdom. Mu-jung Wei's part in the plot was discovered and he was put to death, but Mu-jung Ch'ui proclaimed himself Prince of Yen in 383. His army, led by Mu-jung Liu, captured Chung Shan in 384. Mu-jung Ch'ui made Chung Shan his capital and built a large palace there. In 386 he assumed the Imperial title as ruler of Hou Yen, the Later State of Yen. When he died in 396 he was succeeded by his fourth son, Mu-jung Pao (355–399), whose reign lasted only three years. Defeated in battle by the king of the T'u Pa State of Wei, he sought refuge with Lan Han, but instead of giving him sanctuary Lan Han killed him.

Mu-jung Sheng (373–401), the son of a concubine of Mu-jung Pao, then became King of Yen. He avenged his father and killed Lan Han, but was himself killed in the attack on the palace. His place was taken by his uncle Mu-jung Hsi, who was noted for his cruelty. Among many others, he killed his grand-nephews, the sons of Mu-jung Pao. He himself was killed by Mu-jung Yün, the adopted son of Mu-jung Pao. Mujung Yün ascended the throne in 407 but reigned only two years. He was killed by two of the women of his court. He was succeeded by one of his ministers who ruled until 430 and then by a brother who succumbed in 436 to the attacks of the Kingdom of Wei.

Mu-jung Te, the youngest son of Mu-jung Huang, served under his father and his older brother, Mu-jung Ts'un. He accompanied the latter into captivity and held official position under his captor, Fu Chien. He joined Mu-jung Ch'ui after he had established the State of Hou Yen and also served as a minister under Mu-jung Pao. In 398, however, he rebelled and, following the death of Mu-jung Pao, was able to take over part of the territory of Yen and declare himself the emperor of the Southern State of Yen. His nephew Mu-jung Ch'ao (385–410) succeeded to the throne in 405, but he lost his kingdom and his life in 410 when he was captured by Liu Yü, a general of the Eastern Chin Dynasty and the founder of the Liu Sung Dynasty (420–479).

It was not certain just when, between 399 and 436, the armies of Wei captured Chung Shan. A military headquarters was established there as part of their defenses against the Chinese forces in the south. A new administrative area was set up called An Chou. Later on the name of the area was changed from An Chou to Ting Chou "in order to make the world peaceful or tranquil." This seems to be the first use of the name Ting Chou.

Toward the end of the Northern Wei dynasty, there was fighting around Ting Hsien. Yü Wen-hung, a general under Hsiu Li, led the attack, but was drowned during the fighting along the T'ang river. His son T'ai also served under Hsiu Li and, after the latter's death in 528, under Ke Jung. It is said that Ke Jung assembled a force of one million men and surrounded Yeh Erh Chu Jung, who, however, led 7,000 good soldiers against Ke Jung, defeated and captured him at Fu K'o. The rest of Ke Jung's force then surrendered. Ting Chou and four other chou were then under the control of Yeh Erh Chu Jung. After the death of Ke Jung, Yeh Erh Chu Jung took T'ai into his army and made him a general. Two years after he defeated Ke Jung, Yeh Erh Chu Jung was killed by the Emperor Wei Ti.

In 534 the Northern Wei Kingdom was split into the Eastern and Western Wei. The Eastern Wei was succeeded by the Pei Ch'i, Northern

Ch'i dynasty, the Western Wei by the Northern Chou. In 577 the latter conquered the Northern Ch'i and united north China. Yang Chien established the Sui dynasty by persuading his grandson, the last of the Northern Chou rulers, to abdicate. During the succeeding years Yang Chien was overcoming the forces to the south and in 589 he became the head of a reunited China.

The downfall of the Sui and the establishment of the T'ang dynasty in 618 brought a short period of revolt, but Ting Hsien probably was not greatly disturbed at this time as most of the fighting was to the west and south. For almost three hundred years China knew peace and prosperity. It was one of the great ages in Chinese history.

In 900 Chu Ch'uan Chung commanded his general Chang Ts'un-ching to attack Liu Jen-kung. He captured 20 cities and then, because the road was muddy, he turned west to Ch'i Chou and killed the magistrate there. He then attacked Ting Chou. Wang Ch'u-chih led several tens of thousands of soldiers against Chang Ts'un-ching. They met in battle at the Sha river, which runs across the southern part of Ting Hsien. Wang was defeated; half of the men were killed; the rest fled.

In the latter part of the eighth century the Khitans, a Mongol-speaking Turkish tribe from eastern Mongolia and southern Manchuria, moved down onto the upper part of the North China plain. They carried on raids to the south and at the end of the T'ang dynasty were the chief threat of invasion faced by the Chinese. In 928, led by their chief T'i Yin with 7,000 cavalry, they forced their way as far south as Ting Hsien. In the seventh month Wang Yen Ch'u met and defeated them at the T'ang river, and pursued them to I Chou. As it was the rainy season the rivers were full and many of the Khitans were drowned. Many others were captured and killed by the armies of the later T'ang Emperor. In 936 Shih Ching-t'ang, with the aid of the Khitans, overthrew the Later T'ang dynasty and established the Later Chin dynasty. In 947 Shih's son and successor tried to throw off the suzerainty of the Khitans, but failed and was carried into captivity.

How often the struggle between the Khitans and the Chinese brought fighting to Ting Hsien cannot be determined from the records. Pi Shih, commenting on one of the histories of that time, remarked that the battles lost at the T'ang river were not mentioned—only the victories. It is known, however, that in the 11th month of 988 the Khitans came again to the T'ang river. They had defeated, in the north, the

immense expedition sent against them by Sung T'ai Tsung and had
followed the retreating armies southward, capturing and looting the
towns and villages along the way. They finally camped north of the
T'ang river. The Chinese generals decided that they would not attempt to give battle. Li Chi-lung, however, although previously defeated, insisted on fighting. Helped by Yuan Chi-chung, he led his
forces against the Khitans, defeated them, and pursued them as far as
Ts'ao Chou. Li Chi-lung was rewarded by the Emperor for his victory.

The Sungs and the Khitans were evenly matched and kept up their
border warfare for a long time. In the sixth month of 1003 the Emperor showed the plan of battle to his generals and ordered the soldiers
of Chen Ting, Kao Yang, and Ting Chou to meet at the T'ang river.
There they were commanded to erect brush works so the enemy could
not rush in. They were told that when the enemy came they should
stand against them, that when they saw the opposing forces retire they
should beat the drums, but keep their formation lest they be taken by
surprise. Fighting came again the next year when the Sung general,
Wang Ch'ao, was attacked and beaten. He had to withdraw and
camped at Yang Cheng Ting.

The hsien histories do not tell of fighting in Ting Hsien during the
next three hundred and fifty years, possibly because that part of the
country was held by outsiders for most of that time, first by the Khitans
and then by the Chin dynasty of the Nü-chen Tartars. The Chins first
overcame the Khitans and then marched against the Sungs and captured
their capital, Kaifeng, in 1125. The Chin forces must have gone through
Ting Hsien on their way south.

During the first decade of the thirteenth century the Mongol tribes,
under the leadership of Genghis Khan, broke through the Great Wall
and overran the provinces of Shansi and Hopei. In 1213 Genghis Khan
led an expedition against the Chins and marched in triumph almost
to the end of the Shantung promontory. This expedition undoubtedly
won control of the Ting Hsien area. There was further fighting between
the Chins and the Mongols and later between the Mongols and the
Southern Sung dynasty of the Chinese. As the battle lines were far
south of Ting Hsien, that area probably was not disturbed, except by
the passage of large bodies of armed troops and the exactions and difficulties that attend such movements.

The Mongols made Cambaluc (Peking) their capital, so the surrounding area would be free from disturbances during the time they held power. In 1367 Chu Yuan-chang, who had secured control of a large area in the lower Yangtze Valley, started north against the Mongol rulers. His generals captured Kaifeng and then pressed on to Cambaluc. Its fall in 1368 brought an end to the Mongol dynasty and signalized the beginning of the Ming dynasty. Because of the rapid withdrawal of the Mongol forces, the country did not suffer from long continued civil war, but there is probably little doubt that Ting Hsien suffered at the hands of the ill controlled, defeated Mongol armies.

In 1369 the Emperor Hung Wu took ten villages from Wu Chi Hsien and added them to Ting Hsien. They included the present market town of Hsing I, which used to be the chief city of Hsing I Hsien. Hsing I Hsien had been abolished and its territory given to Wu Chi Hsien soon after the end of the Sung dynasty. After the establishment of the Republic 2,680 mu were transferred from Ting Hsien to Hsin-lo Hsien.

Ting Chou, which included in its boundaries three hsien, Ting, Chü-yuang, and Shen-tse, was a provincial chou and was therefore directly under the central government rather than under first a t'ing, then a fu, then the provincial government, as was the case with most of the chou.

Terrible days came to Ting Hsien soon after the death of the Emperor Hung Wu. After defeating the Mongols and securing control of the country he established his capital at Nanking and sent his several sons to different parts of the empire as princes of the various local states. His fourth son, Chu Ti, was made the Prince of Yen. His capital was at Peking, then called Pei P'ing Fu. When the Emperor Hung Wu died in 1398 he was succeeded by his grandson, as his oldest son, the Prince Imperial, had died in 1392. Chu Ti would not accept his nephew as emperor and rebelled in 1399. He first started for Nanking through eastern Hopei and Shantung, but had to abandon the expedition of 1400 as the loyal troops at Mao Chou held out against him.

The next year, 1401, he again tried to fight his way south. This time he took the road through the western part of Hopei. In the eighth month he surrounded Ting Hsien. In the ninth month he assaulted and captured the city. He apparently slaughtered most of the population, for one record says: "The great plain north of the Yangtze was depopulated, swept by the besom of the Prince of Yen." Another report says that for a thousand li south from Peking he killed many of the

people because he met such resistance there. It is said that only two
people, who had hidden themselves, escaped alive when he took Tinghsien city. Referring to that time, the people recall it as the time when
"the red insects [Yen Wang's soldiers wore red trousers] ate everything"
and as a time when "the swallows nested in the trees [because they could
find no roofs]".

Chu Ti finally was successful in his rebellion, captured Nanking,
and placed himself on the throne in 1402. He took the Imperial title of
Yung Lo. On his return to the north, the new Emperor made a special
point of capturing Mao Chou and taking it to pieces brick by brick.

The Ting Hsien histories do not mention Yen Wang's assault on
Tinghsien and the killing of the population. Evidently it was one of
the events omitted from the official histories, even though the Yen Shan
Hsien history says that Yen Wang killed many people there.

The Emperor repopulated the desolated regions by bringing large
groups of immigrants from Shantung and Shansi. Most of those who
came to Ting Chou were from Shansi and many of the present Ting
Hsien families trace their origin back to Hung Tung Hsien in Shansi.
Two hundred and seventeen of the 529 clans in the Experimental District said their ancestors came from Hung Tung Hsien. One clan said
their ancestors lived in Ting Hsien before 1400 and had escaped Yen
Wang's troops by hiding. The 1730 edition of the Hung Tung Hsien
history reported that there was a great famine in Shansi in 1428 and
that more than 100,000 people moved away.

In 1448 a Mongol general, Yeh Hsien, invaded the north, captured
the Emperor Chen T'ung, and fought his way south through Ting
Hsien. Shih Heng and his son led their army against Yeh Hsien and de-
feated him at Ch'ing Feng Tien, a market town in the northern part of
Ting Hsien. The Emperor, however, was still held captive by other
Mongol officers and did not return to the throne until 1457.

In 1507 a band of bandits headed by Liu Liu and Liu Ch'i came
from Pa Chou and raided the area south of Peking. They were defeated
near Peking and retreated south, reaching Ting Hsien in 1510. The
band did a great deal of damage there before they were driven off.

In 1638 a Manchu force came inside the Great Wall and captured 48
chou cities, including Ting Chou. They went further south, but came
back the next year. They apparently had not attempted to hold Ting
Chou, for on their return the city was held by a Chinese force. The

Manchus again took the city and killed many of the officers and gentry, many more than when they captured the city the previous year.

Fighting came again in 1644, at the end of the Ming dynasty. Li Tzu-ch'eng and Chang Hsien-chung rebelled in Shensi and Shansi. They were so successful that Li Tzu-ch'eng attempted to make himself emperor. He marched on Peking and captured it after the death of the last Ming Emperor, Ch'ung Cheng. Li was soon driven out, however, as Wu San-kuei called in the Manchus and, with their help, defeated Li's forces. He set fire to the palace in Peking and retreated to the south. He attempted to make a stand at Paoting and at the T'ang river, but Wu defeated him there and pursued him further to the south.

In 1650 a Shansi general rebelled at Ta T'ung. He brought his forces to Ting Hsien, robbed the countryside, and finally captured and plundered the city. After that Ting Hsien had peace for the next two hundred years.

In 1853 the T'ai P'ings came north in an attempt to capture Peking. They reached Cheng Ting Fu, south of Ting Hsien, and swinging to the east and north, managed to reach Tinghai, some 20 miles from Tientsin, where they were defeated. Ting Hsien was not touched by the T'ai P'ings, but the unsettled times made it possible for several bands of bandits, led by Lu Erh-lu, Chang Chi-t'ai, Ma Chueh-tzu, and others to make a great deal of trouble throughout the countryside. They were finally captured and beheaded.

In 1862 the Ma Tse, horse thieves, were active south of the T'ang river. There were several hundred men in the band, and they caused considerable local disturbance, but could not have been a very serious threat to the peace of the countryside as they were captured by the local self-defense corps.

The year 1868 was one of local disaster for the bandit Chang Tsung-yu came with his band from Shen-tse Hsien to Ting Chou. The people of Ting Ts'un built a wall around the village and for a time held out against Chang. They were finally overpowered by numbers, the village was captured, and most of the inhabitants were killed. The bandits laid siege to the city, but the people and the soldiers held the wall until the bandits became discouraged and went to Ch'i Chou.

The Boxer Rebellion in 1900 brought trouble to Ting Hsien. The Boxers had several recruiting and training centers in the hsien. As part of their anti-foreign campaign they attacked the Catholic church in

Pei Ch'e Chi, but were unable to overcome the resistance of the church members. After the Boxers left, the church group, for revenge, robbed and burned some 15 villages. The villagers came to the city for aid and got a group of over one hundred men to help them. The church members could not hold out against this force, so one night several hundred men, women, and children attempted to escape to Cheng Ting Fu. The Boxers met them at Kao P'eng Chen and killed many of them.

In the ninth month foreign soldiers came to Tinghsien and occupied the west suburb. Led by some of the Catholic group, they went to Kao P'eng Chen, burned the town, and killed many of the people. Later on, the foreign troops found a force of several hundred Boxers in a temple in Ch'ü Yang Hsien. They drove them out and burned the temple.

Toward the end of 1900 a girl living in Tun Wang Hsi tried to take advantage of the disturbed times. She assumed the title of Emperor and with the help of a group of supporters caused considerable trouble in Ting Hsien before her group was broken up.

In 1901 a group of foreign soldiers were passing Tung Chang Ts'un and wanted to enter the village. The villagers closed the gates in the wall and refused to let them in. The troops were about to move off when one of them was hit by a shot from the village. Tung Chang Ts'un and the neighboring villages were captured and burned and many of the villagers were killed.

The end of the Ch'ing dynasty in 1911 caused practically no disturbance in Ting Hsien. In 1913, the second year of the Republic, the political organization of the country was changed. The fu and chou divisions of the provinces were all abolished, leaving only the provincial and the hsien governments. The three hsien, Ting, Chü-yang, and Shentse, that had been under Ting Chou, came under the direct control of the provincial government.

Taxes were increased after the generals started fighting for the control of the Peking government in 1920. In 1922 Wu P'ei-fu drove Chang Tso-lin north from Peking. In 1924 one of Wu P'ei-fu's generals came to Ting Hsien to collect money and requisition supplies. In January, 1926, Chang Tso-lin's army of Manchurian troops went through Ting Hsien on their way to Honan. In September they came back, retreating before an army from Shansi. The Fengtien army made a stand south of Paoting and drove the Shansi army back to Ting Hsien. They attempted to hold the city, but the Fengtien army came in from the east and, after fighting in the streets, drove out the Shansi troops. The people in the city built dugouts as refuges from the shooting. The victorious army not only levied special taxes for "saving" the city, but there was a great deal of general looting by the troops.

Chang Tso-lin and Yen Hsi-shan fought again in October, 1927. Then in May, 1928, Feng Yu-hsiang and Yen Hsi-shan joined with the Nationalist forces to drive out Chang Tso-lin and his Fengtien army. The Nationalist Revolutionary Army was fighting with the National Pacification Army for possession of Hopei province.

Defeated at Shih Chia Chuang, Chang Tso-lin's army retreated to Ting Hsien. They were driven from there, but only after fighting in the city streets. Before they left, they looted the countryside and levied on the city. Judging from the losses in the Experimental District, the looting and exactions of the armies during the years 1927–1928 amounted to about $1,000,000.

With the capture of Peking the Nationalists completed the unification of the country. They moved the capital to Nanking and changed the name of Peking from Pei Ching, North Capital, to Pei P'ing, North Peace.

There was fighting again in the summer of 1931 when Feng Yu-hsiang tried to start a revolt against the Nationalist government. The battle line was drawn to the north of Ting Hsien, but airplanes flew over and bombed the city. Bombproof cellars were dug for the inhabitants. Trenches were dug for machine gun emplacements on top of the city wall. The revolt quickly collapsed, so Ting Hsien was spared any serious fighting, but it did suffer from the armies as they went through.

The Japanese captured Ting Hsien in 1937, but met heavy resistance from the local forces. It was reported that the city changed hands some seven times before the Japanese were able to hold it. Because of the continued resistance throughout the countryside many of the villages were raided by the Japanese and not a few were burned and completely destroyed.

City Wall

Tinghsien city was surrounded by an old wall that the hsien history said was first built during the Han dynasty. Its length was given as 26 li and 13 pu. Another report gave its length as 21 li (seven miles). It had supporting bastions on both the inside and the outside. Those inside were some 16 feet long. The longest of the outside ones that we measured was 38 feet long.

The wall was pierced by four gates, one on each side of the city. At the east and south gates the wall was 36 feet high, 67 to 70 feet thick at the bottom, and 21 feet thick on top.

In the past the wall was fully faced with brick, both inside and out, and the top was lined with crenelations. Later many of the crenelations had fallen off and on at least two occasions bricks were taken from the wall and used as foundation material for roads. In some places along the wall, sand and dust had been piled so high by the wind that it was easily possible to climb up to the top of the wall.

During the reign of the Ming Emperor Yung Lo outer or enceinte walls were added to the gates. At the south gate there was a double outer wall so that it was necessary to go through three gates to get outside the wall. At the east gate the walls were so arranged that it was necessary to go through four gates. At the west gate the outer walls had been cut through so that the improved road from the station could go directly into the main gate. The doors were still in place in most of the gates, but they were not being used. Above each of the four gates there was a big gatehouse. The hsien history states that all four of them were repaired in 1616. Three were repaired by K'ang Hsi, two by Chia Ch'ing in 1810, and two during the reign of Tao Kuang.

The K'ang Hsi history also speaks of a moat around the wall, 100 feet wide and 20 feet deep. In 1729 water from the city moat was used to irrigate 800 mu of land. When the T'ang river shifted its bed in 1775 it ran through the city moat to the Meng Liang river, but another change in the river's bed in 1801 took the water supply from the moat, leaving it dry except during the heavy summer rains.

Liao Ti Pagoda

According to one report the Sung Emperor Chen Tsung, in 1001, ordered the monk Hui Neng to build the pagoda to commemorate his bringing a set of the Buddhist scriptures to Ting Hsien. Another report says the pagoda was begun in 1004 after a battle with the Khitans at the T'ang river. The building of the pagoda was completed in 1055. It had 11 stories, was 260 feet high and 260 feet around the base. It was built of brick throughout. It took so many bricks that it was said that all the trees of Chia Shan were cut down to provide enough fuel to burn the bricks for the Ting Hsien pagoda.

In the sixth month of 1884 a large section of the outside wall of the pagoda fell down, so that it was no longer possible to go to the top. During the civil war of 1931 the base of the pagoda was used for the storage of ammunition.

Spring Garden

The Spring Garden in the city was said to date back at least to the Sung dynasty. An old stone monument tells of its being a place of great beauty. It included some 20 acres and was surrounded by high walls. Later on the garden was occupied and destroyed by soldiers. The land was then appropriated by the influential people of the city. The land was recovered and the present garden established by the magistrate in 1586. A temple dedicated to Han Wei-kung and Su Tung-p'o, the Snow Wave Stone and Study, and the Emperors' Character Arbor were features of the garden.

Su Tung-p'o's original Snow Wave Study was behind the Confucian Temple in the grounds of the present Girls' Normal School. The ash trees in the courtyard were said to have been planted by Su. Near his study he set up a Snow Wave Stone. It was lost after he left Ting Hsien in 1094 but was rediscovered in 1587 and in 1702 was moved to its present site in the Spring Garden. With it there is another Snow Wave Stone that came from Chao Chou and a stone on which has been carved some of Su Tung-p'o's poetry. A building erected in 1702 near the Snow Wave Stone was given the name of Later Snow Wave Study to commemorate Su Tung-p'o's earlier study.

Han Wei-kung, who was venerated in the same temple with Su Tung-p'o, was magistrate in Ting Hsien before Su. He later became a famous general and a civil and military governor. He was specially remembered for the relief program that he instigated in 1048 for the flood sufferers of Ting Hsien. Prior to 1702 Su and Han had separate temples, but when extra space was needed to house the retinue of the Emperor K'ang Hsi, who stopped in Tinghsien and stayed in the Spring Garden, the two temples were requisitioned for Imperial use. A third temple was then dedicated to the joint worship of the two heroes.

In the Emperors' Character Arbor were several stone monuments on which were carved writings of K'ang Hsi, Ch'ien Lung, and other emperors.

Ting Pottery

Ting Hsien is said to have been the site of a flourishing pottery trade up to the time the Chin Tartars forced the Sungs to retreat to Hanchow. The potters migrated before the invasion, the majority of them going to Ching Te Chen, the pottery center in the Yangtze valley. The white, dark reddish brown, and rare black pieces of Ting pottery are now highly prized. Although Ting Hsien is said to have been the site of the potteries producing this ware, no trace can now be found of any pottery yards or of any clay beds.

CHAPTER XX

Calamities

T HE TING HSIEN histories listed 145 calamities during 1,821 years. An earthquake in 106 A.D. was the earliest. Hail and floods in 1926 were the latest listed. One calamity every 12 or 13 years was the average, but, as some years had more than one calamity, a better average was trouble every 15½ years.

Two centuries, the fourth and 12th, had no disasters or calamities, The bad years were scattered throughout the other centuries, but, as might be expected, more are noted in the later centuries. The records, undoubtedly, have improved and more of the less serious losses are listed. Before 1500 none of the centuries had more than five years with difficulties. After 1500 all had more than 11. Twenty-two years were listed in the 17th century and 25 in the 19th. When completed, the 20th century probably will have the largest number. Twelve of the first 26 years were listed—every year from 1915 through 1926.

Fourteen different kinds of events were included in the list of calamities. In order of frequency they were: flood, drought, locusts, hail, earthquakes, epidemics, good years, thunder, frost, storm, snow, panic at the pagoda, fire, and Boxers. Civil wars, which for the civilian population were disasters comparable with flood or drought, were not listed.

Floods were reported 35 times, an average of once every 52 years. Twenty-eight droughts were listed. Locusts appeared in sufficient numbers to be mentioned 21 times, hail 17 times. There were 14 earthquakes and eight serious epidemics, cholera or plague. It is most suggestive to find that seven good years were included in the list of calamities. Bumper crops evidently made for such low prices that the year was an outstanding one in the minds of the people. The other calamities were all mentioned less than six times.

Although Ting Hsien has been the scene of considerable fighting through the centuries and, in the language of the people, soldiers were one of the scourges of the countryside, they were mentioned only once in the list of calamities. That was Boxer Year, 1900. Evidently, in writing the history of a locality, it has not been "good form" to mention the times the community has suffered from the movements of armed forces. It might reflect on the armies of the emperor.

The earliest flood reported was in 521. There was another in 575, but no more were listed for almost 500 years. The report of the floods of 1048 states that the magistrate Han Ch'i worked out plans for relief. There were heavy rains and floods the next two years, but then no further flood is mentioned until 1407. At that time, the records show, taxes were remitted to help the flood sufferers. In 1553 the floods were so severe that the people sold their children and ate the bark of trees; there was even some cannibalism. Three years later, in 1556, it rained so hard in the sixth month that the leaves fell off the trees, the crops were drowned, and houses were destroyed.

Floods were reported for four consecutive years in 1653–1656. The spring rains of 1654 failed so badly that the early crops suffered from drought, but the fall crops were again flooded by the heavy summer rains.

In the eighth month of 1696 it rained for eight days and nights and destroyed the crops. In 1775 water was running on the land for 40 days. In 1801 some 87 per cent of the families in Tung Pan village emigrated because of the flood. Only some 25 out of 200 families remained. In the seventh month of 1867 it rained for seven days and nights and the ears of grain sprouted.

In 1917 the T'ang and Sha rivers and all the small streams overflowed. Houses were damaged in 302 of the 453 villages and the crops were damaged in 335 villages. One hundred and ninety-seven villages either had no crops, or harvested less than 10 per cent of the usual yield. The smallest damage was 30 per cent, reported by 24 villages. The land damaged was 559,615 mu, about 40 per cent of the farm area. Thirty-five thousand chien (rooms) were destroyed. This was about 8 per cent of the hsien total. The value of the buildings destroyed was some $2,000,000. A total of 99,468 people, some 25 per cent of the population, reported serious or very serious damage.

The floods of 1919 and 1922 damaged only two villages; that of 1926 damaged eight villages. If they were not so recent, the floods probably would not have been included in the list of calamities. Thirteen villages were damaged in 1923, 89 in 1924, and 69 in 1925. The rest of the 35 floods are listed, but are not given any special comment.

It is not until 1801 that the records report the amount of flood relief in terms of money. That year 9,863.62 taels were given for relief. In 1822 relief totaled 3,489.2 tan (bags) of grain and 2,095.83 taels. The next year, 1823, the amount was 2,814.06 tan and 1,542.59 taels. In 1917 the magistrate and the gentry secured some $3,727 by the sale of grain from the village granaries, raised some $1,954 by subscription, and distributed these amounts in cash grants. The poorest adults were given 1,000 cash. This was equivalent to 83 cents silver, as the exchange rate was 1,200 cash for $1.00. Those who were a little better off received 700 cash, 58 cents. Half of these amounts were given to the children of the needy families.

Remission and postponement of taxes have long been methods whereby the government lightened, somewhat, the burden of those who had suffered from disaster. The usual procedure was for the hsien magistrate to report the disaster to the provincial authorities, giving an estimate of the number of villages and the amount of land damaged. The magistrate of a neighboring hsien then was ordered to investigate and report. In 1917 70 per cent of the taxes were remitted for those who had suffered a total loss of their crop. The other amounts were 60 per cent for 90 per cent loss; 40 per cent for 80 per cent loss; 20 per cent for 70 per cent loss; and 10 per cent for a loss of 50 or 60 per cent. Unremitted taxes were not collected that year, but were spread over the two succeeding years. Where the damage was around 40 per cent, the taxes were postponed until the fall of the next year. Similar figures were used in connection with flood damage in 1919 and in the years 1922 to 1926 inclusive.

Chou ch'angs, porridge kitchens, were opened in four villages in 1917 to provide food for some of the neediest people in the four winter months. They could give, however, only a relatively small amount of help as each chou ch'ang could provide for only 120 persons.

The food shortage resulting from the flood of 1917 raised the price of grain. To keep the price at a minimum, a grain office, p'ing t'iao chü, was opened in the city with branches in each of the six districts. Those who were given tickets were allowed to buy a ten days' supply of millet and kaoliang amounting to two he, about one-half pound, a day per adult and 1 he per child. The grain was sold at a price set by the Chamber of Commerce. The price was kept down by remitting all taxes and transportation charges, omitting the commission regularly paid the men who measured the grain, and getting the villagers to transport the grain free of charge. To be eligible for a p'ing t'iao chü ticket a family must be classed as poor or very poor, or have less than 10 mu of land and more than five in the family, or be a peddler or a farm laborer with no land.

A refugee camp was run from January to May in the city Ch'eng Huang temple to care for 120 old or weak persons. Each district was allowed to send 20. The inmates were given two meals a day, but ordinarily were expected to bring their own bedding. The operating cost was met by village appropriations, by contributions, and by the use of some of the money appropriated for the repair of the granaries. The hsien government contributed only if there was a deficit.

The earliest drought listed was in 431. The granaries were opened and grain was given to the people. The drought of 483 must have been very severe for it is reported that the people of Ch'i Chou and Ting Chou fed the refugees on the road. The report specially states that 947,-000 people did not die. From 510 to 938, there was a period of 428 years without a reported drought and then, from 943 to 1290, another long period of 347 years. There were three later periods of more than 100 years between droughts, 1291–1440, 1442–1552, and 1712–1816.

Another authority[1] reports four severe droughts in Chihli province during the first half of the 14th century, but these are not listed in the Ting Hsien histories.

In 1290 the people were given grain for 60 days, starting in the third month. In 1553 there was a drought both spring and fall. There was a great famine in 1561. In 1685 there was a drought in the spring and fall. One third of the taxes paid in grain were remitted. In 1689 the last half of the taxes was remitted and grain was distributed from the 10th month to the 4th month of the next year. The same was true in 1870. In 1877 there was a great famine in North China. There was nothing growing on the land for thousands of li. Many refugees died along the road and the hungry people resorted to cannibalism. There was also a drought in 1878.

In 1920 all of Ting Hsien suffered from drought. One hundred sixty-

1. Raymond T. Moyer, "The Aridity of North China", *Journal of North China Branch, Royal Asiatic Society*, 1932.

three villages, 36 per cent, reported serious damage to the crops. Two hundred and eighty thousand mu of land, 20 per cent of the farm area, were affected. The dry spring made it almost impossible to plant the unirrigated land. Irrigated land was planted, but later on many of the wells went dry and the locusts came in from the neighboring hsien. The villagers tried to kill them for "several tens" of days, but could not keep them from damaging the crops. Ten villages reported 100 per cent loss and 52 villages more than 70 per cent damage. Another 59 villages had 50 to 60 per cent loss and 52 had 30 to 40 per cent loss. Taxes were remitted according to the amounts of damage.

A survey of the hsien found 9,877 very poor families and 7,998 poor families, about 25 per cent of all the families in the hsien. The number of individuals involved was reported as 99,700. Of these, 51.7 per cent were males and 48.3 per cent were females. The average size of the families was 5.1 persons for the very poor families and 6.2 for the poor families. Relief was given by the government and local relief associations and not a little came from outside organizations. One thousand dollars was given by the provincial government. The Hopei and Peking branches of the China International Famine Relief Commission gave 98 bags of wheat seed. The American Board Mission gave 41 bags. A local philanthropist donated 250 suits of cotton clothes. The American Red Cross sent funds to help relieve the distress. Some of this money was used for work relief in the building of the new roads in the city and from the city to the railroad station in the west suburb; some was used to assist in the digging of wells for irrigation in Ting Hsien and five neighboring hsien. With this help, 463 wells were dug in Ting Hsien and 3,109 in the neighboring hsien during the spring and summer of 1921. There was serious drought damage again in both 1922 and 1925. The district to the north and east of Tinghsien city suffered the most. After the 1922 drought the hsien government and the China International Famine Relief Commission both helped to develop the well digging program. The 1925 drought gave added impetus to the well digging.

In 284 rain and hail damaged the crops. In 476 some of the hailstones were said to be about two feet in circumference and to have come down with force enough to kill some of the farmers. In 945 a hailstorm uprooted some of the trees in the Pei Yueh Miao. In the fourth month of 1577 the largest hailstones were like eggs. In 1682 the damage was so severe that the government remitted three-tenths of the grain taxes. In 1858 the largest hailstones were like rice bowls and many of the roof tiles were broken. In May, 1915, hail fell for an hour and damaged the wheat crop of 10 villages. The highest loss was 70 per cent; the lowest under 40 per cent. There was still hope for a fall crop, so the government remitted only 40 per cent of the taxes of one village, 30 per cent for two, and 20 per cent for four villages.

Hail added to the damage from flood in both 1917 and 1926. In 1917 it affected 335 villages and 597,045 mu of land, 42 per cent of the land and 74 per cent of the villages. Relief and remission of taxes were included in the flood relief program.

Some of the hailstones that fell on July 8, 1918, were reported to be as large as eggs and four to five inches thick. In 1923 the largest stones were the size of eggs; the smallest the size of bullets. Forty villages and 16,541 mu of land were affected.

Ting Hsien lies in a region that is not usually affected by frost before harvest time. Only three serious frosts are mentioned. In 463 the damage in the seventh month was so extensive that the taxes were remitted. In 1882 the buckwheat was damaged by frost in the eighth month. In 1922 the spring rains held off until June so many of the fields were planted with buckwheat. In the eighth month, when the buckwheat was in bloom, a storm brought cold and frost. The entire hsien was affected. Ninety-nine villages had 50 to 60 per cent damage. For these villages all of the extra taxes and one-tenth of the regular taxes were remitted. The rest of the regular taxes were to be collected during the next two years.

Locusts were an ever present threat to the Ting Hsien crops as a few were seen almost every year. Some were reported every year except one from 1915 to 1922. In some years only a few villages reported any damage; in 1918 only one village. It was six villages in 1922, 13 in 1919, and 18 in 1915. In 1920, at the time of the big drought, 20 per cent of the villages saw some locusts and the crops were damaged in 64 villages, 14 per cent.

Only the years of serious damage were listed before 1911. From 838 to 1891 only 14 years were listed as bad locust years, an average of one every 75 years. In the fall of 838 the grass and leaves were all eaten. In the fifth month of 1292 the leaves of the mulberry trees were eaten so no silk worms could be raised that year. In the spring of 1591 all the crops were eaten. The worst damage was in the area to the south of the city.

In 1705 the summer locusts flew in such swarms that they covered the sun, but it is reported that they were soon killed. In 1825 so many locusts were flying together that the sun could not shine through. They stayed for three days.

Killing the locusts or scaring them away was about the only protection the farmers had. As soon as any locusts were seen everyone turned out. Gongs and other noise-makers were beaten to keep the locusts from settling on the crops. Beaters of all sorts, spades, forks, flat pieces of wood, shoe soles nailed on sticks, brooms, and bundles of willow twigs were used to kill the locusts. Ditches were dug and the locusts driven into them were buried there. Fires were lighted at night to attract the insects so they could be killed.

The government often offered a bounty to encourage the people to kill the locusts. In the spring of 1915 the rate was 10 cash (0.73 cents) per catty. Only 762 catties were caught. The bounty, plus some special prizes amounting to $3.50, brought the expenditure to $9.05. In the fall of the same year 5,945 catties were caught. As they were caught at the border of the hsien, the reward was doubled. It totaled $82. Eleven dollars food money for the police for the days they helped with the work made the total expenditure $93.

In 1920 64 villages caught 30,656 catties, some 20 tons. That year the reward was 50 cash per catty. It was to be paid half from the tax funds and half from funds secured by the village heads. The police expenditure amounted to $155.73.

There was considerable damage to the main fall crops in 1921. In 1922 the crops of six villages were attacked, but the locusts were quickly caught, so there was not widespread damage. The loss on some 13,859 mu was about 60 per cent. One-tenth of the taxes on that land was remitted, and the remainder spread over the two following years.

Cholera and plague were not frequent visitors to Ting Hsien, at least in epidemic proportions, as only eight visitations were reported in the list of calamities, and three of those were in 1918, 1919, and 1920. Plague was reported in 1554, 1581, 1821, 1918, and 1919, cholera in 1885, 1895, and 1920.

In 1918 Ting Hsien was one of the plague quarantine centers established along the railroad. All small stations were closed and passengers were allowed to board the train at the larger stations only after careful examination, which often included a quarantine of four to five days. Passengers were required to furnish their own food, though the railroad gave some help if the people had no money. Communication was cut between the city and some 47 places to prevent the spread of the disease. The work was carried on under a specially organized plague prevention bureau with a special staff of doctors, nurses, and police. The reported expenses amounted to $4,230, of which $1,452 was for special police service. After the epidemic was apparently well in hand, a new case upset matters, until it was learned that the new patient had broken quarantine by going over the back wall of the isolation house to talk to a sick relative.

The death rate was not given for 1918, but in 1919 some 446 persons died of plague in Tinghsien city and some five or six villages. The police compelled the people to clean the streets and their houses and they also distributed medicine provided by the hsien government.

Fourteen earthquakes were reported, but the records ordinarily made but little comment on them. Ting Hsien, being in the coastal plain, was not in a primary earthquake zone and generally has not been seriously damaged by any earthquakes that have been felt. The earthquake in 106 was the earliest recorded calamity. That quake and the one in 503 are said to have broken the Heng Shan, a mountain some 25 miles northwest of Ting Hsien. The earthquake in 777 lasted for three days. Those of 1679 and 1720 were heavy enough to damage the pagoda. The top of the pagoda was shaken down in 1720. The latest earthquake mentioned was in 1882.

Two storms caused enough damage for them to be entered in the list of calamities. One was in 1723, the other in 1818.

Heavy thunder storms have been included in the list of calamities. One was recorded in 1562. In 1577 the Stone Buddha Temple, Shih Fo Szu, was hit by lightning and "the dragons rose up." In 1666 the pagoda was struck. In 1856 lightning set fire to the back hall of the examination buildings. In the fifth month of 1900, Boxer year, thunder was heard three times although no clouds were seen.

Snow is not an unusual occurrence in Ting Hsien, but ordinarily only a few inches fall at any one time. In 1713 snow fell in the fourth month while in the 12th month of the 24th year of Chia Ching, January, 1820, the snow was three feet deep.

The pagoda has been the scene of two disasters, besides those connected with earthquakes and lightning. On certain of the festival days the people like to go to a high place to get the view. When the pagoda was in repair it was natural that large crowds would climb to the top. On the 16th day of the first month of 1568 and again on the fifth day of the fifth month of 1773, the rumor got around that the magistrate was coming to lock the doors. Panic seized the people and in the scramble to get out many were crushed to death. The toll was 237 in 1568 and over 300 in 1773.

Extra good years, Ta Yu Nien, have been included in the list of calamities. Bumper crops evidently made marketing a difficult problem and forced prices to the minimum. The first of the good years listed was 1051, the third year of the Sung Emperor Huang Yu. The bumper crops were probably influenced by the floods of the previous year. The next good year was 1543, almost 500 years later. In 1562 the records say one tou of grain cost 25 cash and one tou of beans seven cash. In 1690 one tou of rice cost three cents silver and one tou of miscellaneous grains 1.5 cents silver. It seems strange to find this listed as a good year as there was a spring drought that warranted the remitting of the first half of the taxes, and there had also been a drought the year before. One-half of that year's taxes were remitted and grain was given out from the 10th month to the fourth month of 1690. The other specially good years were 1729, 1815, and 1856.

The records report that wild bears were seen in Ting Hsien in 1585.

The hsien histories do not include in their list of calamities the times when Ting Hsien suffered loss at the hands of the military forces, but experience in North China from 1924 through 1931 made it evident that, whenever there was fighting in an area, levies were made on the countryside for carts, animals, manpower, and food. Money was secured by special assessments. Many a community had to pay large sums for being protected from threatening troops, or for being "saved" from the armed forces driven out by the new occupation forces. The amounts lost by the local population apparently varied from a small to a total loss. When Yen Wang "swept the North" the eaves swallows nested in the trees, because no houses were left in the area.

Levies were made on the countryside in October, 1927, when there was fighting between Chang Tso-lin and Yen Hsi-shan, and again in May, 1928, when the Nationalist forces, the National Revolutionary Army, fought with the National Pacification Army for possession of Hopei province.

The amount of the 1927 and 1928 civil war losses suffered by the families in the Experimental District was determined by a survey of the 62 villages. There was looting and requisitioning of property in both years, but not every village was affected. A special assessment, levied in 1928, was collected from all the villages.

The 1927 loss, reported by 42 villages, totaled $20,160. This was an average of $480 for each of the 42 villages affected, or $325 per village for the district. The amounts per village ranged from $20 to $4,400. Six villages reported losses of $1,000 or more. For nine of the villages, the loss was less than $100, for 19 it was less than $200. The loss per family averaged $2.60 for the affected villages and $1.90 for the entire district. If these averages were typical for the hsien, the hsien total was about $145,000.

In 1928 the looting and requisitioning loss was almost twice that of 1927. The amount reported was $39,865 in 40 villages. Twenty-six villages reported losses for both years. Eight villages escaped both years; at least they reported no loss.

The loss per village in 1928 ranged from $10 to $4,340. Only three of the 40 villages lost less than $100. Thirteen villages reported losses of more than $1,000 and eight over $2,000. The average was just under $1,000 per village for those affected, or $643 per village for the 62 villages.

The 1928 figures also gave the number of families that were affected. The total was only 435 out of a total of 6,453, or 6.7 per cent. In one village of 19 families, 18 reported loss. In another village, of 458 families, only four reported any war loss. The average loss was $91.60 for the families reporting, but only $3.80 for all the families in the district.

The $39,865 looting and requisitioning loss of 1928 was divided as shown in the table on page 453.

Relatively few oxen were taken. They probably were too slow for the troops. The other animals were divided very much as was the animal population on the 400 farms in Chapter III, except that the army took proportionately a few more horses and a few less donkeys.

Besides the looting and requisitioning losses, a special assessment was levied on all the villages in 1928. The amounts reported by the village heads ranged from $210 to $3,950. The total was $71,733.30, an average

	Value	Average Value
127 mules	$11,390	$90
144 donkeys	5,815	40
61 horses	2,970	49
10 oxen	345	35
Ransom for cattle	1,145	
Clothes	4,260	
Carts	1,495	65
Crops	84?	
Miscellaneous	3,945	
Money	7,660	
	$39,865	

of $1,157 per village. We have not been able to determine the basis of the assessment. It evidently was not levied according to the number of families or the number of mu in the village area. In the different villages, the amount per family varied from $3.10 to $12.60. The average was $6.90 per family, or about $1.15 per person. The amount per mu varied from 10.4 cents to 92.0 cents per mu of crop area and from 10.1 cents to 89.5 cents per mu of total area. The average was 30.3 cents per mu of crop area, or 28.6 cents for the entire district, crop land, waste land, roads, villages. There may have been some other basis for the levy, but it would appear that the amount levied on each village was arbitrarily fixed.

The combined requisitioning and assessment loss of 1928 totaled $111,595, an average of $1,800 per village and $11.11 per family. In the different villages, the average loss per family varied from $3.10 to $57.50.

If the Experimental District is an average sample, the hsien loss from requisitioning and looting in 1928 was between $270,000 and $295,000. The total special assessment was between $490,000 and $525,000. Together the total war loss for the hsien was between $760,000 and $820,-000. The range in the amounts is the result of figuring them on the basis of two different averages, one the amount per family, the other the amount per village.

The losses for 1927 and 1928 together totaled $131,755 for the Experimental District, an average of $2,125 per village, or $12.60 per family. This would seem to indicate a total of almost $1,000,000 for the hsien. This did not, however, include the $323,440 collected for the anti-Red military campaign by a 100 per cent extra land tax levy in 1926 and a 200 per cent extra levy in 1927, or the $65,718 extra land tax collected in 1928 for rehabilitation and relief.

TABLE 113. CALAMITIES IN TING HSIEN, 106–1926[1]

A.D.		A.D.		A.D.	
106	Earthquake	1441	Drought	1655	Floods
284	Hail	1447	Locusts	1656	Floods
431	Drought	1520	Locusts	1666	Lightning
463	Frost	1543	Good year	1679	Earthquake,
476	Hail	1553	Drought, floods		drought
483	Drought	1554	Plague	1682	Hail
503	Earthquake	1556	Floods	1685	Drought, floods
510	Drought	1560	Locusts	1689	Drought
521	Floods	1561	Drought	1690	Drought, good
528	Earthquake	1562	Thunder,		year
575	Floods		good year	1693	Floods
682	Hail	1568	Pagoda panic	1696	Floods
776	Earthquake	1577	Hail, thunder	1697	Floods,
777	Earthquake	1581	Earthquake,		earthquake
838	Locusts		plague	1705	Locusts
938	Drought	1586	Drought	1708	Drought
943	Locusts, drought	1591	Locusts	1711	Drought
945	Hail	1597	Floods	1713	Snow
998	Hail	1607	Floods	1720	Earthquake
1037	Earthquake	1617	Locusts	1723	Storm, floods
1048	Floods	1623	Earthquake	1724	Floods
1050	Floods	1627	Earthquake	1725	Hail
1051	Good year	1638	Drought	1729	Good year
1268	Hail	1640	Drought	1773	Pagoda panic
1290	Drought	1642	Drought	1775	Floods
1292	Locusts	1645	Floods	1794	Floods
1326	Hail, drought	1646	Locusts	1801	Floods
1327	Hail	1653	Floods	1802	Locusts
1407	Floods	1654	Drought, floods	1808	Floods

[1] Hsien histories.

(continued on next page)

(TABLE 113 CONTINUED)

A.D.		A.D.			
1815	Good year	1891	Locusts	*Totals for*	
1817	Drought	1895	Cholera	*1,820 Years*	
1818	Storm	1900	Boxers, thunder,	Floods	35
1819	Snow		foreign troops	Droughts	28
1821	Plague	1915	Hail, locusts	Locusts	21
1822	Floods	1916	Locusts	Hail	17
1823	Floods	1917	Hail, floods	Earthquakes	14
1825	Locusts	1918	Hail, plague,	Epidemics	8
1829	Earthquake		locusts	Thunder	5
1856	Lightning, good	1919	Locusts, plague,	Frosts	3
	year		floods	Pagoda	2
1858	Hail	1920	Locusts, cholera,	Snow	2
1859	Locusts		drought	Storms	2
1867	Floods	1921	Locusts	Boxers	1
1870	Drought	1922	Locusts, frost,	Good years	7
1877	Drought		drought, floods		145
1878	Drought	1923	Hail, floods		
1879	Floods	1924	Floods		
1882	Earthquake, frost	1925	Drought, floods		
1885	Cholera	1926	Hail, floods		

CHAPTER XXI

Geography

TING HSIEN, one of the 120 hsien of Hopei province and one of the 40 hsien in the Paoting district, lies toward the western side of the North China coastal plain some 135 miles west of the Bay of Chihli, 37 miles south of Paoting, and 128 miles south of Peking. Roughly rectangular in shape, the hsien extends from 38° 19' to 38° 41' north latitude and from 114° 54' to 115° 23' east longitude. Its latitude is approximately the same as that of St. Louis, Washington, and Lisbon.

Beginning in the northwest and proceeding in a clockwise direction, Ting Hsien is bounded by the following hsien: T'ang, Wang-tu, An-kuo, Shen-tse, Wu-chi, Hsin-lo, and Ch'ü-yang. The hsien boundaries include an area of some 4,320 square li, approximately 480 square miles.[1] Exact area figures were not available as no complete and accurate survey had been made of the hsien. Some years ago, when government surveyors were sent down from Peking, they were firmly told to go home.

The climate of Ting Hsien is generally cold and dry in winter, hot and wet in summer. Meteorological records are not available for Ting Hsien, but have been kept by the Hopei University at Paoting. The 37 miles between Ting Hsien and Paoting probably did not make a great difference in the weather. The university records, for the three years 1927–1929, give the average mean temperature as 54.5° Fahrenheit. The monthly averages ranged from 22.8° for January to 80.8° for July. For each of the three winter months, December, January, and February, the mean temperature was below freezing. For the three summer months of June, July, and August, it was 77° or above. (See Figure 2, page 6.) The extreme temperature range for 1927 was 121 degrees, from −12° to 109°. For all three years the temperature range was at least 106 degrees.

1. In 1947 the Ministry of the Interior reported the area of Ting Hsien to be 1,213.55 square kilometers, or 480.1 square miles. The area of Ting Chou had been 973.5 square miles.

The growing season for the area, the number of days with mean temperature continuously above 43°, was some 226 to 230 days, or about March 25 to November 10.

For the years 1927–1929 there was an average of 59 days per year with some precipitation, 10 days with snow and 49 days with rain. There was hail on two days in the three years. The average yearly precipitation was 485.3 millimeters or 19.1 inches. The annual totals varied from 15.5 to 24.2 inches.

Almost 70 per cent of the average rainfall came in the months of July and August and 84 per cent in the four months from June through September. For all three years there was no precipitation in February and either October or November had no rain. For five months of the year the average precipitation was less than one-third of an inch. Only in the four months from June through September was the average over one inch per month.

Rainfall statistics were secured for the years from 1914 to 1926, but unfortunately were incomplete. However, if we use the available figures, omitting from the averages the individual months with no report, the sum of the monthly averages was 412.1 millimeters (16.2 inches), some 15 per cent less than the 1927–1929 average.

The figures for the four months from June through September show some very interesting variations. The average was 14.1 inches, but for the individual years the range was from 0.97 inches in 1921 and 2.5 inches in 1920 to 30.2 inches in 1917 and 32.6 inches in 1924. The year by year variation in the June–September rainfall is shown in Figure 3. The years 1917 and 1924 were flood years. For July, 1924, the rainfall was 24.6 inches. Less than 1.5 inches fell during the preceding six months. In 1917 the July rainfall was 16.1 inches. Both 1920 and 1921 were famine years. In July, 1921, the recorded rainfall was only 1.4 millimeters and the June–September total was only 24.6 millimeters. The drought was so acute in North China that the American Red Cross sent relief funds to help carry the people through to the next harvest. As part of the relief program in Ting Hsien, surfaced roads were built from the railroad station to the city and inside the city wall. Four hundred and sixty-three wells were dug with Red Cross assistance.[2]

The low average rainfall of less than 20 inches and its uneven distribu-

2. China International Famine Relief Commission, Series B #49, *Well Irrigation in West Hopei*, Preliminary Report, December, 1931.

tion throughout the growing season made irrigation necessary for the growing of good crops in ordinary years and as insurance for at least minimum crops in drought years. Ground water was available fairly near the surface and in reasonably sufficient amounts. The water table varied from two to 40 feet below the surface, averaging about 14 feet. How this was developed for irrigation and domestic use is reported in Chapter XI.

Ting Hsien is part of the east China alluvial coastal plain, so there are no natural hills in the area. Dykes had been built to control the rivers and a few mounds had been built up to a height of some 30 or 40 feet. Local tradition says that one of these was piled up by the army to make the enemy believe it was a supply of food. Another appeared to be a large grave mound with a long entrance tunnel. The average elevation is about 100 feet above sea level.

The soil of the area is generally deep and fine textured, calcareous and somewhat saline. Along the river beds there usually is a considerable area covered with coarse sand. Elsewhere the soil is sandy loam, loam, and some clay.

The area is drained by streams that rise to the west, cross Ting Hsien in an easterly direction, and later join the Hu T'o Ho in An-kuo Hsien. That stream flows north to the Pai Ho, which enters the sea near Tientsin. The chief rivers are the T'ang, which runs about three miles north of Tinghsien city, and the Sha, which runs about eight miles to the south. The Meng Liang is a smaller watercourse that runs southeast between the two and joins the Sha in An-kuo Hsien. One branch of the Meng Liang comes up to the southeast corner of the city wall, where it connects with the old, now dry, city moat, which in one of the old records was described as 100 feet wide and 20 feet deep.

The rivers are generally swollen in summer time with the heavy rains, but in winter most of the watercourses are dry. The large Black Dragon Spring in the northwest part of the hsien insures a year round flow in the T'ang. The spring supplies enough water to irrigate some 2,090 mu of rice fields before it reaches the T'ang. There also used to be a large White Dragon Spring, but it was flooded and destroyed in the flood of 1801. The hsien history says that during the reign of Hsien Feng the Black Dragon Spring failed. The dragon king was said to have moved to a village in Ch'ing-yuan Hsien, Paoting, some 35 miles north, because too many people came to the pool to get fish. Later on, the elders of one of the villages near the spring, probably Tung Nan Ts'un, sent a four-horse wagon to bring the dragon king back. After his return the water came back to the spring.

At flood times the rivers have a tendency to break out of the old silted channels. In 1794 the T'ang broke through the dykes to the south and ran past the city wall into the Meng Liang. In the flood of 1801 it took a new channel to the north of its old bed, so that villages that had been on the north bank were then on the south bank. The damage caused by that flood was so extensive and so well remembered that a monument was erected in Tung Pan Ts'un stating:

> In the sixth year of Chia Ch'ing the T'ang took a new bed. The crops were damaged and destroyed so that the people had no clothes and no food. Houses fell down. The people complained. The site of a large village became the bed of the river. The people wanted to escape. The village had about 200 families. About 100 families left. Now [1853] only 20 to 30 families remain.

The T'ang would probably have changed its course after the floods of 1917 and 1924, except that the breaks in the dykes were repaired and the river forced back into its old bed.

In 1810 the people of T'ang Hsien blocked the watercourse and cut off the flow of the T'ang to Ting Hsien. They were sued by the residents of Ting Hsien, but the case was not decided until 1826. Then the decision was in favor of Ting Hsien.

Through the years, the T'ang and Sha have had their part in China's history. Being two of the larger streams crossing the western part of the coastal plain, they have been advantageously placed for defense and have been the scene of numerous battles. The chief of these from the 6th to the 17th century are listed in the historical resumé in Chapter XIX.

The inhabitants of Ting Hsien lived in the walled city and its three suburbs, east, south, and west, 10 market towns, and 443 villages. The towns generally, but not always, had more families than the villages, did more business than the villages, had more stores, and had a larger proportion of non-farm families. All of the towns had markets, but so did 72 of the villages. As the differences between the towns and villages were largely those of degree we have grouped them together in our studies and counted them as 453 politically organized residence and farming areas. How they were distributed in the hsien is shown by the map on page 5.

Each of the villages and towns included a residence area, in which all the families lived and which was regularly surrounded by some sort of protective wall, and the fields adjacent to and surrounding the residence area. Definite boundaries were fixed between the fields of the different villages. The provincial regulations of 1928 required that they be marked by boundary stones. Boundary lines were drawn because each village assessed the land it controlled to provide funds, when needed, for village expenses for schools, home guard, and crop watching.

The amount of arable land controlled by the villages varied from 245 to 32,500 mu. Nineteen per cent had less than 1,000 mu. Some 73 per cent had less than one square mile of farm land. Only 10 per cent had as much as 6,000 mu, 1,000 acres. The average was 3,065 mu. The total farm area of the villages and the city was 1,424,931 mu, approximately 371 square miles. This was 76 per cent of the total area of the hsien.

Although the village boundaries were set and regularly maintained, it apparently was possible for land on the periphery to be transferred to an adjoining village if it was sold to a resident of that village. It was also evident that new villages could be formed and secure control of the surrounding land. The number of villages had been growing during the previous eighty years, for the hsien history of 1849 gave the number as 423 or 30 less than at the time of our study.

We also found 19 residence areas that were not recognized as separate villages but might well be later on. They evidently had been set up because of crowding in the original residence areas, but did not control the surrounding farm lands and did not have separate governments so were still satellite villages.

Seventy-one, 58 per cent, of the 123 villages in the 1st and Experimental Districts (10 villages were in both districts) were given a family surname. Six were named for the Wang family. Some nine different terms were used for village, walled village, castle, residence, camp, hamlet. The most usual one, used 26 times, was ——— chia chuang, village of the house of ———. There were 13 pairs of villages, north-south, east-west, big-little. Fifteen villages were named for physical features, a neighboring river, a bridge, a dyke, a gate, low ground, specially good soil, or white earth. One group of five villages were different goat yards. There was the village of the eight brothers, four families, ten families, eight cornered man, horse's head, old crow, head light, cow village, and cock crowing terrace. One was just Big Village; its companion Little Village. Another pair were Big and Little Growing Village. Three villages were Unusually United. Only one was named for an occupation, paper making.

The hsien history of 1849 reported that in olden times the hsien had been divided into 38 li with the number of villages in each li varying from one to 29. The total number of villages was 430. In 1845, when the pao-chia system was being revived, the name of the division was changed to yueh. At that time there were 44 yueh and 423 villages. Each yueh had from three to 29 villages. After 1912 the villages were divided into administrative areas known first as districts and then as self government districts. At the time of our study there were six districts and 453 towns and villages.[3] Figure 1 shows how the districts were divided.

In the six districts the number of villages varied from 63 to 90, the number of families from 6,555 to 16,010, the average number of families per village from 92 to 220, the amount of arable land from 150,156 to 342,773 mu, the average amount of arable land per village from 2,050 to 4,290 mu, but the average amount of farm land per family was very similar for all six districts. It varied from 19.1 to 23.8 mu per family (see page 22). The hsien average was 20.4 mu per family, or 3.5 mu per person.

Our averages of 20.4 mu of farm land per family and 3.5 mu per person agreed very closely with other reports of land distribution in Hopei. D. K. Lieu and Cheng Chung-min reported an average of 3.5 mu per person for Jehol, Chahar, Suiyuan, Ningsia, Hopei, and Shansi provinces.[4] Cressey gave the average cultivated land per farm household in Hopei as 24 mu.[5] Our average per farm family in Ting Hsien was 21.2 mu.

We found the district divisions convenient when collecting our material and developing our tables, but since the division into districts was primarily for administrative purposes and the study of the figures did

3. The 1934 hsien map had only five districts. The 1st and most of the 2nd had been combined into one. Nine villages from the old 2nd were added to the old 5th to make the new 4th. Only the numbers of the other three districts were changed.

4. "Statistics of Farm Land in China", *Chinese Economic Journal*, March, 1928.

5. George B. Cressey, *China's Geographic Foundations* (McGraw Hill Book Co., New York, 1934).

not show any distinctive and continuous differences between the districts, only occasionally have we given the detailed district figures.

When the Mass Education Movement began its work in Ting Hsien in 1926 it had its headquarters in the market village of Chai Ch'eng, in the east central part of the hsien. It took for its field of work at that time Chai Ch'eng, the neighboring market town of Tung T'ing, and the 60 villages that did most of their trading with Chai Ch'eng and Tung T'ing. This was our Experimental District. The area included in the District is shown in Figure 1. There were 10,445 families in the 62 villages. The reported farm area of the villages was 238,563 mu, an average of 23 mu per family. In the different villages the average amount of farm land per family varied from 11.4 to 50.0 mu.

A 36 foot national road for cart and animal travel came from Paoting and went on south to Shih Chia Chuang. During the Ch'ing dynasty there was a watchman every five li and a watch house every 10 li. It was the watchman's duty to repair the road, especially when the Emperor came out on a trip. After 1911 the watchmen were discontinued and the road fell into disrepair, but it was still being used. In 1916 the unused land in the right of way, amounting to some 60 mu, was allocated by the provincial government to the Girls' School as an endowment. The land was rented and the income used by the school.

Five hsien roads that radiated from the city to the hsien boundaries provided for local traffic and for transportation to the neighboring hsien. The villages were all interconnected by minor roads. Any repairs made on the roads were done by the villagers living nearby. In some villages the alumni association of the Mass Education Movement promoted a program of road repair.

When a necromancer reported that broken feng-shui was the reason for the death of an unusual number of the people living in the houses facing on one of the village roads the regrading of the street became a matter for the entire community. Every family on the street sent at least one man and several also sent carts to help with the work. The feng-shui was broken because part of the road drained to the north and part to the south. The situation was made still worse by the fact that the water that flowed north joined water coming from the northwest and ran off to the east. The necromancer stated that the feng-shui could be restored if the road was regraded so that there was a continuous flow from north to south and the water from the northwest flowed down the street instead of crossing it. If the grading was not too exact and some of the summer run-off stayed in the street, it would be still better for the feng-shui.

Except for the road from the station to the city and some of the main roads inside the city, Ting Hsien had no paved roads.

Open, springless, iron-tired carts made of date, locust, elm, and willow wood, with wheels 3' 8" in diameter, furnished a large part of the local transportation. Their cost ranged from $60 to $80. Other means of transportation were wheelbarrows, rickshas, pack animals, and human carriers. The charge for hauling by cart was $3.00 a day for a one-animal cart and $4.80 for a two-animal cart. This was about 60 cents per 100 catties, as the usual load, when the roads were dry, was about 500 catties for one animal and 800 catties for two. A day's trip was about 80 li. This made the charge per ton mile about 34 cents. For wheelbarrows the charge was about 80 cents per 100 catties per day's travel of 70 li, 50 cents per ton mile. For rickshas, which would carry about 200 catties, the charge was $2.00 per day or some 54 cents per ton mile. Pack and riding mules were rented for $2.00 a day. A day's trip was 80 li. Porters carrying 100 catties of goods charged $1.00 for a day's journey of 80 li, 57 cents per ton mile. Special mule carts for passengers cost $4.00 for a day's trip of 100 li.

General freight transportation was provided by five shipping companies and two mule suppliers.

Rickshas were reported to have first come to Ting Hsien in the 10th month of 1927. Then there were only three. In 1931 there were 79. Their cost ranged from $90 to $120. They rented for $4.00 or $5.00 a month.

The Peking-Hankow railroad furnished north and south rail transportation for passengers and freight. Tickets were first sold in Ting Hsien in 1900. There were three stations in the hsien about 10 miles apart. The one of Tinghsien, about six li from the city, was an express stop. In 1928 the railroad handled some 3,000,000 catties of cotton, 3,000,000 catties of pears, 1,500,000 catties of sesamum oil, 1,000,000 catties of peanuts, and 1,000,000 pieces of cotton cloth.

Five postal routes radiated from the city along the hsien roads. There were postal agents in the market towns and in some of the larger villages. In other villages the business was handled by a local store which received from $1.50 to $15.00 a month for its services. For most of them the amount was about $3.00 a month. Post office boxes were available in some of the stores for $1.00 and $2.00 a season.

Telegraph wires followed the railroad and were available for civilian use. Ting Hsien was a branch of the Paoting office. In the hsien the delivery fee for messages was 25 cents for 10 li. Messages going to adjoining hsien were sent through the post office.

There were four local telephone lines of from 18 to 30 li in length. The exchange had some 25 subscribers. Long distance calls were possible on the lines along the railway. The engineer was paid $20.00 per month. The two workmen received $14.00 and $11.00 per month.

A small generating plant supplied electric current to a few of the stores in the city.

TABLE 114. TEMPERATURE AND PRECIPITATION, MONTHLY AVERAGES, 1927–1929[1]

	Temperature (Fahrenheit)			Rainfall (millimeters)
	Maximum	Mean	Minimum	
January	32.5	22.8	13.5	17.5
February	37.4	28.8	18.5	0.0
March	54.2	43.7	32.7	6.2
April	71.8	58.6	46.2	24.1
May	84.4	72.0	56.8	8.5
June	92.6	79.4	67.0	40.1
July	90.5	80.8	72.5	167.2
August	87.0	77.0	69.8	169.7
September	81.3	68.5	57.5	30.0
October	69.5	55.2	42.8	7.2
November	52.2	40.5	26.6	7.8
December	35.5	25.9	17.8	7.0
				485.3
				(19.1 inches)

[1] From records of Hopei University, Paoting.

TABLE 115. PRECIPITATION, JUNE–SEPTEMBER, 1914–1929
(millimeters)

1914	255.0	1918	237.6	1922	287.6	1926	no data
1915	236.21	1919	319.1	1923	332.1	1927	282.4
1916	326.0	1920	64.0	1924	828.1	1928	549.5
1917	755.4	1921	24.6	1925	no data	1929	389.0

1 September missing.

TABLE 116. CULTIVATED LAND PER VILLAGE

Mu	Villages	Per Cent	Mu	Villages	Per Cent
Under 500	20	4.4	4,000–4,999	42	9.3
500–999	66	14.6	5,000–5,999	25	5.5
1,000–1,499	62	13.7	6,000–6,999	26	5.7
1,500–1,999	41	9.1	7,000–9,999	11	2.4
2,000–2,499	58	12.8	10,000 and over	10	2.2
2,500–2,999	36	8.0	Total	453	100.0
3,000–3,999	56	12.3			

Minimum 245   Maximum 32,500

Index